THE FORGOTTEN GOD

THE FORGOTTEN GOD

Perspectives in Biblical Theology

Essays in Honor of Paul J. Achtemeier
on the Occasion of his Seventy-fifth Birthday

Edited by

A. ANDREW DAS

and

FRANK J. MATERA

Westminster John Knox Press
LOUISVILLE • LONDON

© 2002 Westminster John Knox Press

Scripture quotations, unless otherwise indicated, are from the New Revised Standard Version of the Bible, copyright © 1989 by the division of Christian Education of the National Council of the Churches of Christ in the U.S.A., and are used by permission.

Scripture quotations marked RSV are from the Revised Standard Version of the Bible, copyright 1946, 1952, 1971, 1973 by the Division of Christian Education of the National Council of the Churches of Christ in the U.S.A., and are used by permission.

Grateful acknowledgment is made to Union Theological Seminary and Presbyterian School of Christian Education to reprint photo of Paul Achtemeier.

Book design by Sharon Adams
Cover design by Eric Walljasper

First edition
Published by Westminster John Knox Press
Louisville, Kentucky

This book is printed on acid-free paper that meets
the American National Standards Institute Z39.48 standard. ∞

PRINTED IN THE UNITED STATES OF AMERICA

02 03 04 05 06 07 08 09 10 11 — 10 9 8 7 6 5 4 3 2 1

Library of Congress-in-Publication Data

A Catalog record for this book is available from the Library of Congress

ISBN 0-664-22276-5

Dr. Paul J. ("Bud") Achtemeier

Contents

Contributors

ELIZABETH ACHTEMEIER
Adjunct Professor of Bible and Homiletics, Retired
Union Theological Seminary in Virginia

HAROLD W. ATTRIDGE
Lillian Claus Professor of New Testament
The Divinity School, Yale University

DAVID E. AUNE
Professor of New Testament
The University of Notre Dame

JOHN T. CARROLL
Harriet Robertson Fitts Memorial Professor of New Testament
Union Theological Seminary and Presbyterian School of Christian Education

RICHARD J. CLIFFORD, S.J.
Professor of Old Testament
Weston School of Theology

JOSEPH A. FITZMYER, S.J.
Professor of New Testament, Emeritus
The Catholic University of America

DAVID M. HAY
Joseph E. McCabe Professor of Religion, Emeritus
Coe College

Contributors

RICHARD B. HAYS
George Washington Ivey Professor of New Testament
The Divinity School, Duke University

LUKE TIMOTHY JOHNSON
Robert W. Woodruff Professor of New Testament and Christian Origins
Candler School of Theology, Emory University

LEANDER E. KECK
Winkley Professor of Biblical Theology, Emeritus
The Divinity School, Yale University

JACK DEAN KINGSBURY
Aubrey Lee Brooks Professor of Biblical Theology, Emeritus
Union Theological Seminary in Virginia

JAMES LUTHER MAYS
Cyrus H. McCormick Professor of Hebrew
and Old Testament Interpretation, Emeritus
Union Theological Seminary in Virginia

S. DEAN McBRIDE JR.
Cyrus H. McCormick Professor of Hebrew and Old Testament Interpretation
Union Theological Seminary and Presbyterian School of Christian Education

PATRICK D. MILLER
Charles T. Haley Professor of Old Testament Theology
Princeton Theological Seminary

FRANCIS J. MOLONEY, S.D.B.
Professor of New Testament
The Catholic University of America

PHEME PERKINS
Professor of New Testament
Boston College

Doctoral Students
of Paul J. Achtemeier

"Those who are taught the word must share in all good things with their teacher."—Galatians 6:6

Carl B. Bridges Jr.
Robert A. Bryant
Richard Paul Carlson
J. Knox Chamblin
A. Andrew Das
Casey Wayne Davis
Christopher A. Davis
Philip Knox Gladden
Thomas David Gordon
Roy A. Harrisville
Paul Michael Hedquist
David Paul Henry
David Walter Kendall
Johann Douhyun Kim
J. Nelson Kraybill
Frank J. Matera
Vernon Solomon Olson
Brian K. Peterson
David A. Renwick
C. Thomas Rhyne
Michael Leroy Sweeney
William N. Wilder

Foreword

In Appreciation of Paul J. Achtemeier

I am truly grateful for the opportunity to express my deep appreciation of Professor Achtemeier's manifold contributions to the discipline of biblical study, to the appropriation of Scripture in the life of the church, Roman Catholic as well as Protestant, and to the well-being of the Society of Biblical Literature. No other Protestant New Testament scholar in our generation has matched the range of these contributions.

One thread that runs through his scholarly output (seventeen books, five dozen articles, and over seventy-five book reviews) is a resolute use of the historical-critical method not only to recover aspects of early Christianity but also to make the theological content of the New Testament accessible to colleagues, students, and the general public. Both the historical reconstructions and the theological analyses of this superb exegete are reliable because he has eschewed the lure of exotic theories and faddish interpretations. Readers of his publications on the Synoptics (especially Mark), Paul (primarily Romans) and 1 Peter—to name the best known—benefit from exegetical work that is carefully grounded in the text, that reflects judicious, rigorous historical thinking in the use of other ancient sources, and that never forgets that it is the theological content, broadly understood, that makes these writings significant. Appreciation of this achievement is enhanced when one notes that this scholarship flourished in decades when the value of such work could no longer be taken for granted but needed to be affirmed and exemplified.

While firmly rooted in the Reformed tradition, the ecumenical horizons of Professor Achtemeier's work became concrete in actual tasks. In addition to participating in the Reformed-Roman Catholic Dialogue, he was a member of two other panels (both sponsored by the United States Lutheran-Roman

Catholic Dialogue) that explored two controversial themes, first the role of Peter and then that of Mary in the New Testament. Since his scholarship is neither methodologically sectarian nor confessionally parochial, it is not surprising that in 1985 he was the first non-Catholic to be elected president of the Catholic Biblical Association.

Although he is a member of numerous professional organizations such as the American Theological Society and the international Studiorum Novi Testamenti Societas, it is the Society of Biblical Literature that has benefited most, and longest, from his leadership in virtually all aspects of the Society's endeavors. In addition to giving sagacious guidance to various program segments at its annual meetings, he was—and remains—deeply involved in the administrative affairs of the Society, serving as its executive secretary (1977–1980) and as its president (1989). With these responsibilities in a rapidly growing Society came a key role in guiding the affairs of Scholars Press (alas, no longer extant) through roiled waters. Now, as chair of the Society's Finance Committee and as a member of the Constitution Revision Committee, he contributes his experience and wisdom to the task of shaping the Society's future.

The same qualities that colleagues value in his institutional leadership—professional competence graced with clarity and sound judgment, personal integrity and unwavering commitment to high standards—have characterized also his sundry editorial responsibilities. In addition to being New Testament editor for the commentary series *Interpretation*, he twice served as associate editor of the *Catholic Biblical Quarterly*, and during the 1980s he served as associate editor and editor of the journal *Interpretation*. Especially noteworthy is the fact that under his leadership as general editor, the Society of Biblical Literature launched successfully its first major publication designed to make the results of biblical scholarship available to the general public—*Harper's Bible Dictionary* (1985; revised in 1996 as *HarperCollins Bible Dictionary*). It was natural then that he also served as consulting editor for the Society's next project—*Harper's Bible Commentary* (1988; revised in 2000 as *HarperCollins Bible Commentary*).

During these highly productive years, he taught and mentored students, lectured and preached in colleges and seminaries here and abroad, translated a book and several articles from German, coauthored three books with his wife, Elizabeth—herself a published Old Testament scholar and well-known professor of homiletics—and coparented two children, one of whom (Mark) followed his father into the professorate and is currently teaching theology at the Divinity School of Dubuque University.

For nearly four decades, it has been my privilege to know "Bud" Achtemeier as a treasured friend and colleague and, for part of that time, to have shared in work of the Society of Biblical Literature. Especially do I cherish our ongoing conversations, which began with our mutual interest in the Gospel of Mark and have continued with reference to the theology of Paul. For these years of enriching collaboration, as well as for enduring friendship with this remarkable, gifted Mensch, I am profoundly grateful.

Leander E. Keck

Introduction

Introducing the Forgotten God

A. ANDREW DAS AND FRANK J. MATERA

Over a generation ago Nils Dahl lamented the neglect of theology in the narrow sense of the word. Few if any studies had directly addressed the question of God in the New Testament; theology was usually tackled only indirectly or tangentially. Rudolf Bultmann subsumed theology into anthropology. Oscar Cullmann subsumed it into Christology, and christological studies typically paid little attention to the relationship between faith in Christ and faith in God or to the transfer of divine titles to Christ. The neglect has been understandable because the New Testament contains very few thematic formulations about God. The New Testament authors appear to take for granted in large measure the Old Testament conception of God. Apart from a few doxological or specialized references, the topic of God is generally broached only in contexts treating some other theme. Dahl contended that the New Testament does not provide a uniform doctrine of God but "considerable diversity." "This variety ought, however, to have been a cause for investigation and not for neglect" (1975, 6).

The present volume is a response to Dahl's urgent plea for an investigation into the unity and diversity behind the biblical conception of God, especially within the pages of the Christian Scriptures. It is appropriate that this volume should honor and be dedicated to Paul J. Achtemeier (on the occasion of his seventy-fifth birthday), whose own career has repeatedly returned to this very question. In 1962 Professor Achtemeier authored an important essay on "Righteousness in the New Testament" for *The Interpreter's Dictionary of the Bible*. He demonstrated a prevailing and virtually uniform conception of righteousness throughout the diversity of New Testament writings. God is righteous precisely because God has entered into and faithfully maintained a covenant relationship with humanity. Although this relationship had been jeopardized

1

by human failure and sin, God acted in Christ to restore the relationship. In a sweeping review of New Testament literature, Achtemeier showed the intrinsically relational dimension to God's righteousness. James D. G. Dunn has at various points highlighted this early essay by Achtemeier as formative for his own understanding (most recently in 1998, 342 n. 27). The breadth of Achtemeier's analysis presaged the breadth of a career in which he has published articles, specialized monographs, and commentaries on Gospel literature, especially Mark; the Pauline epistles, including especially Romans; and the Catholic epistles, most notably his magisterial commentary on 1 Peter. In his studies of Mark's Gospel, Achtemeier emphasized how Christ's work manifested God's own glorious reign. Theology provides the proper context for Markan Christology (1986, 1). Similarly in his study of Romans, Achtemeier drew attention to an economy of salvation that he defined as God's plan, enacted through the divine election of Israel as promised to Abraham, to save humanity from the consequences of its sinful rebellion. While the divine plan has a decidedly christocentric shape, Achtemeier qualifies:

> [This] economy remains under the control of God, who is the one who has shaped it in such a christocentric form. That is why Paul continues here as elsewhere to be primarily a theologian rather than exclusively a "christologian." It is *God's* plan that informs Paul's understanding of the "gospel of God" as he has made clear at the outset. God is the one who moves it along its way, and who is also behind its defining moment that consists in the appearance of Jesus Christ. (1997, 12–13; cf. 1985, 4–18)

In his Hermeneia commentary on 1 Peter, Achtemeier championed the perspective that the Petrine author has identified his Gentile recipients as "the new people of God." The theocentric language once applied to Israel has now been appropriated for these Gentile Christians (1996, 68–71). Although "the theological logic of 1 Peter is grounded in the events of the passion of Jesus Christ," what has taken place in Christ conforms to a divine plan that predates creation (1996, 66). God continues to create through the instrument of the gospel word (1996, 67). Theology in the narrow sense has remained a central consideration throughout the writings of Paul J. Achtemeier's career as a theologian. How appropriate that fifteen internationally renowned scholars should continue this work in a volume to honor him, and that it be forwarded by his longtime friend and colleague, Leander E. Keck.

Nils Dahl's classic, programmatic essay offered several suggestions to rectify the neglect of theology proper. He pointed out that the New Testament authors tend to take the conception of God within the Old Testament for granted, even as they simultaneously modified that conception—sometimes quite dramatically—in light of what had happened in the crucified Messiah. As a necessary foundation, then, for the theology of the New Testament, four scholars will in this volume explore the conception of God in the Old Testament. Dahl also maintained that the best approach to the issue will respect both the unity and diversity of New Testament literature. Each author in this volume will therefore explore the distinctive conception of God within the pages of a single biblical author, a related group of authors, or a distinct body of biblical literature. Dahl concluded in a preliminary fashion that one would not be able to treat the God of the New Testament "in isolation from christology, pneumatology, anthropology, and soteriology, and vice versa" (1975, 8). The distinctive dependence or independence of theology from other aspects of an author's or authors' thought requires examination. After the four essays on the Old Testament, ten authors will explore the God of the various New Testament documents with these questions lurking in the background. Finally, Professor Achtemeier's wife and scholarly confrere, Dr. Elizabeth Achtemeier, will offer summative reflections on biblical preaching about God.

S. Dean McBride's essay on the God of the Pentateuch offers a foundation for all the subsequent essays in this volume, since Judaism and Christianity are both constructed on the shared textual base of the Torah. Although the Pentateuchal witness preserves reference to the cosmic consortium of ruling powers, Israel's God revealed as Yahweh alone encompasses and transcends the authority of these ruling powers. God is One and there is no other. This one God has created the world and has acted on a cosmic stage in world history through the flood up to the election of the family of Israel. At that point, the cosmic stage recedes into the background in favor of God's special relationship with Israel and Moses as the mediator of that relationship. Israel thus serves as a "holy nation," a consecrated community, which witnesses the sovereignty of the only true God who stands over all. The narrowed focus on the people of Israel will explode into a renewed cosmic emphasis as God acts to redeem all the nations of the world in Christ.

The New Testament writings draw extensively from the Psalms, the topic of James Luther Mays's essay, although it is the Psalms' Christologies and anthropologies that prove of particular interest to the apostolic authors. The Psalms affirm in agreement with the Pentateuch that Yahweh is the one and only God, a perspective inherited and assumed by the New Testament authors. This God continues to reign as Sovereign over the course of human history and has as Creator fashioned a special people with whom to enter into a relationship. This is a God who proves to be faithful, merciful, and saving. The God of the Psalms proves to be especially faithful to the Messianic King, even in the midst of defeat and death. If God is faithful to the Messianic King, those who place their trust in God for deliverance will not be disappointed. The God of the Psalms is clearly a God whose power is made perfect in weakness (2 Cor

2:8). The New Testament authors in their presentation of God's "Son" will heartily employ the same motifs.

God once again governs the cosmos and the nations within the prophetic corpus. Sometimes, even prominently, this governance involves the wrathful meting out of judgment and punishment, but Patrick D. Miller explains that these displays do more than maintain the "cosmic, human, and cultural order." God's actions model justice for the human community. Even so, the divine anger is mitigated by compassion. Judgment is not God's final word. On the contrary, God heeds the intercessory prayers of the prophets to forestall wrath, even when that wrath is fully deserved for the sake of justice. God resists judgment for as long as possible and, like Abraham, searches for one single person who acts justly. Only with grief and tears does God act in judgment, and even then it is as a potter who destroys the vessel but reshapes the clay to fashion something new and more wonderful. The book of Jonah epitomizes the prophetic view of God when Israel's most hated and undeserving enemy experiences God's mercy and compassion instead of wrath. The New Testament cross of Christ is a natural extension of the prophetic insight into the character of God.

Wisdom literature, according to Richard J. Clifford's essay, does not present God in terms of the covenant relationship with Israel but rather at work in the entire world. The Proverbs convey divine, parental wisdom to humanity, a wisdom that reflects God's creation and ultimate control over the world. The book of Job urges its readers to recognize that divine wisdom and justice, in the face of human suffering, cannot be measured by merely human standards. God does not mechanically mete out punishment and reward. God may at times let the righteous suffer within a larger, divine purpose. Qoheleth, or Ecclesiastes, speaks of the inscrutable God who in this world of turmoil and reversal may be encountered only in the joy of the moment. Human existence is ephemeral and vain in comparison with the vast, ever renewed cosmos. Nevertheless, God gives to human beings out of sheer grace and apart from mortal merit. Sirach agrees with the other Wisdom writings that the universe reveals something of the otherwise incomprehensible God, but Sirach also uniquely integrates the historical traditions of Israel, its history, and the law as incarnations of God's Wisdom. Finally, the Wisdom of Solomon speaks of the Wisdom available especially to the Jews as the agency of God's majestic but hidden governance of the world. God's wisdom, mediated through human intermediaries and within reach of all, reflects a divine rule that takes precedence over human rulers.

The Markan God, whom Jack Dean Kingsbury introduces to his readers, cannot be understood except through Christ as the narrative's central figure. Reading Mark from the point of view of narrative criticism helps avoid the misemphases in past scholarship. Although Christ remains central to the story, a proper evaluation of the Son of God is dependent upon God's reliable evaluative "point of view" as the Father. To adopt any other point of view would be in error and even satanic. God openly announces the divine perspective on Jesus' identity as the Son at his baptism and later at the transfiguration, a perspective that the narrator, Scripture, and Jesus himself likewise echo. What Jesus' Sonship entails, though, will not be fully clear until the cross, when his blood is poured out for many (14:24). Only in recognizing Jesus as the one who was obedient to the will of his Father will readers be prepared to live the same cruciform life. Only in the shadow of the cross comes the first recognition on the lips of a human character within the story of Jesus' full identity as the Son of God. At last a human being's perspective of Christ is in alignment with God's own.

God is certainly not a neglected factor in Luke-Acts, as John T. Carroll shows in his "reader-oriented approach." Both God and Christ are called by the names "Savior" and "Lord," and both remain in an intimate communion even throughout Christ's passion. Christ subordinates himself to the will of God to the point of death on the cross and so serves as the instrument through whom God's Spirit exercises power and forgiveness. Alongside Jesus and the Spirit, God speaks and works through the agency of angels, visions, and prophetic figures. Sometimes God even speaks directly within the story. God's revelation takes place, in the second part of Luke's story, through the church. God is the Savior of Israel who has remembered the covenantal promises to Abraham and David, but surprisingly this salvation brings division and reversal to Israel. The marginalized and the oppressed, even the Gentiles, find themselves included within God's saving plan for Israel, while many in Israel reject the message. The book of Acts records the message of Christ being spread to diaspora synagogues—in the face of rejection—and beyond, to the farthest reaches of the earth. While human and supernatural authorities may resist the divine plan, God's will ultimately prevails at every turn in the story. This faith-inspiring and empowering God as Savior is refashioning a new, worldwide community of people liberated from despair and need.

Christian Trinitarians mined the Fourth Gospel in support of their later systematic reflection. Francis J. Moloney, like Kingsbury and Carroll, prefers a method instead that recognizes the "narrative theology" of the Evangelist: God cannot be abstracted from the story of Jesus. Although no one has ever seen God, the divine Word enfleshed makes God known, especially in the accomplishing of God's saving "work." Johannine Christology ultimately serves theology. While Jesus stands in a unique relationship of love with God, through Jesus believers also enter into a relationship of love and the saving knowledge of God. Such knowledge of God can only take place through the cross, the hour of Christ's glorification when Jesus was "lifted up" for all the world to see, a moment that the entire narrative anticipates. In gazing upon the glory of the crucified Jesus, a new family is gathered into being of those who have experienced God. It is at this moment that one experiences the glory of a God who truly loves, and it is out of that experience that believers are empowered to love one another in the same fashion.

Although Paul's letters to the Galatians and Romans represent an entirely different literary genre from the Gospels, Richard B. Hays discerns an undeniably narrative substructure revolving around God's historic relationship to humanity. While both letters offer a sweeping review of this history, Romans begins the story with God's creation of the world and humanity. Romans also explores God's hardening and God's ultimate plan to save Israel. Both letters trace God's promises to Abraham and the patriarchs as recorded in Israel's Scriptures, and these promises, Paul notes, already included the Gentiles. Prior to the fulfillment of the promises, God provided the Mosaic law as a temporary measure. With the fullness of time God sent forth his Son to rescue humanity "from the present evil age" of slavery and sin through the Son's faithful death. In Jesus' death, one sees God's very own fidelity, reflecting proto-Trinitarian christological (re)definition. In faithfulness to the promises, God raised Jesus from the dead and through the Spirit called and justified both Jews and Gentiles into a new community. Such faithfulness on God's part certainly inspires and evokes a faithful response. The story will conclude with God's judgment of the world and the revelation of his eschatological glory, a glory that also embraces his children.

The first Christians followed the Jews in a staunch insistence upon one God, but according to Pheme Perkins, Paul modified that confession to reflect God's raising of Jesus Christ the crucified one. Like Hays, Perkins recognizes that Paul's approach to God at Corinth reflects the situation there. The Corinthians' "spiritualized eschatology" led to a corresponding failure to recognize God's power in the physical death and bodily resurrection of Christ. In conformance with Jewish tradition God is one, but the one Lord is Jesus Christ "through whom are all things." This monotheism, which stands behind the recognition of the nonexistence of idol-gods at Corinth, flows freely into Christology, and into soteriology and ecclesiology. Consequently, the Corinthian Christians should not harm the faith of those whose consciences are weaker with respect to food sacrificed to idols. In a congregation full of people who consider themselves "spiritual" or "mature" relative to others, Paul invokes the cross as proof that God's power does not enhance worldly status. God gives life through the mystery of a humble cross to what "is not." The Corinthians in their pursuit of spiritual perfection are losing the actual wisdom of God exhibited in crucified weakness. Paul returns to weakness and suffering in 2 Corinthians when he contends that they must view his apostolic suffering and hardship through the lens of divine power again manifested in the cross of a dying Christ.

Colossians and Ephesians are simultaneously theocentric and christocentric according to David M. Hay. God is the author of redemption who is at work in Christ to reconcile an alienated humanity. While worship, prayer, thanksgiving, and praise are directed not to Christ but to God, God can be known only through Christ. The theological emphasis, more frequent in the first half of each letter, yields to Christ the "Lord" in the latter hortatory sections of the letters, although the Christian still acts in conformity to God's will. God remains, then, the ultimate determiner of people's destiny and has been at work behind Christ's resurrection and that of the believers. In the process, God has achieved a military-like victory in Christ as the opposing supernatural forces are defeated and the dividing wall of the law torn down. The Mosaic law no longer obstructs human salvation with its dark record of deeds. Whereas Paul's Christology, according to Hay, appears "subordinationist," Colossians and Ephesians often portray Christ as roughly equal to the Father or close to equal. In Christ, the fullness of the Deity dwells. God is likewise present in the corporate and individual lives of believers in the church. Christians enjoy unlimited access to the immediate presence of God, a blessing open to all who believe, whether Jew or Gentile. This universalistic strand of thought stands in tension alongside the particularistic, as God is gathering up in Christ and within the church all things—the seed for a restoration of all humanity.

Whereas Hay finds Colossians and Ephesians both christocentric and theocentric, Joseph A. Fitzmyer finds each of the Pastoral Epistles decidedly theocentric. In response to polytheism, henotheism, and emperor worship, the Pastorals affirm the one God who is transcendent and sovereign over all humanity in accordance with the Shema of Israel (Deut 6:4). First Timothy 6:14–16 lists seven characteristics that distinguish God as unique, each of which can be traced to the influence of Judaism and early Christianity. God is especially a powerful "Savior" in the Pastorals, in contrast to the gods and deliverers of the Greco-Roman world, and is concerned with the salvation of all humanity, effecting that plan through Jesus Christ, who is also called "Savior." The Pastorals, however, do not equate God and Christ but speak of the two as a coupled pair. Christ reigns in the glorious presence of God and functions as God's envoy and agent of human salvation. Finally, the Pastorals speak of the various relationships of people to God. Those who believe in the one God are the "elect" who should devote themselves to good works. Paul is God's servant, or slave, commissioned by both God and Christ. Church officials are entrusted the divine Scriptures and the care of God's household, the church.

Harold W. Attridge begins his survey of the theology of Hebrews by listing the basic dogmatic claims that the author makes about God: God exists, God creates, God judges, God is the object of propitiation. As a second approach, Attridge traces in Hebrews the history of God's relationship with humanity, especially the patriarchs and Israel. God is not just a distant creator and judge but is intimately involved with an earthly family. Aspects of the story, including the wilderness sanctuary, the sprinkling of blood, and the Sinai theophany at the giving of the law, all point as symbols to Jesus the high priest's sacrifice. In yet a third methodological approach to Hebrews, Attridge briefly considers David A. deSilva's patronage model and finds the approach useful but ultimately unable to account for the entirety of Hebrews' social imagery. God is not just a divine patron offering benefaction or an inheritance; the broker-Son must render that testament valid by death and thereby become the heir. Finally, Attridge discusses the conceit that the author and readers can overhear the conversations between God and the Son and between God and all of God's children. Rather than review the story of Jesus as the Gospels do, these conversations or dialogues employ the language of Scripture. As the Son speaks in response to God, the Son is modeling for God's children a way of dialoguing with God as well as a pattern for living those words of faith in concrete action.

Luke Timothy Johnson explains that James and 1 Peter, as letters that draw upon the language of prayer and exhortation, do not offer the most direct information about God. James is nevertheless perhaps the most theocentric document in the New Testament. While James does occasionally draw upon Jesus' teaching in the Synoptic tradition and looks forward to the coming of the Lord, Jesus is mentioned explicitly only twice in the letter. In undergirding the author's moral exhortations to the rich with respect to the poor, James speaks at length about God and not Christ. The socioeconomic duality is matched by a moral duality within a universe where the world above stands in stark opposition to the "earthly, unspiritual, devilish" below. Johnson thus identifies the heart of the letter in its exclamation, "Adulterers! Do you not know that friendship with the world is enmity with God?" (Jas 4:4). One must choose one's allegiance, whether for God or for the world and its value system. James's statements about God provide warrants for moral exhortation to live as a community apart from competitive envy. First Peter's theology, on the other hand, cannot be severed from Christology. God is the Father of Jesus Christ, and faith in Jesus brings the believer to God and glorifies God. Johnson closes by cataloguing the statements about God in 1 Peter under the categories of titles/epithets of God, actions and ascribed qualities of God, and attitudes/actions directed toward God.

David E. Aune takes as his launching point the two instances of direct speech by God in the Apocalypse of John (1:8; 21:6). These two utterances are embedded within a striking cluster of four related, mutually interpretive divine titles used for God and/or Christ: (1) "[he] who is and who was and who is to come," (2) "the First and the Last," (3) "the Beginning and the End," and (4) "the Alpha and the Omega." Aune develops the Jewish and Greco-Roman background to each title but concludes that ultimately it is the context of the Apocalypse that is decisive for their interpretation. Part of the interpretive context is the understanding of time in the Apocalypse. After a review of the history of research on biblical time, Aune concludes that time is a phenomenon that can be conceptualized in a variety of ways, and differing social and psychological constructions of time may exist side by side. The notion of "restoration," typical in apocalyptic eschatology, captures the sense of time in the Apocalypse. Salvation is the restoration of humanity and the world to its ideal state enjoyed at the beginning. This involves both nationalistic restoration (a new Jerusalem) and universalistic restoration of creation and human society in general (a new heaven and a new earth). The divine titles reflect the Apocalypse's restorative eschatological perspective.

The final essay in the volume makes the transition from biblical theology to biblical preaching. Echoing motifs from the earlier essays, Elizabeth Achtemeier recognizes that the God of the New Testament remains the God of the Old Testament, of Abraham, Isaac, and Jacob. Jesus is the fulfillment of a story that began long before. Since God is at work in the pages of history, the preacher must respect the narrative character of God's self-revelation through time, a narrative that now envelops the present-day congregation. This narrative bespeaks a God who is active and who continues to speak his word afresh through the medium of preaching and teaching. The word of the sovereign God powerfully transforms an individual's worldview in announcing the absolute truth of human sinfulness and the genuine need for redemption within a new community. Achtemeier outlines a method to let the Bible speak its own message anew by the power of the Holy Spirit, which includes close examination of and meditation on the biblical text's rhetorical structures, patterns, and vocabulary. The preacher must remain immersed in the biblical story and text in both worship and life in order to "channel" to the congregation God's revelation rather than human opinion.

In many ways, these fifteen essays and their authors mirror the scholarly life and career of Professor Paul J. Achtemeier. The contributors are all internationally recognized scholars who have come together to honor one of their own. Six of the fifteen essays were authored by Roman Catholic scholars, a tribute to the ecumenical dimension of Professor Achtemeier's work and the distinction of being the first Protestant to serve as president of the Catholic Biblical Association of America. Paul Achtemeier also served as president of the Society of Biblical Literature, and just as that organization and these essays span the scope of biblical literature, he has never neglected the full scope of the Scriptures in his own writings or in his personal life. He married an Old Testament scholar and with her published *The Old Testament Roots of Our Faith*. He has constantly returned to the relationship between the Jewish and Christian Scriptures, most notably in *The Inspiration of Scripture* and in editing two Bible dictionaries and a volume on the Hebrew prophets. Even as each of the essays in this volume offers fresh, scholarly exposition of the Scriptures, the exposition is always in the service of their broader theological content. Virtually every scholarly work from the pen of Paul J. Achtemeier aims at the theological exposition of the Bible. At the same time, his scholarly endeavors have never been purely for the digestion of academicians. He has always sought to reach beyond the academy to engage the interested layperson or student of the Scriptures, as does this volume. Several of his writings are specifically for pastors, and so this volume seeks to make the transition to biblical preaching. On behalf of all of his students throughout the last forty years, two former students here recognize their sincere debt of gratitude for a mentor and *Vater.*

SELECT BIBLIOGRAPHY

Achtemeier, Paul J. 1962. "Righteousness in the New Testament." Pages 91–99 in vol. 4 of *The Interpreter's Dictionary of the Bible*. Edited by G. A. Buttrick. Nashville: Abingdon.

———. 1980. *The Inspiration of Scripture: Problems and Proposals*. Philadelphia: Westminster.

———. 1985. *Romans*. Interpretation: A Bible Commentary for Teaching and Preaching. Atlanta: John Knox.

———. 1986. *Mark*. Proclamation Commentaries. Philadelphia: Fortress.

———. 1996. *1 Peter*. Hermeneia. Minneapolis: Fortress.

———. 1997. "Unsearchable Judgments and Inscrutable Ways: Reflections on the Discussion of Romans." Pages 3–21 in *Looking Back, Pressing On*. Edited by E. Elizabeth Johnson and David M. Hay. Vol. 4 of *Pauline Theology*. Atlanta: Scholars Press.

Achtemeier, Paul J., and Elizabeth Achtemeier. 1995. *The Old Testament Roots of Our Faith*. Rev. ed. Peabody, Mass.: Hendrickson.

Dahl, Nils A. 1975. "The Neglected Factor in New Testament Theology." *Reflection* 73:5–8.

Dunn, James D. G. 1998. *The Theology of Paul the Apostle*. Grand Rapids: Eerdmans.

1

The God Who Creates and Governs

Pentateuchal Foundations of Biblical Theology

S. Dean McBride Jr.

As different as they are in important aspects of overall configuration and contents, the Scriptures of Judaism and Christianity are constructed on a common textual base—the Pentateuch. These initial five books, Genesis through Deuteronomy, have narrative priority by virtue of the antique epochs they survey. Beginning with an overview of primordial times (Gen 1–9), they trace the genealogical antecedents and itinerant careers of the patriarchs Abraham, Isaac, and Jacob (Gen 10–36), and they describe in much greater detail the metamorphosis of Jacob's expanding family into a distinctive political community that is most often known by his other name, "Israel" (Gen 37–Deut 34). But the foundational significance of the Pentateuch is more profoundly theological than chronological. The chief protagonist, whose exercise of cosmic sovereignty is indefeasibly demonstrated in Israel's creation, is the God whose gracious providence and redemptive purposes are honored throughout the rest of Jewish and Christian Scriptures. The Pentateuchal account is shaped by the conviction that ancient Israel was constituted and commissioned through covenant for a perennial vocation in the disciplined service of this God who created it. Accordingly, as the traditional designations "Torah" and "Law" (Greek *nomos*) indicate, the Pentateuchal disclosure of the divine economy has a large prescriptive dimension, which also remains normative for the communities of faith nurtured by this and other scriptural corpora that extend its theological witness (e.g., Josh 1:1–9; Mal 4:4 [3:22]; Sir 24:23; Matt 5:17; John 1:17; Acts 28:23; Babylonian Talmud, *Giṭṭin* 60a–b).

From the perspective of historical-critical scholarship, to be sure, the Pentateuch is not a unitary work but a literary composite, exhibiting a number of stratified sources, each with a discrete provenance and theological emphasis. The oldest of these documentary strata, which may be described as parallel written deposits of archaic Israelite epic lore, are usually labeled "Yahwistic" (J) and "Elohistic" (E). According to majority critical views, J and E are monarchical in date, from approximately the tenth to the eighth centuries B.C.E., and they exhibit some particularities suggestive of their origins in the Judean and north Israelite kingdoms respectively. An enlarged edition of these combined strata, incorporating an early version of Deuteronomy, was perhaps drafted by Judean scribes in the seventh century B.C.E., after the demise of the northern kingdom. A century or so later, in the era of Persian hegemony, the "Deuteronomic" edition may have been supplemented with other traditional lore, by a school identified as "Priestly" (P) because of its conspicuous interests in matters of cultic worship, sacral rites, and covenantal ethics. This penultimate or final form of the Pentateuch seems designed to have served as a theological charter and polity for the Judean restoration that is described in the books of Ezra and Nehemiah.

Whatever its underlying sources and history of composition may have been, the Pentateuch's artful, inter-interpretive network of narratives and prescriptive traditions develops three foundational affirmations: (1) There is only one God, "the LORD [Yahweh]," who created the cosmos and who continues to govern it; (2) "Israel" is God's special possession among the nations of the world, set apart for a ministry of praise, witness, and blessing; (3) Moses is the principal agent through whom God speaks and acts to claim Israel as God's people in perpetuity. Well before the New Testament era, these three affirmations had acquired creedal import in Jewish liturgy (e.g., Pss 104–106; Neh 9; Mishnah *Tamid* 5.1), and they remained of crucial significance in the shaping of early Christian proclamation.

THE LORD, GOD MOST HIGH

In its full extent, the Pentateuch coordinates a portrait of the deity who is most intimately self-disclosed to Israel as "Yahweh" (conventionally represented in many English translations of the Bible by the surrogate honorific "the LORD"). This broad portrait is richly textured rather than uniform. It still displays variegated and occasionally incongruous features of the source materials used in its composition. Some of the literary components are stories that have a fabulous, folkloristic character. They depict a vigorously active and anthropopathic deity whose personal appearances may be palpable as well as corporeal (e.g., Gen 3:8–21; chap. 18; 32:22–32; Exod 4:24–26; 24:9–11; Num 22:22–35). While many other narratives are much more formal, studied, or didactic in their portrayal of divinity, they are usually also conceptually vivid, offering glimpses of an awesomely powerful and always dangerous physical presence that is much safer to attend from a distance than to approach, see, or domesticate (e.g., Exod 19:16–23; 33:18–23; 40:34–38; Lev 10:2–3; 16:2; Deut 4:9–12; 5:23–27). There are a few important cognitive portrayals as well, articulating attributes and honorific appellations that characterize the sublime, incorporeal divine monarch of later Jewish and Christian thought (e.g., Exod 34:6–7; Deut 10:17–18). Though real, these and similar differences of theological perception should not be exaggerated into intractable polarities. They are tolerable as complementary facets of Torah's larger portrait of divine sovereignty and providence.

'Elyon's Assembly

Pentateuchal references to divinities other than Israel's God are overwhelmingly negative. In conformity with the clear proscription in Exod 23:13, such putative "gods" are rarely specified by name (cf. Num 21:29, where Moabites are called "people of Chemosh"). One exceptional instance may be the deity identified as "Baal Pe'or" in the episode of egregious Israelite sacrilege described in Numbers 25 (cf. Deut 4:3–4; Ps 106:28; Hos 9:10). However, this designation is usually taken to be a title referring to the local "Lord [ba'al]"— perhaps a manifestation of Chemosh—venerated at the sanctuary atop the promontory of Pe'or in northwestern Moab (Num 23:28; 31:16; Josh 21:17; cf. Deut 3:29 [bêt pĕ'ôr]). Pe'or's unnamed "Lord" achieves notoriety only because he and his cult exemplify the danger of apostasy; he differs little from the other anonymous "gods" of Egypt and Canaan that Yahweh is said to have defeated (Exod 12:12; Num 33:4; Deut 33:27; cf. Josh 24:14–15; Judg 2:11–13; Ps 97:7). Similarly, the expression "other gods [ʾĕlōhîm ʾăḥērîm]" is commonly used to disparage and proscribe especially Canaanite cults and idolatrous practices, and to condemn any attempts by Israelites to integrate veneration of alien deities into the worship of Yahweh (e.g., Exod 20:3; 23:23–24; 34:11–16; Deut 7:3–5, 16; 13:6–8; 18:20). Often the polemical sense conveyed is that these gods are bogus; they have no identity apart from their manufactured iconic representations (e.g., Gen 31:19; 35:2–4; Exod 20:23; 32:1–4; Deut 4:28; 32:21; cf. also 2 Kgs 19:18; 1 Chr 16:26; Ps 96:5; Isa 45:21).

Especially against the dense backdrop of prohibitions designed to exclude any religious practices that might compromise Israel's devotion to Yahweh alone, a few Pentateuchal witnesses stand out because they suggest that Yahweh's unique sovereignty is congenial with a cosmic consortium of ruling powers. The concept, which is more openly attested by descriptions of heavenly assemblies elsewhere in the Bible (e.g., 1 Kgs 22:19; Job 1:6; 2:1; Dan 7:9–10) and in other religious literatures of the ancient Mediterranean world, accounts for the way Yahweh's victory over Egyptian forces is hymnically celebrated in Exod 15:11 (the translations throughout this essay are my own):

> Who is like you, Yahweh, among the gods [ʾēlîm]?
> Who is like you, majestic among the holy ones,
> splendidly fearsome, performing wonders?

Yahweh's exaltation among or above the other members of the divine assembly is later echoed in confessional form by Jethro, Moses' Midianite father-in-law: "Now I know that Yahweh is greater than all the gods [gādôl . . . mikkol-hāʾĕlōhîm]" (Exod 18:11; cf. 2 Chr 2:5[4]; Pss 86:8; 89:6–8[7–9]).

Another brief but more instructive sketch of divine consortium engaged in its ecumenical work appears in the poetry of Deut 32:8–9:

> When ʿElyon assigned nations (their) domains,
>   when he segmented humankind,
> he delineated the territories of peoples,
>   according to the number of the deities;
> so Yahweh's portion is his very own people,
>   Jacob his allotted share.

This cosmogonic scenario suggests that a heavenly executive, ʿElyon (often rendered "the Most High"), assigned the peoples of the world their individual territorial dominions and delegated oversight of the resulting national hegemonies to a cohort of tutelary "deities" or "godlings" (reading bĕnê ʾĕlōhîm in v. 8b; cf. especially Ps 82:6: "gods, sons of ʿElyon [ʾĕlōhîm . . . bĕnê ʿelyôn]"). At least ostensibly, Yahweh acquires the people "Jacob" in this distribution—just as, in a similar scene described by the Greek poet Pindar, supreme Zeus allots the island of Rhodes as a fiefdom to the sun god Helios (*Olympian Odes* 7.54–64; cf. Deut 4:19; Mic 4:5). Elsewhere, though, "ʿElyon" is included among Yahweh's own names and epithets (e.g., Num 24:16; Pss 7:17; 18:13; 47:2[3]); this encourages the view that Yahweh, as the consortium's chief officer, retained "Jacob" for a personal possession (cf. Jer 10:16). A dramatic encounter reported in Gen 14:17–24 establishes the theological equation. Melchizedek, royal priest of Salem, blesses Abram in the name of ʾEl ʿElyon, "God Most High" (or perhaps, in its primal sense, "Supreme ʾEl"), who is entitled "creator [qōnēh] of heaven and earth" (14:18–20). In Abram's response, these credentials of Melchizedek's divine sovereign are assimilated, by conjoining them to Yahweh's name as a sort of titulary: "I have sworn to Yahweh, ʾEl ʾElyon, creator of heaven and earth . . ." (14:22; cf. Pss 115:15; 121:2).

Plenary God

Jethro's exuberant confession of Yahweh's greatness, together with the synthesis of divine credentials epitomized in Abram's oath, illuminates the Pentateuch's most comprehensive and consequential theological argument: Because

Yahweh's portfolio both encompasses and transcends the exercise of all powers traditionally ascribed to the cosmic consortium, there is no heavenly reason or earthly need to acknowledge the discrete existence of any other deity. The singular divine persona revealed to and invoked by Israel as "Yahweh" is the sum total of true divinity, plenary "God [*ĕlōhîm*]." Nothing that counts as divine is left over.

While the crux of this argument is developed in the lengthy review of Israel's exodus from Egypt and its covenantal sanctification at Sinai-Horeb, the Genesis narratives establish key elements of the thesis. Above all, in the opening sections of the book, which portray the emergence of world order, the consortium's pluriform identity and cosmic functions are allowed to recede into Yahweh's universal sovereignty.

The extraordinary prologue to the Pentateuch in Gen 1:1–2:3 (P) outlines the grand, imperious work of a creator who is identified only and often as "God [*ĕlōhîm*]." This nominal formation itself is plural, and is usually so rendered when it refers to any and all godly collectives (as in Jethro's confession and the expression "other gods"). But in the prologue, and often elsewhere when Israel's divine patron is ostensibly meant, the appellation is regularly construed as a singular entity: "Then God said [*wayyōʾmer ʾĕlōhîm*]" (Gen 1:3); "God saw [*wayyarʾ ʾĕlōhîm*]" (1:4); "God called [*wayyiqrāʾ ʾĕlōhîm*]" (1:5); and so forth. Even so, a still cogent plurality of being is disclosed within this majestic oneness when, in the course of the sixth-day's work, the creator proposes, "Let us make humankind in our image [*bĕṣalmēnû*], according to our likeness [*kidmûtēnû*]" (1:26). Singular "humankind [*ʾādām*]" is inherently here a collective of male and female persons who are designed, literally in concert, by the divine consortium "God." Hence, human beings have the capacity not only to reproduce, like earth's other animate creatures, but to perform the unique service of stewardship that is delegated to them in the form of a special divine blessing (1:27–28). Moreover, even when this blessing is compromised and requires renewal and adjustment, the "image" of the consortium remains indelible in the generations of humankind (5:1–2; 9:6; cf. Ps 8).

Lest there be any misunderstanding of the creator's unique personal identity, the storied account of creation that follows in Gen 2:4–3:24 (primarily J with P editing) regularly identifies the protagonist as "Yahweh God [*yhwh ʾĕlōhîm*]" (2:4–5, 7, etc.). This unusual pairing of divine appellations is an overt theological construction, not an accident of conflated sources. Its use here establishes that "Yahweh" fronts the consortium, largely assimilating or incorporating it, though the internal voice of divine deliberation still acknowledges plurality at a climactic moment (3:22: "like one of us"). Nor is it accidental when the plural appellation makes a brief independent reappearance in the portentous conversation between the serpent and the woman (3:1b–5): "God

[ʾĕlōhîm]" connotes the creator but also the divine company whose ranks primal humanity is prompted by the serpent to join, becoming "like gods [kēʾlōhîm], knowers of good and evil" (3:5). The immediate effort is not without some limited success (3:7, 22). Of course, other consequences are considerably more dubious, involving a decline in earth's productivity as well as in the prerogatives of each of the chief culprits (3:8–24).

From Gen 4:1 onward, through the rest of the book and into Exodus, preferences of the stratified sources do seem to explain, at least in large measure, discrete uses of "Yahweh" and "God [ʾĕlōhîm]" as principal designations for the singular divine protagonist. The consortium is not completely effaced, however (e.g., Gen 18:1; 19:1; 28:12; 32:1–2). Most remarkable is the episode in Gen 6:1–4, where the divine cohort makes a brief, bold, and perhaps even emblematic appearance, specifically identified as a plurality of "the sons of the gods [bĕnê hā ʾĕlōhîm]" (6:2, 4). The unchecked espousals of human women by these conciliar deities account for the rapid increase of human population in antediluvian times, including the births of the super "warriors" who are fabled as "Nephilim" (cf. Num 13:32–33). Already in antiquity this apparent glimpse of polytheistic myth was recast into an elaborate drama of rebellion in ʿElyon's heavenly assembly, which results in the expulsion of members of the angelic host, corrupted by lasciviousness, who nonetheless endure as estranged "watchers," the guardians of outlaw nations (1 En. 6–16; cf. Acts 7:42). However, nothing in the Genesis text indicates behavior by either the deities or their brides that is any more scandalous or ungodly than the act of procreation averred by Eve when Cain is born: "I have created a person [qānîtî ʾîš], together with Yahweh" (Gen 4:1; cf. Jub 4:14; Matt 1:20–21; Luke 1:26–38). Similarly, the executive action taken by Yahweh in Gen 6:3 is not punitive but rather prudential and corrective: It limits longevity of all spirit-empowered human beings—including those individuals who might claim heroic ancestry, an extra measure of superhuman vigor, or superlative achievement—to a maximum of one hundred twenty years (cf. Deut 34:7).

A major turning point in the narratives of Genesis is marked by the devastating flood that cleanses the earth of blood pollution (6:5–8:22), which is followed directly by God's recommissioning of humankind and covenantal pledge of constancy to all creatures preserved alive through Noah's faithful service (9:1–17). This epochal pact is only the first in a coordinated, five-part series of formal divine enactments that extends through the rest of the Pentateuch. The initial covenant anchors the whole series because it secures the cosmic ecosystem against another such dissolution, but it leaves open basic issues of divine governance or, more specifically, the question of how the Noahic remnant of humankind will be enabled to fulfill the creator's renewed and expanded charge to exercise responsible stewardship on earth (9:1–7; cf. 1:28).

The answers that begin to emerge in the genealogical drama of Israel's descent from Shem are introduced in Gen 10:1–11:9 by a detailed, comprehensive overview of human diaspora. It is important to note that this grand ethno-graphical sketch of Noah's segmentary, multicultural offspring resonates strongly with the world order of enfranchised nations whose designated guardians are the members of 'Elyon's heavenly assembly (Deut 32:8–9; Ps 82; cf. again *1 En.* 6–16). To be sure, the international perspective in Genesis 10 is mundane, and when the dispersion of Noahic humanity away from Babel is tersely portrayed in Gen 11:1–9, only Yahweh is named. Even here, though, a vestige of the plenary assembly remains, invoked to implement the executor's plan: "Come, let us go down so that we may confuse their language" (11:7).

The national charter of Jacob-Israel to minister as Yahweh's sanctified people comes into nearer view in the familiar stories featuring Abram and his patriarchal successors. The call in Gen 12:1–3 is a vocational commission, inviting Abram to accept Yahweh's agenda of blessing, which is designed to transform Abram's own heirs into "a great nation [*gôy gādôl*]" but also to enhance through them the well-being of all other "families of the earth." Abram's ready response draws him into the bilateral relationship that is con-solidated in the form of an "eternal covenant" in Genesis 17. Significantly, when this covenant is initiated Yahweh discloses another identity to Abram: "I am 'El Shaddai" (17:1). Often rendered "God Almighty," this appellation— even more so than its formal parallel "'El 'Elyon" (which was first invoked by Melchizedek in 14:19)—seems to connote parental oversight that is charac-teristically manifest through blessing, as it will be for Abram's heirs (28:3–4; 35:11; 43:14; 48:3; 49:25; Exod 6:3; cf. Num 24:4, 16). Yet the terms of the covenant itself emphasize generic divinity: "to be to you God [*lihyôt lĕkā lēʾlōhîm*] and to your descendants after you" (17:7; cf. Exod 29:45; etc.). If Yah-weh's specific credentials include the executive duties of 'El 'Elyon and now also the compassionate patronage of the divine kinsman 'El Shaddai, the com-plete portfolio is still most aptly comprehended by the designation "God."

Beginning with Abram's call, the providence of the plenary God, Yahweh, is disclosed in increasingly interpersonal and intimate ways (e.g., Gen 18:17–19; 25:23; 28:13–15; 46:3–4). Although the ecumenical horizon estab-lished in Gen 1:1–2:3 remains cogent, the Pentateuch's narrative focus has nar-rowed, and it will continue to draw tighter in order to concentrate on Israel's communal formation and the finely woven fabric of its revealed polity.

Early Christians understood themselves to live at a time when the focus of God's providence had expanded again, to clarify the whole of cosmic order and, especially, to include within its purview the redemption of the world's other nations descended from Noah, together with the Jewish heirs of Abra-ham and Moses. This Christian vision of God's ongoing work of creation was inspired by evangelists who identified Jesus as the preeminent "son of the Most High" (Mark 5:7; Luke 1:32; 8:28; cf. Matt 28:18–20) and by apostles who could even use an Athenian memorial to "an unknown god" as an opportunity to elaborate the ancient story of 'Elyon's assembly into a new cosmogonic drama of salvation (Acts 17:22–31; cf. Rom 1:16–3:26).

THE LORD, GOD OF ISRAEL

The wider, international perspective on Yahweh's providential work, so carefully and firmly established in Genesis, is not abandoned in the prolonged account of Israel's transformation from a patriarchal household into a well-ordered sacral community. For one thing, all of the major scenes are played out abroad—in Egypt, Midian, the wilderness of Sinai, Transjordan—that is, outside the boundaries of the territory that has already been set apart by divine allotment to become the national homeland for the family of Jacob among the lineages of Abraham (cf. Gen 15:17–21; 28:13–15; 37:1; Deut 2:2–23; 34:1–4). The extrapatrimonial settings have probative significance: They allow external witnesses, citizens of other nations, to be in attendance when Israel is reclaimed as Yahweh's firstborn and is then reconstituted as Yahweh's people through covenant. Like Jethro, these outside observers can thus attest what the Israelites themselves should know, that something unique has occurred, something much grander than a clandestine escape of foreign slaves from servitude in Egypt, something that on reflection is of decisive importance for an understanding of how and by whom the cosmos is governed (e.g., Exod 7:4–5; 9:29–30; 15:13–18; 18:10–12; Num 14:13–16; 23:7–24; cf. Josh 4:23–24). Furthermore, while the human catalyst for the transformation has a levitical pedigree (Exod 2:1–2; 6:16–25), his early vita identifies him as an internationalist—who is closely affiliated with prominent Egyptian and Midianite families—before he is recruited to oversee a new phase in the program of nation-building that began with the commission of Abram.

The elaborate literary architecture of the books of Exodus through Deuteronomy develops a scenario of Israelite repatriation, which was already sketched in visions to the principal patriarchs (Gen 15:13–16; 46:1–4). The plot has three major narrative segments. The first segment, Exodus 1–18, is the most familiar and dramatic as well as the shortest of the three. It describes how Jacob's descendants are subjected to genocide and harsh exploitation by a tyrannical Egyptian regime, and how their ancestral God, through the agency of Moses, gains their release and leads them to an isolated haven in the wilderness. In the second and longest segment, extending from Exodus 19 through Num 10:10, the former slaves of Pharaoh remain encamped for a year at Mount Sinai or Horeb, in the vicinity of Midian. Here, where Moses had received his own call to serve the ancestral God, they undergo the initial stages of a corporate rebirth, acquiring a new, more comprehensive political identity, polity, and mission. In the third segment, Num 10:11 through Deuteronomy 34, God's fledgling people, with Moses continuing to guide them, travel fitfully from Sinai-Horeb, taking a full generation to reach the eastern threshold of the national homeland promised to their ancestors. Although it is misleading to describe this three-part narrative as a biography of Moses, he certainly plays a unique, authoritative role in the progressive unfolding of the sublime character and intentions of Israel's divine sovereign.

Exaltation of Yahweh and Moses

In Exodus 1–18, the God already known by various names to Israel's ancestors is disclosed anew as Yahweh, first to Moses in Midian and then through him to both the enslaved Israelites and their Egyptian oppressors. The knowledge targeted at each of these parties is strategic. It involves an urgent and radical claim of sovereignty that none of them accepts as authentic until it is shown through experience to be ineluctable. The effect of this demonstration, in individual cases as well as overall results, is to provide an empirical basis for trust in Yahweh's insuperable, secure, and exacting hegemony.

The remarkably fulsome account of Moses' call and investiture in Exod 3:1–4:17 (cf. 6:2–8) emphasizes that God's attentiveness to Israel's immediate plight in Egypt is explicable and reliable as part of a long-term agenda of divine patronage (cf. 2:23–25). The task of emancipating Israel, proffered to Moses by the one who addresses him from a blazing bush, is thus not capricious, nor is Moses' resistance to the assignment, which is only overcome when the preliminary promise of godly presence with him (3:12; cf. Gen 28:15; 46:4) is amplified into a credible vocational endowment. Of first importance, Moses learns that the mysterious speaker is his own and Israel's tutelary deity, whose personal name is "Yahweh." Even though the connotations of the name remain veiled or inchoate here, Moses' acquisition of it has practical, efficacious significance, establishing the way in which the ancestral God may henceforth be invoked. The name's correct use will become the hallmark of Israel's corporate identity and worship "for all generations" (Exod 3:15; cf., e.g., Num 6:22–27; Deut 4:7; 6:13; Mic 4:5). Secondly, Moses negotiates the means to exhibit Yahweh's power through mighty deeds and words, a capacity Israel will memorialize as an unequaled personal distinction (Deut 34:10–12; cf. Sir 45:3).

Neither in his investiture nor in the political encounters that follow is Moses referred to as Yahweh's "prophet [nābîʾ]." That will be Aaron's inaugural role, as spokesman for Moses. Apparently from the outset, Moses himself is coopted into a higher rank of divine service, to be a corporeal extension of Yahweh's discriminating will. He will personify plenary "God [ʾĕlōhîm]" to both Pharaoh and the Israelites (Exod 4:15–16; 7:1–2). Somewhat later, when he is fully tenured as Israel's leader, Moses will be identified as Yahweh's prime "servant [ʿebed]" (Exod 14:31; cf. Num 12:6–8; Josh 1:2), a role that all Israelites will eventually share (Lev 25:42, 55). A rare, metaphysical honorific is associated with Moses only at the end of his career, when he is entitled a spiritually engrossed "man of the gods [ʾîš hāʾĕlōhîm]" (Deut 33:1; cf. Josh 14:6; Ps 90 [heading]; Sir 44:23b–45:2). Without doubt, the Pentateuchal portraits of Yahweh as Israel's only God and of Moses as Yahweh's most trusted confidant form a striking hologram of divine agency in temporal affairs.

What Pharaoh hears initially and then repeatedly from Moses, but can never fully acknowledge, is that Yahweh's claim on the Israelites is proprietary, preceding and superseding Egypt's enslavement of them (Exod 4:22–23; 5:1–2; 7:4–5; 8:1–2). By continuing to constrain Yahweh's cherished "firstborn," Pharaoh defies Yahweh's legitimate exercise of sovereignty. His arrogant obstinacy thus compromises his own rule, even over Egyptian subjects whose lives become forfeit to Israel's more powerful, cosmic sovereign (8:22–23; 9:13–17, 27–30; 10:1–2, 7; 11:4–8; 14:15–18; cf. 13:1–16). Conversely, the series of increasingly deadly plagues inflicted on Egypt and the climactic deliverance of the Israelites—achieved through the defeat of Pharaoh and his chariotry in the battle at the sea—vindicate at once Yahweh's hegemonic claim and the authority of Moses, Yahweh's servant who has persistently represented it (14:30–31). Given this public confirmation of Moses' preternatural status, it is significant that the tradition depicts him after the battle standing at the seaside with the astonished Israelites, to lead them in an anthem extolling the victory of their ancestral God—who now, as the incomparable warrior Yahweh, has demonstrated the prowess to reign supreme "forever and ever" (15:1–18). Jethro's personal confession upon hearing the news merits notice once again because it underscores in context the knowledge that eluded Pharaoh and that the Israelites have finally begun to assimilate: "Now I know that Yahweh is greater than all the gods" (Exod 18:11; cf. 14:10–14).

God Merciful and Gracious

When, in accord with God's signal pledge at the time of Moses' commissioning (Exod 3:12), the refugee Israelites reach Sinai-Horeb, they begin a year-long novitiate in the communal service of Yahweh. The general character of the curriculum and its expected outcome are announced without delay through Moses (Exod 19:4–6a):

You have seen what I did to Egypt; I bore you up on eagles' wings and brought you to myself. And now, if you heed my voice and keep my covenant you shall become my most treasured one among all the peoples. Although the entire earth is mine, you shall be my priestly dominion and holy nation.

Without discounting important differences of language and conceptuality, this familiar proposal bears some resemblance to the cosmogonic work of 'Elyon's assembly sketched in Deut 32:8–9. The critical difference is that here Yahweh and the community of Jacob-Israel are to be conjoined by an expressly bilateral "covenant" rather than a magisterial grant. Still, in both versions Yahweh establishes a discretionary claim in favor of one particular national enclave among the world's separated populations. Moreover, the conditional or reciprocal quality of the bond between God and treasured people indicated in Exod 19:5 (cf. 19:8; 15:26; Lev 26:3–45; Deut 26:16–19) also comes to the fore, and painfully so, in the continuation of the poetic version in Deuteronomy 32. Those who, like Moses himself, are gathered into Yahweh's sacral dominion are privileged by and for the loyal service they perform. The complementary concepts of justification and sanctification are helpful in characterizing the theological foundations of this service.

In the narrative sequence, the primary obligations of the "covenant" proposed in Exod 19:5 are the "words," well known as the Decalogue, addressed to the assembly of Israel by the deity now identified as "Yahweh your God who brought you out of the land of Egypt" (20:1–17). Even before Moses receives the tablets on which this text is inscribed (24:12; 31:18) additional provisions are divinely legislated, with Moses serving as clerk, in order to amplify the principal commands, expanding them into a more comprehensive social charter (20:18–23:33; cf. Deut 4:12–14; 5:1–6:3). The covenant relationship so defined and interpreted in law is then recorded and ceremonially ratified, with emphasis placed on Israel's professions of fidelity (Exod 24:1–8; cf. 19:7–8). But the contract is immediately and almost irreparably violated. While Moses remains in communion with Yahweh atop the shrouded mountain, the apprehensive company of Israelites below becomes ensnared in idolatrous worship (32:1–10). Retribution is severe, as it had been earlier, when Egypt was devastated in order to gain Israel's release (e.g., 12:29; 13:15; 14:30). At Sinai, punitive wrath takes the form of a plague as well as a bloody, fratricidal purge executed by Moses' levitical colleagues (32:25–29, 35). Nevertheless, we are told that Moses' bold, vigorous intercession on Israel's behalf is expiatory, securing a reprieve for a remnant of the people (32:11–14, 30–34). In Exod 33:1–16, Moses presses the case even further. He parlays his personal "favor [ḥēn]" with Yahweh into a commitment that Yahweh's own presence will accompany him and the Israelites—"I and your people"—when they continue the journey to the homeland reserved for them in Canaan. The important implication in this exchange is that the delegated guardianship of an angelic surrogate or subordinate member of the divine assembly would only suffice to make Israel like other nations, whereas Yahweh's executive presence will assure that Israel too will be incomparable, remaining distinct "from every people on the face of the earth" (33:1, 16; cf. 23:20–24; Dan 10:13, 21; 12:1; cf. Num 14:13–16; Deut 4:6–8; 33:29).

What follows in Exod 33:17–34:28 includes the enactment of another covenant, one that modifies in two crucial respects the now defunct agreement that was intimated in 19:3–6 and formalized in 24:1–8. First, while the former covenant presupposed Israel's experience of Yahweh as the stern, demanding judge and uncompromising warrior who had triumphed over Egypt (e.g., 15:3–12, 26), the revised covenant of 34:10–28 is predicated on a much fuller, more nuanced knowledge of Yahweh's essential character and priorities. In response to his request to be shown Yahweh's intimate "ways" and "glory" (33:13, 18), Moses is privileged with at least a clear auditory perception of the "goodness" of the divine being who is encoded by the name Yahweh (33:19; cf. 3:13–14). The theophanous declaration in Exod 34:6–7, which opens with an emphatic repetition ("The LORD! The LORD!"), articulates what the name "Yahweh" henceforth means and makes accessible to worshipers who respect its sanctity (e.g., Num 6:24–27; Pss 103:6–14; 145:8–9; Mic 7:18–20). The deity so invoked in humble, penitent supplication is "God merciful and gracious [ʾēl raḥûm wĕḥannûn]." To be sure, this perennial wellspring of compassion and of grace upon grace is neither erratic nor gratuitous. Because the source has the character of divine personhood—"Yahweh" who is "God [ʾēl]"—its abundant flow is purposeful, directed, calibrated (e.g., Num 14:13–15; Deut 4:31; Joel 2:12–14). The attributes listed in Exod 34:6b–7 reveal the norms by which this benevolent sovereign appropriately metes out mercy and correlates its distribution with justice. Revelation of Yahweh's propensity to "lift up" or "forgive iniquity, transgression, and sin" is especially cogent, even with the qualifications that remain in place (cf. Exod 20:5b–6; 34:14; Num 14:20–24; Deut 7:9–10). Moses is quick to make petitionary use of this knowledge in order to reestablish the unique relationship that had been ruptured by the calf apostasy: "If I have found favor in your eyes, O Lord, then let the Lord go in our midst—even though it is a stiff-necked people—and pardon our iniquity and our sin, and make us [your very own] possession" (34:9). Especially after the singular "I" of the protasis, the plural pronouns of the apodosis—"our midst . . . our iniquity and our sin . . . make us"—are poignant. Moses, whom God had earlier declared worthy of replacing the deeply flawed Israelites (32:10), identifies with them once again. He invokes his own merit as God's faithful servant on behalf of his people, so that they may be forgiven and reconciled with Yahweh through him. Second, and consequently, the covenant that follows is enacted by Yahweh principally with Moses himself (singular "you") and "with Israel" only to the extent that the people are encompassed by or subsist in him (34:10, 27). In order to remain God's most treasured possession among the nations (19:5), the Israel that Moses represents, and for whom he has so effectively interceded, must be saved, justified, and sustained by divine grace.

Alongside the theme of covenant as a diplomatically constituted bond between God and the people Israel is another, more sacramental understanding of the relationship, which defines Israel's vocation in terms of the communal purity, piety, and sacrificial worship that enable it to function in ministry on Yahweh's behalf. This interconnected theme of sanctification is most expansively developed in Leviticus, where it is epitomized by the charge, "You shall be holy, for I, Yahweh your God, am holy" (Lev 19:2). According to this view, Israel is constituted as "a priestly dominion and holy nation" (Exod 19:6) when it conforms to the holiness that is the unassailable attribute of the God who delivered it from Egypt, thereby separating it from the nations (e.g., Lev 11:44–45; 20:26; Num 15:40–41).

Sanctification is the discipline of imitating God's ways that Israel is instructed through Moses to perform, but it is also a gracious gift of consecration that it receives (cf. Exod 31:13; Lev 20:8; 21:1–23; 22:32) so that it may sustain in its midst the real presence of God, which is mediated by "the tabernacle [*hammiškān*]" (e.g., Exod 25:8–9). The intricate design of the tabernacle complex, centered on the ark, and the basic orders of priesthood, liturgy, and expiatory rites crucial to its operation are revealed to Moses on Sinai in Exodus 25–31 and supplemented in Leviticus. Only after the first covenant is broken and the second one is negotiated to replace it are the plans for construction of the tabernacle carefully implemented under Moses' supervision (Exod 35–40). Once the work is complete, the "glory of Yahweh [*kĕbôd yhwh*]," whose exterior veil is the dense cloud that had formerly settled on Sinai, takes up residence within the congregation of Israel (40:34–38; cf. Num 9:15–23). The God who creates has created something new, a living sanctuary set apart in the midst of the world's nations.

Yahweh Alone Is God

By the time of their departure from Sinai (Num 10:11–28), both Moses and Israel have ostensibly been transfigured. They have been drawn into the orbit of divinity and are physically imprinted with God's presence. As episodes narrated in the rest of the Pentateuch will indicate, however, transfiguration is not to be confused with deification, nor does it confer either personal or communal autonomy. The boundaries inherent to Yahweh's sacral order must be respected, even though the degrees of holiness are sometimes difficult to discern.

Moses' transfiguration occurs when, in the climactic encounter at the summit of Mount Sinai, Yahweh passes "across his face [*al-pānāw*]" (Exod 34:6a), which leaves it fearsomely radiant (34:29–35; cf. 33:11). Although different terminology is used, the episode narrated in Num 11:16–30 underscores Moses' sacral empowerment, describing how some of his abundant "spirit [*rûaḥ*]" is allowed by Yahweh to spill over onto the council of elders who assist in the governance of Israel (cf. Num 27:18–23; Deut 1:9–18; 27:1; 34:9). Lest this charismatic enfranchisement suggest a complete relaxation or democratization of divine authority, Numbers 12 reports oracular confirmation of Moses' singular status: He alone is the one to whom Yahweh has entrusted oversight of "my entire household" and through whom Yahweh communicates directly, "mouth to mouth [*peh ʾel peh*]" (12:7–8; cf. Deut 34:10). Apparently only once does Moses, the man renowned for his incomparable humility (Num 12:3), identify himself too closely with the divine persona who acts through him (Num 20:9–12; cf. Deut 32:51).

Israel's corporate transfiguration into a "holy nation" is attested by the schematized arrangement of the camp, as portrayed in Num 1:1–10:10. Here too, authority in matters of sacral politics is guarded and gradated, with the Aaronid priesthood, supported by the lower orders of Levites, playing an instrumental role in the maintenance of communal holiness (cf. Num 16–19) and in the distribution of divine blessing (e.g., Num 6:22–27; cf. Lev 9:22–23; Deut 10:8). The vigilance expected of the clergy is exemplified in the Baal Peʿor episode (Num 25). Phinehas, Aaron's grandson, responds with deadly force to an act of sacrilege, thereby rescuing the integrity of the relationship between Yahweh and consecrated community. His reward is the fourth in the series of five Pentateuchal covenants—the "covenant of peace" that bestows upon his lineage the inalienable right to high priestly office (25:10–13; cf. Exod 6:16–25; Sir 45:24).

The narrative provides an external view of Israel in the post-Sinai era. Jethro's confession of Yahweh's incomparability among the gods (Exod 18:11) has its counterpart in the witness of the prophet Balaam, another non-Israelite, whose four oracles focus on the incomparability of Israel as the singular people of Yahweh (Num 23–24). Themes of national empowerment and of divine blessing and curse that were introduced in the commission of Abram (Gen 12:1–3) have symphonic resonance here (e.g., Num 23:8, 20; 24:9). While this prophetic testimony is eloquent as well as probative for the Pentateuchal portrait of Yahweh's providential work, it is fitting that Moses' own splendid disquisitions provide the theological capstone of Torah.

The three foundational affirmations noted at the beginning of this essay come to forceful cognitive expression throughout Deuteronomy. Each of the book's four major parts, which together comprise Moses' testament, emphasizes that Israel has been uniquely constituted among the world's nations so that through its corporate life it may continue to exemplify the superlative values, integrity, and benefactions of Yahweh's universal sovereignty. Although the Yahwistic Israel addressed by Moses is a stubborn, conflicted work in progress, rather than an immaculate conception of the divine assembly, at least in theory it is endowed through grace with the knowledge and the capacity to become a reification of the image of God in humankind.

Deuteronomy 1:1–4:43 consists in the main of Moses' first-person memoirs, which review key episodes of the prolonged and often troubled journey from Sinai-Horeb to the plains of Moab (1:6–3:29). This is followed by a didactic peroration (4:1–40) that epitomizes the primary argument of Pentateuchal theology. Here, for the first time in Scripture, what Israel is supposed to have learned through its early history as God's covenant people comes to succinct, unqualified expression as a monotheistic creed: "Yahweh is the (plenary) God [*hāʾĕlōhîm*] in heaven above and on earth beneath; there is no other" (4:39; cf. 4:35; 32:39). At the center of the testament, in 4:44–28:68, is "the polity [*hattôrâ*]" whose statutory rulings [*haḥuqqîm wĕhammišpāṭîm*]" articulate systematically the covenantal principles and practices by which Israel is expected to conduct itself and to succeed as Yahweh's people. In retrospect, this promulgation completes the commission that Moses received to amplify the Decalogue into a permanent national constitution (cf. Exod 34:10–28; Deut 1:3; 5:1–6:3; 31:9–13; cf. Josh 1:7–8; Mal 4:4 [3:22]). Similarly, the reciprocal oaths of Yahweh and the assembled people, reported in Deut 26:16–19, ratify the relationship that had been proposed when Israel reached Sinai-Horeb a generation before (Exod 19:3–6). The polity is complemented in 29:1 [28:29]–32:52 by the last of the Pentateuch's five covenants, this one identified in the superscription as "the covenant Yahweh charged Moses to enact with the Israelites in the land of Moab." The Moab covenant bestows upon a broadly inclusive, multigenerational "all Israel" the communal identity and individual accountability under the exclusive rule of Yahweh that Moses has held in trust for the people until the very end of his career. The testament concludes with Moses' blessing of the Israelite tribes (33:1–29), which is followed by a brief account of his departure (34:1–9) and a closing epitaph that professes his incomparability as an instrument of divine providence in Israel's formative history (34:10–12).

THE GOD OF ISRAEL AND THE NATIONS

With the clarity of its Mosaic vision, Deuteronomy knows that the generations of "all Israel" will continue to struggle with their inherited vocational identity as the covenant people of "the LORD," their only God, who also rules the whole cosmos as "God of gods and Lord of lords" (cf. 4:32–40; 10:12–22). Under the tutelage of Moses' Torah, which extends the guidance of Moses himself, these incarnations of Israel will experience the debilitating effects of curse as well as the prosperity of blessing in the land granted to the ancestors (e.g., 4:25–28; 11:13–17; 28; 30:15–20; 32:1–43; cf. Lev 26). Even when Moses' heirs find themselves dispersed in exile among the nations, however, they have the assurance that the divine sovereign revealed as "God merciful [*ʾel raḥûm*]" will never abandon them entirely but rather continue to seek their repentance, reconciliation, and restoration (Deut 4:31; cf. 32:36–43).

Deuteronomy foresees less clearly when and how other nations of the world, whose ostensible guardians are subordinate members of the divine assembly (4:19; 29:26; 32:8–9), will come to acknowledge that "the LORD" alone is God. Sufficient as a foundation for the rest of Scripture—that is, for the Prophets and the Writings but also for the New Testament—is the confidence that Israel's own fortunes will be decisive in this ongoing drama. Above all, the efficacy of Israel's fidelity to Torah should demonstrate to the nations the preeminent sovereignty and providence of the deity it has learned to invoke as "the LORD" (4:6–8).

Claiming a culminating, lucid, and definitive revelation in Jesus Christ (e.g., Luke 24:13–27; Heb 1:1–4), the writings of the New Testament both accept and enlarge the Pentateuchal portrait of God's unique character and sovereign purposes. Thus, when Jesus is asked to identify the Torah's "greatest commandment of all" (Mark 12:29), he begins his response with the Mosaic proclamation of Deut 6:4: "Hear, Israel! Our God is the LORD, the LORD alone." And when addressing the threat of idolatry in the Corinthian congregation, Paul affirms that however numerous may be the purported deities "in heaven or on earth, as indeed there are many (such) gods and many (such) lords, for us there is (only) one God, the Father, from whom all things are and for whom we exist" (1 Cor 8:5–6; cf. Rom 3:29–30). Even the Johannine evangelist, whose high Christology is one of the most important factors in the parting of the ways between Christianity and Judaism, does not retreat from Israel's confession that there is only one God, though he now affirms that in Jesus the Creator's eternal "Word became flesh and tabernacled among us . . . full of grace and truth" (John 1:14).

Neither does the New Testament deny Israel's perennial vocation as God's people, even when it insists that God's reconciling work in Christ now also invites the world's dispersed nations into a new covenantal relationship. Thus, in the Synoptic Gospels, Jesus trains and commissions his disciples to enlarge the boundaries of Israel of old, granting them the authority not only to baptize "in the name of the Father and of the Son and of the Holy Spirit" but to amplify the commandments of Torah in preparation for God's universal kingly rule (Matt 5:17–20; 28:16–20; Luke 24:44–49; cf. Acts 1:8). Although Paul's testimony about Israel and the efficacy of Torah is more ambivalent and diverse, he too avers that God has not rejected Moses' faithful heirs in favor of converts from other nations (Rom 9–11). If some of Abraham's children according to the flesh have stumbled, while the church finds increasing acceptance among Gentiles, that is because of a discrete divine plan whose temporal denouement must include the salvation of "all Israel" (Rom 11:11, 26). This is so because for Paul "God merciful" sustains the lives of Jews and Gentiles alike (Rom 9:14–16; 11:30–32).

Likewise, the writings of the New Testament continue to affirm the foundational significance of Moses' person and ministry. For the early church, Jesus was "the prophet like Moses," whom God had promised to send (Deut 18:15–16; Acts 3:22; 7:37). Moreover, Moses' exaltation as God's preeminent servant, who brings divine presence into Israel's midst, is the model for Jesus' own transfiguration (Matt 17:3–8; cf. Mark 9:2–8; Luke 9:28–36). Like Moses, Jesus thus speaks for, or as, God and performs God's own work (cf. Deut 34:11–12 and Luke 24:19). Once again, Paul's ambivalence is noteworthy. Sometimes, as in Galatians, Paul seems to avoid direct reference to Moses, quite possibly because his Judaizing opponents claimed Mosaic authority on behalf of their ministry to the Gentile congregations of Galatia. In 1 Corinthians 10:1–4, interestingly, Paul refers to Israelites of the exodus generation as "baptized into Moses," which has its counterpart in the new baptism into Christ (12:12–13; cf. Rom 6:3). And 2 Cor 3:4–4:18 argues that Paul and other Christians have been commissioned as "ministers of a new covenant" that expressly supersedes the Mosaic covenant of Exodus 34 (cf. also Heb 8:6–9:22).

The Christian Scriptures, from beginning to end, attest to the unique sovereignty and coherent providence of a divine creator who nurtured Israel's emergence in history and who claimed it through the agency of Moses to be a special possession among the nations of humankind. This is the same God whom Christians know through faith in Christ as Lord and Savior. It is a privilege to offer this essay in tribute to one whose provocative scholarship has always affirmed the importance of remembering the old in order to understand and embrace what is genuinely new.

SELECT BIBLIOGRAPHY

Balentine, Samuel E. 1999. *The Torah's Vision of Worship*. Overtures to Biblical Theology. Minneapolis: Fortress.
Blenkinsopp, Joseph. 1992. *The Pentateuch: An Introduction to the First Five Books of the Bible*. Anchor Bible Reference Library. New York: Doubleday.
Campbell, Antony F., and Mark A. O'Brien. 1993. *Sources of the Pentateuch: Texts, Introductions, Annotations*. Minneapolis: Fortress.

Cross, Frank M. 1973. *Canaanite Myth and Hebrew Epic: Essays in the History of the Religion of Israel*. Cambridge, Mass.: Harvard University Press.

Halpern, Baruch. 1993. "The Baal (and the Asherah) in Seventh-Century Judah: Yhwh's Retainers Retired." Pages 115–54 in *Konsequente Traditionsgeschichte: Festschrift für Klaus Baltzer zum 65. Geburtstag*. Edited by Rüdiger Bartelmus, Thomas Krüger, and Helmut Utzschneider. Orbis Biblicus et Orientalis 126. Freiburg, Switzerland: Universitätsverlag; Göttingen: Vandenhoeck & Ruprecht.

Hurtado, Larry W. 1988. *One God, One Lord: Early Christian Devotion and Ancient Jewish Monotheism*. Philadelphia: Fortress.

Janowski, Bernd. 2000. "The One God of the Two Testaments: Basic Questions of a Biblical Theology." *Theology Today* 57: 297–324.

Kugel, James L. 1998. *Traditions of the Bible: A Guide to the Bible as It Was at the Start of the Common Era*. Cambridge, Mass.: Harvard University Press.

Levenson, Jon D. 1985. *Creation and the Persistence of Evil: The Jewish Drama of Divine Omnipotence*. San Francisco: Harper & Row.

Lohfink, Norbert. 1994. *Theology of the Pentateuch: Themes of the Priestly Narrative and Deuteronomy*. Translated by Linda M. Maloney. Minneapolis: Fortress.

Mann, Thomas W. 1988. *The Book of the Torah: The Narrative Integrity of the Pentateuch*. Atlanta: John Knox.

McBride, S. Dean, Jr. 2000. "Divine Protocol: Genesis 1:1–2:3 as Prologue to the Pentateuch." Pages 3–41 in *God Who Creates: Essays in Honor of W. Sibley Towner*. Edited by William P. Brown and S. Dean McBride, Jr. Grand Rapids: Eerdmans.

Miller, Patrick D. 2000. *The Religion of Ancient Israel*. Library of Ancient Israel. London: SPCK; Louisville: Westminster John Knox.

Mullen, E. Theodore, Jr. 1997. *Ethnic Myths and Pentateuchal Foundations: A New Approach to the Formation of the Pentateuch*. Semeia Studies. Atlanta: Scholars Press.

Smith, Mark S. 2001. *The Origins of Biblical Monotheism: Israel's Polytheistic Background and the Ugaritic Texts*. Oxford: Oxford University Press.

Soulen, R. Kendall. 1996. *The God of Israel and Christian Theology*. Minneapolis: Fortress.

2

The God Who Reigns

The Book of Psalms

JAMES LUTHER MAYS

The book of Psalms is one of the two Old Testament books with the most quotations and allusions in the New Testament. The other book is Isaiah. The relationship is clear evidence for the importance of the Psalms for the writers of the New Testament. But when the quotes and allusions are examined, it is apparent that they are not usually employed to record what these authors believed about God. Their theology, in the specific sense of that term, seems to be assumed.

THE PSALMS AS THEOLOGICAL PROLEGOMENA

When the quotations and allusions are ordered according to the purpose of their use, the majority fall into two groups. The first is christological—the use of psalmic material to disclose, interpret, and illuminate the person, work, and fate of Jesus as God's Messiah. Obvious illustrations are the citation of Ps 2:7 at Jesus' baptism (Matt 3:17; par.), Ps 22:18 in the Passover narrative (Matt 27:35; par.), and Ps 110:4 in the pastoral discourse of Hebrews (Heb 5:6, 10; 6:20; 7:11, 15, 21). The second group is anthropological in function. Descriptions of the enemy and the wicked in the Psalms are used to characterize the fallibility and finitude of the human condition in the human relation to God. Examples are Ps 5:9 in Rom 3:13; Ps 94:11 in 1 Cor 3:20; and Ps 34:12–16 in 1 Pet 3:10–12.

What these groupings (along with other less frequent uses of psalmic material) show is that quotations and allusions are not the best guide to the substance and importance of the knowledge of God in the Psalms for the New Testament. The Psalms themselves, however, contain more direct statements about God than any other book in the two testaments of the Christian canon. God is described and evoked in the hymns, prayers, and instructional poetry of the Psalms by testimony to what God has done and typically does and by assertions of the features of God's character. The works of God and the attributes of God are the constant agenda of the Psalms.

There is a scattered use of the psalmic theological material in the New Testament. Paul cites "The earth is the LORD's and all that is in it" (Ps 24:1) in his instruction to the Corinthians about dietary practices (1 Cor 10:26). The call to "Taste and see that the LORD is good" (Ps 34:8) is echoed in the exhortation in 1 Pet 2:3. In Rev 15:4, "All the nations you have made shall come and bow down before you" (Ps 86:9) is read as eschatological prophecy. The declaration, "The LORD is just in all his ways, and kind in all his doings" (Ps 145:17), is repeated in the heavenly praise around the divine throne in Rev 15:3.

These examples suggest that the identity and character and conduct of God did not need to be a primary agenda for the writers of the New Testament. The knowledge of God is assumed. They appealed to the Psalms and other Old Testament books as a source for the knowledge of God when the need arose in addressing the concerns of Christology, soteriology, and ecclesiology. Otherwise they assumed and read the Psalms as authoritative witness to God.

In the matter of the relation between the witness to God in the Psalms and the theology of the New Testament, the project must be oriented by the New Testament to discern what is assumed. What elements of the Psalms' view of God are necessary and significant for the New Testament, granted that a certain amount of rereading in the light of the developing Christology of the Christian community takes place? The following points to only some of the underground relationships.

"THE LORD IS GOD"

The first and indispensable statement about God in the Psalms must be a sentence in which God is the predicate instead of the subject. The term "god" is a class noun. In the language of biblical and contemporary times it can refer to any being reckoned to belong to the class of designates. *Elohim* in the Hebrew Bible is used for any deity or as a plural for deities in general. In the Psalms, as in the entire Old Testament, the ambiguity is dealt with by the use of a name. The name is used in two ways: first, to establish the identity of the god to whom praise and prayer is offered and, second, to claim the noun "god" exclusively for the name.

The basic and indispensable sentence is "the LORD is God" (Ps 100:3). The subject of the sentence is the name YHWH. In the history of the Hebrew text, the consonants of the name out of reverence were vocalized as *Adonai* (Lord), and this title itself functioned as a name. The sentence says who God is and who is God. It means to identify the God who is the theological subject of the Psalms and to claim the predicate of the sentence exclusively for the one identified in the subject of the sentence. The effect of the claim is that the noun "god" also comes to be used as an identifying name, the practice found in the group of psalms called Elohist psalms, where "God" predominates as the name, rather than "LORD" (Pss 42–83).

The proper name YHWH identifies the God who is known in Israel through his works and words. For the writers of the New Testament, God is the One known through the Scriptures, the Torah and Prophets and Writings. The works and words of the God of Israel so much constitute the knowledge of God and his identity that the name itself becomes a theologumenon. In the Psalms, to pray is to "call on the name of the LORD" and to praise is to "praise the name of the LORD."

In the Psalms, all the elements of the faith and language that know and say who God is are assembled in poetry of praise, prayer, and instruction. The Psalms in the context of the other Hebrew Scriptures are the indispensable prolegomena to the meaning of "God" in the New Testament. It is this prolegomena that makes it possible and meaningful to say "he is one, and besides him there is no other" (Mark 12:32; cf. Rom 3:30).

"THE LORD REIGNS"

The New Testament opens with Jesus' proclamation of the kingdom of God. The theme is expounded and elaborated in his teaching and career. At the conclusion of the New Testament, the book of Revelation opens up the vision of the One whose name is "King of kings and Lord of lords" (Rev 19:16). The hymns and prayers in the Psalter show how theologically comprehensive and significant the theme is. In the Psalms, the organizing theological metaphor is the reign of God. God's relation to all dimensions and aspects of reality is thought of and spoken about as a sovereignty.

In the focal panel of the arrangement of the book of Psalms there is a group of hymns whose theme is *"YHWH malak"* (Pss 93–100). The sentence is both proclamation and confession of faith. It can be translated as a nominal sentence, "The LORD is king" (NRSV) or a verbal, "The LORD reigns" (RSV). The verbal reading brings out better the dynamic active sense intended by the affirmation. The reign of the Lord God is more an activity than an office. It is constituted by what the Lord has done, is doing, and will do. So the language about the Lord's reign in the Psalms allows one to think of it as something accomplished and established, something that occurs in specific events, and something expected.

The Lord's active role is the effective power in shaping the two constitutive spheres of reality. God's power is at work in the very existence of the world and in what happens in the world. The Lord reigns in creation and in history. There are psalms that deal with the two spheres separately. Psalms 29 and 93 concentrate on the exercise of the Lord's royal power to establish the earth in the midst of the chaotic and uncreated floods. Psalms 47 and 98 focus on God's way with the nations and peoples of the world and portray the salvation history of the people of God as the manifestation of God's reign in the world of nations. But the two are coherent and continuous exercises of the same power and purpose, and can be spoken about in the synonymity in which they belong in a proclamation to be made universally: "Say among the nations, 'The LORD is king! The world is firmly established; it shall never be moved. He will judge the peoples with equity'" (Ps 96:10). What the LORD has begun in the creation of the world is being enacted and completed among the peoples of the earth. The realization of the LORD's reign is the theme of all reality.

The hymns and prayers and instructional poetry of the Psalter do not, of course, present a systematic account of the reign of the LORD. But this poetry is based on and reflects a theology of God's conduct and character that is foundational for the New Testament. As creator, the LORD is sovereign over all peoples and every person in the world, and all owe the LORD fealty and depend on him for life. The LORD is working in the history of his people. He has claimed them to reveal and establish his reign in the world over the nations and their gods. The LORD is shepherd (a royal metaphor) of his flock and every person in it. He has designated one person as his anointed to play a special role in his relation to his people and especially the nations. As creator, the LORD has manifested himself as "God of glory." In his dealing with his people he has disclosed his holiness (Ps 9:8), his righteousness and justice (97:2), his steadfast love and faithfulness (98:3), and his way of combining forgiveness with rebuke (99:8).

"THE EARTH IS THE LORD'S"

In the teaching of Jesus, God is represented as creator and human beings are regarded first of all as God's creatures. God is "Father, Lord of Heaven and earth" (Matt 11:25), who "makes his sun rise on the evil and on the good and sends rain on the righteous and on the unrighteous" (Matt 5:45) and knows and provides for all human needs (Matt 6:25). For Paul, "there is one God, the Father, from whom are all things and for whom we exist" (1 Cor 8:6). In believing and deciding, it is fundamental that "the earth and its fullness are the Lord's" (1 Cor 10:26, quoting Ps 24:1).

This confidence that all that exists is the creation of the Lord God and that the identity of human beings as his creations is the truth about their existence and conduct assumes the Old Testament. The Psalms are in this matter the canonical correlate of Genesis 1–2. In what some psalms say and in the very way the book as a whole is arranged, God is viewed in his relation to humans as first of all their creator. God's work in the salvation history of his people is put after and in continuity with the creation work. In this respect, the Psalms are open to a reading that includes the way of God with the peoples of the world as coherent with his way with the people of Israel.

The Psalms are insistent and consistent in holding the identity of the Lord as creator together with the status of human beings as his creation, who in their createdness are dependent on God and responsible to him. Psalm 8 advocates a theocentric view of the universe and an anthropocentric view of God's purpose in it. The One whose glory is set in the heavens is nonetheless concerned specifically with humankind and has given humans a role in relation to the other creatures that is analogous to God's relation to the universe. Yet, as Psalm 104 says, human beings remain one of the creatures incorporated into the ecology of earth and dependent on God for the gift and maintenance of their life. All is and remains the work of the Lord.

The Lord is not only sovereign over human beings because they and the earth in which they live belong to him as creator (Ps 24:1–2), but humans individually are bound to him in an intimate and personal way. God "fashions the hearts of them all, and observes all their deeds" (Ps 33:15). Psalm 139 describes how each person in what one does and thinks and where one goes is "known" by the Lord in a way that includes even the formation of the person in the womb.

The Lord's work as creator establishes the obligation and accountability of all and each to him. Because he spoke and the world came to be, all who live in the earth should fear him (Ps 33:8–9). Psalm 24 joins the accountability of humans for their conduct to the praise of the Creator. Psalm 19 even connects the benefits of the instruction of the Lord to the glorious perfections of creation. And the psalmist of Psalm 119 prays that the God who made and fashioned him would give him understanding "to learn your commandments" (Ps 119:73), another indication that in the psalmic tradition the Torah is being integrated with creation as well as salvation theology.

The way that the two works of God, creation and redemption, are being integrated into one continuous story is evident in all the psalms that recite God's work as creator and God's action in Israel's career as an unbroken sequence (Pss 135, 136, 146, 147, 148). How harmoniously the two have interpenetrated each other is clear in such a couplet as:

The LORD is gracious and merciful,
   slow to anger and abounding in steadfast love.
The LORD is good to all,
   and his compassion is over all that he has made.
                    (145:8–9)

"SO GREAT IS THE STEADFAST LOVE"

The conviction that God can be trusted pervades and underlies what is said in
the New Testament. One can trust oneself and one's destiny to God no matter what one's need or condition. "Your Father is merciful," says Jesus, even
"kind to the ungrateful and wicked" (Luke 6:35–36). What is said about God
in the Psalms draws a portrait of a God who is above all else to be trusted. A
rich vocabulary of typical actions, attributes, and metaphors is employed to
evoke the character of the God to whom the psalmist can say, "O my God, in
you I trust" (Ps 25:2).

The Psalms describe how the Lord acts and may be expected to act. The
Lord's greatness lies in the fact that he "delights in the welfare [*shalom*] of his
servant" (Ps 35:27). He "redeems the life of his servants; none of those who
take refuge in him will be condemned" (Ps 34:22). He is a righteous judge who
does not delight in wickedness. "He judges the world with righteousness; he
judges the people with equity," and so is "a stronghold for the oppressed"
(Ps 9:8–9). He is the salvation and truth of all who rely on him.

The Psalms contain a catalogue of characteristics to concretize the knowledge of God. The Lord is holy, glorious, and mighty, so he is able to be trustworthy. He is just and righteous, good and faithful, so his character justifies
trust. He is gracious, compassionate, and forgiving, so all may trust themselves
to him. "His steadfast love endures forever," a refrain that tells the central
truth about the Lord (see Ps 136).

Metaphors are used to unite the conceptual and the experiential in the
knowledge of the faithful God. The Lord is rock, refuge, fortress, strength and
shield, shepherd, light, guide to right paths—all images that invite trust.

Some psalms seem composed to draw a verbal portrait of this faithful God.
Psalm 103 is an example. It begins with a recital of the ways of the Lord with
those who fear him—forgiving, healing, redeeming, ennobling, fulfilling,
renewing. For the oppressed he works vindication. To the sinner he shows
compassion. To mortals whose destiny is dust, he gives his everlasting steadfast love. So the human condition of vulnerability, fallibility, and mortality is
countered and resolved in the mercy and grace of the Lord. Psalm 25 is
another example. It opens with an assertion of trust in God and then moves
into a declaration of the faith that grounds the trust. The Lord is the God of

salvation. His mercy and steadfast love have always been there. Indeed, the Lord's faithfulness in steadfast love is the path both the humble and sinner may walk. To those who fear him, he grants his friendship and reveals his covenant.

The psalmic theology of the faithful God is epitomized in a beatitude: "Happy are those who make the LORD their trust" (Ps 40:4).

"HE DELIVERS THE NEEDY WHEN THEY CALL"

In the entire New Testament there is an assumption that God is disposed toward those who know their dependence on him and against those who undertake to be autonomous. This theological view is expressed in Jesus' beatitudes that affirm the poor in spirit, those who mourn, the meek, and those who hunger and thirst for righteousness (Matt 5:3–6). It lies behind his instruction to the disciples "about their need to pray always and not to lose heart" (Luke 18:1). In the Psalms there is a virtual library of prayers that are the voice of those who know their neediness.

These prayers by their number and passionate eloquence represent the conviction that prayer is the best confession of the faithfulness of God and the essential response of trust in God. The Lord is in his very identity "you who answer prayer" (Ps 65:2). There is a congruence between true prayer and the being of God.

> The LORD is near to all who call on him,
>   to all who call on him in truth.
> He fulfills the desire of all who fear him;
>   he also hears their cry, and saves them.
>   (Ps 145:18–19)

To denote those whose prayers are "in truth," the psalms use a vocabulary of dependency. "O LORD, you will hear the desire of the meek; . . . you will incline your ear to do justice for the orphan and the oppressed" (Ps 10:17–18). "This poor soul cried, and was heard by the LORD" (34:6). "You deliver the weak from those too strong for them, the weak and needy from those who despoil them" (35:10). "The meek shall inherit the land" (37:11). "For he delivers the needy when they call, the poor and those who have no helper" (72:12). In English translations, the vocabulary can appear in different words: not only "poor," "weak," "meek," "needy" but also "lowly," "humble." Social categories such as "widow and orphan" and "oppressed" are used to the same purpose. The intention of this various vocabulary is always theological, to represent those who by condition, self-understanding, and stance trust themselves to God. The way in which the vocabulary of righteous/wicked is paired with the language of dependence indicates that these terms are more religious than moral. Trust is the first order of righteousness. Autonomous strength, boasting, and self-assertion are habits of wickedness.

The coherence of theology and prayer in these prayer psalms is evident in passages such as the first seven verses of Psalm 86, in which a sequence of petitions are each supported by a grounding clause. The first is "Incline your ear, O LORD, and answer me, for I am poor and needy." The supporting clauses are statements about the dependency of the psalmist on the responsiveness of God, alternated so as to show the inner coherence of the two. The self-designation "poor and needy" is paralleled in subsequent lines by assertions of devotion and trust and penitent prayer to show that the neediness of the psalmist is real in his trust and cry.

"YOU ARE MY SON"

The baptismal word said from heaven to Jesus was the inaugural declaration from the Second Psalm: "You are my Son." In the New Testament, the significance of this revelatory announcement concerns the office and role of Jesus primarily. Its portent is christological. But in the case of this sentence, the one who speaks is as important as the one addressed. The declaration has immense theological weight. It discloses God as one who can have and does have and does acknowledge such an intimate and indissoluble relation with a human person. The bare fact of the declaration raises the question about the possibility and purpose in God that informs the sentence. It is the Psalms first of all that witness to the God who so binds himself to a person.

The background and origin of God's unique relation to a particular person lies in the Lord's election of David. His relation to David was itself a manifestation of the Lord's sovereignty. In an exercise of his free initiative, the Lord chose David from among the people. He "found" him and anointed him and gave him an identity and dependency expressed in the cry, "You are my Father, my God, and the Rock of my salvation!" (Ps 89:26). By the election of David, the Lord disclosed his way and will to vest his reign in the mortality of a man. "I have set my king on Zion, my holy hill" (2:6). In the midst of human history, God wills to have a place and a person to reveal and enact his role. The reign of the Lord was identified with him and he with that reign.

In Messiah David, the Lord's reign was personified and represented. The messiah is God's representative and agent in dealing with the people of the Lord (78:67–72). In their midst he stands for and administers the Lord's justice and righteousness (72:1–2 and 45:6–7). His strength will be the protection of the Lord's people (20:6–9). Through him the Lord will bless his people (72:15–17).

The messiah is also God's regent in dealing with the nations and peoples of the world. Because the Lord rules over all, the role of his messiah concerns all the world and its peoples. He receives power and authority over the rulers of earth as the Lord's royal grant (2:7–12). His strength and invincibility are an aspect of the power of God (18:31–48; chap. 20; 21:8–12). In his exercise of kingship, he will extend the claim of the Lord's kingship over all nations (Ps 110).

Because of the symmetry between the kingdom of God and the rule of David, the relationship is indissoluble. By divine sworn covenant the regal office is guaranteed. It is established forever with David and his descendants. So the fate of the representative role vested in the Davidic line places the faithfulness of the Lord in question (89:1–18). Indeed, the Lord's deliverance of the anointed from the power of death is a revelation of God's faithfulness to his steadfast love (18:1–19, 50). It is through God's salvation of the messiah that the purpose of God in the messiah's kingship is realized (18:43–48).

That God's king should reach the fulfillment of his rule in his salvation from death opens up the great mystery about God's way with the Davidic messiah in the Psalms. Because most of the prayers for help in the Psalter are introduced in the voice of David, two strange things are to be noted about this figure who personifies the rule of God. First, in these prayers this agent of God's power discloses that he is one of and one with the lowly, poor, weak, meek, and humble, whose only strength is their trust in God. He is the afflicted righteous one, the brokenhearted and crushed in spirit (34:15–18) who prays, "O God, be merciful to me, for in you my soul takes refuge" (57:1). Second, the psalmic David can even become the rejected one whose humiliation and degradation contradicts and calls into question God's faithfulness. Indeed, the shame and death of the messiah appears to be the work of God himself (89:38–51, especially 43–45). The messiah can cry out, "My God, my God! Why have you forsaken me?" (Mark 15:34, quoting Ps 22:1). And yet it is in and through the messiah's salvation from the powers of death itself that the lowly are given hope, the people of the Lord renewed, and the reign of the LORD is revealed to the world (Pss 22, 64, 116, 118). Through God's way with the Davidic messiah it begins to become clear that the Lord is a god whose power is made perfect in weakness (2 Cor 2:8).

CONCLUSION

These are some of the topics and themes that display the significant way in which the Psalms form the theological background of the New Testament writings. The relationship between the two is so close and complex that it cannot be reduced finally to a list of topics. The themes are embedded in the

Psalms in a larger sphere of language used to praise and pray and proclaim God. It is not claiming too much to say that this larger world of language is also the home of the theological language of the New Testament. It is because this is so that the Psalms could be taken up as the direct praise and prayer of the early church. It is the reason the Psalms have often been bound in a volume with the New Testament as though the Old Testament book belonged in a special way also to the second part of the Christian canon. The author of this article would like to believe that there is in this commonality and coherence of Psalms and New Testament a kind of analogy for the relationship of friendship and endeavor he shares with the one whom this volume honors.

SELECT BIBLIOGRAPHY

Anderson, Bernhard W. 1999. *Contours of Old Testament Theology*. Minneapolis: Augsburg Fortress.

Brueggemann, Walter. 1984. *The Message of the Psalms*. Minneapolis: Augsburg.

———. 1995. *The Psalms and the Life of Faith*. Minneapolis: Augsburg Fortress.

Holladay, William L. 1993. *The Psalms through Three Thousand Years*. Minneapolis: Fortress.

Kraus, Hans-Joachim. 1986. *Theology of the Psalms*. Minneapolis: Augsburg.

Mays, James L. 1994. *The Lord Reigns: A Theological Handbook to the Psalms*. Louisville, Ky.: Westminster/John Knox.

———. 1994. *Psalms*. Interpretation: A Bible Commentary for Teaching and Preaching. Louisville, Ky.: John Knox.

McCann, J. Clinton, Jr. 1993. *A Theological Introduction to the Book of Psalms*. Nashville: Abingdon.

Miller, Patrick D. 1986. *Interpreting the Psalms*. Philadelphia: Fortress.

———. 1994. *They Cried to the Lord: The Form and Theology of Biblical Prayer*. Minneapolis: Augsburg Fortress.

Rad, Gerhard von. 1962 and 1965. *Old Testament Theology*. 2 vols. New York: Harper & Row.

Westermann, Claus. 1981. *Praise and Lament in the Psalms*. Atlanta: John Knox.

3

"Slow to Anger"

The God of the Prophets

Patrick D. Miller

It is to the prophetic books especially, though not only to them, that Christian theology—in its more sophisticated forms and especially in popular theology—owes its tendency to depict the God of Israel or the God of the Old Testament as a God of wrath and judgment, a kind of Janus-faced deity, sometimes turning toward Israel or humankind in wrath, sometimes turning in mercy and compassion. The former seems to be heavily the tone of the Lord's dealing with Israel in the time of the prophets, but the more loving aspect is acknowledged as also present at times.

Such a depiction of God misrepresents the prophetic word and has so distorted the revelation of the God of Israel as to undermine in significant ways the theological standing of the Old Testament in the Christian community, an outcome that is reflected in the absence of the Old Testament from preaching, theology, and liturgy (apart from the Psalms) as well as a consequent misreading of the New Testament as a revelational corrective of the Old Testament's view of deity.

A proper understanding of the God of the prophets needs therefore to focus particularly on this issue, for all else flows out of it or is shaped by one's understanding of the judgment of God. A coherent but complex perception of the wrath and judgment of God within the message of the prophets needs to recognize several things.

GOD'S WRATH

God's anger and judgment are real and a large part of the prophetic word. One cannot underplay this dimension of the prophet's oracles, especially those in the preexilic period. Text after text speaks "the word of the Lord," often in first person speech with vivid and disturbing imagery, about God's intent to destroy the people, and sometimes other peoples. For example, the Lord declares:

> My anger shall spend itself, and I will vent my fury on them and sat-isfy myself; and they shall know that I, the LORD, have spoken in my jealousy, when I spend my fury on them. Moreover I will make you a desolation and an object of mocking among the nations around you, in the sight of all that pass by. You shall be a mockery and a taunt, a warning and a horror, to the nations around you, when I execute judg-ments on you in anger and fury, and with furious punishments—I, the LORD, have spoken—when I loose against you my deadly arrows of famine, arrows for destruction, which I will let loose to destroy you, and when I bring more and more famine upon you, and break your staff of bread. I will send famine and wild animals against you, and they will rob you of your children; pestilence and bloodshed shall pass through you; and I will bring the sword upon you. I, the LORD, have spoken. (Ezek 5:13–17)

Or in the words of another prophet:

> I will bring such distress upon people
>   that they shall walk like the blind;
>   because they have sinned against the LORD,
> their blood shall be poured out like dust,
>   and their flesh like dung.
> Neither their silver nor their gold
>   will be able to save them
>   on the day of the LORD's wrath;
> in the fire of his passion
>   the whole earth shall be consumed;
> for a full, a terrible end
>   he will make of all the inhabitants of the earth.
>   (Zeph 1:17–18)

Such texts could be multiplied greatly, for the reality of judgment, expressed theologically as God's wrath or anger, is a constant subject of prophetic proclamation. The language is harsh, hyperbolic, disturbing, and relentless. The resultant picture of God as cruel and unbending, as jealous and vindictive, leaves the hearers of the word disturbed. Such language is meant to match the equally disturbing pictures of the sin of the people and of the nations, also articulated again and again in the prophetic preaching. That cor-relation is critical and the reason why it is not theologically proper to encounter these images of judgment and take them on their own apart from the larger context.

A GOD OF JUSTICE AND RIGHTEOUSNESS

The God of the prophets is not a God of judgment but a God of justice and righteousness. The confusion of these two, that is, of judgment and justice, is one of the problems. The reality of judgment is not to be denied, but it is momentary, transient, occasional, and situational. Judgment is not a divine attribute. Justice, however, as a mode of being and acting belongs to the very character of God and is experienced in all sorts of ways, including judgment. One of the most powerful indicators outside the prophets of the centrality of justice for the character of God is Psalm 82, where the other gods, the gods of the nations, are condemned to mortality, that is, to the loss of divinity on one ground alone: their failure to ensure justice for the weak and the poor and their partiality toward the oppressors of the poor and the fatherless. Justice is not simply one of a list of divine concerns; the cosmos depends upon it.

The point is sharply made in Jeremiah when the Lord says that properly to "understand and know me" is to understand and know that "I am the LORD; I act with steadfast love, justice, and righteousness in the earth, for in these things I delight" (Jer 9:24 [Heb. v. 23]). *Hesed*, *mišpat*, and *sedaqâ* are what the Lord does in the world. The *mišpat* (justice) may involve judgment, but the sequence indicates clearly that the great things God is doing in the world are loving, just, and righteous. Even the judgment against one party may be the vehicle for the justice of God to be enacted in behalf of another party. The justice of God is in behalf of the "right" (*saddîq*). In contemporary parlance, the "judgment" of the courts is not regarded as an inherently negative thing nor a reflection of a harsh and oppressive attitude toward the subjects of the court. On the contrary, the judgment of the courts is the public citizen's last best hope for the triumph of justice in the human community. It is thus no accident that the administration of justice in the courts is one of the items at the top of the prophetic agenda of indictment as well as of recommendation. Without trying to make direct connections, I would argue that that human situation is a reflection of what the community knows about the source of justice and the way in which God deals with the human community.

The wrath of God, a motif indeed prominent in the prophets, is an anthropomorphism, or better, anthropopathism, for conveying the highly negative response of God to human sin and to the disobedience and wickedness of God's people or of other nations (e.g., see Isa 5:25; 9:12, 17, 21; 10:5–6; 13:3, 9, 13; 30:27–28; Jer 4:8, 26; 7:20; 10:24–25; 12:13; 30:23–24; Hos 8:5; Ezek 5:13). It is therefore a way of speaking of divine judgment. But that judgment, whether described in terms of the wrath of God or not, is in behalf of God's righteous and just way in the world. This point is made again and again by the way in which the prophetic oracles effect a correspondence in their judgment oracles between the sin for which the people are indicted and the punishment that is to be announced. The prophet calls attention to the justice of God's judgment by the device of "poetic justice." The ubiquity of this schema in the prophets is a testimony to the degree to which divine judgment is an effecting of divine justice and righteousness (for an extended discussion, see Miller 1982). The correspondence is specifically asserted by the Lord in various places, as, for example, in Ezekiel's sermon on Amos 8:2:

> Now the end is upon you,
>> I will let loose my anger upon you;
> I will judge you according to your ways,
>> I will punish you for all your abominations.
> My eye will not spare you, I will have no pity.
>> I will punish you for your ways,
>> while your abominations are among you.
>> (Ezek 7:3–4; cf. vv. 8–9)

One may not like the judgment that comes, but the problem is with the human community, not with the God who judges in order to bring about a cosmic, human, and cultural order in which justice is normative and not spasmodic. A telling articulation of just this point occurs in Isa 26:7–10:

> The way of the righteous is level;
>> straight is the track of the righteous you make level.
> Yea, on the path of your judgments, O Lord, we wait for you;
>> your name and your renown are the soul's desire.
> My soul yearns for you at night;
>> yea, with my spirit within I seek you longingly.
> For as your judgments are wrought on the earth,
>> the inhabitants of the world learn righteousness.
> Should the wicked person find mercy,
>> he will not learn righteousness.
> In a land of uprightness he acts wrongly
>> and does not see the majesty of the Lord.
>> (author's translation)

The way the Lord makes in the world is characterized by righteousness, and such righteousness and justice identify the path that human creatures are to walk. The degree to which this is the case is evident in the "judgments" of God in the world. Through them, the inhabitants learn righteousness. The anticipation and expectation of the community is "on the path of your judgments." That is, hope is not against judgment but on the way of judgment because the community has no hope apart from the justice of God. The point is reinforced by the claim that mercy will not show the wicked the way of righteousness.

That is learned only in a divine order that is itself characterized by righteousness and justice.

Thus, divine judgment is a part of the instruction of the community so that its *imitatio dei* is a reflection of all of God's moves to effect justice in the human community, including those moves that are characterized as judgment because they put down the forces of wickedness, disobedience, and sin—that is, the persons and communities who stand against the will of the God of Israel to effect a just order in the world and a moral ground for comprehending the Lord's way. So it is that the salvific act in behalf of justice for oppressed slaves in Egypt is an act of judgment against the oppressor Egypt and its king. The prophets do not flinch from daring to claim that in the realpolitik of their times, God was at work to bring about justice in and through the agencies of nations and rulers. Their task was to interpret what was going on not as simply unfortunate circumstances but as the activity of a righteous God to deal justly with the human community, an enterprise that involved stopping the various kinds of unrighteousness and injustice operative in the community. That such moves were perceived as punishment was appropriate to the covenantal character of the relationship.

Such punishment=judgment=divine justice and righteousness was always affected by the nature and character of God to show compassion and steadfast love, a claim that was central to the oldest and most common confession of ancient Israel (Exod 34:6–7). While this confession, frequently alluded to in the Psalms, is not a dominant note in the prophets, it does appear in several places (Joel 2:13; Jonah 4:2; Nah 1:3) and lies behind many of the prophetic interpretations of the divine intent and action. In his study "The Character of God in the Book of the Twelve," Paul R. House comments, "[T]he depiction of God in the Twelve does not differ significantly from that of earlier books, nor from earlier summary texts such as Exod 34:6–7" (House 2000, 145).

The priority of the Lord's compassion is indicated in various ways. One sees it, for example, in the vision reports of Amos when, on two occasions, Amos sees a vision of divine judgment and intercedes, first beseeching God's forgiveness (Amos 7:2) and then a second time simply asking God to stop the judgment (7:5). The appeal that Amos makes is, "How can Jacob stand? He is so small!" The significance of that particular appeal is immediately evident. The prophet knows the inclination of the God of Israel to care for the little and the weak and the insignificant. To the extent that he is able to make a case for Israel/Jacob to be viewed in the eyes of God that way, he can expect a merciful response. This inclination is fundamental to the God of the Old Testament, as persistently so in the prophets as anywhere else in that literature. The intercession of the prophet works precisely because it is grounded in the character of God who is bent toward mercy and compassion, not toward anger and punishment. There are, of course, two more vision reports that indicate the judgment will come (7:7–9; 8:1–3). One notes, however, in these instances there is no intercession on the part of the prophet. It is surely not accidental that after the vision of the plumb line by which God measures the faithfulness of the people, the prophet does not seek further relief. From the image one learns that the people are found to be "out of plumb" and so incapable as such of being the "house" that the Lord needs to be God's people in the world. The walls will need to come down and the house be rebuilt if God's way is going to be carried out in the world. So judgment comes, with defeat and exile, not because God's word is finally judgment but because God's way cannot be manifest in the world with a people whose life runs so counter to God's justice and righteousness.

THE OPENNESS OF GOD'S JUDGMENT

The judgment of God is constantly open to the intervention of the prophets. The intercessions of Amos are indicative of this openness, but they are not particularly novel in this regard. Several texts indicate that the prayer for God to hold back judgment is a part of the prophetic calling, expected not necessarily by the people, though they may on occasion seek the prophet's prayers in their behalf (e.g., Jer 42:1–3), but *expected by the Lord.* That is, God assumes, expects, and even desires prophetic intercession to appeal to God's compassion and mercy. The exception to this rule simply proves the point. In Jer 14:11, the prophet is told, "Do not pray for the welfare of this people," and then in the next chapter the Lord says, "though Moses and Samuel stood before me, yet my heart would not turn toward this people" (Jer 15:1; cf. Ps 106:23; 1 Sam 12:23). As in the case of Amos, the situation is so far gone that God's purposes require a punishment. The people have resisted correction again and again (Jer 5:3), and now the Lord must move against them. But the assumption is that the heart of God is fundamentally merciful and affected by pleas in behalf of the people. There is a sense in which God is afraid for Jeremiah to pray for the people because the Lord knows there is an inclination within the heart of God to be moved to mercy by the prayers of the prophets.

Furthermore, the prophetic texts indicate that this vulnerability is not simply something that God puts up with but that it is built into the character and expectation of God so that when there is not intercession that will shift God's judgment to mercy, something is wrong and prophecy is failing in its task, again not because the people say so but because the Lord so declares. One of the responsibilities of the prophet is to stand in the breach and repair the breach, to mend the relationship between God and the people, an act defined as standing in their behalf so that God will be drawn to mercy (Schroeder 1998). Again, one must stress that this is *God's* understanding and expectation (Ezek 22:30–31). The prophet is, in effect, appointed to appeal to the mercy of God (Ezek 13:5) or to represent the people by exposing himself or herself in behalf of others (cf. Isa 58:9b–12). As Christoph Schroeder has pointed out, standing in the breach is not a manifestation of God's insistence on some violent act to turn away the divine wrath.

> God's wrath is not directed against a scapegoat; it is not even directed against the one who stands in the breach. It is rather directed against those who refuse to step into the breach against those who neglect justice, who try to protect their lives instead of risking them for others. God's wrath is not an expression of divine arbitrariness and temper; it has a moral dimension. It is poured out; it breaks out when social cohesion and solidarity break apart. (Schroeder 1998, 20)

The point is that even when divine punishment is just, when the actions of the people merit the wrath of God, there is an openness and an expectation that the prophetic voice will intercede, appealing to the mercy of God (for a fuller discussion, see Miller 1998, 211–32).

The openness of God to a "change of mind" is in no sense a characteristic divine capriciousness or inconsistency on the part of God. All the instances in which the texts report such a change of mind, a relenting on God's part, have to do with situations where divine judgment is an appropriate way of responding to the acts of the people. In nearly all of the instances, as is the case with the vision reports of Amos mentioned above, the change of mind is from judgment to mercy and the deliverance of the people (e.g., Exod 32:14; Jer 18:8 [but see 18:10 for the reverse movement]; 26:3, 13, 19; Joel 2:13–14). That is, there is a divine propensity for merciful response to the people even in the face of their sin and their unwillingness to be corrected. Judgment is a feature of divine justice, but even justice is subject to being overruled by mercy. It does not always happen, but even when the point is made that God will not relent, the tendency of God so to do is emphasized indirectly (e.g., Jer 4:28; Ezek 24:14; Zech 8:14). In one instance, the Lord speaks of having become "weary of relenting" (Jer 15:6), an indicator that such relenting is the operative tendency, enough so as to wear out God because circumstances, that is, the people's sin and stubbornness, bring such change of mind into play so often.

GOD'S AMBIVALENCE ABOUT JUDGMENT

The wrath and judgment of God are thus marked by considerable ambivalence and resistance on God's part. Many of the divine speeches in the prophetic oracles reveal this ambivalence and the degree to which the Lord resists the judgment as long or as much as possible. The signs of such resistance are varied and indicative of the fact that judgment is not simply a matter of divine decree but the outcome of a complex process of divine wrestling, anguish, attempted overtures to the people, calls for repentance, warnings that keep the door open, and the like. The divine soliloquy in Hosea 11 is indicative of the wrestling within the heart of God and the way in which God's holiness is the ground not only for judgment but also for mercy.

> How can I give you up, Ephraim?
>   How can I hand you over, O Israel?
> How can I make you like Admah?
>   How can I treat you like Zeboiim?
> My heart recoils within me;
>   my compassion grows warm and tender.
> I will not execute my fierce anger;
>   I will not again destroy Ephraim;
> for I am God and no mortal,
>   the Holy One in your midst,
>   and I will not come in wrath.
>   (Hos 11:8–9)

The Lord's bent toward compassion is a part of what it means to be God, not just an option among other possibilities. The definition of deity in the prophets is, as throughout the Old Testament, not a logical extrapolation from an a priori definition of the category but a revelation from the story of God's way with Israel. The prophetic understanding is thus consistent again with the ancient revelation: "The LORD, the LORD, a God merciful and gracious, slow to anger . . ." (Exod 34:6; cf. 33:19). Such reticence to wrath in favor of compassion is what it means to be the Lord.

Jeremiah's prophecy is one of the places where the wrath and judgment of God are rampant. Even there, and maybe especially there, one encounters the divine resistance to judgment on the people and all kinds of indications of God's frustration and despair at the way the people continue to sin. Chapters 4–6 ring the changes on the announcement of divine judgment, but they are also filled with indications that God seeks in various ways to avert the judgment and agonizes over the failure to accomplish that end. We hear about Judah refusing the correction and discipline of God and instead making "their faces harder than rock" (5:3; cf. 2:30; 7:28; and see below). Further, there are the call to look for the good way (6:16) and the various queries to the people: "Do you not fear me?" (5:22). God's search for just *one* person who acts justly and seeks truth (5:1) is reminiscent of the conversation with Abraham over whether there is anybody righteous in Sodom and Gomorrah, a conversation that, like this prophetic oracle, indicates God's openness to mercy rather than judgment if there is the slightest human inclination toward righteousness. The one just and truthful person becomes like those who stand in the breach, whose presence in prayer and righteous action is not only capable of averting divine wrath but is what God seeks always in order not to have to come in judgment. Judgment does not come easily for the Lord of Israel. On the contrary, there is a divine anguish reflected in the inner dialogue within the mind and heart of God that comes to the surface not infrequently and very clearly in these chapters. So the Lord says, "Shall I not punish them for these things?" an address to self or to the prophet (5:9). God's inner anguish is even more evident in Jer 4:19–22, which ends with the first-person voice of God in the sentence "my people are foolish, they do not know me (v. 22)." But there is no reason to assume that the earlier first-person cry, "My anguish, my anguish! I writhe in pain!" (v. 19) cannot be the voice of God as much as the voice of the prophet, especially as that outcry flows so clearly out of the preceding divine speech. (For a full discussion of the case for seeing God as the one lamenting in these texts, see Roberts 1992, 361–74.) The anguish and complaint of the prophet is a reflection of the anguish and complaint of God. Judgment is no less unsettling for God than it is for those who view it. Human shrinking in horror from the devastating and destroying wrath of God is already anticipated by the one who so acts.

The mix of divine grief and wrath, of lament and judgment, is evident elsewhere in Jeremiah's prophecy. The divine soliloquy of 5:9 is repeated in 9:9 [Heb v. 10] as the Lord asks the question, "Shall I not punish them for these things?" and answers with both tears and anger, the former in verse 10 as the Lord says, "I will take up weeping and wailing for the mountains, and a lamentation for the pastures of the wilderness," and the latter with the announcement in verse 11: "I will make Jerusalem a heap of ruins, a lair of jackals." (For a discussion of the textual issues and the choice of the MT with its first-person verbs rather than the LXX with its imperative, see Miller 2001). This same complex assortment of responses of anger and sadness is evident also in Jer 12:7–13, which is primarily an announcement of judgment but whose pathos is evident in the frequent references to "my house," "my heritage," "my vineyard," "my portion," and especially in the words "I have given the beloved of my heart [*yedidût nafšî*] into the hands of her enemies" (v. 7). Hidden in that sentence are all the words about divine election rooted in God's faithfulness to the promise and God's love for Israel in Exod 19:3–6 and Deut 7:6–11 and 9:4–5. Again, the divine voice is probably present once more in Jer 8:18–9:1 [Heb. 8:18–23] in the same mix of grief, sadness, and anger at the plight/fate/judgment/punishment of "my poor people." And in Jer 14:17, the prophet is told to lament for the people:

> You shall say to them this word:
> Let my eyes run down with tears night and day,
>   and let them not cease,
> for the virgin daughter—my people—is struck down with a crushing blow,
>   with a very grievous wound.

The prominence of God's sadness and tears in the midst of anger is an appropriate motif in the prophecy of Jeremiah because it is there also where one encounters extensive use of the metaphor of marriage and divorce as a way of speaking about faithfulness and unfaithfulness. Whether on the human plane or in the heart of God, grief and anger are both present in the face of marital unfaithfulness.

A RESPONSIVE GOD

The judgment of God is responsive to the human situation. The point may be an obvious one, but it is central to the whole discussion. In relation to God, judgment is to be understood as an outcome of God's justice, righteousness, and steadfast love (see Jer 9:24). But it is also and totally an outcome of what happens on the human plane. The only modification of that is by the way in which God's compassion may relent from the judgment appropriate to the human situation. The prophets, however, readily point to the flexibility of the divine word and the divine decision, indicating in various ways the openness of the divine activity, so that God's response is deeply dependent upon human response to God's work and God's way. Isaiah's word to Ahaz contains a critical "if": "If you do not stand firm in faith, you shall not stand at all" (Isa 7:9). Ahaz faces a choice, and the choice he makes determines God's response. So also the name of his son, "Shear-yashub," is a symbolic name whose force depends completely upon how the people act. Will it be "[Only] a Remnant Shall Return," or will the name of the child be an indicator that "A Remnant Shall [Indeed] Return" (Isa 7:3; 10:20–23)? In Jeremiah 42, the people ask Jeremiah to pray to the Lord for them and promise that whether God's response is good or bad, they will obey it. Jeremiah does so and reports God's response, which is to the effect that the people themselves will determine completely whether the divine word is good news or bad news, deliverance or disaster. Their decision to stay in the land or to go to Egypt will determine the divine response, for good or for bad.

This same flexibility on God's part is evident in the interpretation of the potter with the clay when Jeremiah visits the potter's house. The Lord says, "Look, I am a potter shaping evil against you" (Jer 18:11). But the point of the text is that the Lord will shape the pot according to the response of the people. At first glance, the Lord's speech seems to show a kind of whimsy: "At one moment I may declare concerning a nation or a kingdom, that I will pluck up and break down and destroy it. . . . And at another moment I may declare concerning a nation or a kingdom that I will build and plant it" (vv. 7–9). What follows each of these statements indicates that the decision is totally dependent upon whether a nation turns from its evil or decides to do evil. There is nothing capricious at all about the momentary decision of the Lord. The way the people act evokes God's response. That such openness is available to the nations of the earth is evident from Jer 12:14–17.

Surely part of the reason so much prophecy of judgment is preserved in the books of the Old Testament prophets is to argue the case for the primacy of justice and compassion over wrath and anger, to make the point that again and again the people went their own way, did not do the will of the Lord, said no when reproved, continued in their sinful ways when specifically called to obedience by the prophets. These oracles heap up not only the words of divine judgment but a virtual catalogue of willful disobedience and resistance to the divine pleas, to the anguished call of God to walk in the good way and to live as "my people" are called to live. Isaiah's repetition of the words, "For all this his anger has not turned away, and his hand is stretched out still" (Isa 5:25; 9:12, 17, 21; 10:4) is accompanied by the repeated indictment of the people for their iniquitous ways.

God's activity vis-à-vis the nation or the nations may be planned or purposed (e.g., Isa 14:24–27; 23:6–9; 46:10–11; Jer 29:10; 49:20; 50:45), but it is not deterministic or irrevocable, at least up to a point (see, e.g., Amos's final two vision reports in Amos 7:7–9 and 8:1–3). There is a malleability comparable to the malleability of clay in the hands of the potter. Human acts and decisions significantly shape the future of God with the people. The sovereignty of God is nowhere compromised by the degree to which it implies freedom and takes account of the human way.

NEVER THE LAST WORD

The judgment of God is not the last word of the prophets or their largest word. There may be some exceptions to this claim, but it is the dominant tendency in the prophetic texts. It is expressed in a variety of ways. The word of God that "I will not make a full end" of the people is repeated in Jeremiah (4:27; 5:10, 18; 46:28). While its force is not altogether clear, it does appear to be a kind of divine caveat in the very midst of the word of judgment. It does not reduce the pain of the judgment; it does qualify its finality. The devastating and unavoidable judgment will come to a disobedient and stubborn people who have failed to respond to God's prior discipline and correction. But even that will not be the final end. That such a word about not making "a full end" is God's open door to a future for the people whose conduct and way does not merit it is underscored by its presence in a salvation oracle in Jer 30:11, where the text is explicit about real punishment not being the end of Judah. (This text indicates there will be a full end of the nations among whom the Lord has scattered the exiles, but that word receives frequent qualification, as, for example, in Jer 12:14–17, where the Lord promises to deal compassionately with the nations if they will "learn the ways of my people.")

Other texts reveal a God who is not only slow to anger but whose anger is not forever. Indicative of this strain in the prophetic portrayal of the Lord of Israel is the word in Isaiah 54. The proclamation of the prophet of good news to the exile comes to a close with his interpretive words:

> For a brief moment I abandoned you,
>   but with great compassion I will gather you.
> In overflowing wrath for a moment
>   I hid my face from you,
> but with everlasting love I will have compassion on you,
>   says the LORD, your Redeemer.
>
> (Isa 54:7–8)

The experience of judgment is real and devastating. It is reflective of the anger of God, the "overflowing wrath" that has consumed this people, resulting in the destruction of their leadership, their loss of land, and their exile in a foreign land. There is no escaping the reality of the judgment. The prophet, however, speaks the voice of God that terrible as such experience of the divine wrath is, it is nowhere like the "everlasting love," God's compassion for this people. The abandonment is brief; the gathering an act of great compassion. One cannot diminish the terror of the judgment, but the prophet says that it cannot compare with the greatness of God's compassion and love. They are both the final word and the larger word.

This is not unlike the divine word in Jer 3:12 when the Lord calls for repentance on the part of the northern kingdom:

> Return, faithless Israel,
>   says the LORD.
> I will not look on you in anger,
>   for I am merciful,
>   says the LORD;
>   I will not be angry forever.

This text echoes the similar word of the psalmist, alluding to Exod 34:6–7:

He will not always accuse,
　　nor will he keep his anger forever.
　　(Ps 103:9)

A JUDGMENT THAT RENEWS

The judgment of God is a part of renewing and reshaping a people for God's own way. God does not give up. Judgment is a stopping place on the way to the reassertion of blessing out of God's compassion. While God's judgment is clearly understood as punishment (e.g., Isa 40:1–2), there are numerous indicators that the punishment serves a larger purpose, to wit, the reshaping of the people toward the intended relationship with their God. A number of notions and images convey such an understanding of divine judgment, for example, the frequent reference to God's "correction" or "discipline" (*mûsar*) in Jeremiah (2:30; 5:3; 7:28; 17:23; 32:33; cf. 6:8; 30:11; 46:28; Isa 26:16). One may compare illustratively the oracle in Jer 31:18–20, where Ephraim is quoted as accepting the divine discipline and becoming ashamed and repenting, resulting in the divine announcement, "I will surely have mercy on him," with the oracle in Zeph 3:1–13, where Jerusalem is depicted as not listening and not receiving correction from past judgments and so experiencing once again the judgment of God. Similar prophetic indications of punishment intended to serve a corrective function and bring the people back to a true and faithful relationship with the Lord are more indirectly indicated in such texts as Isa 1:5–9; 9:8–21 (Heb. 9–20); and Amos 4:6–11. In Jer 30:11, the Lord promises to chastise the people but not to destroy them, to punish but not to make an end of them. Indeed, this word is in the context of an oracle of salvation.

The image of the Lord as the potter molding the clay also suggests the place of judgment in the divine plan (Jer 18:1–12). The process of judgment may itself be the remolding of the clay. The spoiled clay is remolded in the potter's hand as Jeremiah looks on. That becomes a metaphor for God's handling of Judah/the clay. The pot will not work and is flawed as a container until the potter reshapes it to what it is meant to be or to do "in the eyes" of the potter (lit. "as was right in the eyes of the potter to do"; NRSV: "as seemed good to him"). This malformed, misshapen vessel will be reshaped so that it is right in God's eyes.

An equally prominent image is that of the refining fire that tests and refines. In some instances, the refining fire in the smelter seems simply a powerful image for judgment (Jer 6:27–30; Ezek 22:18–20), but elsewhere the image clearly indicates a refining in order to purify and reuse the silver or metal (Isa 1:24–26). The Isaiah text may suggest that the image in all its contexts implies a melting of the dross to refine and purify the metal, again a correcting of the elect people by the fires of judgment so that they are reformed, literally.

Another image of God's judgment to effect a reformation of the people rather than a destruction of them is to be found in the image of the plumb line (2 Kgs 21:13; cf. Isa 28:17). The dimension of reforming the people is only implicit in this image, but it is there in the sense that a norm or standard of judgment is being suggested, against which the people do not measure up. The construction will not work; the wall is out of plumb. The Lord, therefore, will have to tear down the wall because it cannot work when it is out of plumb. Implicit in such an image is the notion of rebuilding the wall, starting the process over with a wall that is properly constructed.

Finally, there is the image of the dish that is wiped clean, turned upside down, and placed back on the shelf:

> [L]ike the image of the plumb line there is a functional or utilitarian dimension that points beyond the judgment and has a larger aim than simply eliminating the food in the dish. It is in order to render the dish, which has a use or purpose, usable again, to make it clean so that Yahweh may use it according to his purpose, may fill it anew. The present food in it is spoiled and rotten. Jerusalem is the dish Yahweh will clean and use again. The image fits perfectly with the historical fate of Jerusalem—wiped clean, turned on its face to be kept till Yahweh is ready to use it once more. (Miller 1982, 137)

Such understanding of judgment as effecting change and renewal needs to take account of a related but different strain of thought found in some of the prophets, an understanding of God's work of renewal growing out of the experience of exile. It is evidence of a kind of tension between the language of repentance and the language of determinism, between a notion of virtuous moral selfhood that assumes and expects the capacity for moral decision in favor of the good and so a turnaround from bad ways to correct ways and a sense that "people are inherently incapable of acting in accord with the good" (Lapsley 2000, 185). This tension has been worked out in some detail with regard to the book of Ezekiel (see Lapsley 2000), but it is present elsewhere, for example, in the prophecy of Jeremiah and in Deuteronomy, which probably at this point reflects a prophetic origin. For Deuteronomy, it is the move from the call to the people to "circumcise, then, the foreskin of your heart, and do not be stubborn any longer" (Deut 10:16; cf. Jer 4:4: 9:26; a related image is that of washing the heart as in Jer. 2:22 and 4:14; see also Ezek 36:25) to the declaration that "the LORD your God will circumcise your heart and the heart of your descendants, so that you will love the LORD your God with all your heart and with all your soul, in order that you may live" (Deut 30:6). While it is unclear whether these two passages reflect a temporal distance, this latter passage certainly reflects the experience of the exile. This may also be the case for Deut 10:12–22, so the difference should not be assumed to be a matter of temporal shift. The tension may be within the same context. Both Jeremiah (see 24:7; 32:39; cf. 31:33) and Ezekiel (see 11:19–20; 36:26–27) speak of God's gift of a new heart and a new spirit that will enable the people to keep the statutes and ordinances. The assumption is at least implicit that only by the Lord's action will the capacity for being and living differently be possible. In like manner, the vision of the dry bones having God's spirit put within them and coming to life reflects this same side of the tension (Ezekiel 37). In the face of the people's complaint that "Our bones are dried up, and our hope is lost; we are cut off completely," the Lord announces the divine intention to bring them up out of their graves and put the spirit of life in them, that is, to transform them from death to life.

Here, therefore, is a significant shift from the images of correction and reshaping out of punishment to the divine gift of a new being. The God who has punished a recalcitrant people will be the means by which the people are able to live in true and faithful relation to the Lord and the Lord's way. But the change is not a matter of taking correction, finally being repentant, but of receiving a new being and a new will as God's gift beyond the judgment.

THE CASE OF JONAH

The book of Jonah is a critique of the misreading of God's character and the misunderstanding of God's judgment. The primary function of this story is not to add to the collection of prophetic oracles out of Israel and Judah's history but to provide basic clues to the character of the God of the prophets and especially to fight the misunderstanding of God as primarily aimed at effecting judgment, especially of the non-Israelite peoples. The attack of the book on Israel's xenophobic propensities is evident and well recognized, but the deeper word is about the character of God and the way in which that character is so heavily oriented toward mercy and compassion that the clearly deserved judgment of Israel's greatest enemy, the hated Assyrians, can be averted. The book presumes significant misunderstanding of the character of God. Repentance takes place, so one would expect, according to the message of the other prophets, that God would withhold judgment. But Jonah assumes, on the one hand, that God's judgment of Israel's enemy brooked no holding back, while fearing, on the other hand, that the Lord of Israel even with a hated enemy might act in character, that is, according to the ancient confessional understanding that affirmed the Lord to be compassionate, slow to anger, abounding in steadfast love (Jonah 4:2). The hero of the book of Jonah is the Lord, and the intention of the book is thoroughly theological. It is a revelatory corrective of the propensity to see God's ultimate aim as judgment and to see the elect people's enemies as God's enemies.

THE CROSS AND GOD'S JUDGMENT

To misunderstand the judgment of God as deeply related to the mercy of God and the vindication of the just and righteous purposes of God is to misunderstand the meaning of the cross as well as the continuing words of judgment that belong to the New Testament. The death of Jesus on the cross is preeminently God's act of judgment, but it is also preeminently God's act of compassion upon humanity. In Christ's emptying of self and obedience unto death, God's way is seen to be so clearly marked by the abundance of steadfast love that it is willing to go even unto death. That the judgment of God is penultimate and not ultimate, a part of the larger purposes for blessing and realization of God's righteous and just rule, is evident in the outcome of Jesus' death. Good Friday and Saturday remind us of the depth of human sin and the terror of divine judgment. There is no escaping that any more than in the prophet's announcements of judgment against ancient Israel. But those days are not the final days any more than the prophetic judgment speeches are the last word about what God was doing with Israel. There is the new life that is given by God and the resurrection from the dead:

> It will be reckoned to us who believe in him who raised Jesus our Lord from the dead, who was handed over to death for our trespasses and was raised for our justification. Therefore, since we are justified by faith, we have peace with God through our Lord Jesus Christ, through whom we have obtained access to this grace in which we stand; and we boast in our hope of sharing the glory of God. (Rom 4:25–5:2)

Such a way of understanding God's work in Christ is already anticipated in the story of the way of the suffering servant of Isaiah 53. It is God's way, a way that does not end in judgment but assumes that the consummation of God's purposes in this world is completely shaped by the character of God, long ago revealed to Israel and persistently insisted upon by "his servants the prophets."

SELECT BIBLIOGRAPHY

Brueggemann, Walter. 1978. *The Prophetic Imagination.* Philadelphia: Fortress.
Heschel, Abraham J. 1962. *The Prophets.* New York: Harper & Row.
House, Paul R. 2000. "The Character of God in the Book of the Twelve." Pages 125–45 in *Reading and Hearing the Book of the Twelve.* Edited by James D. Nogalski and Marvin A. Sweeney. Society of Biblical Literature Symposium Series 15. Atlanta: Society of Biblical Literature.
Lapsley, Jacqueline E. 2000. *Can These Bones Live? The Problem of the Moral Self in the Book of Ezekiel.* Beiheft zur Zeitschrift für die alttestamentliche Wissenschaft 301. Berlin: de Gruyter.

Miller, Patrick. D. 1982. *Sin and Judgment in the Prophets*. Society of Biblical Literature Monograph Series 27. Chico, Calif.: Scholars Press.

———. "Prayer and Divine Action." 1998. Pages 211–32 in *God in the Fray: A Tribute to Walter Brueggemann*. Edited by Timothy Beal and Tod Linafelt. Minneapolis: Fortress. Reprinted in Patrick D. Miller. 2000. *Israelite Religion and Biblical Theology: Collected Essays*. Journal for the Study of the Old Testament: Supplement Series 267. Sheffield: Sheffield Academic Press.

———. "The Book of Jeremiah." 2001. In *Introduction to the Prophetic Literature: Isaiah, Jeremiah, Baruch, Letter of Jeremiah, Lamentations, Ezekiel*. Vol. 6 of *The New Interpreter's Bible*. Edited by Leander E. Keck. Nashville: Abingdon.

Roberts, J. J. M. 1992. "The Motif of the Weeping God in Jeremiah and Its Background in the Lament Tradition of the Ancient Near East." *Old Testament Essays* 5: 361–74.

Schroeder, Christoph. 1998. "'Standing in the Breach': Turning Away the Wrath of God." *Interpretation* 52: 16–23.

4

The God Who Makes People Wise

The Wisdom Literature

RICHARD J. CLIFFORD, S.J.

The Hebrew Bible prefers to speak of God acting on earth rather than reigning in heaven. In the Bible, God deals with the people of the earth, in particular the chosen people Israel. Such is the approach of the Pentateuch, the historical books, the Psalms, and the prophets, but not of the books with which this chapter is concerned—the Wisdom literature. Proverbs, Job, and Qoheleth (the apocryphal Sirach and Wisdom of Solomon excepted) do not mention Israel, its covenant with Yahweh, its leaders, or its institutions. They focus on the daily life of men and women, on how life is to be lived and its problems resolved. The books view the world of men and women as the ongoing work of God, which turns human striving for wisdom and happiness ultimately into a quest to understand God.

Wisdom literature has more in common with the literature of Israel's neighbors than does any other section of the Bible. Its genres and questions are widely attested throughout the ancient Near East. What makes it Israelite is its conception of God. Proverbs' personification of Wisdom reshapes Yahweh's outreach to human beings. In Job, Yahweh proves to be the God of cosmic justice and wisdom and, astonishingly, also of compassionate commitment to Job. Qoheleth's world is opaque, full of contradictions, yet it reveals God acting in the passing moment. Sirach refreshes the old traditions by integrating them with the traditions of Yahweh the God of Israel, and Wisdom of Solomon combines wisdom traditions with Greek philosophy to show how Yahweh rules the world.

This essay on God in the Wisdom literature is intended to honor Paul J. Achtemeier for his critical and faith-informed scholarship, generous contribution to the academy as administrator and editor, and service to the church in its ecumenical breadth.

THE BOOK OF PROVERBS

Proverbs is an anthology of father-son instructions (chaps. 1–9; 22:17–24:34), two-line sayings (10:1–22:17; chaps. 25–29), and miscellaneous poems (chaps. 30–31). A clue to its date and composition is 25:1, which implies that servants of King Hezekiah in the late eighth century B.C.E. already had in their library a Solomonic collection of proverbs (all or part of chaps. 10–22) when they added another (chaps. 25–29). By the late eighth century, then, the two-line saying was an established genre attracting the creative efforts of palace scribes. The instructions of chapters 1–9 were composed later, perhaps in the early postexilic period.

Personified Wisdom in Chapters 1–9

Though probably composed by different authors, the instructions in these chapters have been edited into a drama. The opening (1:8–19) sets the scene for all that follows in chapters 1–9: A youth leaving home is instructed by his parents how to build his house (including choosing a wife). In this liminal scene, they warn him against one of the two great dangers to proper "building"—violent men (always plural) and their ways (1:11–19; 2:12–15; 4:10–19). The other great danger to the young man will shortly be mentioned—the deceptive woman (always singular; 2:16–19; chap. 5; 6:20–35; chaps. 7 and 9). These two enemies of wisdom are not merely occasional tempters; they invite the youth to *join* them, to "throw in your lot among us" (1:11, 14), and the woman offers a sexual *relationship*. The central character is Woman Wisdom, who in three speeches (1:20–33, chaps. 8 and 9) invites the youth to be her life companion. By the end of chapter 2, all the characters have been introduced: the young man (1:10), his father and mother (1:8), the violent men (1:11–14; 2:12–15), the deceptive woman (2:16–19), and Woman Wisdom (1:20–33). The "son" or disciple lives in a tumultuous world of competing calls.

It should be noted that though the original recipient of the instructions was a young man (1:4b), Proverbs expands the audience to include older people ("the wise" in 1:5 would be of mature age), and the Bible expands it even further by envisioning as readers all Israel, female and male, young and old.

The most important and fascinating figure in chapters 1–9 is Woman Wisdom. As her origins shed light on her function, it is worth looking at the current theories: (1) a quality (wisdom) of a deity came to be regarded as a separate entity (hypostasis), (2) a Syro-Palestinian or Egyptian goddess served as a model for her, (3) she is based on the divine or semidivine bringers of culture from the gods to human beings originally found in Mesopotamian mythology (*apkallu, ummānu* in Akkadian). The first theory is excluded because Wisdom never acts independently of Yahweh and is regarded as totally separate. The second is unlikely because there is no solid evidence for a suitable Palestinian goddess, and the Egyptian goddess of order, Maat, is too lifeless to have served as a model for Woman Wisdom. The third theory, culture-bringer, is a good parallel and is supported by good linguistic evidence, for Hebrew *ʾāmôn*, "sage" (8:31) is derived from Akkadian *ummānu*, "sage, scribal expert."

The importance of properly identifying Woman Wisdom as a culture-bringer is that one can see her role in the chain of transmission of heavenly wisdom to human beings on earth. In the ancient Near Eastern conception, the gods made the world exclusively for themselves, and humans were the slaves who tended it. The wisdom (that is, practical knowledge) required for this task belonged to the gods, however, and needed to be mediated to the human race. An example of such mediation in Mesopotamia is the several cosmogonies depicting the creation of human beings in two stages, the first stage without "wisdom" (animal-like existence, no society) and the second stage, with wisdom in the form of *culture* (e.g., kingship, laws) and *crafts* (e.g., metallurgy, writing). This capacity to live at a human level and be fit servants of the gods constituted "wisdom." Much of the wisdom needed by the race was given long ago in the ancestral crafts and culture. Mediation of heavenly wisdom continued into the present through the human institutions of king, scribes (and their writings), and family. The king fought off enemies, rendered just decisions, and set an example, enabling the people to live fittingly in the gods' world. The king's task of making his subjects "wise" was also accomplished through his palace scribes who copied ancient literature, interpreted omens, and wrote compositions such as "wisdom literature." The institution of family was part of the transmission; the head of the family managed his household and imparted wisdom to his children. An indication of how important these institutions are in Proverbs is its mention of the king thirty-three times, and the father (sometimes the mother) twenty-seven times, as unfailing sources of wisdom.

Proverbs makes a great change in the ancient picture that profoundly affects its portrait of God: It personifies Wisdom and gives her a role in God's governance of the human race. She was created first (8:22–31), which in that culture meant taking precedence over all creatures. Her function is derived from her gender, for she brings to humans the very love and gifts she has received from Yahweh (8:30–31). She asks her disciples to do no other act than receive her as guide and friend. She uses the language of love: "I love those who love me, and those who seek me diligently find me" (8:17; cf. Song 1:28; 3:1, 2). Personifying as a woman the wisdom that enables people to live humanely and be good divine servants profoundly affects the concept of God. God is not the wise creator only, but one who lovingly invites everyone—the simple and the wise—into an ongoing relationship in which goods are exchanged and life is enhanced. Personification as a woman has all the more point in that the ideal reader of Proverbs 1–9 is a young man establishing a house and choosing a wife!

Personified Wisdom influenced the New Testament. John 1:1–18 combines the concepts of God's word and wisdom. The Gospel employs Woman Wisdom to interpret Jesus, for example, as Wisdom is with God from the beginning (Prov 8:22–23), so Jesus is the Word in the beginning (John 1:1) and with the Father before the world existed (John 17:5); as she descends from heaven to dwell with humans (Prov 8:31), so does Jesus (John 1:14; 3:31; 6:38; 16:28); as she uses symbols of food and drink and invites people to banquet (Prov 9:2–5), so does Jesus (John 6:35, 51; 4:13–14). The early Christian hymns recorded in Phil 2:6–11 and Col 2:15–20 developed personified wisdom to explain the incarnation.

The Sayings of Chapters 10–31

What does an aphorism do? Is it, say, compressed information? The eighteenth-century essayist Samuel Johnson put it best: "Men more frequently require to be reminded than informed" (*Rambler*, no. 2). Aphorisms help people see things in a new light and suggest fresh analogies for making decisions, as noted by Johnson (on the achievement of Alexander Pope): "new things are made familiar, and familiar things are made new" (*Lives of the Poets*). Sometimes a biblical proverb shows God acting directly; more often the world is presumed to be a self-righting system with divine action implicit or stated in a passive verb ("the divine passive"). The operation of divine justice and wisdom is shown through *types*, often as polar opposites (the righteous and the wicked person, the wise and the foolish person, the rich and the poor person). The fate of each type (not of each individual) illustrates the justice and wisdom of God's rule.

The sayings below illustrate how biblical proverbs engage and provoke the reader through irony, paradox, humor, satire, and ellipsis. They excite the curiosity and stretch the imagination. To appreciate the sayings, a highly literal translation (such as my own translation in this section) is recommended. JPSV or NAB are similarly literal and recommended.

> In every place, the eyes of Yahweh
>   are watching the wicked and the good.
>   (15:3)

The saying does not simply say God is all-seeing, but that in every place—holy or profane, hidden or public—God observes human beings. Good and evil are determined by God's standards, not by human ones. The saying is a mini-meditation on divine sovereignty.

Who pursues righteousness and kindness
  will find life and honor.
                    (21:21)

Ironically, intense pursuit attains something other than its original object. Some things are too precious to be seized directly; they must be given. To gain them, therefore, pursue something other than them (e.g., virtue, as in Matt 6:33: "First seek the kingdom of God and its justice and all these things will be given to you").

Common sense derived from experience by itself is not adequate to understand the world that does not belong to human beings but to God. Hence the importance of paradox, a seemingly contradictory statement that turns out to have unexpected meaning and truth.

Who returns evil for good—
  evil will not depart from his house.
                    (17:13)

Normally, one gets rid of what is unwanted by putting it somewhere else. In the case of evil, however, transferring it to one who has done us good ensures that it will stay with us. New Testament injunctions to forgive enemies develop observations such as this one.

One person gives freely and ends up with more,
  another holds back what is due and grows poorer.
                    (11:24)

Generosity to the poor leads to more wealth and stinting on giving makes one poorer. The paradox is also found in the New Testament: "To anyone who has, more will be given and he will grow rich; from anyone who has not, even what he has will be taken away" (Mark 4:25; Matt 13:12; Luke 19:26).

Many sayings cannot be categorized. Some impose themselves because of their unadorned statement of a profound truth—"Rich person meets poor person—the Lord made them both" (22:2) or "Better a serving of vegetables where love is than a fattened ox where hatred is" (15:17). Other sayings are "zingers," sharp-edged statements of unfashionable truths—"The horse is readied for the day of battle, but victory belongs to the Lord" (21:31) or "Who blocks his ears from the cry of the poor will call out but go unheard" (21:13).

It requires effort for modern readers to appreciate the interactive and sophisticated world that produced the sayings. One senses in the sayings wonder at the created world, faith in its mysterious self-righting capacity, hope that the truth will win out. In Proverbs, truth is reached dialectically. Hence, the person who is isolated, arrogant, or defensive can never become wise.

The world of the sages who wrote Proverbs resembles the world of Jesus. He did not hand out abstract wisdom, but engaged people in genuine conversation and moved respectfully with their answers. Like the sages, Jesus knew that the world was God's; nothing in it was alien to him. To reveal that world to others, especially its hidden theocentric dimension and timetable, he used instructions and proverbs that were inspired in part by the book of Proverbs.

THE BOOK OF JOB

If Proverbs is an example of the didactic side of Wisdom literature, Job is decidedly an example of its questioning side. Ancient Near Eastern literature had many works that questioned divine justice and satirized the gods. *The Babylonian Theodicy* (ca. 1000 B.C.E.), for instance, is a dialogue between a sufferer and a sage. The sage offers advice (admit your error and seek God!) but no sympathy. The tension is only resolved when the sage finally agrees with the sufferer's words that the gods "bring him to a horrible end, they snuff him out like an ember." This work probably influenced Job, though the Joban author brings the dramatic tension to new levels by having an angry and eloquent sufferer directly confront the God responsible for *all* events, not only Job's case. The book of Job cannot be dated securely because it refers to no dateable event. Many suggest the period of the sixth-century exile, when Job might have served as a symbol of national suffering.

The Character of Job

Job is the first recorded "righteous sufferer" in history. In ancient Near Eastern religion, the invariable response to unexpected suffering would have been, What have I done wrong? One simply assumed one had offended the gods, even if inadvertently. Against all precedent, however, the afflicted Job maintains his innocence, asserts it is God who is in the wrong, and demands that God answer his questions.

The book is not, however, a treatise on innocent suffering and divine justice, but a story about a man named Job. Like any drama, Job has a beginning (God's decision to allow Job to be afflicted and Job's initial reactions), a middle (Job's arguments that his afflictions are not punishment for sin, and the friends' rejection of his arguments and, gradually, of him), and an end (God's storm appearance, Job's retraction, and God's judgment that Job is righteous). Measured in discourse time (the time required to tell the story), the middle section of three cycles of speeches of Job and the friends (chaps. 3–37) requires thirty-five of the book's forty-two chapters and thus must be regarded as extremely important. Modern readers may be tempted to skip or scan the speeches, but the author delights in airing all views and displaying every feeling. Speakers respond to each other indirectly through allusions and wordplay, and repeatedly circle back to arguments made earlier. The dialogues are about relationships as well as ideas. The friends begin devotedly as they sit silently with Job for seven days, but are soon offended by Job's explosion of anger (chap. 3) and unwillingness to admit wrongdoing (chaps. 6–7). As the friends' alienation increases, Job gradually gives up on them and demands instead an interview with God. By the end of the third cycle (chaps. 22–27), the friends have dropped out of the picture and Job is talking only to God (chaps. 29–31).

The pervasive irony of the book affects its portrait of God. The prologue, with its heavenly scenes (1:6–12; 2:1–6), lets the reader in on something Job and his friends are unaware of: God is afflicting Job because of a bet with the Satan (a kind of inspector who is suspicious of moral heroes like Job) that Job will curse God when trouble comes. So the reality is that Job is suffering not because of his sin but because of his righteousness! Readers thereafter see an ironic depth unintended by the speakers. For example, Job three times expresses the hope for a heavenly figure who would take his part before God (9:32–35; 16:18–22; 19:23–29), but the reader knows that the only other heavenly figure is the malevolent Satan and that God is actually on Job's side.

The Portrayal of God in Job

Though Job is the protagonist, God is present in every scene as subject of every speech or as actor. In a sense, there are four portraits corresponding to the four parts of the book: the prologue, the speeches of Job, the speeches of the friends (including Elihu in chaps. 32–37), and Yahweh's speeches plus the epilogue. Only at the end do the parts add up to a rounded portrait.

The prologue (chaps. 1–2). Despite reservations from some scholars, the prologue (chaps. 1–2) and epilogue (42:7–17) are original, for without them the drama is left hanging. Perhaps no scene in Job is more disturbing than Yahweh betting with the Satan, handing over Job's family and finally Job himself to the malevolent Satan in a wager on whether Job reveres God for love. Shocking, too, are Yahweh's words to the Satan after the first trial: "[Job] still persists in his integrity, although you incited me against him, to destroy him for no reason" (2:3). What kind of God would do such things? Some scholars excuse the coldness by pleading the author is constrained by the genre of heavenly assembly scene (which required give and take among the members), but the author elsewhere masters genres. The author exploits the traditional scene to show that God acts exclusively for God, in this case to win a wager. God takes an interest in heroes like Job and one can hear admiration, even love, for Job. What is "good" and "bad" for Job, however, is determined by divine standards. Job calls his affliction "bad" (2:10), but it is "good," for it is God's testing.

The deity acting out of pure self-regard—testing human beings, determining what is good and what is bad—will return later in the book in the two speeches and epilogue (chaps. 38–42). Meanwhile, this deity will be the subject of the speeches.

The speeches of Job. Job's acceptance of the destruction of his property, family, and his own health (chaps. 1–2) is explosively reversed when he curses the day of his birth and longs for death (chap. 3). As the friends grow cold, Job's desire to meet God face to face increases, though he believes God's capriciousness and volatility rule out justice in his case. Job even parodies a hymn "praising" God's justice and wisdom (chap. 9). He comes to realize that God is more pitiless a pursuer than the friends (21:21–29). The world is arbitrary and violent, God is an enemy, and a just man in straits can only rail.

The speeches of the friends. The friends can only understand Job's case by assuming he has offended God, though perhaps inadvertently. To them, God's world is too reliably made for a truly just person to suffer as grievously as Job. If Job will only own up to the wrong that he must have done, he will find God, loyal friend of the just, only too eager to forgive and support a new beginning. Job's claim of righteousness is obstinate and sacrilegious. God is consistent.

The speeches of God and the epilogue (chaps. 38–42). Though some regard Yahweh's speeches in the storm as a deliberately irrational assault on Job's rational quest, the speeches are in fact a carefully framed answer to Job, whom God elsewhere regards with respect and affection. The first speech (38:1–40:5) answers Job's charge that God did not create *in wisdom*, and the second speech (40:6–42:6) answers Job's charge that God did not create *in justice*. The opening line of each speech (translated properly) is its topic sentence: (1) 38:1: "Who is this who obscures my plan in darkness, / presenting arguments without knowledge?"; (2) 40:8: "Will you pervert my justice? / Will you prove me wrong so that you may be in the right?" (my translation).

In the first speech, God's questions come down to one: Did you bring the world into being? Job's charge that the creation of the earth was random and without design (9:5–6) is revealed as baseless because Job was not there to witness the foundation of the earth laid with great skill (38:4–7). No human being can judge that the world lacks design, for things must conform to divine design. For example, the fabulously stupid ostrich is stupid by design (39:13–18). The speech shows that the world includes the useful, the bizarre, and even the playful, all by God's design.

Justice in the second speech is not the passive and impartial concept of Western culture, but the biblical concept—active and partial, that is, upholding the righteous and putting down the wicked. Job had accused God of being unjust in this sense by allowing the wicked to prosper and the righteous (like Job) to suf-fer. The rebuttal demonstrates God *can* control ultimate cosmic evil (symbolized by the land beast Behemoth and the sea beast Leviathan) but does not necessar-ily exercise control for the benefit of human beings. The two beasts have a place in God's universe though they fulfill no evident function, cannot be domesti-cated, and do not serve human beings. God allows them to exist under divine control, despite their potential for evil. The world is God's, not man's (Job's).

Job's response to the speeches is brief: "I had heard of you by the hearing of the ear, but now my eye sees you; therefore I retract and repent of dust and ashes" (42:5–6, my translation). Far from despising himself and repenting (NRSV), Job simply drops his suit now that he has encountered God and rec-ognized his own limits. In the epilogue, Yahweh's anger is directed not against Job for his relentless attacks, but against his friends who "have not spoken of me what is right, as my servant Job has" (42:8). Job intercedes and God for-gives them. Yahweh restores to Job twice what he had before and gives him a new family, functionally a "resurrection" in that Job will now live through his descendants. The story ends with a great banquet of restoration.

The rounded portrait of God. The book skillfully plays off the portraits of God drawn by Job and by the friends against the portrait of the prologue, divine speeches, and epilogue. The friends insist that the world is created and directed with a wisdom and justice they can understand. Punishment and reward are the consequences of evil and good deeds, though the friends allow for delays and unseen retribution. (Unwittingly, they agree with the Satan's determinist views.) Job, on the other hand, holding God to strict standards of human jus-tice, expects to be upheld as the righteous man he is. Finding support neither from God nor friends, he rails against a world he finds arbitrary and unjust.

The prologue-epilogue narrative is consistent with the divine speeches. Against the friends' view, God is revealed as unconstrained by a mechanical reward-punishment scenario, acting freely for purposes beyond the knowl-edge of human beings. Job's righteousness, for example, is actually the reason why he is suffering. Despite the friends' pretensions, God cannot be figured out from the course of human events. Against Job's view, his sufferings are the result of circumstances (the wager) of which he knows nothing; the world is indeed ruled by wisdom and justice, but they do not conform to human stan-dards; God is not Job's enemy but his admiring friend and patron, eager to return to him all that he has lost. In summary, God is sovereign and free, uncontrolled by human action, yet, astonishingly, is fascinated by human beings, especially the loyal upon whom he looks with admiration and love. The book is, ultimately, about God, not Job. Yet Job remains for all ages the model votary of this inscrutable, gracious, and loving God and is so remembered by the New Testament (Jas 5:11).

THE BOOK OF QOHELETH (ECCLESIASTES)

The book of Qoheleth is a series of observations on life and the wisdom tradition written by a strong-minded individual who bills himself as "king over Israel in Jerusalem" (i.e., Solomon, not named in accord with the typifying tendency of wisdom literature). Most scholars date it between the early fourth and the mid-third centuries. Opinions differ as to whether it is partly a response to the Hellenistic culture introduced by Alexander the Great (d. 323 B.C.E.).

Structure of the Book

Though scholars disagree on the precise structure of the book, there is some consensus on the demarcation of the major units. The outline below attempts to stay within the consensus.

1:2–3	Frame (cf. 12:8)
1:4–11	Cosmology: change, duration, and forgetting
1:12–2:26	I the king and the results of my search
3:1–22	Times are predetermined, fooling the human mind
4:1–16	Striving leaves one unsatisfied
5:1–7 (Heb. 4:17–5:6)	Religious duties
5:8–6:9 (Heb. 5:7–6:9)	Enjoy life, avoid greed
6:10–7:14	Despite wise sayings, no one knows what is good
7:15–29	Righteousness and justice elude us
8:1–17	Arbitrary world
9:1–10	The same fate comes to all, enjoy today
9:11–10:15	Life is risk
10:16–11:6	How to live with political and economic risks
11:7–12:8	Old age and death are coming, enjoy the present
12:8	Frame (cf. 1:2–3)
12:9–11	Epilogue

Message of the Book

The book is framed with the motto "vanity of vanities" in 1:2–3 and 12:8. "Vanity" is the traditional rendering of *hebel* (lit. "breath"), which means, according to context, insubstantial or transient, wrong or repugnant. The opening cosmology in 1:4–11 sets the stage for human life by contrasting the movement of the ever renewed cosmos with ephemeral human life. The transition from impersonal universe to human life is v. 8: "all words are wearying [in preference to NRSV: "all things are wearisome"]; a human being cannot express it," that is, there is a fundamental inability of the mind to understand reality and express it accurately. What the prologue states about the limits of language and wisdom will be affirmed again in 3:11 (see below).

The king makes his appearance in 1:12–2:26 and provides the book with a voice, that of the old king who has seen all things. Like kings in royal inscriptions of the time, he proudly gives his name and title: "I am Qoheleth. I have been a king over Israel in Jerusalem" (my translation). He narrates not his conquests and political success, as one might expect from the genre, but his life-long quest for wisdom. There are two allusions. One is to Solomon the wise king of wisdom literature whose career is described in 1 Kings 3–11. The last chapter in the Kings account tells us, however, that Solomon failed as a sage at the end of his life, bedazzled by women and unable to hand on to his son the full kingdom of his father David. The other allusion is to King Gilgamesh, hero of the great Mesopotamian epic poem *Gilgamesh*. Embarking on a heroic quest for immortality and failing to find it, Gilgamesh returns to his city "weary but at peace" to spend his last days. The standard version of the epic makes the heroic warrior into the wise teacher, adding a forty-line introduction in which the old king addresses the reader as "you" who can learn from "my" travels. Though the persona of the king is less explicit after chapter 2, it continues through the book. When Qoheleth emphasizes the inability to hand on one's legacy to one's children (chapter 2; 6:1–3), one thinks of Solomon, who could not transmit his kingdom to his son. When Qoheleth reflects that death comes to wise and fool alike, one thinks of Gilgamesh, who was urged to give up the quest for eternal life by Siduri the alewife in words very similar to Eccl 9:7–9: "Go, eat your food in pleasure and drink your wine with a merry heart, for God long ago approved whatever you do. Always let your garments be white and let not oil be lacking upon your head. Enjoy life with your beloved spouse all the days of your vain life" (NRSV altered).

Three texts in Qoheleth forcefully state the inability of even wise human beings to achieve mastery over their lives. At the end of the king's life of seeking wisdom (2:24–26), he reports that

> there is nothing better for a human being than to eat and drink, and find enjoyment in his toil. This also, I saw, is from the hand of God; for apart from him who can eat or who can have enjoyment? For to the one whom it seems good to him, God gives wisdom and knowledge and joy; but to the one who misses (such favor) he gives the work of gathering and heaping, only to give it to one whom it seems good to God. (my translation)

Qoheleth sees no clear and consistent relationship between toil and reward; the decision remains with the inscrutable God. The same point is made in the most famous passage of Qoheleth, 3:1–15, which begins, "For everything there is a season, and a *time* for every matter under heaven: a *time* to be born, and a *time* to die." The single "time" is contrasted with the "sense of past and future" (Heb. *ʿōlām;* RSV "eternity") in the mind: "[God] has made everything suitable for its *time*; moreover he has put a sense of past and future into their minds, yet they cannot find out what God has done from the beginning to the end" (3:11). It is not surprising that Qoheleth is skeptical about praying to a God who has not given to human beings the capacity to range much beyond the present moment: "God is in heaven, and you upon earth; therefore let your words be few" (5:2; Heb. 5:1).

Qoheleth is best seen not as a philosopher or thinker but as a clear-eyed observer of his society and world. He has an extraordinary confidence in his own observations, which trump inherited wisdom traditions. What he observes affects his picture of God. Palestinian life in the fourth century and early third centuries was evidently subject to rapid and unpredictable change, with a huge potential for sudden gain and sudden loss in business dealings. Qoheleth sees that people, at least those of his own social class, cannot cope with the volatile and dangerous pace of life, and he accordingly advises them to lay aside grandiose ambitions and enjoy the present moment. He uses commercial terms such as "toil" and "profit" as metaphors for the labor put in and the profit taken from life. For Qoheleth, much more of life is "given" than people realize. Most events simply happen; no one plans or orchestrates them. Acceptance of reality therefore is a divine imperative. One has a duty to experience or "see" life.

Qoheleth differs from Proverbs regarding the quest for wisdom. In Proverbs, wisdom belongs to the gods and is mediated to the human race through the king, sacred writings, and heads of families. The heavenly wisdom intended for human beings is personified, taking on a life of its own. It can be pursued and nurtured as one pursues and nurtures a wife. Qoheleth, on the other hand, does not urge people to seek wisdom but to enjoy the moment. The king, who in Proverbs is a mediator of wisdom, declares the quest does *not* attain wisdom, for the moments of life are hidden with God (3:1–8).

If one compares Qoheleth to Job, one sees that both sages are keenly aware that things are crooked (Eccl 7:13), but only Job demands the crookedness be straightened out. Qoheleth simply says that's the way things are: "What is crooked cannot be made straight" (1:15).

Qoheleth's Portrayal of God

Qoheleth's skepticism does not allow him to speak with the confidence of Proverbs or even of Job about God's activity in the world. Other authors may speak about seeking the face of God, but Qoheleth can only point to the hand of God, which is closed to human view and gives only one moment at a time. There is a time for everything. The sense of past and future in the human mind is an illusion. The surprising thing, however, is that Qoheleth is not a nihilist, but believes one can in a sense encounter God by accepting the moment.

Accepting the moment gives joy, and, surprisingly, the sage speaks of joy again and again (e.g., 2:26; 3:12, 22; 5:20; 9:7–9; 11:9–10). Scholars differ on the relative pessimism of Qoheleth, with some opting for a message of complete absurdity and meaninglessness. One can, however, also read the book as clearing away inflated claims about wisdom and allowing God to be God in a world that is, to be sure, opaque, but not without meaning.

Qoheleth did perhaps hand on one legacy to the New Testament: His denial of the principle of retribution can be regarded as a harbinger of Paul's insistence that God's gifts are not earned, but given with complete graciousness.

SIRACH

Sirach is the name given to the collection of the writings of Jesus son of Eleazar son of Sirach of Jerusalem (Sir 50:27), usually called Ben Sira, who lived in the late third and early second century B.C.E. He is the only wisdom writer to have signed his writings; others wrote anonymously in the ancient Near Eastern custom. He may have conducted a school if Sir 51:23 is not metaphorical: "Draw near to me, you who are uneducated, and lodge in the house of instruction." The book consists of essays on traditional topics such as wisdom, prudent speech, friendship, wealth, and family, and new topics such as the Mosaic law and the history of Israel.

The huge anthology is organized into two parts each with four sections: The first part includes 1:1–4:10; 4:11–6:17; 6:18–14:19; and 14:20–23:27. The second part includes 24:1–33:18; 33:19–38:23; 38:24–42:14; and 42:15–50:24. The conclusion is 50:25–51:30. Each section is introduced by an essay on wisdom (e.g., 1:1–10; 24:1–33).

Theology of the Book

Wisdom and historical traditions. Though Ben Sira is a traditionalist who receives the wisdom legacy with respect, he integrates it with the historical traditions of the Bible. The two most important texts combining wisdom with the historical traditions are chapter 24 and 42:15–50:24. Chapter 24 develops Proverbs 8, associating wisdom with God's word (v. 3), placing her in the Jerusalem temple (vv. 10–12) and its liturgical celebrations (vv. 13–14), identifying her with "the book of the covenant of the Most High God, the law that Moses commanded us" (v. 23), which (in a change of image), like the four rivers of Genesis 2, makes the whole world bloom.

In 42:15–50:24, nature (42:15–43:33) and history (of Israel, chaps. 44–50) proceed according to God's creative word, which expresses divine wisdom. The remarkable harmony of the world as a system shows the influence of Stoicism, according to which the universe is ruled by the immanent divine Logos or word and the human race is invited to join that harmony. The phrase "He is the All" (43:27) occurs also in the famous Stoic Hymn to Zeus, though Ben Sira distances himself from the immanentism of Stoicism by his next verse: "he is greater than all his works." The history is divided into three periods, linked by two transitions in 46:1–12 and 49:11–13: (1) the period when covenants were established (44:16–45:25; "covenant" occurs seven times), (2) the period of the kings (46:13–49:10), and (3) the Second Temple period (49:14–50:24). Notable is the enormous coverage of the high priests Aaron and Simon and their temple rituals involving light, water, and fruit (45:6–22 and 50:1–21). Why the emphasis on the temple ceremonies? Perhaps because the temple liturgy makes visible the Wisdom who dwells in the temple (24:13–15, cf. 50:9–12)—worship furthers the rule of wisdom.

Woman Wisdom, inherited from Proverbs, is given "a local habitation and a name." She is incarnated in actual institutions: the Mosaic law, the Jerusalem temple and its rituals, and in the work of the sage (24:30–34; 38:34–39:11; 51:13–30).

Ben Sira's probing of God's ways. Wisdom literature accepted the world as given; it never advocated reform of the world (though it had a skeptical side as in Job). The questioning side appears from time to time in Ben Sira, who otherwise is confident in God's rule. An example is the discussion in 15:11–20 of divine sovereignty and human freedom, which was not traditionally regarded as a problem. Ben Sira criticizes common ways of putting the problem: "Do not say, 'It was the Lord's doing that I fell away'" (15:11); similarly in 16:17: "Do not say, 'I am hidden from the Lord.'" He comes down emphatically for both human freedom and divine sovereignty, reasoning from the Scriptures, custom, and, mostly, from the divine character.

Portrayal of God

Ben Sira is the first of the wisdom writers to speak descriptively and at length of God. He has an obvious sense of the grandeur of God, which for him consists of omniscience and omnipotence, mercy and severity. Human beings encounter God within a world that is vast, harmonious, and beyond their comprehension; as mortals (human mortality is asserted again and again), they can only respond to God in submission and confidence. Though Ben Sira is aware of problems and possible contradictions, his contemplative impulse overrides them, and he customarily speaks of God with undisguised delight and wonder.

God is omniscient, seeing all acts of human beings, good and bad, and judging them (e.g., 15:18–19; 16:16–19; 23:19–20; 39:19–20). "The God of all" (36:1) issues commands (39:18; 43:26) so sweeping that humans cannot fathom them (18:1–6). All things come from the divine bounty: wisdom to the sage (37:21), wealth to the poor (11:12–13), and healing to the sick (38:2, 9). Even Israel has received its chosen status from God (10:4 and 17:14; cf. Deut 32:8).

Divine omnipotence does not, however, elicit craven fear, for God's purpose is consistently positive toward the human race. Confidence is the only response. God loves those who assist the widow and the orphan (4:10), and protects those who revere him (2:13; 33:1), observe the law (15:1; 17:11), and seek wisdom (1:16; 25:10). Mercy is allied with omnipotence (18:4), which is appropriate in view of human fragility and inclination to evil (17:25–27; cf. Gen 6:5; 8:21). Ben Sira's emphasis on God's greatness and mercy accounts for his repeated injunctions to pray and for his many models of prayer: for overcoming the tyranny of sexual passion (23:1–6), for the defeat of Israel's enemies (36:1–7), in thanksgiving for salvation (51:1–12). Prayer is a capacity given to human beings by which they can fulfill the purpose of their creation (17:8).

Sirach in the New Testament

The direct influence of Sirach can be detected only in the letter of James (e.g., compare Jas 1:5 with Sir 18:18 and 20:15; Jas 1:6 with Sir 1:25 and 2:12). Sirach's emphasis on suffering as testing (Sir 15:11) is echoed in Jas 1:13. Sirach was immensely popular in the early church, and one may suppose that Ben Sira's portrayal of a grand, purposeful, merciful, if occasionally harsh, God influenced early Christians.

WISDOM OF SOLOMON

Wisdom of Solomon is an anonymous work of the first century B.C.E. or early first century C.E., composed in Greek for a Jewish audience. The work singles out for praise the virtue of wisdom (both a perspective and an energy animating the world) and a people, Israel, whose history and behavior embody wisdom. In genre, the work has been described by some as a protreptic, which is an extended advertisement to adopt a particular way of life (Judaism), and described by others as an encomium of wisdom and her benefits to a particular people. The purpose of the work is clear—to show the hidden governance of the world through divine wisdom and the special availability of wisdom in Judaism. The author makes the case for Judaism in a Hellenistic marketplace of religious ideas where religions were validated by their miracles, their antiquity, and the immortality they offered. The author was a committed and learned Jew, perhaps from Alexandria, who aimed to persuade young compatriots and others of the beauty and truth of Judaism.

Outline of the Book

The author makes a coherent case that is best shown by the outline below.

Part 1		(1:1–6:21): The Two Worlds
A		Exhortation: Seek God's wisdom (1:1–12)
	B	The thoughts of the wicked (1:13–2:24)
		C	Examples of the blessed life (chaps. 3–4)
	B	Retraction by the wicked (5:1–23)
A		Exhortation: Seek God's wisdom (6:1–21)

Part 2		(6:22–10:21): Wisdom and the Way to It
A		The origin of Solomon is like that of any human being (7:1–6)
	B	Solomon prays for wisdom (7:7–12)
		C	Grant of wisdom to Solomon (7:13–22a)
			D	Praise of wisdom, its nature, origin, action; its twenty-one attributes (7:22b–8:1)
		C	Solomon will marry wisdom, who lives with God (8:2–9)
	B	Thoughts of the young Solomon (8:10–16)
A		Young Solomon will ask for wisdom (8:17–21)
		Prayer of Solomon (chap. 9)
		Eight heroes of wisdom (chap. 10)

Part 3 — **(11:1–19:22): The Exodus: Seven Comparisons**
(Italicized type below refers to the Egyptian experience, and roman type to the Israelite experience)

1. 11:6–14	*Flowing water*/water from the rock
Two digressions:	(1) the moderation of God toward Egypt and Canaan (11:15–12:27) and (2) a critique of worshipers of other gods (in three parts: 13:1–9; 13:10–15:13; 15:14–19)
2. 16:1–4	*Frogs*/quails
3. 16:5–14	*Flies and locusts*/bronze serpent
4. 16:15–29	*Storm and hail*/manna
5. 17:1–18:4	*Darkness*/light
6. 18:5–25	*Death of first-born*/Israel spared
7. 19:1–9	*Drowning in the Red Sea*/passage through the Sea
19:10–22	Summary

The Portrayal of God in the Wisdom of Solomon

Even more than other wisdom books, the Wisdom of Solomon finds God in the world, for wisdom is the knowledge of the spirit that animates the world and guides the righteous. Part 1 (chaps. 1–6) has been aptly called "the two worlds." One world is the world of appearances, ruled by Gentile kings, violent and destined to pass away, whereas the other is hidden, ruled by divine wisdom, and eternal. Each world has its citizens. The citizens (always plural) of the world of appearances express their philosophy of life in chapters 2 and

5, whereas the citizen of the eternal world, the righteous person, also called the child of God (2:13, 16; always singular) appears in chapter 2 and 5:1–2. As in Proverbs, the fate of the contrasting types (reward for the wise/righteous person, punishment for the foolish/wicked person) reveal God as the just and wise ruler of the world. The author transposes the ethical dualism of the Bible to a cosmic level. Instead of good versus evil people, the conflict is between a good eternal world versus an evil transient world. Though borrowing from Middle Platonism the contrasts of temporal and eternal, of spiritual and material, the author retains the biblical belief in a personal and transcendent God.

Part 2 is about wisdom itself. First, wisdom lies within the reach of all. Even that paragon of wisdom, King Solomon (singular in contrast to the pagan kings; not named in accordance with the typifying tendency of the book), had to pray for wisdom. According to the famous description in 7:22–8:1, wisdom is a subtle energy, capable of entering human beings to be their guide as well as directing the course of the world. Indeed, chapter 10 interprets history from Adam to Moses as a process guided by individuals whom wisdom has entered to guide the world through them.

Part 3 focuses on the constitutive event of Israel, the exodus, to show that Israel is the "son" of God in the world (18:13) whose fate reveals the just and wise God. The drama of the wicked and the righteous individual in chapters 2–5 plays out on the historical and corporate plane in the Israelite exodus, where the Egyptians are the wicked and Israel is the righteous son (11:6–14; 16:1–19:9).

In summary, no other biblical book makes wisdom so reflective of God's very self and so intimately involved in the operation of the world, for she is "a breath of the power of God, and a pure emanation of the glory of the Almighty; . . . a reflection of eternal light, a spotless mirror of the working of God, and an image of his goodness" (7:25–26). Since the Lord animates the world, all that has come to be preserves its being (1:14b). God did not make death, for it came in through the devil's envy (2:24). The world of appearances, characterized by violence and death, is slated to pass away, but before it does, the kings ruling this world are invited to repent and recognize the true ruler. The just, however (identified with Israel), are guided by wisdom and can look forward to eternal life.

God is almost too majestic to be described. Wisdom, who reflects God so sensitively, presents God to us, and, moreover, guides us to the kingdom of God.

SELECT BIBLIOGRAPHY

General

Clifford, Richard J. 1998. *The Wisdom Literature*. Interpreting Biblical Texts. Nashville: Abingdon.

Crenshaw, James L. 1998. *Wisdom Literature: An Introduction*. Rev. ed. Louisville, Ky.: Westminster John Knox.

Murphy, Roland E. 2002. *The Tree of Life: An Exploration of Biblical Wisdom Literature.* 3d ed. Grand Rapids: Eerdmans.

The Book of Proverbs

Boström, Lennart. 1990. *The God of the Sages: The Portrayal of God in the Book of Proverbs.* Coniectanea Biblica, OT Series 29. Stockholm: Almqvist & Wiksell International.

Clifford, Richard J. 1999. *Proverbs.* Old Testament Library. Louisville, Ky.: Westminster John Knox.

Fox, Michael V. 2000. *Proverbs.* Anchor Bible 18A. New York: Doubleday.

Murphy, Roland E. 1999. *Proverbs.* Word Biblical Commentary 22. Dallas: Word.

Van Leeuwen, Raymond C. 1997. "The Book of Proverbs: Introduction, Commentary, and Reflection." Pages 17–264 in *Introduction to Wisdom Literature: Proverbs, Ecclesiastes, Song of Songs, Book of Wisdom, Sirach.* Vol. 5 of *The New Interpreter's Bible.* Edited by Leander E. Keck. Nashville: Abingdon.

The Book of Job

Habel, Norman. 1985. *The Book of Job.* Old Testament Library. Philadelphia: Westminster.

Newsom, Carol A. "Job." 1997. Pages 317–637 in vol. 4 of *The New Interpreter's Bible.* Edited by Leander E. Keck. Nashville: Abingdon.

Perdue, Leo, and W. Clark Gilpin, eds. 1992. *The Voice from the Whirlwind: Interpreting the Book of Job.* Nashville: Abingdon.

The Book of Ecclesiastes (Qoheleth)

Crenshaw, James L. 1987. *Ecclesiastes.* Old Testament Library. Philadelphia: Westminster.

Fox, Michael V. 1999. *A Time to Tear Down and a Time to Build Up: A Rereading of Ecclesiastes.* Grand Rapids: Eerdmans.

Murphy, Roland E. 1992. *Ecclesiastes.* Word Biblical Commentary 23. Dallas: Word.

Seow, Choon-Leong. 1997. *Ecclesiastes.* Anchor Bible 18C. New York: Doubleday.

The Book of Sirach

Collins, John J. 1997. *Jewish Wisdom in the Hellenistic Age.* Old Testament Library. Louisville, Ky.: Westminster John Knox, chs. 2–6.

Crenshaw, James L. 1997. "The Book of Sirach." Pages 601–867 in vol. 5 of *The New Interpreter's Bible.* Edited by Leander E. Keck. Nashville: Abingdon.

Skehan, Patrick W., and Alexander A. Di Lella. 1989. *The Wisdom of Ben Sira.* Anchor Bible 39. New York: Doubleday.

The Wisdom of Solomon

Kolarcik, Michael. 1997. "The Book of Wisdom." Pages 435–600 in vol. 5 of *The New Interpreter's Bible.* Nashville: Abingdon.

Reese, James M. 2000. "The Wisdom of Solomon." Pages 749–63 in *Harper's Bible Commentary.* 2d ed. Edited by James L. Mays. San Francisco: HarperSanFrancisco.

Winston, David. 1979. *The Wisdom of Solomon.* Anchor Bible 43. Garden City, N.Y.: Doubleday.

5

"God" within
the Narrative World of Mark

Jack Dean Kingsbury

It gives me great pleasure to write this article in honor of Paul J. Achtemeier. Almost twenty-four years ago, he was instrumental in my coming to Union Theological Seminary (Va.). Since then he has been not only colleague and friend but also confrere here at Union. I wish both him and his wife, Elizabeth, every joy and blessing in their retirements.

Christology lies at the heart of Mark's gospel story because Jesus is the protagonist. In fact, unless one has a firm grip on Christology, one will not understand Jesus' relationship to God, to the disciples, to the religious authorities, to the crowds, to the little people, or to the future. Neither will one understand how the plot of Mark's story unfolds. Although the goal of this article is to explore the figure of God, we nevertheless begin with Christology. In the last two decades, the approach to Markan Christology has changed radically. Here at the outset, therefore, I shall review succinctly the debate over Markan Christology. This in turn involves discussion of the two most prominent ways in which Mark's Gospel has been read in the twentieth century.

In Gospel research, the method of narrative criticism is still new, having only entered onto the stage in the early 1980s. Nevertheless, the impact that use of it has had in shaping attitudes about how to read the canonical Gospels is already out of proportion to its youthful age. Until twenty years ago, the near consensus among scholars was that the key both to grasping the Christology of the Synoptic Gospels and to reading them aright lay in determining how best to interpret the title "the Son of Man." This pursuit itself generated enough literature to fill a library.

In narrative-critical purview, the Gospel of Mark is a narrative that comprises *story* and *discourse*. The story is that of Jesus Christ from baptism to death and resurrection. A major aspect of the discourse is *point of view*. In the recent debate over Markan Christology, the application of point of view has played a decisive role. It has, in fact, resulted in a reconception of Markan Christology. Such reconception, in turn, has opened the way to a fresh reading of the gospel story as a whole. Together, this reconception and fresh reading constitute the basis on which we shall explore the figure of God. In the past, interpreters have paid relatively little attention to God within Mark's story. Instead, they have concentrated on using Mark's Gospel as a resource for recovering the historical Jesus, or they have focused on the Jesus of the Gospel itself, or on the disciples, or on the community of Mark. Within the world of his narrative, however, Mark understands God as in control both of this world and of the gospel story he tells.

GOD'S POINT OF VIEW

In the twentieth century, the dominant approach to Markan Christology centered on Jesus as "the Son of Man." Correlatively, this title owed its prominence to the importance of the theory of correction. According to this theory, Mark invites readers in the first half of his Gospel (1:1–8:26) to identify Jesus with the pagan, Hellenistic image of the divine man. In the second half of his Gospel (8:27–16:8), Mark then "corrects" this false image through use of the passion predictions and the narration of the passion story (chaps. 14–16). The importance of the title "the Son of Man" derives from its prominence in the passion predictions.

The bogeyman in this corrective theory is Mark's presentation, in the first half of his story, of Jesus as "the Son of God." Indeed, as early as the opening verse Mark identifies Jesus as "the Christ [Messiah], the Son of God," with accent on the latter title. Although this is likely the correct textual reading of verse 1, one cannot be certain of it. Nevertheless, even if "Son of God" is dropped from verse 1, readers reach the episode of the baptism only a few verses later (1:9–11), and here Jesus is depicted still more forcefully as the Son of God (1:11). Regardless of how one decides the textual reading of verse 1, however, Mark can clearly be seen to use the introduction to his gospel story (1:1–13) to present Jesus as the Son of God.

Scholars who follow the corrective theory postulate that Mark presents Jesus as the Son of God in the introduction of his story so that readers will construe "Son of God" in terms of the Hellenistic image of the divine man. Supposedly, the divine man was a heroic figure in the ancient world who was thought of as possessing supernatural power in both word and deed but was in no sense associated with suffering and death. Mark's strategy, therefore, was to have readers in the first half of his gospel story identify Jesus, the Son of God, with the figure of the divine man with whom they were familiar from their pagan, Hellenistic environment. To accomplish this, Mark describes Jesus as powerful of word (1:23) and powerful of deed (4:35–5:43; 6:35–56; 7:24–8:9; 8:22–26) but avoids direct mention of any suffering and death. In this way, Mark leads readers to meld the image of Jesus as the powerful Son of God with the Hellenistic image of the powerful divine man. The theology underlying this image is that humans, right in the here and now, can experience the glory of a higher world.

In the second half of his Gospel (8:27–16:8), Mark "corrects" this powerful Son-of-God, divine-man image of Jesus. Instead of picturing Jesus as accomplishing a salvation of glory, Mark tells of him as accomplishing salvation through suffering and death on the cross. The crucial implication of such salvation is that discipleship, too, is to be understood not as partaking of a sphere of bliss but as following Jesus to the cross and leading a cruciform life.

To correct these false Hellenistic images of Jesus and of discipleship, Mark makes use of passion predictions and narrates the passion story found in chapters 14–16. In the passion predictions, Jesus refers to himself as "the Son of Man" whom God has destined to go to Jerusalem and there to suffer and die (8:31; 9:31–32; 10:32–34). Subsequently, Mark describes Jesus in the passion story as fulfilling in all detail the passion predictions he has already made. By the end of his gospel story, therefore, Mark has accomplished his goal: He has corrected the untruth of the Hellenistic image of Jesus as the powerful Son of God and divine man with the truth that Jesus is the Son of Man whom God willed to accomplish salvation through suffering and death on the cross.

By the early 1980s, the corrective theory of Markan Christology held a near stranglehold on the way in which scholars read the Gospel. Principally, this was due to the fact that this theory, which had been around in rudimentary form for most of the century, had been polished to perfection as a large jewel in the crown of redaction criticism. Redaction criticism is the method that, following World War II, rose to become absolutely dominant in Gospel research. With scholarly interest focused especially on Mark's Gospel, the dominant method of redaction criticism had refined the dominant theory for interpreting the Christology of Mark and had produced the dominant approach to the reading of Mark's Gospel.

In the early 1980s, however, another major event took place in Gospel research: Narrative criticism jelled as a comprehensive method of interpretation. Moreover, one of the chief triumphs of narrative criticism in its infancy is that it provided the tool by means of which the stranglehold that the corrective theory had held on Markan Christology was decisively broken. Moreover, this took place so quickly, so simply, and with such lack of notoriety that scholars seemed to wake up one day to find it self-evident that the corrective theory had all along made for an impossible interpretation of Markan Christology and therefore an impossible approach to the reading of the Gospel. Indeed, the abandonment of the corrective theory seemed to occur so swiftly that a novice in Markan studies could almost have thought that the theory had never existed.

What narrative criticism brought to the table of Gospel research in a manner that had previously not been exploited was the literary device of point of view. This device calls attention to the standpoint or perspective that a narrator of a story or any given character within it takes regarding time, space, phraseology, psychology, and theology or ideology. Apply this device to the reading of Mark's Gospel, and the corrective theory disintegrates after one has covered only the first eleven verses. The clear recognition of this explains the simplicity, power, and effectiveness with which narrative criticism overthrew the dominant corrective theory.

As has been indicated, the first verse of Mark's text reads, "The beginning of the gospel of Jesus Christ [Messiah], the Son of God" (RSV), with emphasis on "the Son of God." If this textual reading stands, the corrective theory does not even survive this verse. The reason is that verse 1 is uttered by the narrator of Mark's story, and this narrator is reliable in that he never conveys false or misleading information to the reader. If, however, "Son of God" must be deleted from verse 1, then the corrective theory survives only until verse 11: "and a voice came from heaven, 'Thou art my beloved Son; with thee I am well pleased'" (RSV). Within the narrative world of Mark, this heavenly voice is that of God, so it is God who declares Jesus to be his Son. Without question, the point of view of God in Mark's gospel story cannot be adjudged to be misleading or false. In contrast, however, the corrective theory requires precisely that the interpreter understand God's declaration to be both misleading and false. This is because "the Son of God" is to be taken as a stand-in for the pagan, Hellenistic, heroic divine man. Emerging from his baptism, Jesus is said to be regarded by readers as the powerful Son of God and divine man. He emerges from the water as a radiant, divine figure of glory.

Nevertheless, once one recognizes that God's point of view concerning the identity of Jesus cannot be interpreted as anything but true, the whole idea that Mark has used the first half of his Gospel to identify Jesus, the Son of God, with the figure of the Hellenistic divine man so as, in the second half of his Gospel, to overthrow this image through use of passion predictions featuring "the Son of Man" and the passion story itself, collapses like rotted timber. In Mark's gospel story, not only is the title of the Son of God not tainted but it also contains within it—because it constitutes God's understanding of Jesus— the deepest mystery of Jesus' person, namely, the mystery of his relationship to God. Furthermore, unless one can rightly comprehend Jesus' relationship to God, one is at a loss to comprehend Jesus' relationship to any of the human characters in Mark's story. Comprehension of Jesus' divine sonship is the necessary foundation for comprehending Jesus' relationship to humanity.

If this be clear, it also becomes clear how Mark would have his gospel story read. First, Mark uses the story's introduction to inform readers immediately of Jesus' identity, that he is the Messiah, the Son of God (1:1, 11). In contrast, no human character within the story—including Jesus himself!—is so informed, which makes of Jesus' identity a mystery. Second, Mark enables readers to look on throughout the rest of the story as major human characters struggle mightily to penetrate the mystery of Jesus' identity. Third, not until the end of his story does Mark depict a human character as actually penetrating the mystery of Jesus' identity by confessing him at death to have been the Son of God (15:39). Finally, at this precise point, readers, having been privy to Jesus' identity all along, can at last comprehend both fully and rightly what it means for him to be the Son of God. Indeed, readers can comprehend both fully and rightly the relationship of Jesus both to God and to human beings.

As for the term "the Son of Man," this is the designation the Markan Jesus uses to refer to himself without at the same time revealing his identity. When it comes to the question "Who is Jesus?" Mark employs messianic titles to give answer. "The Son of Man," however, is not a messianic title in Mark's Gospel. Overall, Jesus' identity is that of the Messiah-King (of the Jews) from the house of David, the royal Son of God.

GOD'S VIEW OF JESUS AND JESUS' VIEW OF GOD

The claim Mark dares to make is that he writes the whole of his gospel story from the point of view of God. This claim comes to clear expression in the sharp rebuke Jesus gives Peter following the first passion prediction and Peter's repudiation of it: Says Jesus to Peter, "Get behind me, Satan! For you are not thinking the things of God but the things of humans" (8:33, my translation). Noteworthy is the triple contrast one finds in this saying. To begin with, Jesus asserts that only two viewpoints exist in the whole of this world, that of God and that of humans. For humans to adopt a third, fourth, or fifth viewpoint is not even possible. Again, Jesus contends that the viewpoint of humans is not just misguided or wrong but evil, or Satanic. Conversely, to be aligned with the viewpoint of God is to "think" about things as Jesus himself, the one who utters this saying, does. And last, to "think" about things from the viewpoint of God and of Jesus is, implicitly, to think about things from the viewpoint of the one who knows what Jesus has said and can report this saying, namely, Mark as implied author and narrator of his gospel story.

Mark's ultimate claim, therefore, is that the point of view that is normative in his gospel story is God's point of view and that both Jesus and he as narrator, because they "think the things of God," are thoroughly reliable representatives of God's viewpoint. This means we must now explore the relationship Mark establishes in his story between God on the one hand and Jesus and the narrator on the other. Then we can look at how other characters in Mark's story relate to God and ask, finally, what Mark is up to in writing his Gospel.

To begin with Jesus, he is, we know, preeminently (not exclusively!) identified as the Son of God, which touches on the deepest mystery of his person. Already in the introduction of his story (1:1–13), Mark characterizes Jesus' relationship to God along these lines: God has, respectively, anointed Jesus as King ("Messiah"), the Son of God (1:1), foretold through Isaiah of Jesus' "way" (1:2–3), empowered Jesus with the Spirit (1:10), personally acknowledged him to be "my Son" (1:11), and, through Jesus' empowerment, enabled him to resist Satan's forty-day temptation in the wilderness (1:12–13). By the end of Mark's introduction, therefore, readers already know that Jesus' relationship to God is that of God's anointed royal Son, that God has foretold his ministry in Scripture, that God has supremely empowered him for messianic ministry, that God has personally acknowledged his identity as the Son of God and consequently as the one in whom God acts decisively, and that God has inaugurated, through Jesus and within human history, the eschatological age of salvation. It is, therefore, as the royal Son of God who inaugurates God's eschatological salvation that Mark pictures Jesus, in the first act of his public ministry (1:14–15), as proclaiming "the gospel of God" and pointing to himself as the bearer of God's kingdom, or rule, the one who invites Israel to be saved by repenting and believing in the good news he preaches.

As the Son of God, Jesus' relationship to God is furthermore marked by perfect obedience. Mark shows this throughout his gospel story but nowhere more poignantly than toward the end. As Jesus, in Gethsemane, stands before death, he prays to God as the Son who appeals to his Father: "Abba, Father, all things are possible to thee; remove this cup from me; yet not what I will, but what thou wilt" (14:36 RSV). This saying of Jesus rhymes perfectly with his teaching in the first passion prediction: To go to Jerusalem to suffer and to die is "God's will" (8:31). Elsewhere, Mark depicts Jesus as enunciating God's point of view by quoting from the Old Testament, God's very word. For example, Jesus asks the religious leaders, "Have you not read this scripture: 'The very stone which the builders rejected has become the head of the corner; this was the Lord's doing, and it is marvelous in our eyes'?" (12:10–11 RSV). Jesus, in fact, quotes from the Old Testament far more often than does any other character in Mark's story.

In addition, Mark narrates episodes in which Jesus freely acknowledges the superiority of God, his Father, to him, the Son. In conversation with the rich man who addresses him as "Good Teacher," Jesus says, "Why do you call me good? No one is good but God alone" (10:18). In speaking with James and John, Jesus declares, "To sit at my right hand or at my left is not mine to grant, but it is for those for whom it has been prepared [by God]" (10:40). Of his return in heavenly splendor, Jesus affirms, "Of that day or that hour no one knows, not even the angels in heaven, nor the Son, but only the Father" (13:32). And in repudiating the religious authorities, Jesus pits their point of view, not against his own, but against that of God: "You have a fine way of rejecting the commandment of God, in order to keep your tradition!" (7:9 RSV).

In telling readers of Jesus' messianic ministry, Mark deftly correlates this ministry with his identity as the Son of God. It is as brackets around Jesus' entire ministry that Mark shapes the culmination of both the introduction of his story and its ending. The introduction reaches its culmination in words God utters: "Thou art my beloved Son" (1:11 RSV). The ending of Jesus' public ministry reaches its culmination in the confession with which the centurion responds to Jesus' death: "Truly, this man was the Son of God!" (15:39). Such bracketing with climactic statements binds Jesus' messianic ministry and his identity together; the two are fused and intertwined.

The centurion is the first human character in Mark's story to penetrate the deepest mystery of Jesus' identity, that he has been (and at the resurrection will be!) the Son of God. Contrariwise, readers heard God's announcement of Jesus as being "my Son" already at the baptism. Between divine announcement and human insight, however, note what has transpired: Jesus has carried out his messianic ministry to Israel by preaching, calling disciples, teaching, healing, and exorcising demons, and has thus invited Israel to repentance, belief in the gospel, and life in the sphere of God's rule. Jesus has even guided the disciples, in the person of Peter, to confess him correctly as being the Messiah (8:29).

What the disciples in no way understand, however, is Jesus' passion predictions. This is why, in the aftermath of the first prediction, God enters into the world of Mark's narrative a second time, at the transfiguration (9:2–8). God announces, this time to the three disciples on the mountain with Jesus, what they do not know and resist knowing, namely, that it is insufficient to confess Jesus to be the Messiah who has preached, called them, taught, healed, and exorcised demons. God intends for them to know that Jesus is "my Son" and that they are to hear him, to give ear to the passion prediction he has given them. As Jesus journeys to Jerusalem and delivers two more passion predictions, the disciples still understand nothing. When Jesus, in Jerusalem, enters upon suffering that leads to the cross, the disciples evince their ignorance even more pronouncedly: They apostatize and leave Jesus to die utterly alone. Upon Jesus' death, however, the centurion suddenly responds by exclaiming, "Truly, this man was the Son of God!" Not the disciples but this centurion, at the end of Jesus' messianic ministry, becomes the first human being to penetrate the deepest mystery of his identity.

The critical piece for solving Mark's puzzle is still missing: What is the significance of Jesus' death on the cross? Why is it so crucial for Mark that the deepest mystery of Jesus' identity should not be revealed to a human being until Jesus has completed his destiny? And what does Jesus' death say about his relationship to God? Mark has answered these three questions in words Jesus also spoke to the uncomprehending disciples, at the Last Supper: "This is my blood of the covenant, which is poured out for many" (14:24 RSV).

When Jesus, only verses later, does pour out his blood on the cross, he accomplishes salvation for all of humanity—not only for Jews such as the disciples but also for Gentiles such as the Roman centurion—through God's expiation of sins on account of which humans may not despair of forgiveness (2:1–12). Still, it is only through the death of "my Son," the one who is perfectly obedient to God, that God accomplishes such salvation. Identity as the Son of God, perfect obedience unto death, and salvation for all hang together in Mark's story of Jesus. To be sure, it is not unimportant for comprehending the identity of Jesus to confess him to be the Messiah who has, in anointment with the power of the Spirit, proclaimed, called disciples, taught, healed, exorcised demons, and summoned Israel to become his disciples and live in the sphere of God's kingdom. But to grasp the identity of Jesus fully and rightly, readers must comprehend his relationship to God not only as encompassing these acts but also as one of perfect obedience unto death on the cross and the salvific significance of his messianic ministry. Only as readers do this will they likewise comprehend what their own relationship to God is: one of becoming a disciple of Jesus, the crucified Son of God, in the sphere of God's kingdom by following him in leading the cruciform life.

Because Jesus is the protagonist of Mark's gospel story, dominates the story completely, and relates to God throughout his messianic ministry as the Son who is perfectly obedient even unto death on the cross, readers become persuaded to identify Jesus' point of view with God's point of view. Further, as a result of the salvation God accomplishes through Jesus' cross, readers themselves are enabled to relate to God as disciples of Jesus. Notwithstanding all of this, the scope of Mark's claim on behalf of Jesus is vaster yet.

In the last episode of his story, Mark tells of God as resurrecting Jesus, the Son of God, from death to new life (16:6). The significant thing to observe here is that Mark construes Jesus' resurrection, not apart from his messianic ministry, but as part and parcel of it (8:31; 9:31; 10:32–34). Mark's own peculiar position in history, as implied author and narrator of his gospel story, lies beyond Jesus' resurrection but short of his second coming (8:38–9:1; 13:24–27). From this position, Mark looks back upon the ministry of Jesus. In doing so, however, he does not construe the resurrection as some colossally strange event tacked on to an otherwise earthly ministry. No, the resurrection is the final event in a ministry all of which, including death and resurrection, was messianic. Mark posits continuity between Jesus the Son of God who is baptized and crucified and Jesus the Son of God who is risen. As the risen one, Jesus the Son of God remains the baptized and crucified one (16:6). Mark stresses the oneness of Jesus' person both prior to death and after death.

In writing his gospel story, Mark does not always permit readers to see, or even to catch a glimpse of, the glory of Jesus as the risen one, which has nothing to do with any pagan, Hellenistic myth of the divine man. The reason Mark hesitates to depict Jesus in the glory of his Father is that Mark's aim is to describe the baptized Jesus as on his way to crucifixion, the cross being the climactic event of his entire gospel story. Sometimes, however, Mark does let this glory of Jesus shine forth, whether more faintly or more brightly. This happens, for example, at the baptism and temptation, when the glory of God is poured out upon Jesus in dove-like descent to empower him and to declare his identity so that he, in turn, inaugurates the eschatological age of salvation in the presence of tamed beasts and ministering angels. It is this glory of Jesus that shines forth when he teaches with astonishing authority, or when demons cry out his identity as the Son of God, or when he performs miracles, or when he is transfigured atop the mountain, or when he is publicly coronated on the cross, under the guise of literary irony, as both the King of the Jews and the Son of God, or when he is outright depicted by Mark as coming in splendor to usher in the consummated kingdom of God.

To recognize that Jesus is one throughout Mark's story is crucial for interpreting both his relationship to God and the stupendous claim Mark makes on his behalf. Mark pictures God as Creator and Ruler (10:6, 9; 12:26–27; 13:19) and Jesus as the baptized, crucified, and risen Son of God who will "come in the glory of his Father with the holy angels" to bring in the kingdom of God "with power" (8:38–9:1; also 13:24–27). In the latter picture, Jesus the Son of God is described as God's regent, as one who rules in God's stead. This means, therefore, that Mark posits oneness not only between the baptized, crucified, and risen Jesus but also between this Jesus and Jesus as God's cosmic regent. Jesus, therefore, relates to God in such fashion as that he is the baptized, crucified, risen, and cosmic Son of God. Such is the oneness of his own person that, in terms of his relationship to God, it can also be called "oneness," though now expressing a closeness that Christian theology, even to this day, has never been able fully to explicate.

GOD'S POINT OF VIEW
AND THE MARKAN NARRATOR

Along with Jesus, the narrator also conveys God's point of view in Mark's gospel story. The narrator is the reliable, silent voice belonging to Mark as implied author that readers hear telling them the story. One could wish to argue that the narrator is even more important than Jesus in projecting God's point of view. After all, the narrator shapes the plot of the story for readers, including the role played by Jesus. Because the place from which the narrator speaks lies between the resurrection and Jesus' second coming, he has a bird's-eye view in overlooking the whole of Jesus' public and messianic ministry from a futuristic perch. He is also omniscient and omnipresent. He knows with accuracy everything that happens in the story, including what any given character says, thinks, or feels. He can position himself wherever he likes: with Jesus alone at his baptism, with the disciples in the boat, amid the crowds by the sea, or with the religious authorities as they convene to place Jesus on trial. And he can privilege readers with information not known by human characters within the story, which he does in the introduction when he identifies Jesus as the Messiah—King from the house of David, the royal Son of God (1:1). In this way, he ties readers to his narration of the gospel story and persuades them of its truth. Nevertheless, the narrator himself cedes to Jesus the position of being most important in the story. He does this by showing Jesus to be God's Son, through whom God accomplishes salvation and intends that his kingdom will come in glory.

The narrator reveals within the first three verses of the gospel story that he "thinks the things of God." Not only does he introduce Jesus to the readers as the Messiah, the Son of God (1:1), but he immediately launches into a recitation of God's own word as spoken through the prophet Isaiah: "Behold, I send my messenger before thy face, who shall prepare thy way; the voice of one crying in the wilderness: Prepare the way of the Lord, make his paths straight" (1:2–3 RSV). The passage is transparent: The "I" who makes this announcement is God; the one who is "my messenger" is John the Baptist; the one referred to by such expressions as "before your face," "your way," "the way of the Lord," and "his paths" is Jesus, who acts as the "Lord God," that is to say, as the Messiah, the Son of God, in whom God's very kingdom impinges upon the present for salvation and will come in the future in splendor. Just as the prepositional phrase "before your face" and the clause "the voice of one crying in the wilderness" point to the ministry of John the Baptist, so the terms "way" and "paths" point to the messianic ministry of Jesus.

If one combines these various observations, one discovers that within these first three verses, Mark as narrator has summarized the whole of his gospel story, to wit: The God of Isaiah sends John the Baptist as the forerunner of Jesus Messiah, the Son of God, to prepare Israel for the messianic ministry of the Son, who will act in perfect concert with God. Having thus summarized the gospel story he will tell, the narrator has prepared the way for readers to hear this story. Immediately, therefore, the narrator launches into his telling of John the Baptist's ministry of preparation (1:4–8). Then he completes his introduction of Jesus: God anoints Jesus the Son of God with the Spirit for his messianic ministry and personally declares him to be "my Son." In turn, Jesus the Son of God gives demonstration of his spiritual empowerment and of his divine sonship by resisting Satan and inaugurating the eschatological age of salvation (1:9–13).

On this high note, Mark as narrator moves to the middle phase of the gospel story by telling of Jesus' messianic ministry to Israel whereby he preaches, calls disciples, teaches, heals, and exorcises demons (1:14–8:26). Following this, the narrator embarks on the long ending of his story (8:27–16:8): Jesus journeys to Jerusalem, where he suffers and dies in perfect obedience to God and is resurrected from the dead by God, exactly as Jesus himself predicts in the course of his journey (8:31; 9:31; 10:32–34). With the death and resurrection of Jesus, the narrator has told the whole of his story that, again, he summarized in the first three verses. The narrator's relationship to God, therefore, is that he "thinks the things of God," and his relationship to Jesus is that he knows both the identity of Jesus and his destiny. Next to Jesus, the narrator is the most important figure in Mark's Gospel.

GOD'S POINT OF VIEW
AND THE CHARACTERS OF MARK'S STORY

Finally, Mark as implied author and narrator also uses other characters within his gospel story either to express God's point of view or to bring it to bear on situations. Crucial to Mark's story is that Satan, the fountainhead of all evil, be bested by Jesus Messiah, the Son of God. Satan tempts Jesus for forty days in the wilderness only to succumb to Jesus' power to resist him (1:12–13). As Mark shows elsewhere, Jesus must bind the strong man Satan before he can plunder Satan's kingdom (3:22–27). Further, demons are the minions of Satan who do his evil will by afflicting humans. Facing destruction in confrontation with Jesus, they repeatedly cry aloud during Jesus' ministry that he is the Son of God (1:23–24; 3:11; 5:7). As soon as they cry aloud, however, Jesus suppresses their cries, the upshot being that human characters do not hear them and the mystery of Jesus' divine sonship is not made known (1:25–27; 1:34; 3:12; 5:1–13). The purpose the demons serve with their loud but suppressed cries has to do with readers: The demonic shouts remind readers over and over, first, that Jesus is in fact the Son of God ("they knew him," 1:34) and, second, that his identity, though known to supernatural beings, is a mystery human characters cannot penetrate. Literarily, the cries of demons not heard by human characters function in Mark's story like private asides to readers.

The disciples in Mark's gospel story are a pitiable lot. The trend with them is downhill, from ignorance to apostasy. More often than not, they "think the things of humans." Indeed, it is to Peter as spokesperson for the disciples, after he repudiates Jesus' first passion prediction, that Jesus vehemently asserts, "Get behind me, Satan, for you are not thinking the things of God but the things of humans!" (8:33, my translation). Two shining moments, however, do belong to the disciples. The first is when Peter, on behalf of all, confesses to Jesus, "You are the Christ [Messiah]!" (8:29). Although Jesus commands Peter and the disciples to be silent about this (8:30), the confession is nevertheless correct. This is because it corresponds to what Mark as reliable narrator has told readers in the opening verse of the story: Jesus is the Messiah. The reason Jesus commands silence following Peter's confession is that this confession, though correct, is also insufficient: It is not only as Israel's anointed King that the disciples must confess Jesus but also as God's own Son. For the disciples, however, this will not be possible until after Jesus has been raised from the dead (9:9). Only then will the disciples comprehend who Jesus is and what he was about: He is the Son of God who died on the cross to accomplish God's salvation for all, which truth God attests to by raising "my Son" from death to life and to cosmic rulership.

The aftermath of the resurrection, therefore, becomes the second shining moment for the disciples. This is the case, however, because of the promise that God gives them through the "young man in dazzling white" and the three women: Mary Magdalene, Mary the mother of James, and Salome. Inside the empty tomb, the young man tells the astonished women, "You seek Jesus of Nazareth who has been crucified and remains the crucified one. He has been raised [by God]. But go, tell his disciples and Peter that he is going before you to Galilee; there you will see him, as he told you" (16:6–7, my translation). As readers of Mark's story know, a prediction by an agent of God or by Jesus himself necessarily comes to fulfillment. The compelling inference, therefore, is that Peter and the disciples do in fact see the crucified and resurrected Jesus, the Son of God, in Galilee. In so doing, they comprehend what Jesus told them following the transfiguration, that they would not comprehend until after the resurrection (9:9), that is, Jesus' identity as "my Son" (9:7) and his destiny, which will attain to its fulfillment only in the fulfillment of the passion prediction God commanded the three disciples atop the mountain to "hear" (9:7; 8:31). It will be in comprehension of Jesus' identity and destiny that the disciples will do as Jesus has told them to do in his eschatological discourse: Preach the gospel to all nations (13:10).

Other human characters as well are used by Mark as narrator to convey the point of view of God. Excellent examples of "little people" the narrator so uses are the Syrophoenician woman (7:24–30), the father with the demoniac son (9:14–29), and blind Bartimaeus (10:46–52). All three are persons of great faith whose faith leads them to persist in overcoming obstacles in order to have Jesus heal daughter, son, or self. Blind Bartimaeus sits beside the road on which Jesus, disciples, and a great multitude pass by. Hearing that Jesus is in the throng, Bartimaeus shouts out, "Jesus, Son of David, have mercy on me!" Told by the crowd to be silent, Bartimaeus shouts out all the more, "Son of David, have mercy on me!" Jesus stops, recognizes Bartimaeus, summons him to him, and asks, "What do you want me to do for you?" Replies Bartimaeus, "Rabbi, let me receive my sight." Says Jesus, "Go your way; your faith has made you well." Mark's intent in this episode is to show great faith in action. In his appeals to Jesus as Israel's Davidic king, Bartimaeus reveals that he is aligned with God's point of view, that he thinks the things of God. Readers are to take note and to emulate the great faith of Bartimaeus.

Finally, Mark cleverly employs irony to describe even human opponents of Jesus as thinking the things of God. Perhaps the best illustration of this is in the episode of Jesus on the cross (15:24–39). In the name of the Roman state, Pilate declares to all the world in the inscription placed above Jesus' head, "The King of the Jews." The crowds of passersby assert, "You who would destroy the temple and build it in three days . . ." The religious authorities cry out, "He saved others . . . the Messiah, the King of Israel . . ." The two who are crucified with Jesus speak about him, Mark says, along these same lines. And last, the Roman centurion exclaims, "Truly, this man was the Son of God!" From their own standpoint, all of these human characters have a hand in putting Jesus to death. From the standpoint of Mark as narrator, however, they all unwittingly speak the truth about Jesus. Hence, even the human opponents of Jesus attest to the veracity of God's point of view.

CONCLUSION

My thesis is that Mark shows God to be in absolute control of the narrative world of his gospel story. John the Baptist carries out his ministry of preparation and Jesus his messianic ministry in fulfillment of God's will. The characters within Mark's story show themselves either to "think the things of God" or to "think the things of humans," which is evil or Satanic. Ironically, even the opponents of Jesus do God's will or give voice to God's point of view. The culmination of Mark's gospel story comes in the episode of Jesus' death on the cross as the Messiah King, the Son of God. Jesus' death, however, is God's triumph, for through the cross of Jesus, God accomplishes salvation for all of humanity. In raising Jesus the Son of God from the dead, God establishes Jesus as his cosmic regent whom God has also chosen to come again to usher in the kingdom of God in splendor.

At first blush, the thesis that Mark shows God to be in absolute control of his narrative world may seem commonplace, until one reviews the history of Markan scholarship. In the last two centuries, the liberal approach to Mark has reigned supreme. Mark has been excavated as the main source by which one can sketch the earthly ministry of the so-called historical Jesus. Rigorously, the element of eschatology has been expunged from the text of Mark. Nor did the application of redaction criticism at the level of Mark as theologian or of his community assist in a proper reading of Mark. Under the aegis of redaction criticism, scholars arrived at a near consensus that the way to read Mark's Gospel was in terms of the myth of the Hellenistic divine man or at least in terms of construing Jesus as "the Son of Man." Also, Markan scholarship has had to endure all those theses about Mark as taking a theological stand against his community. It is no accident that these theses regarding Mark as rebel flourished in the 1970s at the time the Vietnam War was still raging and America's younger set was rebelling against established authority of every kind. To be sure, narrative criticism is by no means a silver bullet that can solve all problems; no single method suffices to do this. Nevertheless, narrative criticism has assisted in placing some false readings of Mark on the shelf, if one is inclined to believe at all that such a thing as a false reading exists. For myself, I am willing to settle for a better reading of Mark, and this, I believe, is a goal worth pursuing.

SELECT BIBLIOGRAPHY

Achtemeier, Paul J. 1986. *Mark*. Proclamation Commentaries. 2d rev. and enlarged ed. Philadelphia: Fortress.

Best, Ernest. 1983. *Mark: The Gospel as Story*. Studies of the New Testament and Its World. Edinburgh: T. & T. Clark.

Betz, Hans Dieter. 1968. "Jesus as Divine Man." Pages 114–33 in *Jesus and the Historian: In Honor of Ernest Cadman Colwell*. Edited by F. T. Trotter. Philadelphia: Westminster.

Bieler, Ludwig. 1935–36. *Theios Aner*. 2 vols. Vienna: Oskar Höfels.

Bultmann, Rudolf. 1951-55. *Theology of the New Testament*. Translated by Kendrick Grobel. 2 vols. New York: Charles Scribner's Sons.

Donahue, John R. 1973. *Are You the Christ?* Society of Biblical Literature Dissertation Series 10. Missoula, Mont.: Scholars Press.

Holladay, Carl H. 1977. *Theios Aner in Hellenistic Judaism: A Critique of the Use of This Category in New Testament Christology.* Society of Biblical Literature Dissertation Series 40. Missoula, Mont.: Scholars Press.

Hooker, Morna D. 1991. *The Gospel according to Saint Mark.* Black's New Testament Commentaries. Peabody, Mass.: Hendrickson.

Juel, Donald H. 1999. *The Gospel of Mark.* Interpreting Biblical Texts. Nashville: Abingdon.

Kingsbury, Jack Dean. 1983. *The Christology of Mark's Gospel.* Philadelphia: Fortress.

———. 1989. *Conflict in Mark: Jesus, Authorities, Disciples.* Minneapolis: Fortress.

Malbon, Elizabeth Struthers. 2000. *In the Company of Jesus: Characters in Mark's Gospel.* Louisville, Ky.: Westminster John Knox.

Perrin, Norman. 1974. "The Christology of Mark: A Study in Methodology." Pages 104–21 in *A Modern Pilgrimage in New Testament Christology.* Philadelphia: Fortress.

Petersen, Norman R. 1978. *Literary Criticism for New Testament Critics.* Guides to Biblical Scholarship. Philadelphia: Fortress.

Rhoads, David, and Donald Michie. 1982. *Mark as Story.* Philadelphia: Fortress.

Telford, William R. 1999. *The Theology of the Gospel of Mark.* New Testament Theology. Cambridge: Cambridge University Press.

Tiede, David L. 1972. *The Charismatic Figure as Miracle Worker.* Society of Biblical Literature Dissertation Series 1. Missoula, Mont.: Scholars Press.

Tolbert, Mary Ann. 1989. *Sowing the Gospel: Mark's World in Literary-Historical Perspective.* Minneapolis: Fortress, 1989.

Wetter, Gillis P. 1916. *"Der Sohn Gottes."* Forschung zur Religion und Literatur des Alten und Neuen Testaments 26. Göttingen: Vandenhoeck & Ruprecht.

6

The God of Israel
and the Salvation of the Nations

The Gospel of Luke and the Acts of the Apostles

JOHN T. CARROLL

God may be the "neglected factor in New Testament theology" (Dahl 1975), but the fault does not belong to Luke. Readers of the Gospel of Luke and its sequel, Acts, encounter a decidedly theocentric narrative (cf. Brawley 1990, 40–41). In this two-part story, God—the covenant-keeping deity of Israel—purposes and, through various agents and means, announces and accomplishes salvation for all peoples of the earth.

This study of the presentation of God in Luke-Acts will be organized thematically, drawing together relevant materials from both Luke and Acts. While these are distinct books, each with its own narrative and set of characters, Acts continues the story begun in the Gospel of Luke, as the preface to the second volume clearly indicates (Acts 1:1–2). Many questions and expectations raised by book one are resolved only in the sequel, notably the destiny of Judas, the apostles' role as judges of the twelve tribes of Israel (Luke 22:28–30), proclamation and witness "to all nations," and divine power to enable it (24:44–49).

A reader-oriented approach to characterization that constructs the character of God on the basis of a sequential, first-time reading of the text is legitimate and helpful. My discussion, however, will develop a picture that would result from repeated reading, or hearing, of the narrative over a period of time—the sort of engagement that might have occurred in an early Christian community that treasured Luke's two books "to Theophilus."

MODES OF DIVINE ACTIVITY AND PRESENCE

God is an active character in the Lukan narrative. The noun *Theos* ("God") appears 122 times in the Gospel and no less than 168 times in Acts (Thompson

91

2000, 92–93; Green 1995, 37). The divine presence, however, is evident in many ways beyond the use of the name "God." Attention to the names and epithets given to God and the ways in which God is present within the story exhibits the close connection between theology and Christology: Luke-Acts is simultaneously theocentric and christocentric. The saving initiative of Israel's God in human history comes to sharp focus in the person and work of Jesus.

Divine Names

God is Savior (e.g., Luke 1:47), and so is Jesus (e.g., 2:11; Acts 13:23). God is the Lord (*Kyrios*, e.g., Luke 4:18), as is Jesus (e.g., 1:43; 2:11; Acts 2:36). In extolling God as Savior, Mary points to God's grace for the lowly (Luke 1:47–48). Zechariah then proceeds to praise God for sending a Savior (Jesus) to deliver the people from their enemies (1:71, 74) and, through forgiveness, from their sins (1:77). As the story unfolds, it becomes evident that neither God nor Jesus is Savior in a way that rids the Jewish people of Roman rule. Rather, salvation has to do with restoration to the community of God's people through healing of sickness, forgiveness of sin, and acceptance of the lowly and despised.

God is "Lord of heaven and earth," as Jesus begins one prayer (Luke 10:21). Jesus also has universal lordship, according to Peter in Acts (10:36). God is sovereign, and shares dominion with Israel's Messiah and king. As the one who sets the course of human history, God exercises sovereign rule not only in Israel and not only among the nations but also in the whole creation (Acts 17:26–27; cf. 1:7; 14:16). A prayer of the gathered community addresses God as the Lord of all creation (4:24). In his polemic against the notion that God resides in the temple, Stephen deploys Isa 66:2 to point to God as Creator (7:48–50). Paul emphasizes before pagan audiences that God is Creator of heaven and earth (14:15; 17:24), and the source of life for all human beings (17:25). The Gospel customarily speaks (in the voice of Jesus) of God's reign or sovereign rule (*basileia*). In view of the fundamental Jewish affirmation of God as the ruler of the universe, this surely implies God's sovereignty as universal Creator. The theme comes to explicit expression, however, only in Acts.

The other primary name for God in Luke-Acts is "Father." Virtually all these references to God as Father occur in the Gospel, not surprising since Jesus is the character who ordinarily uses the name. It appears in Acts only three times (1:4, 7; 2:33), and two of these report the words of the risen Jesus (1:4, 7; cf. Thompson 2000, 92–93). Jesus' first clear (though implicit) mention of God as "my Father" is spoken, appropriately, in the temple when he is on the threshold of adulthood (2:49). Earlier, however, his identity as "Son of the Most High," associated with his role as the royal descendant of David, was disclosed to Mary by an angel (1:32, 35). In Luke, therefore, the baptism of Jesus confirms rather than reveals his identity as God's son (3:22), an insight later given disciples who observe the transfiguration, again by the "voice of God" (9:35).

Jesus links his eschatological glory as "Son of Man" to the glory of "the Father" (9:26). And when the seventy-two report their successful mission of healing and exorcism (as well, presumably, as proclamation, though only exorcism is mentioned)—a foretaste of the final defeat of Satan—Jesus addresses to God as "Father" a prayer of praise celebrating the resolve of God to reveal these mysteries to the lowly (10:21–22). God is "Father" also of the disciples, a relationship that entails benevolent grace for them: "[I]t is your Father's good pleasure to give you the kingdom" (12:32). The kindness of "the heavenly Father" far surpasses the generosity of human parents, and the gift of the Holy Spirit is the decisive proof (11:13).

Throughout the passion narrative, Jesus remains in intimate communion with God as his "Father." He prays that the cup (of his suffering) may be removed, though he submits to God's will (22:42). He asks his "Father" that his persecutors be forgiven, in a prayer that, though textually uncertain, is probably authentic (23:34; see Nolland 1993, 3:1141–42; Marshall 1978, 867–68; Johnson 1991, 376). And he commits his spirit to God his Father with his last words (23:46). Attentive readers are not surprised that the intimate parent-child relationship between Jesus and God does not spare him suffering and death. In the exchange with the devil at the story's beginning, Jesus had countered the devil's interpretation of Ps 91:11–12—which invoked Jesus' status as Son of God to urge him toward reliance on miraculous protection by God's angels—with his own scriptural quotation (Deut 6:16). Not even God's Son has a right to put God to the test (Luke 4:10–12).

Jesus

The fact that God and Jesus share the crucial titles of "Lord" and "Savior" in Luke and Acts shows that a primary mode of the divine activity in the story involves the agency of Jesus. As the beloved son of God, he is the definitive prophetic voice of God. The voice from heaven at the transfiguration echoes Deut 18:15: "[L]isten to him!" (Luke 9:35). As the Messiah, he has been anointed by the Spirit of God for his mission of proclamation, liberation, and healing (programmatically at 4:18; cf. 3:22; 4:1, 14). As Peter puts it in Acts, "God anointed [him] with the Holy Spirit and with power, . . . [and] he went about doing good and healing all who were oppressed by the devil, for God was with him" (Acts 10:38). And so, as the one through whom divine power flows to heal the sick and exorcise demons, he also brings the claim and liberating power of God's sovereign rule (e.g., Luke 11:20; 17:20–21). The invitation to a meal at his table enacts symbolically the eschatological banquet of God's realm (e.g., 14:15–24). The forgiveness he offers *is* divine forgiveness, expressing the compassionate mercy of God (5:17–26; cf. 7:48; and the parabolic elaboration in chap. 15).

Holy Spirit

Jesus' activity in the narrative expresses the divine purpose because the Spirit of God guides and empowers him. Before Jesus' ministry, and after his ascension in Acts, the Holy Spirit is the primary vehicle of divine presence and action in the story.

The angel who startles Zechariah with news that he will have a son predicts that John will be Spirit-filled even before birth, a prophecy fulfilled only a few verses later (1:15, 43–44). Jesus is conceived when the Holy Spirit encounters Mary, and it is God who is at work (1:35). Simeon, guided by the Holy Spirit, welcomes the infant Jesus in the temple and marks him as the one who embodies God's salvation for the people (2:25–32). Beginning with the baptism of Jesus and his encounter with the devil in the wilderness, the Holy Spirit fills Jesus (3:22; 4:1, 14). If there was any doubt that the activity of the Holy Spirit is the activity of God, the account of Jesus' baptism dispels it. The Spirit descends from an opened heaven upon Jesus, and then heaven (that is, God) declares Jesus to be the beloved Son of God (3:22). The Spirit—God—defines and empowers the mission of Jesus, a point that Jesus borrows words from Isaiah 61 to make in his inaugural speech at Nazareth (4:18–19).

Explicit mention of the Holy Spirit scarcely recurs in Luke's Gospel. Jesus does speak with joy prompted by the Spirit (10:21) and pictures Spirit-enabled boldness in witness before adversaries such as the apostles will display in Acts (Luke 12:10–11). Nevertheless, the stamp placed on Jesus by the Holy Spirit at the outset of his ministry (3:22; 4:1, 14, 18) indicates clearly that the entire ministry—particularly powerful acts of healing—is driven by God's Spirit (cf. Green 1995, 44–46). In an evangelistic speech before Cornelius and his household in Acts, Peter forges this very link between the Spirit's anointing of Jesus and the concrete acts of Jesus' ministry (Acts 10:38).

Although Jesus surrenders ("commends") his "spirit" to God at his death (Luke 23:46), he proceeds in Acts to impart to the apostles, as well as the larger circle of disciples, this Spirit that had enabled and empowered his own ministry (Acts 1:2, 5, 8; 2:33). Now it is the followers of Jesus who are "filled" with the Holy Spirit (2:4). They speak at the Spirit's prompting (4:8, 31; 11:28; 13:9; 21:4, 11), and their journeys and decisions are guided by the Spirit (8:29, 39; 10:19; 11:12; 13:2, 4; 15:28; 16:6–7; 20:22–23).

The Spirit is not explicitly linked to the healing activity of the apostolic community. In Acts, healing is associated with Jesus and his "name" (3:6, 16; 9:34). Nevertheless, the Spirit is a potent force, impressive enough to capture the attention of Simon Magus ("the Great," 8:14–24). At Pentecost, and again at Cornelius's residence and in Ephesus, the Spirit explodes onto the scene (2:4; 10:44–47; 19:1–7).

In the Pentecost discourse, Peter interprets the Spirit's presence as an eschatological sign: "In the last days it will be, God declares, that I will pour out my Spirit upon all flesh" (2:17). Luke enhances the passage from Joel by adding the phrase "God declares." As Israel's story begins its final chapter, it is clear that God—the God of Israel—is the author of the story, the author of human history and of its end. The passage Peter quotes from Joel (3:1–5 LXX) attributes to the Spirit the declaration of the prophetic word, which will be given to both men and women (2:18). As with Zechariah and Simeon in Luke 1–2, the Spirit enables the task of prophetic proclamation in Acts. Moreover, scriptural witness to the promises and work of God is also ascribed to the Holy Spirit (e.g., Acts 4:25; 28:25). God is behind the events Luke narrates, the prophetic testimony in the Jewish Scriptures that anticipated these events, and their interpretation and proclamation by the apostolic company.

Angels

Heaven-sent messengers appear in Luke's narrative, primarily in the opening chapters of the Gospel and in Acts, to deliver a message from God, or as agents of divine guidance, protection, and deliverance (Luke 1:11–20, 26–38; 2:9–15; 24:4–7, 23; Acts 1:10–11; 5:19–20; 8:26; 10:3–8; 12:7–11; 27:23–24; cf. Luke 4:9–12). In one instance, the death of Herod Agrippa I, an angel is sent to perform a punitive miracle (Acts 12:23).

During the account of Jesus' public ministry, explicit mention of the activity of angels or of the Holy Spirit is lacking (after Luke 4:18). Jesus has been endowed with divine power by the very "finger of God" (5:17; 11:20) to heal and forgive, and therefore he needs no other assistance in mediating divine presence. As one who has God's Spirit in full measure, he heals, and it is God's work that is accomplished (8:39). Rejection of God's Spirit-anointed Messiah amounts to a tragic failure to recognize divine visitation (19:44; cf. 9:48; 10:16).

The single exception to this pattern of angelic absence is the textually uncertain appearance of an angel to support Jesus in his time of anguished prayer on the Mount of Olives (22:43). Ordinarily, the lines of communication between Jesus the "Son" and God his "Father" remain open and free of interference. And the power of God is at Jesus' fingertips to heal, embrace in compassion, and welcome into God's realm.

There is some fluidity in the presentation of these modes of divine presence and activity. One can apprehend the Spirit or the approach of an angel in the form of a vision (e.g., Acts 10:3–7, 9–17, 19). In the case of Ananias, two forms of perception merge when a vision becomes the vehicle for audition of the word of the "Lord" (Jesus), who sends Ananias to a stricken Saul (9:10–17). This merging of the sounds and sights of revelation occurs even more dramatically in the scene immediately preceding, when the risen Lord interrupts Saul's journey to Damascus. Reminiscing later with King Agrippa about this encounter with the divine, Paul describes this as a "heavenly vision" (26:19). According to Peter, one meaning of Pentecost is that the Holy Spirit enables and empowers not only declarations of the prophetic word of God but also dreams and visions that open eyes of faith to the working of God (2:17).

The Prophetic Word

In a Lukan touch that distinctly echoes Israel's prophetic scriptures, God's word comes to the people in the voice of prophets. Mary and Zechariah implicitly perform this role when they deliver their Spirit-inspired messages, and Zechariah prophesies that his newborn son will be God's prophet (Luke 1:76). The word of God does indeed come to John (3:2), prompting him to begin his mission of summoning the people to repentance.

Acts makes clear that as the anointed Messiah of God, Jesus also speaks and acts as prophet, a role he embraces in his Nazareth speech (4:24, and implicitly by association with Elijah and Elisha in vv. 25–27). It is a role he then enacts in the ensuing narrative (see Johnson 1991; Tannehill 1986, 1:96–99). Jesus speaks for God. He is in fact the "prophet like Moses" who Moses had assured would be sent to Israel (Acts 3:22–23; 7:37; echoing Deut 18:15). To continue to participate in the covenant people, one must now "listen to him" (in Acts, through his apostolic witnesses). The Lukan transfiguration scene captures this point when the heavenly voice charges the disciples (and readers looking on over their shoulders): "This is my Son, my Chosen; listen to him!" (Luke 9:35). Jesus has been "sent," above all, to proclaim the message of God's sovereign rule (4:43–44)—reorienting life, liberating from domination by the forces of evil, and reclaiming the world for the strange ways of God.

In Acts, the apostles (e.g., 6:2) and then Paul (e.g., 13:46) carry the prophetic message from God to Israel, and ultimately to the "ends of the earth." At the end of Luke's two-volume story, Paul foresees that God's salvation will continue to go to the Gentiles (or nations), and "they will listen" (Acts 28:28).

Direct Speech of God

In two pivotal moments in Luke's narrative, the distance between earth and heaven collapses, and God's voice is heard directly. At the baptism of Jesus and again at the transfiguration, a voice from heaven or from the cloud (i.e., the voice of God) identifies Jesus as the beloved (or chosen) Son of God (Luke 3:22; 9:35). The divine will is also conveyed by a voice originating in heaven in the account of the conversion of Cornelius (Acts 10:13, 15; cf. 11:7, 9). And the risen Jesus confronts Saul on the road to Damascus (9:4–6; cf. 22:7–10; 26:13–18). God appears most directly in Luke's story to provide unequivocal affirmation of the identity and role of Jesus, the Son of God.

GOD, SAVIOR OF ISRAEL

The opening chapters of the Gospel of Luke root the story deep in the history of Israel. Through Spirit-inspired proclamation by angels and humans alike, the God of Israel calls to remembrance the ancient covenantal promises to Abraham and David. Beginning with the births of John and Jesus, the era of definitive fulfillment of these promises has arrived.

An "angel of the Lord" interrupts the temple service of the pious and aging priest Zechariah to give him the stunning news that he will have a son (John) who will "turn many of the people of Israel to the Lord their God" (1:16). When Zechariah later finds his voice, at the birth and naming of his son, the Holy Spirit prompts him to prophesy John's role with precision. He will be regarded as "prophet of the Most High" and will ready the way for the Lord (Jesus), orienting God's people to the salvation they will experience through the forgiveness of their sins (1:76–79). John will be God's prophet, but the Savior God is sending to Israel—fulfilling ancient prophetic witness and keeping the covenantal promises to Abraham—will be another, one who descends from David (1:68–75).

With this claim, Zechariah reinforces the declaration the angel Gabriel had already been sent by God (1:26) to deliver to Mary. She would soon give birth to a son and name him Jesus, and he would come to be esteemed "Son of the Most High"—a fitting title of honor for the one who would occupy David's throne until the end of time, thus fulfilling the promise given King David (1:31–33, recalling 2 Sam 7:12–16; cf. Acts 2:30). His very conception is the result of direct divine intervention (Luke 1:35). Mary gets it right, therefore, when she responds to Elizabeth's blessing of her and her future child by celebrating divine mercy and faithfulness (1:54–55). The promises long ago heard by Abraham are on the verge of realization.

After Jesus' birth, Simeon and Anna add their voices to the chorus: Salvation and redemption have come to Israel. Simeon, however, also under the Spirit's impulse, discerns a division within Israel in response to the one who embodies salvation for the people. He is "destined for the falling and the rising of many in Israel, and to be a sign that will be opposed" (2:34). Not all within Israel will embrace the divine grace that meets them in the ministry of Jesus.

Division begins already with John the Baptizer; the narrator interrupts Jesus' retrospective commentary on John's prophetic ministry by noting the divergent reactions to John. Unlike the Pharisees and lawyers, "all the people who heard this, including the tax collectors," had embraced the divine purpose by receiving baptism from John (7:29–30).

The same pattern marks Jesus' ministry. Meal fellowship with Jesus anticipates the eschatological banquet of God's realm (e.g., 14:15–24; cf. 13:23–30). The exorcisms Jesus performs "by the finger of God" are evidence of the mighty rule of God in the present (11:20). The drama of forgiveness and life-change (repentance) enacted as "sinners and tax collectors" encounter Jesus draws persons from the margins of the religious community into the center of God's household. As the story unfolds, it is invariably the people on the margins who embrace the salvation Jesus offers, whatever concrete form it may take: healing from sickness, liberation from oppression, forgiveness of sins, or restoration to the community. Persons at the center of things—the wealthy, those who take their religion seriously, people who possess social standing and honor—consistently spurn Jesus' invitation and protest when Jesus welcomes those apparently less deserving of God's favor. To the "righteous," the vision of God voiced and enacted by Jesus is disturbing and offensive. This cannot be the way the Holy One of Israel is present and active in the history of the covenant people!

Jesus' inaugural message at his hometown synagogue in Nazareth sets the tone for the ensuing narrative. Isaiah defines Jesus' role and program in the jubilee era of fulfillment (61:1–2; 58:6; cited in Luke 4:18–19). Bringing good news for the poor, sight for the blind, and release for the captive and the oppressed, Jesus is the one anointed by the Spirit of God and sent to help Israel. But like Elijah and Elisha before him, this Spirit-impelled agent of divine succor for the people refuses to restrict his concern to his own town and people. No, prophets meet rejection at home, and it will be no different for Jesus (4:23–24). The examples of Elijah and Elisha suggest that while Jesus embodies divine salvation and "glory" for God's people Israel, by the end of the story Gentiles will know divine benevolence as well (4:25–27). This programmatic scene ends on a note of hostile rejection, confirming Jesus' prophetic insight (vv. 28–30).

At Nazareth, the motif of Gentile blessing points ahead to the Acts narrative more than to Jesus' own activity in the Gospel (though see Luke 7:1–10;

8:26–39). Nevertheless, the pattern of inside-out reversal dominates his ministry. "Sinners" and "righteous" within Israel trade places. Tax collectors, for example—even the wealthy chief tax collector Zacchaeus—answer Jesus' call to discipleship and find acceptance in God's household (5:27–32; 15:1–32; 19:1–10). A similar reversal of roles occurs when Jesus receives hospitality from a "sinful woman" rather than from the Pharisee who is hosting him (7:36–50). Pharisees, and on one occasion the general public, respond with indignation and dismay (5:30; 15:2; 19:7; and cf. 7:39). Jesus explains in parable this surprising reversal of circumstance for conspicuous sinner and honored righteous. In a spirit of compassionate, merciful grace that offends the dutiful, God welcomes prodigals home (15:1–32). God vindicates the sinner who worships in penitent humility, rather than the model of virtue who counts himself better than others (18:9–14).

What does all this have to do with Israel and its God? Jesus' endorsement of the penitent Zacchaeus is eloquent: "Today salvation has come to this house, because he too is a son of Abraham" (19:9). When Jesus brings salvation to Israel, the "lost" among the people come home.

Perhaps the signature parable on this theme is delivered, aptly, at a dinner hosted by a Pharisee. Jesus rewrites the rules governing honor and reciprocity: guests should seek the lowest place at a banquet (14:7–11), and one hosting a dinner should invite persons unable to reciprocate (14:12–14). Ironically, one dinner guest gets the connection—it is a social world redefined by God's sovereign rule that Jesus is picturing—though likely by presuming to be among the beneficiaries he may have missed the point entirely: "Blessed is anyone who will eat bread in God's realm" (v. 15, my translation). Jesus counters this confident declaration with a parable about a dinner attended by none of the originally invited guests; instead, the host welcomes the poor and disabled, and finally even persons beyond the margins of the town (vv. 16–24). The house is filled, yet "none of those who were invited will taste my dinner" (v. 24).

Jesus has come bearing hope, deliverance, forgiveness—salvation—for God's people, just as the Spirit-inspired speakers of the Gospel's opening chapters expected. Especially the last, lost, and least have found a place at the table and a home within the community of God's people. Yet many within Israel have turned away (see also 13:23–30).

"All the people," in fact, finally repudiate Jesus' kingship (23:13–25)—no surprise to the reader after the advance commentary provided by Jesus himself in the parable of the pounds, particularly through its throne claimant motif (19:12, 14–15a, 27). As that parable suggests, Jesus must journey into a distant country (heaven) to receive royal honors as king, Messiah, and Lord (cf. Acts 2:36). His own people would deny him those honors. Hence the shattered hopes of Easter afternoon: "We had hoped he was the one who was about to redeem Israel" (Luke 24:21, my translation). God purposes Israel's restoration, but not without ironic reversal of expectations.

The second part of the story extends the pattern: hearing the summons to repentance issued by Peter, many join the apostolic company, while others, including the powerful elite at Jerusalem, remain hostile. Drawing from the scriptural promise of a "prophet like Moses," Peter shows what is at stake. Those who fail to heed the message of the prophet sent by God (Jesus)—which is conveyed now by his followers who bear witness to him—forfeit their place in the covenant people (Acts 3:22–23; echoing Deut 18:15–20 but borrowing a key phrase from Lev 23:29).

In the same speech, Peter also recalls that the divine promise to Abraham concerned blessing for all families of the earth. The God to whom the Lukan narrative points is Israel's Savior, though many of the people resist this divine offer mediated by the Messiah Jesus. Yet the covenant-keeping God of Israel, it turns out, has long purposed the salvation of all peoples. Acts begins to narrate that development, but the Gospel has already prepared the way.

GOD, SAVIOR OF THE WORLD

Salvation comes to God's covenant people in the story Luke tells, but it presses beyond the borders of Israel to reach the whole world. Peter's speech to the crowd gathered at Cornelius's house could not be more emphatic: God is impartial, and receives persons in every nation who manifest authentic piety (Acts 10:34–35); moreover, Jesus is "Lord of all" (10:36). James later interprets the divine initiative evident in Peter's encounter with the Gentile soldier: "God first looked favorably on the Gentiles, to take from among them a people for [God's] name" (15:14, with support in vv. 16–17 from Amos 9:11–12). And although the narrative places Paul again and again in diaspora synagogues, resistance to his message there drives him to more receptive Gentile audiences (13:46–48; cf. 18:6; 28:23–28)—fulfilling the prophetic promise of light for the nations (or Gentiles), of salvation reaching to the ends of the earth (Isa 49:6, quoted by Paul in Acts 13:47).

Lest there be any doubt whose purpose is being enacted, Paul's report on the eve of the Jerusalem conference (as summarized by the narrator) is clear. Paul recounts "all that God had done with them; and how [God] had opened a door of faith for the Gentiles" (14:27). Fulfilling the covenantal promise to Abraham, God extends grace to all peoples. God is Savior of Israel, and therefore of all who have faith in every nation. God is the chief actor in the narrative.

For readers who come to Acts fresh from Luke's Gospel, there is nothing surprising here. Almost from the beginning of Luke, the universal scope of

God's saving concern has been evident. Holding in his arms the infant who embodies God's "salvation," Simeon sees Israel's glory but also revelatory light for Gentiles (2:32). John the Baptizer's call to repentance prepared the way for the Messiah, whose own mission would result in everyone (lit. "all flesh") seeing the salvation that comes from God (3:6). The fulfillment of this prophecy begins in earnest in Acts, when Peter cites a passage from Joel to declare that "all flesh" will receive God's prophetic Spirit "in the last days" (Acts 2:17, quoting from Joel 3:1–5 LXX). It is therefore fitting that the ancestry of the Son of God be traced to the progenitor of the whole human family, Adam (Luke 3:38).

As we have seen, Jesus' inaugural discourse highlights God's benevolent care for Gentiles (4:25–27). Although his own ministry is not specifically directed to Gentiles, he does offer healing to the household of a Gentile centurion whose confidence in Jesus' healing power would be extraordinary even for a Jew, and to a demon-possessed man who makes his home among the tombs (7:1–10; 8:26–39). Samaritans, too, benefit from Jesus' healing power (17:11–19), questioning of conventional cultural barriers (10:25–37), and patience (9:52–56). A successful mission among Samaritans is only a book away (Acts 8). It is no wonder that Jesus can envision people from every corner of the earth at the eschatological banquet emblematic of God's sovereign rule (Luke 13:28–29).

As the narrative begins, Caesar may pretend to be able to issue orders that direct the steps of every person in the inhabited world (the census in 2:1–3). But the nations now have a new Savior, a new Lord—the Messiah born in David's city (2:11). In the person and work of Jesus, God's mighty rule has exerted itself in the human story. God's salvation has come to Israel, and extends to the farthest reaches of the earth.

AGENTS AND FORCES OPPOSED TO GOD

The signal importance in the Lukan narrative of the divine plan of bringing salvation to Israel and to the nations means that forces opposed to God's gracious ways with the world will also play an important part in the story. The people need a Savior, or deliverance, because of the powers that harm, distort, and oppress.

The catalog of political leaders enumerated by Luke at the outset reveals that the divine drama of salvation involves many powerful players (2:1–2; 3:1–2). These and other "rulers" of the people figure prominently in the passion narrative, as well as in Acts. The emperor of Rome may reign over "all the world" (cf. Luke 2:1), and the high priest and his cronies may call the shots at Jerusalem (even a Roman governor who knows better cannot thwart their will; 23:13–25). Nevertheless, God's purposes are accomplished even when the powers that govern appear to have decisively defeated God's servants (e.g., 9:22; 24:25–27; Acts 9:15–16).

In the early chapters of Acts, when the new leaders of Israel groomed by Jesus confront the political establishment in Jerusalem, it becomes clear just who is serving the purposes of God. Peter explains the apostles' refusal to follow the orders of the council: "We must obey God rather than any human authority" (5:29). In an appeal for restraint and due process, Gamaliel then unwittingly provides the justification for the exchange of leadership roles Luke is narrating. "[I]f this plan or this undertaking is of human origin, it will fail; but if it is of God, you will not be able to overthrow them—in that case you may even be found fighting against God!" (5:38–39). The powers at Jerusalem or Rome may resist the ways and purposes of God, but they will not finally succeed.

Human authorities who oppose God and threaten and harm God's servants do not act on their own. The words with which Jesus submits to the "crowd" that had come to the Mount of Olives to arrest him are haunting: "[T]his is your hour, and the power [or 'authority'] of darkness" (Luke 22:53). Satan is the architect of the countermovement that seeks to undermine the divine project of salvation.

The devil administers the first stringent test of Jesus' fidelity to God (4:1–13). Jesus' exegetical acumen demonstrates that he truly is "God's Son" (cf. 4:3, 9), but his divine sonship will not pursue displays of power. And the passion narrative commences when Satan returns to finish the job, entering Judas to prompt the act of betrayal that will lead to Jesus' arrest, and attempting to undermine the faith of the rest of the Twelve as well (22:3, 31).

Jesus' acts of exorcism and healing expose the futility of Satan's efforts (e.g., 4:33–36, 41). Jesus is the "stronger man" who liberates people from Satan's domination (11:14–26; cf. 13:16). Even the disciples (the "seventy-two") have the devil's minions on the run (10:17–20; cf. Acts 16:16–18; 19:11–19). The presence of God's mighty rule in the ministry of Jesus means the vanquishing of the most potent forces hostile to God's people (Luke 11:20). Not even the death of God's Messiah in dishonor on a Roman cross can frustrate the plan of God.

Fidelity to God and a place in God's realm find more mundane but equally difficult obstacles in the story. Family can stand between a disciple and God (9:59–62; 14:26; 21:16). Especially dangerous is the lure of wealth. Appropriate use of one's possessions—releasing them for the sake of the poor—signals divine blessing and a place in the company of the saved (e.g., 12:33–34; 14:33; 19:1–10; Acts 4:32–37). But preoccupation with wealth and failure to use it to meet the needs of the poor show one to be closed to the salvation a generous and benevolent God bestows (e.g., Luke 8:14; 12:16–21; 16:14–15, 19–31; 18:22–27; Acts 5:1–11). Service of wealth and service of God are mutually exclusive (Luke 16:13). This requirement of discipleship is nothing new; Moses and the prophets expected as much of God's people (16:27–31).

FAITHFUL RESPONSES
TO DIVINE PRESENCE AND ACTIVITY

God's people are to mirror the generosity of a benevolent God. God's mercy is to be emulated by the disciple (6:35–36; 11:4; cf. 10:37; 15:1–32; and, in contrast, 9:52–55; see Thompson 2000, 104; Forbes 2000, 253–54). Community relationships should not feature reciprocal exchange—with persons asking what they will obtain in return for their generosity—but in benevolent care for the needy, who cannot repay (14:12–24). A society reconfigured according to the norms of God's sovereign rule will place a premium on compassion and mercy, without thought of reward.

Since the God to whom Luke's narrative points, and whose ways Jesus enacts in his ministry, is generous, kind, and gracious far beyond what human beings deserve, it is not surprising that the customary human response to God's presence and activity is praise. How else would one welcome the news that God's promises to Israel are rushing to fulfillment in the era of salvation that dawns with the births of John and Jesus? As the story begins, joyful praise finds eloquent expression in Mary (1:46–47), Zechariah (1:64, 68), a chorus of angels (2:13), shepherds (2:20), and Anna (2:38). And joyful, thankful praise of God courses through the narrative of Jesus' public ministry, especially in response to his acts of healing (5:25–26; 7:16; 13:13; 17:15, 18; 18:43; 19:37). Even at the crucifixion of Jesus, the centurion is moved by the way this righteous man has faced death to offer praise to God (23:47). After Easter, the apostles' ministry of proclamation and healing also elicits praise of God (Acts 2:47; 3:8–9; 4:21; 11:18; 21:20).

When the word of God—or the message of God's sovereign rule—is announced, whether by an angel (e.g., Luke 1:38, 45), by Jesus (e.g., 10:16), or by the disciples (e.g., 10:8–11), welcoming the message in belief and trust is the appropriate response. In each case, the one who is received in trust is God. Faithful response to God's word means more than passive listening, however. Jesus insists that the one who hears must perform God's will in obedience (8:21; 11:28; cf. Acts 4:19; 5:29, 32). In fact, Jesus will accept nothing less than single-minded commitment to the demands of God's realm, or of discipleship (Luke 9:59–62; 14:25–33; 18:18–30).

More often than not, lives addressed by God's word have been off course; consequently, the word has hit the target when the listener is moved to repentance. The remarkable breadth of divine grace and mercy does not give God's people reason for presumption (e.g., 13:1–9). The mission speeches of Acts amplify this theme, with the recurring summons to repentance (2:38; 3:19; 8:22; 17:30; cf. 5:31; 11:18; 20:21; 26:20). No wonder that, for the narrator, persons who refused to submit to John's baptism—signifying repentance—were resisting the purpose of the just God (Luke 7:29–30).

If the ministry of Jesus represents God's saving project among the people of God, readers of Luke are prompted to imagine a world reclaimed by the ways and working of the sovereign God—a world of surprising and unsettling reversals that exhibits no respect for the status quo, a topsy-turvy world in which rich and poor, powerful and powerless, righteous and sinner exchange places (Green 1995, 76–94). In keeping with such a strange vision of God's reign on earth, Jesus singles out a child as paradigm and pattern of God's realm (9:47–48; 18:16–17). It is persons of low status who enjoy honor in the household where God is in charge (cf. also 22:24–27).

THE DIVINE CHARACTER: BENEVOLENT GRACE

As we have seen, Luke's Gospel presents bold claims. Heaven has disrupted the customary patterns of political and religious life, God's sovereign rule has begun to refashion human society, and the coming of God's peace disturbs the powerful. It is the time of salvation—not only for Israel but for the nations as well. Yet the salvation that comes from God goes unrecognized by many; it brings astonishing reversals of place and honor, but this is more in parable and banquet than in social reality.

Within Luke's narrative, God's salvation looks quite different from political or military liberation. Yet neither does it bless the status quo. If the characterization of God, particularly in the Gospel of Luke, highlights God's gracious benevolence toward human beings—and especially toward the lowly and needy—this portrayal of God inevitably undermines the conventional practices of human societies and their political institutions (cf. Luke 22:24–27). The narrative suggests that the vision of God's rule advocated and enacted by Jesus has profound social and political implications, but these are left to Luke's readers to pursue. For the first generation of readers, that would not have been an easy task, as they came to terms with their increased prominence—and vulnerability—in a world still dominated by Rome.

Hope in God, in such a context, meant affirmation of God as the one who raises the dead. After all, God vindicated Jesus, whom religious and political authorities had crucified, through resurrection (e.g., Acts 2:32; 5:30). Israel's hope, too, remains resurrection (24:15; 26:6–8).

The divine project of salvation both within Israel and among the nations, therefore, does not proceed according to expectations, although it does proceed according to plan—God's plan (see Squires 1993). God's ways are not human ways, and the God of Luke-Acts is full of surprises: death and resurrection as path to glory, justification for sinner instead of the righteous, honor for the marginalized, Gentiles at table in God's realm. On closer scrutiny, however, none of this is surprising. God remains true to the divine character and to the divine promises revealed in the ancient scriptures of Israel.

The God of Israel and of Luke's narrative is gracious and merciful, boundless in generosity toward the people. This God shows kindness to the undeserving (Luke 5:35–36). Heaven trumpets this God's joy at the restoration of the lost to the community (15:1–32). This God hears the prayers of the penitent, whether a toll collector's appeal for mercy in the temple or a dying criminal's desperate, trusting plea (18:9–14; 23:39–43). One can with some confidence anticipate the reply of this God to Jesus' request that mercy extend even to his executioners (23:34).

Through a lesser-to-greater argument in his parables, Jesus depicts God as generous and kind on analogy with human behavior, but in a way that far surpasses the human exemplar. Even reluctant neighbors provide bread when it is needed, and parents give their children good things, not snakes or scorpions (11:5–8, 11–13). Even a corrupt judge will finally vindicate a persevering widow out of his own self-interest (18:2–5). God's benevolent grace toward the people of God is incalculably more reliable. Bread, forgiveness, and protection will assuredly come to the one who prays as Jesus taught (11:2–4). For those willing to surrender all in service to God, participation in God's realm is assured—along with the things needed in life (12:22–32). Such a God inspires confident trust and faithful service.

SELECT BIBLIOGRAPHY

Achtemeier, Paul J. 1987. *The Quest for Unity in the New Testament Church: A Study in Paul and Acts*. Philadelphia: Fortress.

Brawley, Robert L. 1990. *Centering on God: Method and Message in Luke-Acts*. Literary Currents in Biblical Interpretation. Louisville, Ky.: Westminster John Knox.

Carroll, John T. 1988. *Response to the End of History: Eschatology and Situation in Luke-Acts*. Society of Biblical Literature Dissertation Series 92. Atlanta: Scholars Press.

Conzelmann, Hans. 1961. *The Theology of St. Luke*. New York: Harper & Row.

Cosgrove, Charles H. 1984. "The Divine DEI in Luke-Acts: Investigations into the Lukan Understanding of God's Providence." *Novum Testamentum* 26: 168–90.

Dahl, Nils A. 1975. "The Neglected Factor in New Testament Theology." *Reflection* 73.1: 5–8.

Fitzmyer, Joseph A. 1981 and 1985. *The Gospel according to Luke: Introduction, Translation, and Notes*. 2 vols. Anchor Bible 28–28A. Garden City, N.Y.: Doubleday.

Forbes, Greg W. 2000. *The God of Old: The Role of the Lukan Parables in the Purpose of*

Luke's Gospel. Journal for the Study of the New Testament: Supplement Series 198. Sheffield: Sheffield Academic Press.

Gaventa, Beverly Roberts. 1988. "Towards a Theology of Acts: Reading and Rereading." *Interpretation* 42: 146–57.

Green, Joel B. 1995. *The Theology of the Gospel of Luke*. New Testament Theology. Cambridge: Cambridge University Press.

———. 1997. *The Gospel of Luke*. New International Commentary on the New Testament. Grand Rapids: Eerdmans.

Jervell, Jacob. 1972. *Luke and the People of God: A New Look at Luke-Acts*. Minneapolis: Augsburg, 1972.

———. 1996. *The Theology of the Acts of the Apostles*. New Testament Theology. Cambridge: Cambridge University Press.

Johnson, Luke T. 1991. *Luke*. Sacra Pagina 3. Collegeville, Minn.: Liturgical Press.

Marshall, I. Howard. 1978. *Commentary on Luke*. New International Greek Testament Commentary. Grand Rapids: Eerdmans.

Marshall, I. Howard and Peterson, David, eds. 1998. *Witness to the Gospel: The Theology of Acts*. Grand Rapids: Eerdmans.

Matera, Frank J. 1999. *New Testament Christology*. Louisville, Ky.: Westminster John Knox.

Nolland, John. 1989 and 1993. *Luke*. 3 vols. Word Biblical Commentary 35A–C. Dallas: Word.

Shepherd, W. 1994. *The Narrative Function of the Holy Spirit as Character in Luke-Acts*. Society of Biblical Literature Dissertation Series 147. Atlanta: Scholars Press.

Squires, John T. 1993. *The Plan of God in Luke-Acts*. Society for New Testament Study Monograph Series 76. Cambridge: Cambridge University Press.

Tannehill, Robert C. 1986 and 1990. *The Narrative Unity of Luke-Acts: A Literary Interpretation*. 2 vols. Foundations and Facets. Minneapolis: Fortress.

Thompson, Marianne Meye. 2000. *The Promise of the Father: Jesus and God in the New Testament*. Louisville, Ky.: Westminster John Knox.

Tiede, David L. 1980. *Prophecy and History in Luke-Acts*. Philadelphia: Fortress.

7

Telling God's Story

The Fourth Gospel

FRANCIS J. MOLONEY, S.D.B.

It would be possible to approach the task of uncovering "the forgotten God" of the Fourth Gospel by starting from Christian tradition. The Fourth Gospel presents God as the one who has created the universe, through the agency of the Word (see John 1:3, 10). There is no Johannine presentation of God at the end of time, sending the Son of Man as final judge. But Jesus will return to the glory that was his with the Father before time began (17:5), and he prays that all believers will join him in the unity of love that links him to the Father (17:24–26). In a uniquely Johannine fashion, for both Jesus and the believer, God stands at the beginning (1:1–2) and the end (17:24–26) of human experience. A further rich vein that could be tapped is the importance of the Spirit-Paraclete in this Gospel (see especially 14:15–17, 25–26; 15:26–27; 16:7–11, 12–15), and the beginnings of a theological tradition that would eventually lead to the Christian tradition of the Trinity. The Fourth Gospel clearly affirms that the Father sends, the revealing action of the Son saves, and the Spirit instructs, guides, and continues to nourish the life of the believer in the absence of Jesus. More than any other New Testament document, the Fourth Gospel lays the foundations for the doctrine of a coequal Trinity. Equally interesting is the link made in this Gospel between the death of Jesus and the gift of the Spirit (see 7:39; 19:30), the bold affirmation that "God is Spirit" (4:24), and the nature of the relationship between Jesus, the Son, and the one who sent him, whom he calls both God and Father.

But these essential elements of later Christian theological reflection and tradition do not lie at the heart of the Johannine *story*, and a discussion of God from this perspective would lead into a systematic rather than a biblical reflection. They are our concerns, rather than those of the Johannine storyteller. The Fourth Gospel presents what could be called a "narrative theology." The story of Jesus tells the way God has entered history in and through the person of Jesus, written to persuade rather than inform a reader. The following study respects the Johannine narrative rhetoric, asking whether this Gospel's presentation of God is persuasive.

The Gospels of Matthew, Mark, Luke, and John tell of the birth (Matthew and Luke), life, teaching, death, and resurrection of Jesus of Nazareth. Jesus is the character who dominates almost every event in each story. This is perhaps even truer for the Fourth Gospel than for the three so-called Synoptic Gospels. However, the Prologue to the Fourth Gospel (John 1:1–18) is a surprising indication that the story of Jesus is not primarily about Jesus; it is about what God has done for the human situation in and through Jesus. The opening affirmations of the Prologue take the reader outside history, before all time, into the presence of a unique union between the Word and God. God and the Word preexisted all the events of the human story, united in a union so intense that what God was, the Word also was (vv. 1–2). The author uses Koinē Greek carefully to insist that the Word (*ho logos*) and God (*ho theos*) have their own identity. This is shown by the use of the definite article (*ho*). Both "*the* Word" and "*the* God" have the article, even though it is not attached to "God" when rendering the Greek into English. The use of the two articles insists that the Word and God be seen as separate characters, existing before all time, one intimately related to the other (v. 1: *kai ho logos ēn pros ton theon*). But their shared divinity is shown in the statement insisting that what one was, the other also was (v. 2: *kai theos ēn ho logos*). The Greek sentence is again carefully formulated. The complement (*theos*) of the third person singular imperfect of the verb "to be" (*ēn*) is placed before the verb *without* an article, while the subject (*ho logos*) follows the verb *with* an article. By means of this carefully wrought sentence, the writer maintains the separate identities of "God" and "the Word," but claims that they are both divine. What God was, the Word also was. (I will follow the translation of the New Revised Standard Version in this essay, except in places where my reading of the original Greek suggests an alternative, as here.) Once that affirmation has been made, the reader has no option but to accept that the action of the Word will represent the presence of the divine. This oneness between the Word and God determines the story of Jesus. If what is said of the Word in 1:1–2 were false, the claims throughout the story of Jesus, the Word become flesh (v. 14), would be blasphemous. "The Jews," not having read the Prologue, regard them as such. The reader is called to a decision for or against the revelation of God's action in Jesus.

The Word entered the human story (vv. 5, 9–14) and he had a human name: Jesus Christ (v. 17). The final statement of the Prologue is but the logical consequence of all that has been said thus far. Repeating a well-grounded Jewish belief, the author insists that no one has ever *seen* God. But Jesus Christ, the preexistent Word who was one with God (vv. 1–2), has told the story of God (v. 18). An interesting Greek verb (*exēgēsato*) lies behind my paraphrase of the Prologue's description of Jesus' role as the one who told the story of God (v. 18). This Greek verb is the source of the English word "exegete." Jesus is the exegete of God. His life story makes God known. The Fourth Gospel, through its intense focus upon Jesus Christ, tells the story of God. Tracing "the forgotten God" in the Fourth Gospel, therefore, must also tell the story of Jesus as it is found in this particular narrative.

The reading of Jesus' story that follows will focus upon questions central to the Fourth Gospel's presentation of God: the task of Jesus to make known a God who loves, through the event of the cross. By means of the cross, God is revealed and Jesus is glorified. A brief conclusion reflects upon the ongoing relevance of the Johannine *theology* of the cross. With a sense of privilege, I offer these reflections upon the God of the Fourth Gospel in honor of Paul Achtemeier, an exegete whose Christian life and scholarly contributions have also strained to tell the story of God.

THE TASK OF JESUS

On three occasions during the Fourth Gospel, Jesus addresses the question of his task. Toward the end of Jesus' first foray into Samaria, a non-Jewish world, his disciples bring provisions and the Samaritan woman returns to her village, leaving her water container behind. She will be back, but the disciples are shocked that Jesus should be speaking to a Samaritan woman. The situation worsens when he refuses to take any of their food (4:31–32). They suspect that he has even eaten with her (see v. 33). The narrator's earlier comment on the relationship between Jews and Samaritans is still operative in the narrative: "Jews do not share things in common with Samaritans" (4:9). Playing upon their perplexity, Jesus transcends their concerns, thus explaining why he was with the Samaritan woman and why he has no need of food: "My food is to do the will of him who sent me, and to complete his work" (v. 34). Two important expressions appear for the first time in the Gospel: Jesus is on a mission to do the will of God, the one who sent him, and this means that he must bring to completion—to perfect (*teleiēsō*) a certain "work" (*to ergon*)—a task which forms part of God's design: "his work" (*autou to ergon*).

As the ministry progresses, Jesus defends his mission against "the Jews" who have decided that he must be slain because he offends Sabbath law (see 5:17–18). He tells them, "The works that the Father has given me to complete, the very works that I am doing, testify on my behalf that the Father has sent me" (5:36). God's design, that Jesus bring to perfection the work of the Father, made visible in the works of Jesus, legitimates Jesus' words and actions in the face of all contrary suggestions and accusations. Jesus' life and ministry do not make Jesus known, but reveal the design of God.

At the conclusion of Jesus' final encounter with his disciples, as he goes to the cross, looking back across the ministry, he tells the Father: "I glorified you on earth by finishing the work that you gave me to do" (17:4). Key expressions reappear: "having finished, having brought to perfection" (*teleiōsas*) "the work" (*to ergon*). One of the features of Jesus' final prayer is its wandering in and out of the time sequence of the narrative. Having made the claim that the work has been accomplished in 17:4, Jesus goes on to explain how he has done this: "I have made your name known to those whom you gave me from the world. They were yours, and you gave them to me, and they have kept your word. Now they know that everything you have given me is from you; for the words that you gave to me I have given to them, and they have received them and know in truth that I came from you; and they have believed that you sent me" (vv. 6–8). But this assessment of the disciples is somewhat flattering. Events lie ahead that are even more part of Jesus' perfection of the work of the Father than his having made known the name of God to his disciples. They will not understand him, deny him, and betray him, but he will love them "to the end" (13:1: *eis telos*).

However one handles the critical problem that arises from the "timing" of 17:4, the author's point of view is made clear in 4:34, 5:36, and 17:4: Jesus regards his life as determined by the will of the one who sent him. His task is to bring to perfection the work of the Father. What is becoming evident is that—despite the remarkable things that are said about Jesus in the Fourth Gospel—his life, death, and resurrection function as once-and-for-all moments in the realization of God's design for the human story. The Gospel may be about Jesus, but Jesus is about God's business. To use theological language, Johannine Christology is not an end in itself. It is in service of the author's major concern, namely, theology. In simpler terms, the story of Jesus is really a story of God's action, and thus it makes God known (see 1:18).

This becomes even more obvious when another text from John 17 is considered. Jesus makes clear what it means for the Son to do the will of the Father: "to give eternal life to all whom you have given him. And this is eternal life, that they may know you, the only true God, and Jesus Christ whom you have sent" (17:2b–3). The task of Jesus now emerges clearly. His task is to do the will of the Father who sent him (see 4:34) by bringing to perfection the work of God (see 4:34; 5:36; 17:4). The will of the Father is that eternal life be made a reality for all who come to know the one true God through Jesus Christ, the sent one (17:2–3). But if Jesus does the will of God and brings to perfection the task God has given him by making God known, what sort of

God does Jesus make known? To state the question in more theological terms, if the Christology of the Fourth Gospel is determined by its theology, what is its theology? What is said about the God and Father of the Son, Jesus Christ?

WHAT SORT OF GOD?

Some have claimed that 1 John 4:8, 16 ("God is love") is a Johannine attempt to define God, but the use of the word "love" hardly fits what formal logicians would call a definition. In the Fourth Gospel, as in almost all biblical narratives, God is in relationship, and God acts. The relationship which exists between God and Jesus is articulated in the Prologue (1:1–18) and taken for granted from that point on in the narrative: "And the Word became flesh and dwelt among us, the fullness of a gift which is truth. We have gazed upon his glory, glory as of the only Son from the Father. . . . No one has ever seen God; the only Son, who is turned toward the Father, he has told God's story" (1:14, 18; my translation). The relationship between the Father and the Son is fundamental to Jesus' unique role in the human story: making God known.

Toward the end of the Gospel, Jesus asks the Father that believers be swept into the relationship with God that he has had from all time: "Father, I desire that those also, whom you have given me, may be with me where I am, to see my glory, which you have given me because you loved me before the foundation of the world. . . . I made your name known to them, and I will make it known, so that the love with which you have loved me may be in them, and I in them" (17:24, 26). The love that has existed from all time between God and the Word, between the Father and the Son, has burst into the human story. Jesus has made it known so that others might be swept into that same relationship.

The Fourth Gospel always speaks of God's action, and the most consistent expression used to speak of the action of God is that God "sends." Two verbs are used for the sending action of God (*pempō* and *apostellō*), and many have argued for a nuance of meaning between them. I doubt if this distinction can be maintained, and it is important to be aware that God also "sent" John the Baptist (1:6: *apestalmenos para theou*) to bear witness to the light. The Baptist is the only other character in the narrative to be sent by God, but both the words of the Prologue that introduce him (1:6) and his own witness (1:18–34; 3:27–30) point out that he is sent to bear witness. Jesus is, supremely, the "sent one" of God, the "sent one" of the Father. We have already encountered two passages that link Jesus' being the sent one of the Father with his mandate to do the will of the Father, to bring to perfection his "work." "My food is to do the will of *him who sent me* and to complete his work" (4:34); "The very works

that I am doing, testify on my behalf that *the Father has sent me*" (5:36). But
God's sending action does not cease with the witness (1:7) and Jesus (e.g., 4:34;
5:36). Toward the end of the Gospel, Jesus prays that the disciples also be
caught up into the sending action of God. They are not "sent" by God, but by
Jesus, the unique "sent one" of God. "As you have sent me into the world, so
I have sent them into the world" (17:18). The ultimate responsibility of the
Father for the mission of the Christian disciple is rendered by the "as [*kathōs*]
. . . so also [*kagō*]."

A further action of God determines even more radically the Johannine presentation of the person and actions of God: "For God so loved the world that
he gave his only Son, so that everyone who believes in him may not perish but
may have eternal life" (3:16). It is God's love for the world that determines the
sending of the Son so that the world might have eternal life. We have seen the
author's definition of eternal life in the prayer of Jesus in 17:3: "This is eternal life, that they know you, the only true God."

The task of Jesus is to make God known and to create the possibility of eternal life, but our only access to Jesus' revelation of a God whom no one has ever
seen (see 1:18; 6:46) is through Jesus' words and actions. The Fourth Gospel
makes clear that God has a relationship with the Son and has sent the Son so
that others may enter that relationship and continue the mission of Jesus (see
13:34–35; 15:12, 17; 17:17–19, 20–23). Above all, the motivation for God's
sending of the Son is his love for the world (3:16; see also 15:34–35; 17:20–23).
Little wonder that an elder from the Johannine community of early Christians,
in a period which slightly postdates the Gospel, could twice affirm, "God is
love" (1 John 4:8, 16). To describe God as "love" is to tell very little about the
essence of God. It goes no further than the Gospel's affirmation, "God so loved
the world" (3:16). The God of the Johannine Jesus cannot be known in his
essence, or his being, but only through his actions: relating, sending, and loving. The task of Jesus is to make God known. However, the text shows that
God is to be understood as the one who so loved the world that he sent his only
Son. If the task of Jesus is to make God known, then he must *make love known*.

TO MAKE LOVE KNOWN

Jesus' revealing mission is fulfilled in his words and in his actions. It would
require more space than we have at our disposal to analyze the words of Jesus
throughout this Gospel, and especially the magisterial discourses of John 5, 6,
7–8, 10:1–14, 14:1–16:33, and the prayer of 17:1–26. Jesus' words in the
Fourth Gospel focus entirely upon several relationships: between the Father
and the Son, between the Son and "his own," and between the Son and those

who reject him. To a lesser extent, but still present, the discourses describe the tragedy of the absence of a relationship between God, the Son, and the powers who reject Jesus. For the purposes of this reflection, however, I would like to focus upon the crucial *action* of Jesus' life: his death. The Fourth Gospel is unique in the New Testament in presenting the death of Jesus as his most significant achievement. For the Fourth Evangelist, the cross brings to perfection the task given to Jesus by the Father, the one who sent him. *On the cross* Jesus glorifies God, and *by means of the cross* he achieves his own glorification.

A brief glance at two other New Testament witnesses will serve as contrasts. The Gospel of Mark has often been described as a passion narrative with a long introduction. Jesus marches courageously to Jerusalem, prophesying his oncoming death (see Mark 8:31; 9:31; 10:32–34). He is arrested, tried, and hammered to a cross from which he cries, "My God, my God, why have you forsaken me" (15:34). But that is not his only cry from the cross. The narrator recalls that, at the moment of his death, "Jesus gave a loud cry and breathed his last" (15:37). It is not until *after* he has been ignominiously put to death that a series of more positive events, realizing the promises of the Gospel's prologue (1:1–13), begin to take place. The curtain of the temple is rent from top to bottom, a Gentile confesses that Jesus was a Son of God (15:37–39; see 1:1, 11), women discover God's messenger in an empty tomb and hear the Easter proclamation (16:1–8). God's immediate intervention into the events of the story indicates that Jesus' cry from the cross has not been in vain: He has not been abandoned by his God (16:6; see 1:11). The risen Jesus is going before his disciples into Galilee (16:7; see 14:28).

In the hymn found in the second chapter of Paul's letter to the Philippians (Phil 2:6-11), the Apostle of the Gentiles traces Jesus' career. He did not regard his equality with God something to be grasped to himself jealously and selfishly, but he emptied himself, taking on the form of a slave, born into the human condition (Phil 2:6–7). At the center of the hymn he comes to his lowest moment: "He humbled himself and became obedient to the point of death— even death on a cross" (v. 8). The hymn then proceeds to proclaim that as a *consequence* of this humility and humiliation God highly exalted him and gave him the name that is above every name, that every knee should bend, and every tongue confess Jesus as Lord (vv. 9–11). For both Mark and Paul, the experience of the cross is the *lowest moment* in Jesus' human experience, and his exaltation is the *consequence* of this unconditional commitment to the will of God.

This is not the case in the Fourth Gospel. From its earliest pages, Jesus begins to speak of his oncoming death as a "lifting up," an exaltation:

> Just as Moses lifted up [*hypsōsen*] the serpent in the wilderness, so must the Son of Man be lifted up [*hypsōthēnai dei*], that whoever believes in him may have eternal life. (3:14–15)

When you have lifted up [*hypsōsēte*] the Son of Man, then you will realize that I am he. (8:28)

"And I, when I am lifted up [*hypsōthō*] from the earth, will draw all people to myself." He said this to indicate the kind of death he was to die. (12:32–33)

The verb Paul used in Phil 2:9 to speak of God's exaltation of Jesus *as a consequence of* his preparedness to humble himself unto death, even death on a cross (*hypsōthēnai*), is used in the Fourth Gospel to speak of Jesus' being exalted *upon the cross*. In its Pauline context it only has one possible meaning: God's exaltation of Jesus is the result of the unconditional obedient self-gift of the crucified one. Mark does not use the verb "to lift up," but his understanding of a glory that follows the death of Jesus (see Mark 8:31; 9:31; 10:33–34) repeats the Pauline idea.

In the Fourth Gospel the verb has two meanings. It means both the physical act of "lifting up" on a stake, as is obvious from the use of the verb in the parallel description of Moses' lifting up the serpent in the desert (3:14: "Just as [*kai kathōs*] . . . so also [*houtōs*]"). But it also retains the meaning in Phil 2:9 of exaltation. The crucifixion of Jesus is at one and the same time both the physical lifting up of Jesus from the ground on a cross, and his exaltation.

Other elements in the Gospel begin to gather more meaning. As Jesus and his disciples accompany the mother of Jesus to a wedding at Cana, his mother points out that they have no wine. Jesus replies, "Woman, what concern is that to you and me? My hour has not yet come" (2:4). Despite the rebuke, the mother of Jesus has limitless faith in the efficacy of Jesus' word, and she tells the attendants, "Do whatever he tells you" (2:5). The miracle which follows is a symbol of the messianic fullness promised by the prophets: an abundance of wine, happiness, and good things (see Isa 25:6–8; 62:4–5). The best will be kept till last (see 2:10). The "hour" of Jesus will be associated with a final messianic gesture, of which the marriage feast is an anticipatory sign. At the celebration of the Feast of Tabernacles, Jesus' brothers insist that he go up to the feast, to manifest himself by means of his wonderful miracles. Jesus replies, "My time has not yet come, but your time is always here. . . . Go to the festival yourselves; I am not going to *this* festival, for my time has not yet fully come" (7:6, 8). The "hour" of Jesus will not take place at *this* feast, but it will come at *another* feast. On another occasion during this same celebration of Tabernacles, as Jesus points to his unique unity with the Father, his opponents attempt to arrest him, but they are not able to do so "because his hour had not yet come" (7:30). Still in the temple precincts, he accuses his opponents of not being able to know God because they do not know him. "But no one arrested him, because his hour had not yet come" (8:20). In the end, they take up stones and drive him out of the temple (8:59). Not only will "the hour" be associated with the messianic event (2:1–12), but it points forward to a later feast of the Jews (7:6–8) when those who would violently lay hands upon him will have their way (7:30; 8:20, 59). Until that time, however, his hour has not yet come.

In 11:55 the narrator announces, "Now the Passover of the Jews was near." The temporal aspect of a narrative that has moved rapidly through at least a two-year cycle of the festive celebrations of Israel—the four days of preparation (1:19–51; see *Mekilta* on Exod 19:1–2, 3–8, 9–10) and the celebration of Pentecost "on the third day" (2:1–11; see Exod 19:10–11, 15, 16, 20), two Passovers (2:13; 6:4), Tabernacles (7:2), and Dedication (10:22)—almost comes to a stop. While John 1:1–11:54 covers two years, 11:55–20:31 fills only a few days. On the first of these days, some Greeks come to see Jesus. Jesus announces, "The hour has come for the Son of Man to be glorified" (12:23). A further theological theme has now been associated with "the hour" of Jesus: his glorification. The hour of Jesus is also the moment of his glorification. Although we will return to this important passage, Jesus' words to his disciples on the reason for Lazarus's illness can be recalled: "This illness does not lead to death; rather it is for God's glory, so that the Son of God might be glorified through it" (11:4). The raising of Lazarus triggers the coming of the Greeks, the decision of "the Jews" that he must die (11:49–50), and Jesus' proclamation that "the hour" has come for his glorification.

The theme of the hour dominates Jesus' final days. It marks the beginning and the end of his last night with the disciples. The narrator begins the account of this final encounter with the comment, "Now before the festival of the Passover, Jesus knew that his hour had come to depart from this world and go to the Father. Having loved his own who were in the world, he loved them to the end" (13:1). As he closes the evening, Jesus prays, "Father, the hour has come; glorify your Son so that your Son might glorify you" (17:1). At the cross, Jesus consigns his mother to the Beloved Disciple and the Beloved Disciple to his mother. In a fashion typical of this Gospel, the narrator explains the result of Jesus' words using Greek syntax that has two possible meanings. Whenever these double entendres occur in the Fourth Gospel, the reader should remain open to *both* possible meanings. John 19:27 is universally translated, "*And from that hour* the disciple took her into his own home." This is a legitimate translation, as the use of the Greek preposition *apo* followed by a noun in the genitive case generally has a temporal meaning. However, that is not the expression's only possibility. It can also indicate causality, and this possibility would produce the English sentence, "*And because of that hour [ap' ekeinēs tēs hōras]* he took her into his own home." A new family of God is founded by the exalted and crucified Jesus from that time on, "because of that hour."

Another theme points to the cross for its consummation: the gathering of the children of God who are scattered abroad. Although hinted at earlier in the narrative, it is first explicitly stated within the context of Jesus' discourse on the Good Shepherd who lays down his life for his sheep. In a discourse shot through with images that have their roots in the traditions and symbols of Israel, Jesus announces, "I have other sheep that do not belong to this fold. I must bring them also, and they will listen to my voice. So there will be one flock, one shepherd" (10:16). Hard on the heels of this discourse, the raising of Lazarus leads Caiaphas to instruct his faltering colleagues: "You know nothing at all! You do not understand that it is better for you to have one man die for the people than to have the whole nation destroyed" (11:49b–50). To this the narrator adds, "He did not say this on his own, but being high priest that year he prophesied that Jesus was about to die for the nation, and not for the nation only, but to gather into one the dispersed children of God" (11:51–52).

The raising of Lazarus remains a problem for the leaders of "the Jews," and they plot steadily to put both Jesus *and* Lazarus to death (see 12:10). "It was on account of him that many of the Jews were deserting and were believing in Jesus" (12:11). The entrance of Jesus into Jerusalem generates even further anxiety, as they comment, "You see, you can do nothing. Look, the world has gone after him!" (12:19), and in fulfillment of those words, some Greeks ask to see Jesus (vv. 20–22). This news not only enables Jesus to announce the advent of the hour of his glorification (12:23) but to explain further, "Unless a grain of wheat falls into the earth and dies, it remains just a single grain; but if it dies, it bears much fruit" (v. 24). Jesus elaborates: "Now is the judgment of this world; now the ruler of this world will be driven out. And I, when I am lifted up from the earth, will draw all people to myself" (vv. 31–32). The narrator adds, "He said this to indicate the kind of death he was to die" (v. 33). The theme of gathering, so intensely developed over the final episodes of the public ministry, is resolved in the gift of the mother of Jesus to the Beloved Disciple and the Disciple to the mother at the cross (19:25–27). Only then can Jesus call out in death, "It is finished" (19:30a: *tetelestai*). Jesus has brought to perfection the task (*to ergon*) given him by the Father (see 4:34; 17:4). The hour has come and a new family of God has begun at the foot of the cross. It is upon this family that he pours down the Spirit (v. 30b: *paredōken to pneuma*) and gifts them with the blood and water that flow from his side (vv. 34–35).

THE GLORY OF GOD
AND THE GLORIFICATION OF JESUS

As the section closes that deals with Jesus' making love known on the cross, the theme of glory and glorification emerges. In a unique fashion, the Fourth

Gospel uses the noun "glory" (*doxa*) and its verbal form, in the active mood, "to glorify" (*doxazein*), and also in the passive mood, "to be glorified" (*doxas-thēnai*). The regular appearance of these expressions in the Fourth Gospel indicates that it has two possible meanings. Predominantly in the Greek language, from the classical period down to the time of the simpler, more commercial Koinē Greek, which was the common tongue of much of the first-century Mediterranean world, the expression referred to human achievement. A successful person in any sphere, from athletic games to political achievements, merited glory, esteem, praise, and honor. All these English words could be rendered in Greek with the expression *doxa*. However, some two hundred years before the Christian era, the Hebrew Bible was translated into Greek so that it might be used in the diaspora (the community of Jews living outside the confines of Israel and thus more culturally attuned to the surrounding Greek world). This translation was called the Septuagint (LXX). It also made the Hebrew Bible available for the edification of non-Jewish readers. In this translation, the expression *doxa* was used in a surprisingly new fashion.

The Septuagint regularly translates an important theological concept, "the glory of God," found throughout the Hebrew Bible, with the Greek expression *hē doxa tou theou*. It is difficult to be certain when ancient biblical theological perspectives have their origin. However, the evidence points to the experience of the exodus as the most likely context for the generation of a Hebrew idea of "the glory of God," which was expressed in Hebrew with the words *kĕbôd YHWH*, referring to the visible, experienced presence of YHWH in guiding, supporting, nourishing, and punishing the people. The original meaning of the noun *kābôd* came from the verb *kābad*, which means "to be heavy, to be weighty." This probably was the etymological reason for the LXX translators' use of *doxa*, as the Hebrew verb also has the extended meaning of "to be respected or mighty." But throughout the Old Testament the expression is used in a theological sense associated with the experience of the revelation of God present among the people of Israel. This meaning was foreign to the widespread use of *doxa* in the Greek-speaking world, and yet with remarkable consistency Israel reflected upon the visible, experienced care of YHWH for the nation, and referred to that experience as *kᵉbôd YHWH*.

In the account of the gift of the Law, a cloud (*kābēd*) was visible on Mount Sinai (see Exod 19:16). The Septuagint renders this as *doxa*. When the book of Deuteronomy makes reference to Sinai, *kābôd* is again applied to this foundational moment of YHWH's presence to Israel. This probably reflects the growing awareness in Israel of the central importance of the event of Sinai as revelation of "the glory of the Lord": "Look, the LORD our God has shown his glory [*kĕbodô*] and greatness, and we have heard his voice out of the fire"

(Deut 5:24). Throughout the account of the exodus, the expression "the glory of the LORD" is used to describe experiences: God's saving power against the might of Pharaoh (see Exod 14:4, 17, 18), the gift of the manna (16:7), and the numinous presence of God among the people (see 16:10; 24:16, 17; 33:18, 22; 40:34–35). Its use even extends to the makeshift tent and altar that served as a sanctuary (see 29:43). From these origins, it is used across all the many books and different literary forms of the Old Testament to speak of a revelation of God the people could experience. It is never a *notion* about a saving God, but the *experience* of that God. Even the skies cry out the glory of the Lord (see Ps 19:1). The Rabbis, and along with them the translators of the Hebrew into Aramaic (the Targumists), developed the tradition further. They communicated this sense of the experience of God initiated at Sinai and continuing throughout Israel's story and its institutions, especially the Torah, with their use of the expression *šěkînâ* (among the Rabbis) and the Aramaic *yiqrāʾ* (in the Targums). Both expressions can be translated into English as "glory."

Against this background, the Fourth Gospel presents Jesus as the revelation of the "glory of God" (*hē doxa tou theou*). Perhaps the clearest articulation of this Johannine concept is found at a crucial moment in the story, as the narrator asks why "the Jews" rejected Jesus (John 12:43). He makes a play upon the secular meaning of *doxa*, side by side with its biblical meaning, commenting, "For they loved the glory of men [*tēn doxan tōn anthrōpōn*] rather than the glory of God [*tēn doxan tou theou*]" (my translation). In their rejection of Jesus, "the Jews" have settled for their human achievements and honor (*tēn doxan tōn anthrōpōn*). (The meaning of *doxa* here derives from the pre-Septuagintal use of the term "glory.") In doing so, they have rejected Jesus, the visible presence of God among them (*tēn doxan tou theou*). They preferred the esteem they could measure, touch and enjoy, over against the visible manifestation of God in the person of Jesus, whom they have rejected. This important assessment of the performance of "the Jews" in the Fourth Gospel comes as the narrator asks the question that bedeviled the early church: Why did Israel fail to accept Jesus (see especially Rom 9–11)? Its meaning depends entirely upon the Johannine belief that the story of Jesus, and especially the mighty acts of Jesus, are the revelation of the glory of God (see 1:14; 2:11; 11:4, 40).

Unlike "the Jews," Jesus will never be compromised by a quest for human *doxa* (see 5:41; 7:18; 8:50, 54), as his life is determined by his hour, his response to the will of the one who sent him, the perfection of the task. Thus, as the Gospel unfolds, it becomes clear that Jesus' death will be the revelation of the glory of God and that Jesus will be glorified by means of it. As already mentioned, this is most clearly stated in the lead-up to Jesus' raising of Lazarus (see

11:4). This key passage now calls for further investigation. Informed of the ill-ness of his friend, Jesus announces, "This illness does not lead to death [*pros thanaton*]; rather it is for God's glory [*hyper tēs doxēs tou theou*], so that the Son of God may be glorified through it [*hina doxasthē/ di' autēs*]" (11:4). There is subtle irony and profound theology in these few words. It is true that the ill-ness will not lead to the death of Lazarus. He will be raised to life (see 11:43–44), but the miracle initiates a process whereby a series of events is set in motion ensuring that one man will die for the nation (see vv. 45–50). Lazarus will live, but by means of this illness (*di' autēs*), Jesus turns toward his death. The death of Jesus, therefore, explains what is meant by the rest of his words. His death will reveal the glory of God, and the Son of God will be glorified by means of it. The cross is the place where God is finally revealed in a consum-mate fashion (v. 4b; see 19:30). However, *by means of* the crucifixion, part of "the hour," Jesus returns to the glory that he had with the Father before the world was made (v. 4c; see 17:5).

Once this has been stated in 11:4, Jesus comes back to it regularly. As the Greeks ask to see Jesus, "the hour," which has always been in the future, has come. However, the theme of Jesus' glorification is associated with the hour: "The hour has come for the Son of Man to be glorified" (12:23). The hour, the glorification, and the gathering of the children of God coalesce as Jesus tells of the need for the grain of wheat to fall into the ground that it might bear much fruit (v. 24). Jesus asks that the Father's glory shine forth in v. 28a: "Father, glorify your name." A voice from heaven responds, indicating that Jesus' life and ministry have already revealed the glory of God, and that his imminent death will bring that glorification to its high point: "I have glorified it, and I will glorify it again" (v. 28b). Now is the judgment of this world. Now is the hour for the Son of Man to be lifted up, to draw everyone to himself (vv. 31–32). There can be no mistaking what event triggers the consummation of the hour, the glorification, and the gathering: "He said this to indicate the kind of death he was to die" (v. 33).

At the final meal, as Judas leaves the room to enter the darkness, Jesus turns toward the cross and explains to his disciples, "Now is the Son of Man glori-fied, and in him God is glorified; if God is glorified in him, God will also glo-rify him in himself, and glorify him at once" (my translation). This complex affirmation states that the time is at hand for God's final action in and through Jesus. In the death of Jesus, the glory of God will shine forth, and Jesus, the Son of Man who must be lifted up (see 3:14, 8:28; 12:32) will return to the glory that was his before the world was made (1:1–2; 17:5). The cross is the glory of God and the means by which the Son of God will be glorified (11:4). Jesus' telling the story of God depends upon the Johannine understanding of the cross as the revelation of the glory of God.

THE CROSS AS THE REVELATION OF GOD

The Johannine reinterpretation of the death of Jesus claims that Jesus brought to perfection the task given to him by his Father (see 4:34; 5:36; 13:1; 17:4) in his death on the cross. As he dies he announces, "It is brought to perfection" (19:30: *tetelestai;* my translation). The themes of the "lifting up," "the hour," "the gathering," and "the glorification" of Jesus all play their part, but they are subordinated to the major concern of the storyteller: Jesus' death on the cross reveals the glory of God (see 11:4; 13:31–32; 17:1–5). Jesus' final discourse is framed by two affirmations of his love for "his own." It begins with a comment from the narrator: "Having loved his own who were in the world, he loved them to the end" (13:1). The Greek behind the English "to the end" (*eis telos*) is yet another of the double-meaning words found in this subtle Gospel. It can mean "to the end" in a chronological sense (i.e., until his very last breath), or "to the end" in a qualitative sense (i.e. in a most consummate fashion). As often in the interpretation of the Fourth Gospel, one must not choose one over the other. Both meanings blend as the narrator tells the reader that the death of Jesus is also the time and the place where Jesus reveals his unconditional love for his own. In the final words of the prayer that closes the evening with the disciples, Jesus prays, "I made your name known to them, and I will make it known, so that the love with which you have loved me may be in them, and I in them" (17:26). The author believes passionately that God is love and that the love of Jesus for his own has made God known so that they might be swept into the oneness of love that unites the Father and the Son. But how is this possible? The answer is very simple: "No one has greater love than this, to lay down one's life for one's friends" (15:13).

The God of Jesus is a God who so loved the world that he sent his only son so that everyone could have eternal life. Jesus did not come to judge the world, but to offer it life (see 3:16–17). This life is possible because Jesus has made God known (see 17:3). Knowledge and understanding of the revelation of the God of Jesus is found by gazing upon the lifted up, pierced, Son of Man. As the narrator comments in the final words of the passion narrative, "They will gaze upon the one whom they have pierced" (19:37, my translation). The Johannine storyteller affirms that to gaze upon the pierced one is to see the revelation of a God of love. The original Johannine community could not have imagined the later practice of the veneration of an icon of the cross. Instead, they gazed upon the pierced one in their self-giving love for one another, living the example Jesus had given them (see 13:15). They were known as disciples of Jesus by their obedience to the new commandment he had given them:

that they love one another as he had loved them (see 13:34–35; 15:12, 17). They gazed upon the pierced one as they crossed the road from the security of their former ways to enter the kingdom by being born again by water and the Spirit (see 3:3–5; 19:34). They recognized the revelation of the God of Jesus in the broken body of Jesus and the spilt blood in the fragments that were gathered at the table of the Lord (see 6:1–15, 51–58; 19:34). But that story, telling of the believers' response to the God of Jesus, reaches beyond the limits of this study.

CONCLUSION

Is the Johannine understanding of God persuasive? What has this understanding of a God who is made known in the loving self-gift of Jesus to do with me? The Johannine theology of the cross proclaims God's love and the foundation of a Christian community of believers and lovers. For many reasons, an understanding of the cross as a place where Jesus reveals God's glory and is himself glorified in the foundation of a believing and loving community "because of that hour" has not played a great part in Christian spirituality. Yet, in the day-to-day life of so many Christians, it is an understanding of the cross that underpins much of what we do and how we do it.

The theology of the cross that I have outlined addresses Christianity, as a Christian life is lived in the belief in the revelation of love that shines forth from the steady, day-to-day commitment to the messiness of life. As Gerard Manley Hopkins wrote in *The Windhover*,

> Sheer plod makes plough down sillion
> Shine.

But it is not only Jesus of Nazareth whose death can be understood as the supreme moment of his life, the time and the place where he makes known a God of love, and is himself glorified. Glory and pain, love and suffering, self-gift in the moment of self-loss entwine in the death of all those who have taken to heart the words of Jesus: "No one has greater love than this, to lay down one's life for one's friends" (John 15:13). There is more to the final lines of Hopkins's *The Windhover*, subtitled "To Christ our Lord." They catch the heart of both Johannine theology and Johannine Christianity:

> No wonder of it: sheer plod makes plough down sillion
> Shine, and blue-bleak embers, ah my dear,
> Fall, gall themselves, and gash gold-vermilion.

SELECT BIBLIOGRAPHY

Barrett, Charles Kingsley. 1982a. "Christocentric or Theocentric? Observations on the Theological Method of the Fourth Gospel." Pages 1–18 in *Essays on John*. London: SPCK.

———. 1982b. "'The Father is greater than I' John 14:28: Subordinationist Christology in the New Testament." Pages 19–36 in *Essays on John*. London: SPCK.

Borgen, Peder. 1997. "God's Agent in the Fourth Gospel." Pages 83–95 in *The Interpretation of John*. Edited by John Ashton. Studies in New Testament Interpretation. 2d ed. Edinburgh: T. & T. Clark.

Bühner, Jan-Aolf. 1977. *Der Gesandte und sein Weg im 4. Evangelium: Die kultur- und religionsgeschichtlichen Grundlagen der johanneischen Sendungschristologie sowie ihre traditionsgeschichtliche Entwicklung*. Wissenschaftliche Untersuchungen zum Neuen Testament 2. Reihe 2. Tübingen: J. C. B. Mohr (Paul Siebeck).

Bultmann, Rudolf. 1955. Pages 3–92 in vol. 2 of *The Theology of the New Testament*. 2 vols. Translated by Kendrick Grobel. London: SCM Press.

Cadman, William Healey. 1969. *The Open Heaven: The Revelation of God in the Johannine Sayings of Jesus*. Edited by George Bradford Caird. Oxford: Basil Blackwell.

Forestell, J. Terence. 1974. *The Word of the Cross: Salvation as Revelation in the Fourth Gospel*. Analecta Biblica 57. Rome: Biblical Institute.

Kelly, Anthony J., and Francis J. Moloney. 2003. *The Opening of Heaven: The Experience of God in the Johannine Writings*. Mahwah, N.J.: Paulist Press. In Press.

Koester, Craig. 1989. "Hearing, Seeing, and Believing in the Gospel of John." *Biblica* 70: 327–48.

Larsson, T. 2001. *God in the Fourth Gospel: A Hermeneutical Discussion of the History of Interpretation*. Coniectanea Biblica: New Testament Series 35. Lund: Almqvist.

Moloney, Francis J. 1998. *Glory Not Dishonor: Reading John 13–21*. Minneapolis: Fortress.

———. 2001. "'God So Loved the World': Jesus in the Fourth Gospel." Pages 167–80 in *"A Hard Saying": The Gospel and Culture*. Collegeville, Minn.: Liturgical Press.

Moody Smith, Dwight. 1995. *The Theology of the Gospel of John*. New Testament Theology. Cambridge: Cambridge University Press.

O'Day, Gail. 1986. *Revelation in the Fourth Gospel: Narrative Mode and Theological Claim*. Philadelphia: Fortress.

Painter, John. 1996. "Inclined to God: The Quest for Eternal Life—Bultmannian Hermeneutics and the Theology of the Fourth Gospel." Pages 346–68 in *Exploring the Gospel of John: In Honor of D. Moody Smith*. Edited by R. Alan Culpepper and C. Clifton Black. Louisville, Ky.: Westminster John Knox.

Pollard, T. E. 1970. *Johannine Christology and the Early Church*. Society for New Testament Studies Monograph Series 13. Cambridge: Cambridge University Press.

Reinhartz, Adele. 1992. *The Word in the World: The Cosmological Tale in the Fourth Gospel*. Society of Biblical Literature Monograph Series 45. Atlanta: Scholars Press.

———, ed. 1999. "God the Father in the Gospel of John." *Semeia* 85: 1–202.

Thompson, Marianne Meye. 2001. *The God of the Gospel of John*. Grand Rapids: Erdmans.

Zumstein, Jean. 1989. "L'évangile johannique, une stratégie du croire." *Recherches de science religieuse* 77: 217–32.

8

The God of Mercy Who Rescues Us from the Present Evil Age

Romans and Galatians

RICHARD B. HAYS

> Grace to you and peace from God our Father and the Lord Jesus
> Christ, who gave himself for our sins to set us free from the pre-
> sent evil age, according to the will of our God and Father, to whom
> be the glory forever and ever. Amen.
>
> *(Gal 1:3–5)*

Thus begins Paul's urgent message to the Galatian churches. If, as Nils Dahl
has perceptively suggested, the doctrine of God is "the neglected factor in
New Testament theology" (Dahl 1991, 153–63), it can only be because we have
not been paying attention to what Paul says. Paul insistently places God at the
center of his proclamation, a message that he characterizes as "the gospel of
God" (Rom 1:1). The word *theos* (God) appears 153 times in Romans alone;
furthermore, Paul frequently refers to God using other descriptive formulations, such as "the one who justifies the ungodly" (Rom 4:5), "the one who
raised Jesus from the dead" (4:24), "the one who searches the heart" (8:27),
and "he who did not withhold his own Son, but gave him up for all of us" (8:32).

Perhaps New Testament scholarship has tended to overlook this central
theme of Paul's theology because, in viewing Paul's letters through the
hermeneutical lens of Christendom, it has assumed that the meaning of *theos*
is axiomatic and uncontroversial. This was not so, however, in the missionary
context where Paul lived, worked, and wrote: He preached the gospel in the
world of Hellenistic paganism, where no assured preunderstanding of "God"
could be assumed. At the same time, he was engaged in complex ongoing conversations with his own Jewish heritage, and his interpretation of the God he
knew from Israel's Scriptures was deeply impacted by the events of Christ's
death and resurrection. Consequently, to reexamine Paul's proclamation about

God in Romans and Galatians will require us to think more carefully about the historical context of Paul's writings and about the battles he was fighting.

Paul's letters are not systematic theological treatises but pastoral responses addressed to specific occasions and problems; therefore, his language about God always has specific argumentative purposes (see Moxnes 1980 for detailed discussion of this claim with regard to Romans). For this reason, there is something to be gained by examining the letters one by one and asking how Paul shapes his teaching about God in each letter as he addresses particular concerns. Accordingly, in this chapter we will consider Galatians and Romans individually before offering some synthetic reflections about the portrayal of God that emerges when we read these letters together within the New Testament canon.

As we approach these texts, we must always bear in mind that Paul was a missionary seeking to bring about a conversion of the imagination in his readers—Jews and Gentiles alike (Hays 1999). He sought to lead Gentiles, the primary audience of his missionary preaching, into a new symbolic world in which they would come to understand themselves as children of the one God of Israel. At the same time, he sought to lead Jewish readers—including the Jewish Christians whose missionary work paralleled and partly opposed his— into a new symbolic world in which they would understand God's embrace of Gentiles qua Gentiles as the climactic revelation of the character of the one God worshiped by Israel. In both cases, he was seeking to transform the conceptions of the divine previously held by his hearers. Indeed, the desired transformation was so radical that it would necessarily create a transformed community of readers (the *ekklesia*) in which the one God was known and glorified in unprecedented ways by Jews and Gentiles together.

This kind of communal transformation could occur, Paul was convinced, not merely through the power of persuasive rhetoric but through the proclaimed gospel of Jesus Christ (cf. 1 Cor 1:18–2:5). This proclamation necessarily takes the form of recounting the *story* of what God has done to rescue human beings from alienation, violence, and death. Thus, the truth about God can be known and communicated only in narrative form. (Achtemeier [1985, 10] makes a similar point: "the logic of the structure of Romans is more nearly the logic of history than the logic of doctrine." Subsequently, Achtemeier glosses the phrase "the logic of history" by a fuller formulation: "the logic of the story of God's dealing with his rebellious creation" [14]. Cf. also Keesmaat 1999.) Paul is not a philosopher seeking to articulate general truths about God's character; rather, he is a missionary tirelessly telling the story of the one God's astounding specific acts of self-giving grace. Thus, he narrates the Gentiles into Israel's story; he insists, for example, that they should hear in the story of Abraham a prefiguration and paradigm for the grace of God they have come to know in their own lives (Gal 3:6–29, 4:21–5:1; Rom 4:1–25). As he retells this story, however, he reshapes the portrayal of God that Israel historically had found in the story, by insisting that the cross and resurrection require a dramatic rereading of the scriptural story's meaning.

The import of these observations is that we can best approach Paul's understanding of God by attending to the characterization of God within the story that Paul tells (or sometimes implies) in these letters. We know God solely through what God has done. My treatment of Galatians and Romans will, therefore, trace the narrative structure of Paul's convictions about God. (On the narrative substructure of Paul's theology, see Hays 2001.)

As we shall see, this approach leads to two conclusions that constitute an epistemological revolution in theology. First, in Paul's gospel story, the identity of God is definitively embodied and disclosed in the man Jesus, who is acclaimed by Paul as *kyrios* ("Lord"), the name that the Old Testament ascribes to God alone. Second, within this story the identity of God is bound inextricably to the covenant promises, and therefore to the covenant people; consequently, the transformative, sanctifying work of the Spirit of God in the people of God is intrinsic to the revelation of God's character. These startling claims will be considered more fully in the final section of the present essay. The first task, however, is to trace the portrayal of God in Galatians and Romans.

GALATIANS: THE GOD WHO
RESCUES US FROM THE PRESENT EVIL AGE

God Our Father

Three times in the salutation of his letter to the Galatian churches, Paul refers to God as Father (Gal 1:1–5). While this is a standard element in Pauline letter openings ("grace to you and peace from God our Father and the Lord Jesus Christ"), the threefold naming of God as *patēr* in the opening verses of Galatians is thematically significant in a letter that seeks to persuade Paul's Gentile converts in Galatia that they are authentically children of God (3:26–29; 4:3–7; 4:28–5:1)—that is to say, they stand in the same relation to God as did Israel in the many Old Testament texts that describe the relation between God and his covenant people metaphorically as a relation between a father and his children (e.g., Exod 4:22–23; Deut 32:6; Isa 63:15–16; 64:8–9; Jer 3:19; 31:9; Hos 11:1–3; Mal 2:10). Indeed, as Paul declares later in the letter, God has sent the Spirit of his Son into the hearts of believers, enabling them to cry out to God, "Abba! Father!" (4:6), confirming their status as God's children and heirs.

Thus, by calling God "our Father" in the opening sentences of the letter, Paul signals that God is a merciful paternal figure who embraces Gentiles and Jews together within his covenant family, "the Israel of God" (6:16).

The central concern of Paul's discussion of adoption and of God's "father-hood" is that those who are God's adopted children are the recipients of the inheritance promised to Abraham. Thus, as Marianne Meye Thompson has demonstrated, Paul's "Father" language points not primarily to an experience of emotional intimacy between God and believers but to God's action of faith-ful care and provision for those he claims as his children (Thompson 2000, 116–32). To say that God is "Father" is to confess that he is protector, provider, and the giver of an inheritance—a theme that figures prominently later in Galatians. In Gal 1:1–5, however, Paul does not mention the theme of inher-itance. Instead, God the Father is portrayed as one who reaches out to rescue his people from captivity: He sends Jesus to rescue us from the grasp of the present evil age (1:4; cf. 4:4–5), and he sends Paul as an apostle to announce the good news of this rescue operation (1:1; cf. 1:15–16a).

Against the backdrop of this introductory characterization of God, we may now trace the story, as Paul unfolds it in Galatians, of how God the Father has acted to set things right in a world that has gone wrong. Because Galatians is a pastoral letter written to communities where Paul had already proclaimed the gospel, he does not simply begin from the beginning and retell the story. Rather, he alludes to and comments upon it both directly and indirectly throughout the letter. The order of our exposition will follow the plot of the story, rather than the order in which references to it appear in Paul's argument. This will yield a rough reconstruction of God's role in the gospel story that Paul had taught the Galatians, a story that he now marshals in rebuttal to the claims of the Jewish-Christian missionaries who were troubling them.

God in Paul's Gospel Story in Galatians

God made promises to Abraham. The earliest element in the story that Paul alludes to in Galatians is God's gracious word of promise to Abraham (3:6–9, 15–18). Unlike Romans, which frames the story of Israel within the wider epic of creation and Adam's primal fall into sin, the letter to the Galatians treats God's promise to Abraham as the beginning of the story. Almost certainly, Paul's focus on Abraham is conditioned by the polemical setting of the letter: The rival missionaries were pointing to Abraham as the father of proselytes and urging the Galatians to be circumcised, like Abraham, as a sign of the covenant with God (Gen 17:9–14; for a detailed reconstruction of the message of the missionaries, see Martyn 1997, 117–26, 302–6). Thus, the primary issue that Paul is confronting in this letter is whether Gentiles must be circumcised to be counted among the people of God. In order to stake out his counterposition, Paul renarrates the story of Abraham and gives it his own distinctive spin. The thing that matters most about the story, Paul insists, is that God promised Abraham a great inheritance, and Abraham trusted God's promise. All of this happened long before the Law came into the picture four hundred and thirty years later (3:17). Therefore, God reckoned Abraham righteous entirely apart from Law or circumcision. Indeed, the form in which God delivered the promise to Abraham was a proleptic proclamation of the gospel: "All the Gentiles shall be blessed in you" (3:8). Thus, God is a God who has willed from the beginning to embrace Gentiles within his promised blessing. God takes the initiative to make gracious promises and can be trusted to keep them. (Gal 3:18b can be translated literally, "God graced Abraham through promise.") Abraham's response of trust, as narrated in Gen 15:6, is therefore the paradigm for right relation to God.

Two observations about Paul's account of the promise to Abraham are noteworthy. First, God speaks through Scripture, and God's voice in Scripture pronounces a blessing (3:8–9). Second, the God of whom Paul speaks in Galatians is the God of Abraham and Isaac (Jacob is not mentioned specifically in this letter, but see Rom 9:10–13). These observations, taken together, decisively rule out any Marcionite or Gnostic misreading of Paul. The God who promises and blesses, according to Paul's gospel, is the God of Israel's Scripture, a God who must be known in and through the retelling of Israel's story. The promise that God made to Abraham can be described as a covenant (*diathēkē*; 3:17), and all those who are called by God stand within the sphere of God's covenant promise.

God gave the Law. This part of the story is notoriously murky in Paul's allusive retelling—so murky, in fact, that some interpreters have suggested that Paul regarded the Sinaitic law as given by angelic beings acting apart from God's purposes (3:19). This suggestion, however, is almost surely a misinterpretation. The passive verbs "added," "ordained," and "given" in Gal 3:19, 21 refer to God's action, and Paul emphatically asserts that the law is not opposed to the promises of God (3:21). The argument of Galatians is that God gave the law as a temporary restraining and protecting measure until the coming of the promised "seed"—that is, Christ—who would receive the inheritance and make it available to Jews and Gentiles alike. (For fuller exposition of this difficult passage, see Wright 1991, 157–74; Hays 2000.)

Paul's account of the purpose of the Law is one of the things that distinguishes him most sharply from other Jewish interpreters of his time. We hear little or nothing, especially in Galatians, of the Law as a blessing or a revelatory treasure. Here again, the polemical setting of the letter is crucial to understanding Paul's notably restrained statements about the Law. Paul was reacting against the demands made by the missionaries in Galatia that Gentile converts be circumcised and observe at least some of the Torah's requirements (cf. Acts 15:1). Paul saw this as an oppressive demand imposed upon Gentile believers by ethnocentric teachers oblivious to the liberating effects of Christ's death: In their hands, the Law—with its specific demands of circumcision, dietary practices, and calendar observances—had been turned into an instrument of Jewish cultural imperialism. Paul does not dispute that God gave Moses the Law, but he insists that it had no power to give life (3:21); it was designed only as a *paidagōgos*, a "disciplinarian" to keep Israel in protective custody until the coming of Christ (3:23–26). With regard to the understanding of God, an important claim is made here: God is bigger than the Law. God used the law for a certain purpose, but God is neither defined by the Law nor bound to it. God is free to act in a new way, and that is just what Paul declares he has done.

God sent his Son. Galatians never gives an explanation of how human beings came to be under the power of "the present evil age" (1:4), but this language expresses an apocalyptic worldview. Somehow the world became enslaved under "beings that are not gods," whom Paul calls the *stoicheia tou kosmou* ("elemental spirits of the world," 4:3, 8–9). In this dire situation, the only hope for liberation from slavery was that God would intervene to rescue us. That is what God has done, Paul announces: "When the fullness of time had come, God sent his Son, born of a woman, born under the law, in order to redeem those who were under the law, so that we might receive adoption as children" (4:4–5). The verb translated "redeem" here is *exagorazō*, a term used to describe the emancipation of slaves from the slave market. Paul pictures God as one who dispatches the Son on a mission to liberate us from bondage (5:1), or as J. Louis Martyn renders Gal 1:4, "to snatch us out of the grasp of the present evil age" (Martyn 1997, 90–91). Israel knows well that God is a rescuer. The same verb that Paul uses in Gal 1:4 is used in Exodus (LXX) to describe God's deliverance of Israel from slavery in Egypt (e.g., "I have come down to *rescue* them from the hand of the Egyptians" [Exod 3:8]).

How did the Son, Jesus Christ, accomplish this rescue mission? In striking contrast to the exodus story, God saves his people not through powerful signs and wonders but through the ignominious death of his Son. Paradoxically, the rescue was accomplished through his death on the cross. Through this horrible death, "Christ redeemed us from the curse of the law by becoming a curse for us" (3:13). The event of Jesus' death brings the old world of slavery to an end, and by participating in his death, God's people pass out of an old life into a new world. "I have been crucified with Christ; and it is no longer I who live, but it is Christ who lives in me" (2:19b–20a). Paul can even make the remarkable claim that through the cross, the world has been crucified: The death of Jesus is an apocalyptic event that ends one age and ushers in a new one

(6:14–15). That is why Paul's initial proclamation to the Galatians focused on Jesus Christ crucified (3:1; cf. 1 Cor 2:1–5).

One other aspect of the Son's mission is highlighted when Paul writes of "the faith of the Son of God who loved me and gave himself for me" (2:20, see footnote in NRSV). The Son of God's *pistis* (i.e., faith, trust, or faithfulness) is embodied in his self-sacrificial death for the sake of humanity. This faithfulness parallels Abraham's *pistis* (or, more precisely, Abraham's *pistis* prefigures the faithfulness of Jesus), but at the same time the faithfulness of Jesus is also an expression of *God's* faithfulness to his promises. As Paul puts it in 3:22, that which was promised (by God) was given "through the faithfulness of Jesus Christ to those who believe" (again, see NRSV footnote). This formulation strongly suggests that Jesus' faithfulness unto death was in some sense an action of God, an action through which God fulfilled the promise to Abraham. That point becomes clearer in Romans than it is in Galatians, but there can be no doubt that Paul sees God at work through the cross.

God raised Jesus from the dead. The letter to the Galatians makes little direct reference to the resurrection, but the opening sentence of the letter makes it clear that the cross cannot be understood as a saving event apart from the resurrection: Paul was given his apostolic commission "through Jesus Christ and God the Father, who raised him from the dead" (1:1). The resurrection is portrayed as a direct action of God the Father, an expression of God's sovereign power that brings into being a new creation (6:15). The resurrection is not merely the resuscitation of a dead body under the conditions of the old creation; rather, it is the sign of God's power bringing a new world to birth.

God justifies the Gentiles through the faithfulness of Jesus Christ (3:8; 2:16). The world of God's new creation is one in which Gentiles receive God's blessing (3:14), so that the distinction between Jew and Greek melts into insignificance (3:28). Scripture had already foreseen this and proclaimed it in the blessing of Abraham (3:8). This theme receives more reflective development in Romans, but it is fundamental to the argument of Galatians, and it receives especially pointed expression in Paul's account of his confrontation with Cephas at Antioch (2:11–21). When we read Paul's statements in the context of the controversy over table fellowship at Antioch, it becomes clear that "justification" refers not only to a forensic declaration of acquittal before God but also— indeed, primarily—to being set in right relation to God within the covenant community of God's people (Hays 1992; Baker 1999).

This motif is very closely connected to the letter's image of God's "adoption" of men and women, Jews and Gentiles alike, as his own children (3:26–29; 4:4–7). The images of justification and adoption are complementary and point to the same reality of inclusion in God's family.

God calls us into participation in the new covenant community. God is one who calls. He calls us into life and into relationship with himself and the community of others whom he has called. This conviction, one of Paul's central beliefs about God, appears several times in Galatians. God called Paul through his grace (1:15) and used Paul as an instrument to call others. God called the Galatians in the grace of Christ, though Paul is now astonished at their defection from the grace into which God had summoned them (1:6). They were called by God to freedom (5:13), but now they are relapsing into slavery. When Paul deplores the persuasive influences that have prevented the Galatians from obeying the truth, he exclaims, "Such persuasion does not come from the one who calls you" (5:8). His use here of the present participle suggests that God continues to call the Galatians; the call of God is not a one-time event but an insistent summons, beckoning us again and again to the freedom that God intends for our lives. One of the most important aspects of this emphasis on God's calling is that it highlights God's initiative in bringing human beings into right relation. Paul carefully safeguards the priority of divine initiative over human efforts to come into relationship with God. Perhaps the most striking illustration of this is his midsentence self-correction in 4:9: "Now, however, that you have come to know God, or rather to be known by God . . ." God knows us before we know God, and God makes the first move to call us into relationship.

In Galatians, because of the challenge to Paul's apostolic teaching and authority, we find a special emphasis on God's calling of Paul to his apostolic mission. God set Paul apart from his mother's womb for the work of proclaiming the Son of God among the Gentiles (1:15–16; cf. 2:7–8). In response to this call, Paul now lives "to God" (2:19), conveying God's grace and peace and mercy (1:3; 6:16) to all who will listen.

God supplies the Spirit. The freedom in which we are to live is guaranteed and sustained by God's Spirit, which God has now sent into our hearts. The Spirit bears witness that we are God's children and heirs (4:6–7). The Spirit also leads and guides us in so distinct a way of life that we no longer need the Law to provide direction. We are to live (lit. "walk") by the Spirit, and the Spirit overcomes the flesh and produces the fruit of righteousness (5:16–25). Furthermore, the Spirit is a palpable presence in the Galatian community, an experienced reality to which Paul can appeal as decisive evidence of the transformation that God has brought about. Through the Spirit, God "works miracles among you" (3:2–5). At the same time, the Spirit sustains hope in a community that still awaits the final manifestation of God's redemptive power: "For through the Spirit, by faith, we eagerly wait for the hope of righteousness" (5:5). There is no evidence in Galatians that Paul reflected about the Spirit as a divine hypostasis, but he does seem to identify the Spirit with Christ (the risen Christ?): "God has sent the Spirit of his Son into our hearts" (4:6). Thus, in some manner, the Spirit is the presence of God as experienced in the community of faith.

God will judge. Although eschatological judgment is not a major theme of Galatians, the latter portions of the letter make passing reference to the conventional expectation that God will judge human beings at the last day. Those who do the works of the flesh "will not inherit the kingdom of God" (5:21). Paul employs the metaphor of sowing and reaping as a way of evoking the final assize where rewards and punishments will be given out by God's impartial judgment: "Do not be deceived; God is not mocked, for you reap whatever you sow" (6:7). It is in this context also that the otherwise puzzling remarks of 6:4–5 are to be understood: Paul's statement that "all must carry their own loads" is a proverbial allusion to the last judgment (Kuck 1994).

God is the ultimate recipient of glory. The letter's introductory formula touches very lightly on a narrative motif that will be greatly expanded in Romans: In the end, God will be glorified (1:5). Paul does not elaborate here, but it is important to recognize that this is the necessary eschatological conclusion of the story that underlies Galatians. The drama of promise, redemption, and new life in the Spirit leads finally to the goal of the glorification of God. The glory of God is bound up together with "the hope of righteousness" (5:5) and "new creation" (6:15), for God's glory is fully manifest in the restoration of all things to right relationship (cf. 1 Cor 15:20–28; Phil 2:9–11; Col 1:15–20). In Galatians, however, the grand conclusion of the epic receives only passing, allusive attention. This is one more indicator of the focused, occasional character of the letter: Paul is concentrating on the controversy over circumcision and Law observance, and his principal arguments hang upon the themes of God's promise, God's act of redemption through the cross, and God's gift of the Spirit.

ROMANS: THE GOD OF PEACE AND MERCY

In contrast to the polemical tone of Galatians, Romans seeks to sketch a comprehensive framework within which Paul can appeal for harmony among the Christians in Rome, and for their support of his longer-range missionary plans. Whereas Galatians stoutly rejects the necessity for Gentile converts to be circumcised, Romans defends with equal passion the unbroken fidelity of God to Israel. Thus, in Romans Paul must paint his portrayal of God on a canvas large enough to show how God's saving designs from creation to the eschaton have embraced Jews and Gentiles, and how the anomalous phenomenon of Jewish rejection of the gospel fits into the wider redemptive story. Galatians focuses on God's action in the climactic central chapters of the story; Romans backs the camera off for a more panoramic view of God's action from beginning to end.

Because Paul's rhetorical aims in Romans are conciliatory, he highlights God's merciful character. Within the unfolding of the gospel story, God's wrath is finally taken up into a more comprehensive characterization of God's grace. That is not to say that Romans downplays the judgment of God; on the contrary, God's judgment is the essential presupposition of the argument. Nonetheless, the story that Paul tells moves toward a climax in which God's mercy has the final word. Through the proclamation of the gospel, God's faithfulness is declared to the world. As we did in Galatians, let us chart out the logic of the story that Paul retells and explicates in the letter to the Romans.

God in Paul's Gospel Story in Romans

The one God is the Creator of the world. In accordance with the Shema, Paul affirms that God is one (Rom 3:30). This one God worshiped by Israel is the Creator (1:25) of all things visible and invisible, for "from him and through him and to him are all things" (11:36). Even though human beings may rebel and refuse to acknowledge God, "his eternal power and divine nature" have been manifest ever since the creation of the world in the things he has made (1:20). This God is no demiurge who molds formless matter into various shapes; he creates the world *ex nihilo*, for he is the one who "gives life to the dead and calls into existence the things that do not exist" (4:17).

This Creator God, furthermore, has foreknown from the beginning the destiny of all creation. His ultimate design is that "the creation itself will be set free from its bondage to decay and will obtain the glorious freedom of the children of God" (8:21). This design will surely be realized, for he has foreknown, predestined, called, justified, and glorified those who are to be conformed to the image of his Son (8:29–30). Thus, already in the structure of creation the eschatological consummation of all things is foreshadowed. God, "the only wise God" (16:27), possesses a wisdom and knowledge that exceed all human comprehension (11:33–36).

The world is alienated from God. Even though human beings should have recognized God from the wonders of his creation, they have not done so: "they did not honor him as God or give thanks to him," and so they have fallen into confusion, idolatry, and violence (1:18–32). The scope of this predicament is indicated by Paul's tracing it back to Adam (5:12–21); it is the pervasive human condition. "They exchanged the truth about God for a lie and worshiped and served the creature, rather than the Creator" (1:25). Because of this idolatry, "the wrath of God is revealed from heaven against all ungodliness" (1:18). God's wrath, however, takes the surprising form of abandoning idolatrous humans to their own self-destructive devices and desires (1:24–31). The consequences are dire: No one is righteous, no one seeks God, and there is no fear of God in the world (3:10–18). Such ideas are common in Hellenistic Judaism (cf. Wisdom of Solomon), but Paul radicalizes the indictment to include even devout Torah-observant Jews (like himself in his former life), "so that every mouth may be silenced, and the whole world may be held accountable to God" (3:19). Israel, along with the pagan world, is caught in the plight of Adamic humanity.

God made promises to Abraham. In Romans 4, the content of the promise is that Abraham or his descendants would "inherit the world" (4:13) and that Abraham would be "the father of many nations" (4:17, quoting Gen 17:5—a chapter of Genesis that Paul assiduously avoided in Galatians). The promise of God is utterly reliable, and Abraham's trust in the divine word of promise, even in the face of his own advanced age, is the faith that is reckoned to him as righteousness. It is this reliability of God's promise that constitutes the leitmotif of the whole letter and of chapters 9–11 in particular. Despite the contemporary unbelief of Israel, "it is not as though the word of God had failed" (9:6), and God can be counted on to do something to make the promises come true, despite all appearances to the contrary.

As we saw in Galatians, so also in Romans, Paul treats Scripture as a reliable witness of God's word of promise. Moses, Isaiah, and Hosea are quoted by name as prophetic witnesses to the gospel (e.g., 9:33; 10:19–21). This claim looms large in Romans, which begins with the affirmation that "the gospel of God" was "promised beforehand through his prophets in the holy scriptures" (1:2). Accordingly, Romans has far more Old Testament quotations than any other Pauline letter: According to one count, there are eighty-nine Old Testament citations in the corpus of uncontested Pauline letters, fifty-one of which appear in Romans (Koch 1986, 21–24).

God's saving will is expressed through election. God's beneficence is not expressed in undifferentiated generosity to all; rather, Paul finds in Scripture a consistent witness to God's selective purpose. Abraham's true descendants are named through Isaac (9:7); God loved Jacob and hated Esau (9:13); God hardened Pharoah's heart, showing that he is free to have mercy on whomever he chooses (9:15–18, quoting Exod 33:19). This motif once again highlights the divine initiative in salvation: "it depends not on human will or exertion, but on God who shows mercy" (9:16). God is compared to a potter who can do whatever he likes with the lumps of clay that he molds (9:19–24).

Paul maintains that none of this implies injustice on God's part. God is free to do what he chooses and to unfold his saving plan however he chooses, no matter how unfathomable it may be to us. Still, one thing is sure: God is true, faithful, and just, no matter how unfaithful his human creatures may be (3:3–8).

God gave the Law. In this letter, Paul never explicitly formulates a sentence that says God gave the Law to Moses, but he carefully ascribes to the law great authority and holiness, and he calls it "the law of God" in which he delights (7:22). The Jews, he says, were "entrusted with the oracles of God" (3:2). The Law has the effect of holding the whole world accountable (3:19); those who break the Law dishonor God (2:23). "The law is holy, and the commandment is holy and just and good" (7:12). All of this adds up to a more positive construal of the Law than can be found in Galatians. Paul makes it clear that the Law points toward the obedience that God desires, even if human beings continually fall short.

In Romans, however, Paul pursues a plot complication not developed in Galatians: The Law is powerless to effect the righteousness toward which it points, and it therefore becomes an instrument in the hands of sin (7:13–24). The Law is not merely a temporary restraining power, but it actually deepens the human dilemma of alienation and slavery. (This may be implied, though not explained, in Gal 4:5 and in 4:9, where Paul seems to class the law as an accomplice of the *stoicheia tou kosmou*.)

God sent his Son. Out of the plight of captivity to sin, Paul cries out, "Who will rescue me from this body of death?" The answer comes immediately: "Thanks be to God through Jesus Christ our Lord!" (7:24b–25a). As in Gal 4:4–5, Paul retells in Romans the story that God sent his own Son. In Romans, however, the significance of this sending is interpreted less in terms of the Son of God's act of liberating us from slavery and more in terms of the condemnation and destruction of Sin ("sending his own Son in the likeness of sinful flesh, and as a sin offering [see Wright 1991, 220–25], he condemned sin in the flesh, so that the just requirement of the law might be fulfilled in us"), along with the revelation of the righteousness of God (3:21–26). This is not a matter of contradictory stories in the two letters; rather, it is a difference of imagery and emphasis in describing the effects of God's sending the Son.

In Romans, as in Galatians, the redemptive action of God occurs through Jesus' death for our sake (e.g., 3:25; 4:25; 5:8; 8:32; 14:15)—though, surprisingly, Romans contains no specific reference to the cross or crucifixion as the manner of Jesus' death. As in Galatians, the mysterious efficacy of Christ's death is understood in terms of our participation in that death, a theme that receives extended consideration in Romans 6. Even more clearly than in Galatians, "the faithfulness of Jesus Christ" is the key to the saving significance of his death, and that faithfulness is interpreted as a vindication of the faithfulness or righteousness of God (3:21–26). Indeed, the obedience of the man Jesus (which may be taken as synonymous with his *pistis* ["faithfulness"]) is set in explicit antithesis to the disobedience of Adam (5:12–21). Thus, in the

Christology of Romans, Jesus becomes the paradigm for fidelity and the pattern of the newness of life in which we are called to walk.

The thing that distinguishes Paul's treatment of these themes in Romans, however, is that he insistently portrays the faithfulness and death of Jesus as actions that disclose God's identity. There is a mysterious sense in which the actions and suffering of Jesus *are* the actions and suffering of God; through these acts, the love of God becomes embodied and revealed. This breathtaking claim is articulated in Rom 5:8: "But *God* proves his love for us in that while we still were sinners *Christ* died for us." Here the agency of Christ becomes fully identified with the agency of God. We find a similar direction of thought in Rom 8:31–39, which affirms that God "did not withhold his own Son, but gave him up for all of us" and moves to the confession that nothing in all creation "will be able to separate us from the love of *God* in *Christ Jesus our Lord.*" Throughout Romans we find a similar dialectic between statements that describe Christ as the instrument through whom we receive reconciliation (e.g., 3:24; 4:25; 5:1) and statements that seem to identify Christ with God, at least with respect to agency. For that reason, the notoriously difficult syntax of 9:5 at least admits of the possibility that Paul places the phrase "God blessed for ever" in apposition to *ho Christos* ("the Messiah"), so that the sentence identifies Christ explicitly with God. (The arguments of Dunn [1988, 528–29] against this reading are outweighed by the positive considerations adduced by Fitzmyer [1993, 548–49].) Whether that is a correct reading or not, it remains clear that Paul understands the death of Jesus as a revelation of the identity of God and as the loving act through which God reconciles the fallen creation to himself.

God raised Jesus from the dead. Resurrection is a significant theme of Romans, for God is portrayed in this letter as the one who "gives life to the dead" (4:17; cf. 8:11). The resurrection of Jesus was "for our justification" (4:25), and it empowers us "to walk in newness of life," since we will be united with Christ in a resurrection like his (6:4–5). The resurrection has significant implications also for our understanding of the relationship between Christ and God. Through raising Jesus from the dead, God declared him "Son of God with power" (1:4), and Christ Jesus who was raised now "is at the right hand of God" interceding for us (8:34). Because of this exalted position, Jesus Christ can now be acclaimed as "Lord [*kyrios*] of both the dead and the living" (14:9), an epithet which surely can apply rightly to no one other than God alone. Indeed, the title *kyrios*—the LXX's translation for the divine name—is unambiguously assigned to Jesus in Rom 10:9–13:

> If you confess with your lips that Jesus is Lord [*kyrios*] and believe in
> your heart that God raised him from the dead, you will be saved. . . .
> The scripture says, "No one who believes in him will be put to shame"
> [Isa 28:16]. For there is no distinction between Jew and Greek: the

same Lord [*kyrios*] is Lord of all and is generous to all who call on him.
For, "Everyone who calls on the name of the Lord [*kyrios*] shall be
saved" [Joel 2:32].

Here Paul has explicitly identified Jesus as the Lord, the God of Israel of whom
the prophet Joel spoke (on the interpretation of this passage, see Rowe 2000).
This extraordinary claim requires fresh reflection on the way in which this sort
of "christological monotheism" developed within Second Temple Judaism (see
Bauckham 1998; cf. Hurtado 1998).

God calls and justifies Gentiles. Because God is one, he is God of Jews and
Gentiles alike, and he justifies the circumcised and the uncircumcised on the
same basis (3:29–30). Therefore, though the gospel is the power of God for
salvation to the Jew first, it is also for the Greek (1:17). God has now called
Gentiles as well as Jews, saying to those who once were not his people that
they are now children of the living God (9:23–24). That is one thing that Paul
means when he describes God as the one "who justifies the ungodly" (4:5):
God justifies Gentiles, like Abraham, who previously "did not strive for righteousness" (9:30). One of the principal effects of Christ's work is "that the Gentiles might glorify God for his mercy" (15:9a, followed by a string of Old
Testament citations [15:9b–12] showing that the inclusion of the Gentiles in
worshiping God was always God's purpose, now fulfilled in Christ).

God hardens Israel. Here we encounter a surprising complication of the
story. The story of God's action to save the world does not march in a straight,
triumphal line. God's own elect people Israel have refused to accept the
preaching of the good news of Jesus Christ. Paul attributes even this unsettling development, however, to the activity of God. God has laid a stumbling
stone in Zion (9:33, quoting Isa 28:16 + 8:14) and sent a sluggish spirit (11:8,
quoting Deut 29:4 and Isa 29:10) to produce a "hardening" on the part of Israel
(11:25). The effect of this unexpected development is to make more room for
Gentiles to be grafted in, like wild olive branches grafted onto a tree from
which the natural branches have been broken off (11:17–24).

God will save Israel in the end. The hardening of Israel provokes the theological crisis with which Paul wrestles in Romans 9–11. He asks whether God
has rejected his people, and the answer is "By no means!" (11:1). God has the
power to graft them in again, and indeed once the full number of the Gentiles
has come in, "all Israel will be saved" in the end (11:25b–27). The gifts and the
calling of God are irrevocable (11:28), and so even Israel's unfaithfulness cannot finally negate the faithfulness of God (3:3–4a). Here lies a key to the characterization of God in this letter: He is persistently faithful and gracious, even
to "a disobedient and contrary people" who have rejected him despite his
hands being outstretched all day long (10:21). God is faithful, true, and righteous, and nothing can finally thwart his will to deliver Jacob and take away

their sins. In this strange dialectic of hardening and ultimate salvation, we see that Paul's portrayal of God is fully continuous with the depiction of God in Deuteronomy 32 and in the Old Testament prophetic literature: God pronounces judgment and destruction on an unfaithful and idolatrous covenant people, but always there remains the promise of ultimate restoration.

God is at work in the church through the Holy Spirit. As in Galatians, the Spirit plays the role of confirming our status as God's children and heirs (8:14–17, a passage closely parallel to Gal 4:4–7). Through the Spirit, God's love is poured into our hearts (5:5), assuring us that our hope is not in vain. The Spirit of God is now actually dwelling in believers (8:9), giving life and providing guidance. In one remarkable sequence of sentences, Paul seems to use the terms "Spirit," "Spirit of God," "Spirit of Christ," and "Christ" as though they were synonymous and interchangeable (8:9–11). This passage comes as close as anything in Paul to an explicitly trinitarian understanding of God. In any case, the Spirit of which Paul writes here empowers our obedience and submission to God and serves as a promise of the resurrection life in which the Spirit "will give life to your mortal bodies."

One other function of the indwelling Spirit is to "intercede for the saints according to the will of God" and to enable prayer even beyond our power to articulate what we need (8:26–27); implied here is a sort of sympathetic harmony between the indwelling Spirit of God and "God who searches the heart."

God hears prayer. Paul prays for the Romans and asks them to pray earnestly for him (1:9–10; 15:30–33). The language of prayer contains some of Paul's most moving characterizations of God. God is "the God of steadfastness and encouragement" (15:5–6), "the God of hope" (15:13), "the God of peace" (15:33). The prayers associated with these descriptions of God ask for God to bring harmony, unity, joy, peace, and hope. Indeed, the loving community envisioned in these prayers is precisely the aim of God's reconciling action in Christ. Thus, Paul's characterization of God in these prayers corresponds to the persuasive aim of the letter to bring about harmony and cooperation among the Roman Christians. Lest we grow too sentimental about such epithets, though, we should remember that Paul also expresses the confident expectation that "the God of peace will shortly crush Satan under your feet" (16:20)—a helpful reminder that Paul's imagination never strays far from the arena of apocalyptic conflict. Paul's anxiety about his own impending fate in Jerusalem (15:31) is a sobering reminder that the God who hears prayer may also send his servants on dangerous missions.

God calls us to obedient service. Romans is far more explicit than Galatians in calling for the readers to present themselves to God in obedient service. Paul uses various images, but all of them presuppose that God awaits and expects an appropriate response to what he has done through the death and resurrection of Jesus. A couple of examples illustrate the point clearly: "No longer present your members to sin as instruments [lit. 'weapons'] of wickedness, but present yourselves to God as those who have been brought from death to life, and present your members to God as instruments [lit. 'weapons'] of righteousness" (6:13). Or again, "I appeal to you therefore, brothers and sisters, by the mercies of God, to present your bodies as a living sacrifice, holy and acceptable to God, which is your spiritual worship" (12:1). Elsewhere, Paul uses the metaphor of himself as a priest ministering to the Gentiles so that their (self-) offering might be acceptable to God (15:16). This motif of God's expectation for our fit service, however, must be kept in the closest possible dialectical linkage with the next element of the story.

God wills and works in the church. We discern the will of God only by having our minds renewed by the transforming power of God (12:2). God gives various gifts in the one body of the church, which are to be employed for the common good (12:6–8). Indeed, the community itself can be spoken of as "the work of God," in the sense that it is God's own lovingly crafted construction (14:20). Even Paul's own apostolic accomplishments are rightly to be described as "what Christ has accomplished through me . . . by the power of the Spirit of God" (15:18–19).

God will judge the world. Even though Paul can speak of reconciliation as already accomplished in Christ (5:11), several passages in Romans indicate that God's final judgment of human beings remains in the future. In Rom 14:10–12, Paul declares that "we will all stand before the judgment seat of God," and early in the letter he warns of "the day of wrath, when God's righteous judgment will be revealed" (2:6; see 2:1–16; 3:6). The prospect of God's coming judgment informs several of the letter's ethical directives in chapters 12–15, including the renunciation of vengeance in order to "leave room for the wrath of God" (12:19). In the same context, Paul also cautions that those who resist the authorities appointed by God will incur judgment, presumably God's judgment (13:2).

Nonetheless, Paul remains deeply confident that those who are in Christ, who have been justified by Christ's blood, "will be saved through him from the wrath of God" (5:9). The confident and inspiring declarations of 8:31–39 also allude to the scene of final judgment and place Jesus Christ in the position of advocate and intercessor rather than judge. "Who will bring any charge against God's elect? It is God who justifies. Who is to condemn?" (8:33–34a).

God receives eschatological glory. Paul speaks eagerly of "the glory about to be revealed to us" (8:18). Here he is thinking of the revealed glory of the children of God in the redeemed creation that is still to come, but this glory is finally a reflection of the glory of God. Several doxological passages intimate that ultimately God will receive glory forever (e.g., 11:36; 16:27), and the Old Testament quotations that stand at the conclusion of Paul's central argument (15:9–12) envision Christ with a throng of God's people, made up of Jews and Gentiles together, singing praises to God's name. The *telos* of all creation, at the end of the great story of rebellion and redemption, is summarized by Paul's citation of Isa 45:23: "As I live, says the Lord, every knee shall bow to me, and every tongue shall give praise to God" (Rom 14:11). It is perhaps no accident that Paul elsewhere applies precisely the same passage from Isaiah to the exalted Jesus: ". . . so that at the name of Jesus every knee should bend, in heaven and on earth and under the earth, and every tongue should confess that Jesus Christ is Lord [*kyrios*], to the glory of God the Father" (Phil 2:10–11). When God is truly glorified, the identity of Jesus Christ with God, which we have seen emphasized elsewhere in Romans, will at last be revealed in the praise of all creation.

CONCLUDING REFLECTIONS

Romans and Galatians presuppose substantially the same story about God. The story world of Romans does include some distinctive features: Paul refers to God's creation of the world and develops an account of the world's rebellion against God through Adam's sin in a way that has no parallel in Galatians. Additionally, in Romans Paul explores the mysterious subplot of God's hardening of Israel and God's ultimate design to save them, a plot that no one could have guessed from reading Galatians, though the concluding wish for peace and mercy upon "the Israel of God" (Gal 6:16) can be read retrospectively, in light of Romans 9–11, as a foreshadowing of this story. Apart from these distinctive elements in Romans, however, the two letters tell the story of God in ways that are closely parallel. The story may be summarized briefly as follows:

> God long ago gave trustworthy promises to Abraham, promising to bless all nations. God gave the Law to Israel as an intermediary measure until the time when the promises were to be fulfilled. In the fullness of time, God sent his Son to rescue human beings from slavery and sin, through his faithful death. God raised Jesus from the dead. God calls and justifies Jews and Gentiles alike, who join together in a new reconciled community, the church, where God is at work. God supplies the Spirit to the members of this community, empowering them to walk in newness of life. God will ultimately judge the world and reveal his eschatological glory.

In light of this summary, it is not difficult to see why Paul characterizes his message as "the gospel of God" (Rom 1:1). God is the primary actor from start to finish.

The scope of the present essay does not permit exploration of the minor variations in detail between the two letters (for example, the precise role of the Law), but I will offer several concluding reflections on the portrayal of God in the story that Romans and Galatians proclaim.

First, the God and Father of Jesus Christ, the God who sent Paul to proclaim the gospel to the Gentiles, is the same God whose story is narrated in Israel's Scripture. Indeed, the gospel of God's saving grace was already proclaimed—or at least prefigured—in Scripture (Rom 1:2; 3:21; 15:4; Gal 3:8), even though it was fully revealed only in light of the death and resurrection of Jesus. This means that Scripture is rightly read as the vehicle of God's self-disclosure. Furthermore, the God who made promises to Abraham is faithful and will not abandon his people. This means that God has bound himself to his covenant people Israel in such a way that his identity cannot be separated from Israel (cf. Moxnes 1980, 99). It is impossible to overemphasize the importance of these points: We know no God apart from Scripture, no God apart from Israel. Even if God's power should be in principle knowable in the grandeur of creation (Rom 1:19–20), in fact we have failed to know God rightly in this way, and God has in fact chosen to make himself known as the God of Abraham, Isaac, and Jacob. This excludes all notions of a God who is merely a First Cause, or "the ground of being," or a vague spiritual presence. Our knowledge of God in these actions is of course far from exhaustive, for his ways remain above our understanding (Rom 11:33–36). Nonetheless, our knowledge of the story of Israel's God is to be relied upon: God is the one who pronounced a blessing on Abraham, led Israel out of Egypt, and ultimately will "banish ungodliness from Jacob" (Rom 11:26, quoting Isa 59:20 LXX).

Second, God's love was embodied in Jesus Christ. "God proves his love for us in that while we were still sinners Christ died for us" (Rom 5:8). In a variety of passages in both letters, the self-sacrificial death of Jesus is, for Paul, nothing less than God's own saving act. Furthermore, Jesus Christ, raised up by God's power, is the *kyrios* on whom we call and to whom every knee shall finally bow. In short, Paul proclaims that Jesus Christ is the embodiment of God—or, to put it the other way around, God is revealed in Christ. This christological (re)definition of God is paradigm-shattering in its implications, particularly when we hold this point in close conjunction with our first observation above: God is the one God of Israel, *and* Jesus Christ is Lord. In Christ, who became a curse for us and died for us, the one God of Israel was at the same time rescuing us and revealing himself (on the latter point, see especially Bauckham 1998, 45–79) in a shocking but definitive new way, as the one whose sacrificial love justifies the ungodly.

Third, when we place alongside this picture the passages in which Paul speaks of the Spirit of God almost interchangeably with Christ (especially

Rom 8:9–11), we can hardly avoid the conclusion that Paul's understanding of God is proto-trinitarian. Paul of course did not know the doctrinal formulae worked out in the fourth-century church's theological reflection about the one God in three persons, but his prayers, praises, and narratives about that God point to the same complex reality with which the ecumenical councils later grappled. That is why Francis Watson can rightly speak of "the radical trini-tarian logic already present in the God-language of the Pauline texts" (Wat-son 2000, 123; cf. Rowe 2000, 170–73). In an important discussion of God and 2 Corinthians, Frances Young and David F. Ford have explained how this can be so: A person does not need to know theoretical grammatical constructs in order to speak grammatically. In fact, it is the reverse: "Grammar" is devel-oped to explain the linguistic practices of those who speak a complex language with unreflective fluency. In the same way, the later doctrine of the Trinity is an attempt to describe and analyze the way in which Jesus Christ and the Spirit had "become intrinsic to Paul's way of referring to God." As Young and Ford put it, Paul's gospel "exerted a pressure on his talk of God which he himself did not analyze but which is consonant with a differentiation and relationality in God" (Young and Ford 1987, 256–57). As we have seen, these observations about 2 Corinthians hold true for Galatians and Romans as well.

Fourth, the Western tradition's concentration on salvation as a quasi-legal acquittal from condemnation captures only a sliver of Paul's discourse about God. Especially in Galatians, Paul focuses more strongly on God's act of lib-erating us from bondage than on the remission of sins. While forensic imagery is certainly prominent in several important passages in Romans (e.g., 2:1–16; 3:21–31; 8:31–34), it hardly encompasses the full range of Paul's portrayal of God's action; indeed, after chapter 4 the forensic language recedes into the background, and Paul can summarize his proclamation in the letter's climac-tic peroration (15:7–13) without using "justification" language at all. (Note that the same is true of Gal 6:11–18.) To be sure, God's final judgment is a cru-cial part of the story, but Paul's God is far more than a judge. God is also the one who reaches out for us ("all day long I have held out my hands" [Rom 10:21, quoting Isa 65:2]), suffers in order to save his people, and adopts us as his children.

Finally, above all, God is a God who can be trusted. God's deep fidelity to his own word ensures the persistence of his mercy. Paul memorably phrases the argument: "What if some were unfaithful? Will their faithlessness nullify the faithfulness of God? By no means!" (Rom 3:3–4a). That is why, with Paul, we can affirm that "the sufferings of the present time are not worth compar-ing with the glory about to be revealed" (Rom 8:18). Our longing for freedom from bondage to decay will be answered by a God who will not abandon the creation, a God who has raised Jesus from the dead and will bring about the new creation, the redemption of our bodies. The ultimate revelation of God's glory—a glory that embraces us—is sure, for from him and through him and to him are all things.

SELECT BIBLIOGRAPHY

Achtemeier, Paul. 1985. *Romans.* Interpretation. Atlanta: John Knox.
Baker, Mark D. 1999. *Religious No More: Building Communities of Grace and Freedom.* Downer's Grove, Ill.: InterVarsity.
Bassler, Jouette M. 1982. *Divine Impartiality: Paul and a Theological Axiom.* Society of Biblical Literature Dissertation Series 59. Chico, Calif.: Scholars Press.
———, ed. 1991. *Thessalonians, Philippians, Galatians, Philemon.* Vol. 1 of *Pauline Theology.* Minneapolis: Fortress.
Bauckham, Richard. 1998. *God Crucified: Monotheism and Christology in the New Testament.* Grand Rapids: Eerdmans.
Dahl, Nils A. 1991. *Jesus the Christ: The Historical Origins of Christological Doctrine.* Edited by Donald H. Juel. Minneapolis: Fortress.
Donfried, Karl P., ed. 1991. *The Romans Debate.* Rev. ed. Peabody, Mass.: Hendrickson.
Dunn, James D. G. 1988. *Romans.* 2 vols. Word Biblical Commentary. Dallas: Word.
———. 1998. *The Theology of Paul the Apostle.* Grand Rapids: Eerdmans.
Fitzmyer, Joseph A. 1993. *Romans.* Anchor Bible 33. New York: Doubleday.
Guthrie, Donald, and Ralph P. Martin. 1993. "God." Pages 354–69 in *Dictionary of Paul and His Letters.* Edited by Gerald F. Hawthorne et al. Downers Grove, Ill.: InterVarsity.
Hay, David M., and E. Elizabeth Johnson, eds. 1995. *Romans.* Vol. 3 of *Pauline Theology.* Minneapolis: Fortress.
Hays, Richard B. 1989. *Echoes of Scripture in the Letters of Paul.* New Haven and London: Yale University Press.
———. 1992. "Justification." Pages 1129–33 in *The Anchor Bible Dictionary.* Vol. 3. Edited by David Noel Freedman. New York: Doubleday.
———. 1999. "The Conversion of the Imagination: Scripture and Eschatology in Corinthians." *New Testament Studies* 45: 391–412.
———. 2000. "The Letter to the Galatians." Pages 181–348 in vol. 11 of *The New Interpreter's Bible.* Edited by Leander E. Keck. Nashville: Abingdon.
———. 2001. *The Faith of Jesus Christ: The Narrative Substructure of Galatians 3:1–4:11.* 2d ed. Grand Rapids: Eerdmans.
Hurtado, Larry W. 1998. *One God, One Lord: Early Christian Devotion and Ancient Jewish Monotheism.* 2d ed. Edinburgh: T. & T. Clark.
Keesmaat, Sylvia. 1999. *Paul and His Story: (Re)Interpreting the Exodus Tradition.* Journal for the Study of the New Testament: Supplement Series 181. Sheffield: Sheffield Academic Press.
Koch, Dietrich-Alex. 1986. *Die Schrift als Zeuge des Evangeliums: Untersuchungen zur Verwendung und zum Verständnis der Schrift bei Paulus.* Beiträge zur historischen Theologie 69. Tübingen: Mohr (Siebeck).
Kuck, David. 1994. "Each Will Bear His Own Burden: Paul's Creative Use of an Apocalyptic Motif." *New Testament Studies* 45: 289–97.
Martyn, J. Louis. 1997. *Galatians.* Anchor Bible 33A. New York: Doubleday.
Matera, Frank J. 1992. *Galatians.* Sacra Pagina 9. Collegeville, Minn.: Liturgical Press.

Moxnes, Halvor. 1980. *Theology in Conflict: Studies in Paul's Understanding of God in Romans*. Novum Testamentum Supplements 53. Leiden: Brill.

Richardson, Neil. 1994. *Paul's Language about God*. Journal for the Study of the New Testament: Supplement Series 99. Sheffield: Sheffield Academic Press.

Rowe, C. Kavin. 2000. "Romans 10:13: What Is the Name of the Lord?" *Horizons in Biblical Theology* 22: 135–73.

Thompson, Marianne Meye. 2000. *The Promise of the Father: Jesus and God in the New Testament*. Louisville, Ky.: Westminster John Knox.

Watson, Francis. 2000. "The Triune Divine Identity: Reflections on Pauline God-language, in Disagreement with James D. G. Dunn." *Journal for the Study of the New Testament* 80: 99–124.

Wright, N. T. 1991. *The Climax of the Covenant: Christ and the Law in Pauline Theology*. Edinburgh: T. & T. Clark.

Young, Frances, and David F. Ford. 1987. *Meaning and Truth in 2 Corinthians*. Grand Rapids: Eerdmans.

9

God's Power in Human Weakness

Paul Teaches the Corinthians about God

PHEME PERKINS

Most theology courses begin by asking what makes it possible to believe in God. Does God really act to change the material world, or is God an inner, psychological reality that inspires people to lead extraordinary lives of virtue and self-sacrifice? So my students are often surprised that their textbook on Paul's theology (Dunn 1998) only devotes fifty of over seven hundred pages to the nature of God. Of course, a check of the index shows that God will be discussed later in sections on the image of God, Christology, Israel, divine judgment, and the like. Other recent books on 1 and 2 Corinthians have no entry at all for God in the index (Horsley 1998; Murphy-O'Connor 1991). That does not mean that it is possible to describe Paul's theology in these epistles without referring to statements that Paul makes about God. Only a few sections lack any reference to God (Dunn 1998, 28). It is possible to argue that the statements Paul makes about God are axioms that he takes for granted in order to talk about something more pressing, such as what it means to live an authentic human life (Bultmann 1969), how salvation occurs in Christ through the cross (Murphy-O'Connor 1991), or how belief in Christ challenged the established, oppressive powers of the Roman Empire (Horsley 1998). So it is not surprising that New Testament scholarship is sometimes charged with neglecting the foundational theological question: What does Scripture have to say about God? (Dahl 1991).

Since no one in the ancient world doubted the existence of divine powers who both maintained order in the world and could intervene for or against human beings, New Testament writers do not answer modern doubts about God directly. They lived in cities full of gods and goddesses. Jews were thought rather strange, even stubbornly irrational in their devotion to a single God. Pagan critics could accuse Jews of being atheistic because they would not worship the gods who brought the empire its prosperity (Josephus, *Against Apion* 2.167). Jews replied that God is creator of all things and can be known through his works (Dunn 1998, 31, 39–41). So the task facing the early Christians was not whether persons should believe in God but which God (or gods) and why? It is hardly surprising, then, that the New Testament highlights what God has done in Christ and its significance for the present and future of those who entrust their lives to this God. Christians had to distinguish their understanding about God's actions from those of fellow Jews. No wonder, then, that Christ as the key to God's salvation for humanity stands in the forefront of any discussion.

Paul makes basic statements about God in the Corinthian letters that are completely in accord with Jewish belief (Dunn 1998, 30–44). God is the creator of all things and is at work throughout that creation (1 Cor 8:6; 10:26; 11:12; 12:6; 15:28; 2 Cor 5:18). God is one (1 Cor 8:4, 6). There are no other gods (1 Cor 10:20). God is the source of peace and blessing for all who believe in God (1 Cor 1:3; 7:15; 14:33; 2 Cor 1:2; 13:11, 13). People should give God praise and thanksgiving (1 Cor 1:4; 14:18; 2 Cor 1:3; 2:14a; 4:15; 6:1; 8:16; 9:11, 13, 15; 13:7). God is faithful (1 Cor 1:9). God's wisdom and power are greater than anything human beings can conceive (1 Cor 1:19-21; 3:19). God will judge all humanity (1 Cor 5:13; 2 Cor 4:2). God is opposed to immoral and unjust conduct (1 Cor 6:9; 2 Cor 6:4, 7, 16). People must keep commands given by God (1 Cor 7:19). God cannot be deceived because God knows what is in the depths of a person (1 Cor 14:25; 2 Cor 11:11, 31).

Paul asserts that this God called him to preach belief in Christ among the Gentiles. This would have required a major shift in understanding God's plan of salvation for Israel (Donaldson 1997, 81–106). However, that topic does not surface in the Corinthian letters. Here we find Paul dealing with a number of concrete religious problems that sprung up in a church of Gentiles. Since one issue concerns how Christians should relate to the sacrificial meat and banquets connected with pagan gods (1 Cor 8–10), Paul may be repeating fundamental axioms about God to fix these beliefs in their minds. However, Paul also moves beyond these axiomatic statements. At several points, he challenges the Corinthians to change their understanding of God. They readily associated God with power and sought forms of religious experience by which individuals were granted divine empowerment. Evidence of the Spirit in Paul's evangelization played a crucial role in their conversion (1 Cor 2:4; Horsley 1998, 29–38). In 1 Corinthians, Paul addresses a number of situations in which the competitive individualism of religious experience in Corinth was tearing apart the fabric of the community. In 2 Corinthians, Paul responds to sustained, severe attacks against his personal authority as an apostle. The letter as we have it is a composite. Chapters 8 and 9 serve as an appeal for the collection Paul is taking up to aid poor Christians in Jerusalem. Chapters 1–7 defend Paul's missionary activity in the context of a return to friendly relationships between the apostle and the community. Chapters 10–13 contain an angry tirade against outsiders, false apostles who once again threaten to turn the Corinthians against Paul (Furnish 1984, 29–54).

Since Paul's letters often deal with particular problems in a given church, scholars recognize that no single letter gives a full picture of the apostle's views. One approach is to seek theological principles and arguments that underlie the arguments peculiar to a given letter. What is the core from which Paul's other theological insights are generated? Professor Achtemeier, whom we are pleased to honor in this volume, has contributed to this discussion with considerable insight. In order to qualify as the core of Paul's theology, Achtemeier argues, a topic must not only occur frequently in Paul's letters but must take the same conceptual form when it does (Achtemeier 1996, 136–37). Consequently, he discards such common themes as justification, the cross, and God's end-time victory, and argues for the conviction that "God raised Jesus from the dead" (1 Cor 7:14; 15:14–20; 2 Cor 1:9; 4:14) as the core of Paul's theology (Achtemeier 1996, 140–45). This affirmation that "God raised Jesus from the dead" cannot be divorced from the cross without risking a theology focused only on believers as recipients of divine power that overwhelms the constraints of this world. At every turn, 1 Corinthians addresses problems that have arisen as a result of inflated views of spiritual perfection. Fee describes the Corinthian view as "spiritualized eschatology" (Fee 1987, 12). It has even led to denial of the future eschatological hope for bodily resurrection. Therefore, resurrection without the cross is an ambiguous sign of divine power. In this essay, we will not examine every statement Paul makes about God in 1 and 2 Corinthians. Instead, we will focus on Paul's use of the cross and resurrection as the key to a new revelation about God.

Almost 50 percent of the references to God in 1 Corinthians appear in the first four chapters (Furnish 1999, 28), many of them in emphatic grammatical expressions (Richardson 1994, 107). Here Paul opposes the mystery of the cross to Corinthians who boast in their spiritual superiority to others. References to God in 2 Corinthians focus on the apostle. God's resurrecting power enables him to endure life-threatening persecution (2 Cor 1:9; 4:14) and the hostile accusations of persons at Corinth (2 Cor 1:20–21). Paul treats his entire ministry as an apostle as evidence for the power of God at work in weakness (Richardson 1994, 135; Thiselton 2000, 65–66). Therefore, I propose to treat Paul's references to God in the Corinthian correspondence as an ongoing problem of "code-switching," whereby he teaches the Corinthians how to understand God's power in light of the cross and resurrection. The problem is not in their recognition of certain theological tropes about God, Christ, and salvation. The problem is an inability to see that what that familiar language means has been radically changed in light of the cross. Their false reading of God's power leads the Corinthians to erroneous conclusions about themselves and apostolic ministry (Keck 1996).

Rather than lump the entire correspondence together, we will treat the various elements separately. At least two letters to Corinth were never preserved: a letter antecedent to 1 Corinthians (mentioned in 1 Cor 5:9) and a letter that caused the Corinthians grief, which was written after 1 Corinthians and a disastrous visit to Corinth (2 Cor 7:9). The surviving letters allow us to observe the apostle's use of this theological motif in diverse situations over a year (Thrall 1994, 77) or two (Furnish 1984, 54–55), from the spring of 54 C.E. until the winter of 55/56, which he spent in Corinth writing Romans, preparing to take the collection to Jerusalem and journey from Jerusalem west through Rome to Spain (Rom 15:24–28; Murphy-O'Connor 1996, 278–323). Paul had spent a year and a half establishing the church in 50/51 C.E. It is easy to see a growing disappointment with the community's failure to perceive what is at stake in Paul's preaching some five years later.

UNDERSTANDING GOD ANEW: 1 CORINTHIANS

If Paul's theological understanding of God's power in weakness remained difficult for the Corinthians to grasp, not everything that he says about God falls under that rubric. There is a shared way of speaking about and to God that is familiar and not at issue. God appears in formulas of greeting, blessing, and prayer as we have noted. The Corinthians must have learned another conviction about God from their own conversion: God is the one who called them from their former idolatry to faith (1:4, 24, 26; 7:17). The Corinthians would not be surprised by Paul's claim that God had sent him for the purpose of bringing people into an association centered on belief in Christ (1:1; 2:1–5; 12:28). Cult associations in honor of foreign deities were commonly introduced into ancient cities by persons said to be sent by the god in question. Therefore, God is solely responsible for the growth of the church in Corinth (3:6–7; 12:18, 24, 28). Paul and his associates can claim to be "fellow workers" with God, who is the real power at work in bringing the church into being (3:9). Standard phrases such as "church of God" (1:2; 10:32; 11:16, 22; 15:9) serve as familiar tags to designate the community of believers. In turning away from their former belief in gods and goddesses, the Corinthians also agreed that God is the creator whose power extends throughout the universe (8:4–6; 10:26; 12:6; 15:28).

These axioms are so firmly established across the spectrum of religious belief at the time that hardly anyone would be surprised at such statements.

Other affirmations are rooted in the religious traditions of Judaism. Non-Jews could take offense at the monotheistic attack on idolatry as we have seen. Conversion required that Gentiles break off a lifetime of complex relationships—personal, social, and civic—that centered on worship of the gods. First Corinthians 8–10 shows that the Corinthians had various difficulties in drawing this line (Fee 1987, 357–92, 441–91; Horsley 1998, 116–51; Thiselton 2000, 608–786). Christians in Asian and African countries today often find themselves in similar situations. How far can their belief in God be stretched to accommodate inherited religious traditions such as veneration of ancestors or New Year celebrations? In 1 Corinthians 8–10 Paul addresses the claim that as long as Christians realize that such rites are not addressed to a real divinity, they can do whatever they wish. Since this discussion involves the fundamental confession that God is one, we will consider it before turning to God's power as revealed in the cross and resurrection. Libations, feasts, sacrifices, even the decoration of civic space and private homes, all pointed to gods and goddesses. Does Paul believe in them? No. But he concedes the reality they have in peoples' lives with the concession that there are "so-called" deities around (1 Cor 8:5), though not for believers (v. 6a). He warns the Corinthians against thinking it is permissible to attend the banquets that followed sacrifices in a temple with a reference to the offense caused to God if one shared sacrifices offered to demons (10:19–21). Since the Lord's Supper joins believers together in the body of Christ, feasting in the temple of a god or goddess offends against the new reality. One is pretending to have a "fellowship" with persons not part of the new covenant in Christ's body and blood (11:24–25). Such a turn away from God constitutes idolatry even if the Christian does not believe in the reality of the idol in whose honor the meal is celebrated. God may inflict the same judgment on idolatrous Christians as on the Israelites in the wilderness (10:22; Fee 1987, 464–75).

Paul in no way concedes that other gods and goddesses actually exist. He makes these comments as part of the pastoral imperative facing him in Corinth (Dunn 1998, 36–37). The issues do not require an explanation of the beliefs and practices of the majority in the ancient city who were neither Jews nor Christians. Paul is concerned with divisions that have arisen within the church. His ultimate goal is to draw the divided parties back together in common thanksgiving to God even if they differ over what it is permissible to eat (10:30–11:1; Murphy-O'Connor 1978). We may leave reconstruction of the various social pressures and conflicts to the commentaries. Paul's teaching on God comes to the fore in 8:1–6. Paul opens by citing what appears to be a slogan used by one group: "all of us possess knowledge" (v. 1a). He goes on to correct how such persons view their knowledge before revealing the division between Christians: "It is not everyone, however, who has this knowledge"

(v. 7a). Yet all Christians are presumed to agree with the creedal formula, "there is no God, but one" (v. 4b) and "one God, the Father, from whom are all things . . . and one Lord, Jesus Christ, through whom are all things" (v. 6).

The Corinthians are not divided over this theological axiom but over the practical conclusion some have drawn from it. If idols have no reality, then meat that has been offered to them is no different from other meat sold in the market. Whether or not Christians eat meat sold from such sacrifices is indifferent (8:8). Paul agrees in principle. However, he immediately clarifies the norm that should determine Christian action: the love they should recognize in God's call (v. 3; Thiselton 2000, 627). Love enters the discussion because other Christians experience the accusations of a pained consciousness as though they had worshiped those so-called gods and lords (v. 7). Even observing a fellow believer eating such food could cause the "weak" to lose their faith (v. 10). Paul recognizes that repeating theological axioms will not ease a troubled conscience. He never suggests that compelling social motives, whether family ties or relationships with a patron, require that Christians eat such food. So the only necessity is imposed by the danger of causing fellow-believers to lose faith. Unlike the Greco-Roman tolerant universalism, belief is a matter of life or death. Thus, Paul speaks dramatically about the danger of destroying another Christian (v. 11).

Paul requires that those whose theological insight fosters eating idol food without qualms give up the practice when another's faith is threatened (v. 13). He does not base this conclusion on the earlier statements about God. Instead he turns to the cross (vv. 11–12), which for Paul is the uniquely Christian revelation of God's love for humanity. Richardson (1994, 304) describes this shift as characteristically Pauline. Language about God is amplified by that about Christ. Because believers are identified as "body of Christ" in their communal life or as "in Christ," Paul's conclusion that sinning against a fellow Christian is simultaneously against Christ (v. 12) follows easily (Thiselton 2000, 653–56). This example shows how readily Paul moves from God to Christology, soteriology, and ecclesiology.

The creedal formula in 1 Cor 8:6 presents another issue concerning the confession that God is one. Do the parallels in the second half derived from Jesus as "one Lord" show an emerging Trinitarianism? The formula "all things *from whom . . . through whom . . .*" has its parallels in Hellenistic philosophical theology and its appropriation by Jewish authors such as Philo of Alexandria. The divine origin (God), which is the source of all that exists, operates through a mediating power (Wisdom). Jewish monotheism has not been breeched by identifying Christ with Wisdom (Horsley 1998, 119–20; based on Horsley 1978a). From the other side, Gordon Fee argues that an incipient Trinitarianism can be discerned in Paul's descriptions of the roles of Father, Son, and

Spirit. "One God" and "one Lord" preserve the personal identities of Father and Son while retaining the monotheistic confession. Therefore, Fee concludes, "The second clause places the work of Christ, and our relationship to him, in the closest kind of relationship to God. Although Paul does not here call Christ God, the formula is so constructed that only the most obdurate would deny its Trinitarian implications" (Fee 1987, 375).

However, many scholars remain unpersuaded by this argument. Furnish points out that the two-part formula of 1 Cor 1:3 is more characteristic of Paul. It highlights the soteriological benefits received from God and Christ. Paul uses formulae that suggest a subordination of Christ to God. The eschatological importance of this subordination becomes evident in the end-time return of all things to God, in 1 Cor 15:24–28. As believers belong to Christ, so Christ belongs to God (3:23). As Adam is head of his wife, Eve, so God is head of Christ (11:3). Christ crucified is the revelation of God's saving power. Paul never refers to the Spirit as the source of revelation or revealer per se. Therefore, the basic concepts necessary for later Trinitarian theology are absent (Furnish 1998, 96). The primary focus of Paul's second clause derives from the experience of salvation, not from consideration of the powers of God in creation but the salvation that draws humanity back to God (Thiselton 2000, 636–38).

Though idol food may be an indifferent matter as long as one's eating does not cause another to lose faith, participation in the actual banquets that follow a sacrifice is not (10:1–22). Paul appeals to episodes in Exodus and Numbers to warn that such conduct invites divine retribution (v. 5). The notion that a deity would attack those who violate the sanctity of his or her shrine, cult, or devotees would not have been foreign to the Corinthians. Paul had introduced his converts to the Jewish apocalyptic vision of God's end-time judgment (5:13). When he employs the image of divine retribution for those who fail to preserve the holiness of the temple, that is, the believer or the community as the locus of God's Spirit (3:16–17; 6:19), Paul may be referring to an end-time condemnation of Christians. However, his comment on the consequences of profaning the body of Christ by shaming lowly believers at the Lord's Supper (11:29–31) suggests more immediate forms of retribution (Thiselton 2000, 896–98). Both apostolic reprimand and divine retribution may serve to preserve the community from condemnation at the judgment. Warnings that immoral persons will not inherit God's kingdom use established Christian language about the end-time division between God's elect and the wicked (6:9–11; 15:50).

These examples invite Paul's audience to construe divine power in familiar patterns. God uses it to benefit those who are pleasing to the deity and to punish offenders. When Paul warns that the kingdom or reign of God consists not in word but in power (4:20–21), he appears to threaten those whose inflated view of their own religious status makes them resistant to correction. The power in question does not belong to the apostle, but to the God he serves (pace Horsley 1998, 77, who accuses Paul of arrogant authoritarianism). Rather than viewing this reference to power as a threat of divine judgment backing up the apostle, some exegetes conclude that the elliptical phrase refers to the Corinthians. When Paul arrives, they had better have deeds to match their inflated claims (Thiselton 2000, 377). In either case, such remarks confirm the culturally pervasive view of divine power. God may use it directly to bless or punish, or may enable a divinely chosen messenger to employ that power against God's enemies. As we shall see, attacks on the apostle in 2 Corinthians exploit Paul's perceived weaknesses as evidence against his apostolic authority.

Paul does not accept this view of God's power as the truth revealed by the gospel, however. As we have suggested, the cross and resurrection lead Paul to a new understanding of how God's power can be effective in weakness. His first extended theological section (1 Cor 1:18–2:16) contains twenty-five references to God, almost 25 percent of the total in the letter. The cross demonstrates that human ideas of wisdom and divine power are false (Furnish 1998, 28–29). Scholars disagree over the specific nature and cause of the conflicts or divisions that cropped up in Corinth, some suggesting that a more sophisticated preaching by the Alexandrian-educated Apollos could have been a key factor (see Horsley 1998, 33–47). A few partisans may have infected the whole church with an anti-Paul sentiment by charging that Paul had been preaching a gospel for the immature. They considered themselves "spiritual" or "mature" Christians, able to lead others to a higher wisdom. They may have backed up their claims by asserting that such spiritual gifts as speaking in tongues demonstrated a spiritual endowment superior to the apostle's (14:37; Fee 1987, 10–11). Whatever the causes of the disorder Paul seeks to correct, he has to challenge culturally accepted behavior patterns. Competition for individual superiority over others, partisanship, interest in wisdom (whether philosophic or conveyed through initiation in a religious cult), and displays of rhetorical skill were all desired cultural achievements among persons with sufficient wealth and leisure to aspire to them. Others may be drawn into the competition between their respective patrons. Paul opens by chiding the Corinthians for just such divisions (1:10–17).

Paul crafts an argument that sets the saving power of God in the cross over against the wisdom, religious enlightenment, and rhetorical skill valued in Corinth (1:18–19). The axiom that God's wisdom and power is greater than anything humans can devise would not be considered unusual, as Paul's citation of Isa 29:14 in verse 19 indicates. However, to invoke the cross as evidence of divine power does throw down the gauntlet to those who expect God's power to enhance their status in human terms (Thiselton 2000, 165–79). So Paul introduces the category of folly, weakness, low birth, even nothingness, to describe the human perspective on those persons whom God has called to salvation. By working in such persons, God puts the well-born, wise, and powerful to shame (1:25–28). The view that God's saving power would be exercised in overthrowing the wisdom and power of persons who oppress God's elect forms a staple of Jewish apocalyptic, as commentators have observed. But in this instance, Paul is not speaking to the Corinthians as God's faithful ones, suffering and oppressed by persons or powers hostile to God. Paul is speaking to persons most of whom were of no account when God called them (v. 26). The cross indicates that God did not come to save by swapping the "have nots" for those who are powerful in human terms. Rather, God's creative power is such that God can give life and existence to what "is not" (v. 28). Therefore, the only appropriate response is for all to praise God for gifts received (vv. 29–31; Thiselton 2000, 183–91).

Playing on the register of social status, power, and influence, Paul uses the description of God's election of those who are nothing in human terms to put the Corinthians firmly in their place. How such a rebuke would be received depends upon the status of the speaker relative to his audience. Paul rejects what appear to be the self-designations of some of the Corinthians, "the perfect" (2:6) or "spiritual persons" (2:13, 15; 3:1). They are not mature adults but mere infants (3:1–2). Paul sets himself above the immature Corinthians by insisting that his teaching does not derive from human reasoning or socially prized traits such as rhetorical skill. He has the wisdom that comes from God and the Spirit (2:12–13). Paul even appears to reject what human beings might consider "spirituality" (Thiselton 2000, 225). The citation of Jer 9:23 (LXX) in 1 Cor 1:31b, which concludes the first section of this argument, returns when Paul defends against an explicit attack on his apostleship in 2 Cor 10:17. In addition to the explicit citation, which Paul has shortened to boasting "in the Lord," other elements in the context provide verbal links to the language of 1 Cor 1:18–31. Jeremiah 9:22 (LXX) warns the wise, the strong, and the rich against boasting in their respective endowments. Paul addresses the "wise" (*sophoi*) and the strong (*ischyra*), but appears to have substituted "well-born" (*eugeneis*) for "the rich" (vv. 26–27), perhaps indicating that no one in his audience belongs to that stratum of society. Those who peddled rhetorical wisdom in the ancient cities claimed that their wisdom made them "wise, powerful, and well-born" so that the Corinthians might claim these attributes on the basis of their Christian wisdom (Fee 1987, 80). Jeremiah 9:24 instructs such persons in their proper boast: "understand and know me, that I am the LORD; I act with steadfast love, justice, and righteousness in the earth, for in these things I delight, says the LORD." Thus, Paul's instruction concerning the nature of God in this section reverts back to a section of Scripture that Paul may have introduced in his preaching at Corinth.

First Corinthians 2:1–5 contrasts the style of Paul's preaching and ministry with that of the purveyors of rhetorical wisdom, which he describes as "lofty words or wisdom" (*hyperochēn logou ē sophias*). In 1:18, Paul summarized the topic of his preaching as "the message of the cross." Here he introduces another phrase: "mystery of God" (2:1). Ordinarily Paul uses the Greek word for "mystery" in accord with the Semitic term *raz* that it translates. The Essene commentary on Habakkuk explains that the prophet did not know when or how his words reflected the end-time actions of God. God revealed "all the mysteries of the words of His servants the prophets" (1QpHab 7:1–8) to the sect's founder (Bockmuehl 1997, 46–47). This meaning fits Paul's claim that the cross discloses what God's plan of salvation is. The two phrases "word of the cross" and "mystery of God" are functionally equivalent in the apostle's theology. Paul will develop an argument in 2:6–16 in support of the claim that he did reveal the "mystery" to those able to grasp it. The "mystery" is not in fact some deeper, hidden form of Christian wisdom. It is the message of God's saving power through the death of Jesus on the cross, the same gospel Paul has preached all along (Thiselton 2000, 241–57).

A convoluted irony runs through this argument as Paul adopts terms that were being bandied about among the Corinthians. They apparently understood phrases such as "mystery of God" and "preeminence of wisdom" as references to a higher wisdom that could be taught to an elite. Their use of "mystery" may have been closer to Philo of Alexandria's description of allegorical interpretation of Scripture. Using terminology from religious cult initiation, Philo speaks of the allegorical meaning as "the greater mysteries" (*Somn.* 1.164). Insight into these mysteries also facilitates the soul's approach to the essence of God. Paul parodies the Corinthians' interest in such a vision of God by remarking that only the Spirit penetrates the "depths" of God (1 Cor 2:10; Thiselton 2000, 257). Philo infers that the Egyptian Essenes, the Therapeutae (*Contempl.* 28), are engaged in the same religious quest to move the soul out of its attachment to the material world toward the divine (Bockmuehl 1997, 76–78). Paul insists that he is a "steward of God's mysteries" (4:1). Since the mystery in question focuses on the cross, Paul argues that his ministry in Corinth must represent the power of God acting through what is weak and of no account. His presentation of the gospel was not rhetorically powerful. Instead, signs of the Spirit at work accompanied the conversion of the Corinthians (2:4). The antithesis, a faith based on human wisdom over against a faith based on the power of God (v. 5), pries apart two values that the Corinthians saw combined in their devotion to wisdom and spiritual gifts. By pursuing wisdom as a source of spiritual perfection, some Corinthians are losing the actual wisdom of God (Fee 1987, 99).

In part, this division over how God is known depends upon divergent readings of who God is shown to be in Scripture, as Paul's use of Jer 9:23 and Isa

64:4 (2:9) suggests. In part, it stems from a very different understanding of God's relationship to the world. The platonizing allegories of Philo of Alexandria presume that God, the creator, is the transcendent source of all being, order, and goodness. The soul aspires to know this source and, in so doing, its own likeness to the divine. Paul's vision of God is that of a creator dynamically engaged with humankind in the process of bringing the present evil age to its conclusion. The cross and resurrection of Jesus are the central acts in that drama, which reflects God's eternal plan of salvation (2:7). Paul does not think about God apart from these convictions concerning what God has revealed on the cross and is doing in the present to bring this story of salvation to its conclusion.

Since God's plan is hidden or folly to those with knowledge and power in the present age, it must be revealed by God. Paul states explicitly that the Spirit made it known to the apostles (2:10–13; 4:1; 13:2; Bockmuehl 1997, 164–65). The "we" who possess the "mind of Christ" (2:16) and hence are recipients of proper knowledge about God (Isa 40:13 LXX) refers to the apostle and those with the spiritual maturity to recognize God's wisdom in the "word of the cross." So far the Corinthians fail the test of their own sloganizing (3:1–5; Thiselton 2000, 271–86). Paul proceeds to depict the growth of the church as God's activity in which the various apostles have roles assigned them by God (3:4–23). Once again readers are reminded to put aside human honor and wisdom for the foolishness that comes from God (3:18–21). Paul makes the point that all things are ordered to God by adapting a Corinthian slogan, "All things belong to the wise" (see v. 22), so that all believers are "of Christ" who is "of God" (v. 23). The word "God" concludes the argument in chapter 3, underlining the fact that God's will and judgment determine all things (Richardson 1994, 116).

Paul indicates that he intends to correct the way in which the Corinthians view God's apostles (4:1–5, 14–15, 16–21). As the founder of the community in Corinth, Paul is responsible for the integrity of their faith, which has been compromised by this new preoccupation with religious wisdom. Paul mocks the pretensions of "the wise" to exaltation over others as "filled, wealthy, ruling" (v. 8). Were that true, the apostle should share those gifts most of all. Instead, God expects his apostles to exhibit the weakness of the crucified. They are the antitype to those advocates of sophisticated wisdom prized by the Corinthians (4:10). Like captives in an emperor's triumphal parade, they are put on display like those doomed to death in the arena (4:9; Thiselton 2000, 360). What the Corinthians may think about religious teachers who are subject to such humiliation is irrelevant. Paul knows that he will have to answer to the Lord at the judgment (4:5). In that context, Paul reminds the Corinthians of another fundamental axiom: God knows all the secrets of the human heart and judges each person accordingly (Thiselton 2000, 342).

The Corinthian focus on divine power as the source of self-exaltation in their present experience may have contributed to other communal and moral lapses that Paul addresses. He reminds them that the final judgment is near. The preoccupation with God as the source of religious power available to believers apparently led the Corinthians to neglect the fact that God's plan of salvation was not yet complete. Christians live in the end of days (7:29; 10:11; Dunn 1998, 41). First Corinthians opened with the cross. It concludes with the resurrection, whose truth is also denied or distorted in Corinth (15:12). We are not concerned with the various reconstructions of what was being challenged in Corinth or of Paul's reply (see Holleman 1996). Paul uses "who raised Christ from the dead" as a divine epithet. It appears in moral condemnation of those who think sex with prostitutes is indifferent. The body shares an eschatological destiny that God has already initiated with the resurrection of Jesus (6:14). That "God raised Jesus" is given with the creed Paul transmitted to the Corinthians as tradition (15:3–5). To compromise that message by denying God's power to provide believers with a share in that bodily resurrection would make the claim that God raised Jesus a lie (15:15).

What Paul had not said in the earlier discussion of the cross becomes explicit in 1 Cor 15:16–20: The folly and scandal of the cross only stand as evidence of God's transforming power because God raised Jesus from the dead (Thiselton 2000, 1171). The new theological insight about God's saving power in 1 Corinthians 15 emerges with the apocalyptic schema that stretches from the resurrection of Christ to the end-time resurrection of God's elect. When the final victory over death is won, all things will be returned to their creator (15:23–28; Holleman 1996, 49–65). The divine necessity with which Christ rules until handing all things over to God (v. 25) indicates that the end-time victory occurs as a further act of God's power (Thiselton 2000, 1233–35). However, Paul does not conclude that the "end" is a monistic return of all things into the divine substance from which they emerged as in the cyclic conflagrations of Stoic cosmology. The resurrection bodies God creates from the old, decayed seed for believers guarantees their individuality in the world that exists after the end time. Similarly, the fact that Christ returns all things to the Father does not imply that confessing Christ as Lord will no longer be appropriate (Thiselton 2000, 1231; see p. 1238 on the later history of these texts in the Arian controversy). Weakness reflects the transient condition of a world marked by sin and death (vv. 42–43a; Thiselton 2000, 1274).

Undoubtedly the Corinthians would agree with the abstract statement that God's power enables believers to overcome sin and mortality. They appear to have interpreted various forms of religious experience as evidence that God has already bestowed such gifts on members of the community. For Paul, God's power in this world remains configured according to the pattern established by the cross. The Corinthians are denying the centrality of the cross and resurrection for bringing this age to its end (Thiselton 2000, 1274).

THE GOD OF ALL CONSOLATION:
2 CORINTHIANS 1–8

Second Corinthians alludes to a number of events that had soured relations between Paul and the Corinthians since the dispatch of 1 Corinthians. However, many of the particular items addressed in 1 Corinthians disappear from the scene. So there is no reason to understand 2 Corinthians as reinforcing those earlier arguments (Furnish 1984, 27–28; Sampley 2000, 9–11). Other missionaries, with impressive letters of recommendation, have fueled anti-Paul sentiments in the community (2 Cor 3:1–3). Someone in the Corinthian church either insulted and publicly humiliated the apostle during a visit to Corinth (2:5–11; 7:9–11; Furnish 1984, 160–68), or may have committed an actual crime against him (perhaps stealing funds from the collection, so Thrall 1994, 68–69). Paul dispatched a "letter of tears" (2:1–4), which took the Corinthians to task in sharp tones (Sampley 2000, 50). Thanks to God's effective intervention, the rebuke had a salutary effect. The community disciplined the offender (2:5–11) and sought to restore its previous relationships with the apostle (7:5–13). At this point, Paul picks up an epithet for God introduced in the opening blessing. God is the one who comforts the afflicted or downhearted (1:3–11; 7:6). Paul repeatedly uses the theme of God as comforter in these sections: ten times in 1:3–11 and five in 7:5–16 (Sampley 2000, 109). Titus has brought Paul this good news from Corinth. In replying, Paul assimilates the anxiety, despair, and grief over the situation in Corinth to the physical sufferings he has undergone during an imprisonment in Asia (1:8–11; Furnish 1984, 122–24). Both serve as reminders that God's saving power can bring life to those who are near death. Paul does not see this consolation as a personal reward from God. He is rescued for the sake of others, who will also see the sufferings of Christ enacted through the apostle (1:4–5; Thrall 1994, 98–110).

Between these two sections that focus on God as the one who provides strength and comfort to the suffering apostle, Paul defends his ministry (1:12–22; 2:14–7:4). He uses the axiom "God is faithful" (1:18) and the reference to God's promises (v. 20) as oath formulae to defend his integrity despite a cancelled visit to Corinth (Thrall 1994, 144–51). Paul repeats his insistence that his ministry is authorized and supported by God (3:4–5), as the Corinthians who have experienced the spiritual benefits of that ministry should attest (Sampley 2000, 62–64). Not surprisingly, Paul returns to the theme of apostolic weakness as evidence that God's power works through the apostle. Those put on display in the arena in 1 Cor 4:9b are here described as the captives being led in the imperial procession (2 Cor 2:14). However, like the cross itself, this display is received according to the mode of those who witness it (Thrall 1994, 199). Those destined for salvation catch the scent of Christ; those headed for damnation, the smell of death (vv. 15–16). Thrall suggests that if one focuses on the destiny of such captives, a slim chance of imperial pardon awaits some in the arena (1994, 195). Paul thus continues to evoke the image he established in the opening benediction. During his trial in Asia, he despaired of life itself but was delivered by God "who raises the dead" (1:8–9). The correlation between apostolic suffering and life takes on another aspect in 4:7–15. God, the creator, called Paul to this ministry, which initiates the eschatological revelation of God's glory (4:6; Murphy-O'Connor 1991, 43–45). However, the apostle's life is given over to the cross, to suffering and death, so that life will be awakened in those who believe the gospel (4:7–12). The hardship catalogue (vv. 8–9) shows the superior power of God in that the apostle endures afflictions without suffering the consequences to which they ordinarily lead. He quickly returns to affirm God's life-giving power in the resurrection of Jesus (v. 14a). Paul expands the formula in verse 14b to imagine an eschatological future in which the apostle and the Corinthians are united in the Lord's presence at the judgment (Furnish 1984, 286). Suffering, weakness, affliction, and death describe the apostle's appearance in the present age. Such hardships cannot be avoided. But they are bringing into being the community of the elect, which will give praise, thanksgiving, and glory to God (v. 15). Thus, Paul has shifted the audience's attention from the immediate issue of reconciliation with the apostle to their eschatological destiny with God.

Reiterating the paradox of external hardship and internal orientation toward eternal life (4:16–18) leads to an apparent reformulation of the apocalyptic scenario in 1 Cor 15:2–58. A complex metaphor involving dwellings and garments (2 Cor 5:1–5) suggests that the apostle does not anticipate being alive at the final judgment. Nor does he assume that the dead are in some suspended state awaiting the end time (Thrall 1994, 398). Some scholars resolve this dilemma by treating this language as another metaphorical description of Paul's deliverance from hardships (so Furnish 1984, 293–99). We need not resolve the exegetical difficulties here. Whichever reading one adopts, Paul anticipates God's continued life-giving power to triumph over suffering and death. He also anticipates that his apostolic ministry, which conforms to God's standards, will be vindicated at the judgment (v. 10).

The awareness that he stands under God's judgment guides the apostle and should make his integrity evident to those who have criticized him (v. 11; Thrall 1994, 401–3). God the source of all things (v. 18) has entrusted the apostle with the message that God is reconciling the world to God's self in Christ (vv. 19–20). Reminding the Corinthians once again of the God who called them through the apostle, Paul almost speaks as though he were making his missionary appeal for the first time (Thrall 1994, 438). However, this hearing is not the first time. The Corinthians must become reconciled to God's ambassador before the opportunity is no longer available (6:1–2, citing Isa 49:8; Sampley 2000, 97). Titus's report has convinced Paul that his earlier letter has elicited repentance and a genuine desire for reconciliation. So he can affirm that God has provided comfort for the afflicted once again (7:5–16; Sampley 2000, 108–11). A piece of unfinished business remains, namely, the collection for the poor Christians in Jerusalem. Although some scholars treat both chapters 8 and 9 as part of a single appeal (Furnish 1987, 41–44), I concur with those who treat chapter 9 as a separate letter (Thrall 1994, 38–43). Aside from identifying Macedonian generosity as a sign of God's grace (8:1) and using the term *charis* ("grace," "favor") for the collection effort (vv. 4, 6, 7), Paul does not use axioms about God in formulating this appeal. Rather, he invokes the self-offering of Christ on the cross (v. 9; Thrall 2000, 534).

THE GOD OF ALL GENEROSITY:
2 CORINTHIANS 9

Sometime after the dispatch of 2 Corinthians 1–8, Paul has become sufficiently apprehensive to send another note of appeal (Thrall 2000, 563). This time, Paul not only poses the possibility of public embarrassment should the Corinthian contribution appear stingy, he also draws on God-language to make the case for generosity. God is the source of every act of generosity (*charis*, v. 8) and good work, because God provides the material prosperity necessary to practice such virtues (Murphy-O'Connor 1991, 91–93). In the social conventions of the day, a generous gift that the other party could not return in kind created a patron-client relationship. Paul subtly avoids the suggestion that the Jerusalem Christians would become "clients" of these Gentile churches by substituting a good work toward God as the end result, the overflowing of praise and thanksgiving (vv. 12–14). Thus, the Corinthians will return to God what God has given, not only in providing for the poor among God's people but in drawing the recipients and others to acknowledge God's goodness.

THE GOD OF POWER IN WEAKNESS:
2 CORINTHIANS 10–13

Clearly all did not go well with the collection. When Paul finds himself viciously attacked by outsiders, persons whom he calls "super-apostles" (11:5; 12:11) or "false apostles" (11:13), accusations that he collected money under false pretenses lie just below the surface (11:7–11; Sampley 2000, 134; Thrall

2000, 699–708). Paul's angry self-defense employs familiar items in his repertoire of God-talk, with some new rhetorical twists. The military language
switches from the suffering apostle as captive in an imperial triumph to the
apostle as God's military commander (2 Cor 10:3–6). The Corinthians should
not be deceived by the apostle's gentleness in dealing with them. He wields
God's power to protect true knowledge of God by subduing opposing thoughts
and attitudes, presumably those being fostered by the opposing missionaries
(Furnish 1984, 460–64). Not surprisingly, he charges the intruders with boasting in personal achievements and not recognizing that the Lord is the source
of all achievement (10:17–18; again citing Jer 9:23 LXX; Thrall 2000, 652–53).

Paul's most dramatic expansion of the "divine power working through apostolic weakness" occurs in 2 Cor 11:1–12:18, the "fool's speech" (Thrall 2000,
654–55). To unseat the adversaries Paul must speak in a worldly fashion, like
a fool. His catalogue of hardships proves that there is no criterion by which
they could claim to be superior (11:22–33; Thrall 2000, 721–23). The climactic contrast sets Paul's indirectly stated claim to heavenly visions and revela-
tions, whose content he will not disclose, against Paul's physical or human
weakness (12:1–10; Thrall 2000, 772–73). External criticism compels him to
allude to his direct experiences of God, but he rejects the possibility of using
such visions as the foundation for a higher teaching about God. Instead, he
asserts that no one is permitted to speak about such things (v. 4b; Thrall 2000,
794–98). He can boast that God has refused to heal the human weakness or
physical affliction from which he suffers. Whether the weakness in question
refers to chronic illness, the physical toll of all his apostolic hardships, impris-
onments and beatings, or the psychic toll of repeated opposition to his ministry, one cannot determine (on the various theories, see Thrall 2000, 809–18).
God could relieve any or all of these as the "God of consolation" sections in
the earlier letter demonstrate. That leaves an opening for Paul's opponents to
construe apostolic suffering as evidence of God's displeasure. Paul returns to
the motif of God's power, here identified as "the power of Christ" operating
through weakness (12:9–10). He may expect his audience to recognize a philosophical topos: the wise man who is content in all circumstances (Epictetus,
Diatr. I.1.110–13; Thrall 2000, 822).

CONCLUSION

Much of what Paul says about God in the Corinthian correspondence derives
from highly charged debates over the apostle's own ministry in the community. Paul's theological convictions about the cross and resurrection as the
inauguration of God's end-time drama of salvation make it impossible for him

to accept criteria for religious experience, wisdom, and authority proposed by others. As creator, God is the source of all things (1 Cor 8:6). The epithet for God, "who raises the dead" (1 Cor 7:14; 15:14–20), highlights the link between God's creative and salvific power. The various mistaken views advocated by the Corinthians assume that believers experience God's presence in demonstrations of divine power wielded by human agents. They could point to speaking in tongues, to powerful rhetorical preaching, to miracles and the like as proof that individuals were endowed with God's Spirit. Paul consistently disagrees. His central conviction that God's power is effectively working through weakness, through persons of "no account," cannot be credited to extraordinary success. As we have seen, Paul continually reaffirms his vision of God despite serious challenges to his credentials as God's apostle. Paul remains grounded in his belief that God called him as an apostle (1 Cor 1:1) and is at work in building the church at Corinth (1 Cor 1:4). Paul's faith remains grounded in the axioms that "God is faithful" and "God raised Jesus from the dead." What is true of Jesus is true for those in Christ. As long as his preaching and ministry conform to this pattern, Paul remains confident that he will be vindicated by the God who knows what is in the human heart and rewards persons as their labors on God's behalf deserve.

Though claiming not to do so, Paul's convictions and even "boasting" give the impression of arrogance, as though Paul were the only one capable of discerning God's will. Paul does not know as we come to the end of the correspondence whether God will console him with another reconciliation or humiliate him with another painful visit (2 Cor 12:19–21; Thrall 2000, 866–67). He is not confident in the moral condition of the church at Corinth and evokes the cross as evidence for God's power in weakness a final time (2 Cor 13:1–4) while reminding the Corinthians that he continues to wield God's power to build up the church. The ending of the letter (2 Cor 13:11–14) holds out the option that the Corinthians themselves will undertake the process of reform. Paul's vision of salvation looks past his present setbacks, even past the power of Christ's resurrection, to the culmination of God's creation, when all will be one with God (1 Cor 15:28).

SELECT BIBLIOGRAPHY

Achtemeier, Paul J. 1996. "The Continuing Quest for Coherence in St. Paul: An Experiment in Thought." Pages 132–45 in *Theology and Ethics in Paul and His Interpreters: Essays in Honor of Victor Paul Furnish.* Edited by Eugene H. Lovering and Jerry L. Sumney. Nashville: Abingdon.
Bockmuehl, Markus N. A. 1997. *Revelation and Mystery in Ancient Judaism and Pauline Christianity.* Grand Rapids: Eerdmans.

Bultmann, Rudolf. 1969. "What Does It Mean to Speak of God?" Pages 53–65 in *Faith and Understanding: Collected Essays*. New York: Harper & Row.

Dahl, Nils Alstrup. 1991. "The Neglected Factor in New Testament Theology." Pages 153–63 in *Jesus, the Christ: Historical Origins of Christological Doctrine*. Edited by Donald H. Juel. Minneapolis: Fortress.

Donaldson, Terence L. 1997. *Paul and the Gentiles: Remapping the Apostle's Convictional World*. Minneapolis: Fortress.

Dunn, James D. G. 1998. *The Theology of Paul the Apostle*. Grand Rapids: Eerdmans.

Fee, Gordon D. 1987. *The First Epistle to the Corinthians*. New International Commentary on the New Testament. Grand Rapids: Eerdmans.

Furnish, Victor P. 1984. *II Corinthians: Translated with Introduction, Notes, and Commentary*. Anchor Bible 32A. New York: Doubleday.

———. 1999. *The Theology of the First Letter to the Corinthians*. New Testament Theology. Cambridge: Cambridge University Press.

Holleman, Joost. 1996. *Resurrection and Parousia: A Traditio-Historical Study of Paul's Eschatology*. Novum Testamentum Supplements 84. Leiden: Brill.

Horsley, Richard A. 1978a. "The Background of the Confessional Formula in 1 Kor 8:6." *Zeitschrift für Neutestamentliche Wissenschaft und die Kunde der alten Kirche* 69: 130–35.

———. 1978b. "Consciousness and Freedom among the Corinthians. 1 Corinthians 8–10." *Catholic Biblical Quarterly* 40: 574–89.

———. 1998. *1 Corinthians*. Nashville: Abingdon.

Keck, Leander E. 1996. "God the Other Who Acts Otherwise: An Exegetical Essay on 1 Cor 1:26–31." *Word and World* 16: 276–85.

Murphy-O'Connor, Jerome. 1978a. "1 Cor VIII,6—Cosmology or Soteriology?" *Revue Biblique* 85: 253–67.

———. 1978b. "Freedom or the Ghetto (1 Cor VIII:1–13, X:23–XI:1)." *Revue Biblique* 85: 541–74.

———. 1991. *The Theology of the Second Letter to the Corinthians*. New Testament Theology. Cambridge: Cambridge University Press.

———. 1996. *Paul: A Critical Life*. Oxford: Oxford University Press.

Richardson, Neal. 1994. *Paul's Language about God*. Sheffield: Sheffield Academic Press.

Sampley, J. Paul. 2000. "The Second Letter to the Corinthians." Pages 3–180 in vol. 11 of *The New Interpreter's Bible*. Edited by L. Keck. Nashville: Abingdon.

Thiselton, Anthony C. 2000. *The First Epistle to the Corinthians*. New International Greek Testament Commentary. Grand Rapids: Eerdmans.

Thrall, Margaret E. 1994 and 2000. *The Second Epistle to the Corinthians*. 2 vols. International Critical Commentary. Edinburgh: T. & T. Clark.

10

All the Fullness of God

Concepts of Deity in Colossians and Ephesians

DAVID M. HAY

In one compressed formulation, Ephesians identifies God as the one "who is above all and through all and in all" (4:6). What is said there about the universe might also be said of that letter as well as Colossians: God is not simply one subject among many in these writings—rather, God permeates all subjects and assertions. Time and again discrete references to God seem intended to remind readers or hearers of the letters that everything they say is backed by infinite and irresistible authority.

In the following essay no assumptions are made about the authorship of either Colossians or Ephesians. I am inclined, however, to think that Colossians was written either by Paul (indirectly) or a Paulinist rather soon after his death. Ephesians, I suspect, was written by a Paulinist a considerable time later, probably between 70 and 90 C.E., more as a work designed for general circulation than as an epistle to a particular church. The remarkable combination of similarities and differences between the letters probably cannot be explained by any simple hypothesis (Best 1998, 20–40; Dahl 2000, 39–48), but I think with many scholars that the writer of Ephesians had access to Colossians as well as to other Pauline letters and traditions (Lincoln 1990, xlvii–lviii; Perkins 1997, 18). Each of the two letters offers a concise but comprehensive presentation of the Christian message from a Pauline perspective. In addition, Colossians seeks to guard its intended readers against a false teaching that encouraged ascetic practices (2:16–23). Ephesians does not refer to the special problems of a particular congregation, though it argues for Jewish-Gentile unity within the Christian community (2:11–18), posts a general warning against deceitful doctrines (4:14), and may allude to alternative interpretations of Scripture, especially in 5:25–33.

Without attempting systematic comparisons between Colossians and Ephesians on the one hand and other writings in the Pauline corpus on the other,

I will seek to show that the concepts of God in these two letters preserve a strong continuity with ideas in the undisputed letters and also develop them in ways that helped make the apostle's image and teachings meaningful for later times.

Paul Achtemeier has made a series of important contributions to biblical studies over a long career of scholarship and teaching. It is a pleasure to offer this essay in honor of those contributions and the man of rare insight, energy, and warmth behind them.

OBSERVATIONS ON LANGUAGE AND RHETORIC

The following chart provides data relevant to our topic. It is based on the text of *The Greek New Testament* (4th rev. ed.; United Bible Societies, 1998). Columns A and B present frequencies of usage of terms in Colossians and Ephesians. Column C indicates the ratio of each term's usage in Colossians divided by the frequency in Ephesians (rounded off to two decimal places). The total number of Greek words in Colossians is 1,583, while Ephesians has 2,427 (the ratio is 0.65). Thus, the table immediately shows that the use of the term *theos* for God is proportionately about the same in the letters, whereas *patēr* as a term for God occurs somewhat less often in Colossians proportionately.

Greek term	A. Colossians	B. Ephesians	C. Ratio
Theos (God)	21	31	0.68
Patēr (Father—for God)	4	8	0.50
Christos (Christ)	25	46	0.54
Iēsous (Jesus)	7	20	0.35
Kyrios (Lord—for Christ)	14	24	0.58
Pneuma (Spirit—for Holy Spirit)	2	13	0.15

By far the most common term for the deity in both letters is simply "God" (*theos* or *ho theos*). The only other noun often used to designate God is "Father." God is referred to as "Father" more often in Ephesians than in any other Pauline letter (Thompson 2000, 121–22). God is called "Father" four times in Colossians and eight times in Ephesians, but in a variety of expressions: "God the Father of our Lord Jesus Christ" (Col 1:3), "The God and Father of our Lord Jesus Christ" (Eph 1:3), "God our Father" (Col 1:2; Eph 1:2), "the Father" (Col 1:12; Eph 2:18; 3:14), "God the Father" (Col 3:17; Eph 5:20; 6:23), "the God of our Lord Jesus Christ, the Father of glory" (Eph 1:17), and "one God and Father of all, who is over all and through all and in all" (Eph 4:6). The term *huios* ("son") is applied to Jesus only once in Ephesians (4:13) and once in Colossians (1:13). In both cases he is identified as Son of God, but only in the Colossians passage does the context speak of God as "Father." Paul Meyer remarks that the undisputed Pauline letters never speak of God as "Father" and Jesus as "Son" in the same passage, and this pattern is almost perfectly paralleled in the Fourth Gospel as well (Meyer 1996, 263, 271 n. 51). The use of the simple expression "the Father" to refer to God in Col 1:12 and Eph 2:18; 3:14 has only rare and imperfect parallels in the undisputed letters (Rom 6:4; 8:15; Gal 4:6).

Only once in each letter, and then in the letter opening, is God identified as the Father of Jesus Christ (Col 1:3; Eph 1:3). More often God is identified as Father to believers (Col 1:2, 12; 3:17; Eph 1:2; 2:18; 5:20; 6:23), though not always with an explicit "*our* Father." Ephesians, but not Colossians, speaks of believers as God's children (5:1; cf. 5:8); both speak of the future fulfillment of salvation as an inheritance from God (Col 3:24; Eph 1:14, 18; 5:5). Twice Ephesians refers to God as Father of the universe (3:14; 4:6). Along with Acts 17:29, these appear to be the only New Testament passages that speak of God as "Father" to all creatures, not simply Christ or Christians.

Sometimes God is referred to by a periphrasis: "its creator" (Col 3:10), "him who accomplishes all things according to his counsel and will" (Eph 1:11), "him who by the power at work within us is able to accomplish abundantly far more than all that we ask or imagine" (Eph 3:20). Ephesians 3:9 offers a summary description of God as the one "who created all things," and 3:15 speaks of the Father "from whom every family in heaven and on earth takes its name." Ephesians 4:6 concludes a creed-like statement with the words "one God and Father of all, who is above all and through all and in all." Very occasionally an expression might refer to either God or Christ (e.g., Col 1:29 speaks of the giver of energy to Paul; other texts, notably 1:11 and 2:12, make it likely that God is the one in view). The best textual reading of Col 2:2 contains the odd phrase "the knowledge of the mystery of God, of Christ," which could be taken to equate God and Christ, though that conflicts with the writer's usual practice of distinguishing them.

The term "Lord" (*kyrios*) is several times explicitly linked with Jesus or Christ or Jesus Christ (Col 1:3; 2:6; 3:17, 24; Eph 1:2–3, 15, 17; 3:11; 5:20; 6:23–24), and references in both letters simply to "the Lord" consistently seem to refer to him rather than God (in a few cases human slave masters are called "lords" [*kyrioi*]—Col 3:22; 4:1; Eph 6:5, 9).

References to God are more frequent in the first half of each of the letters, including opening greetings and the thanksgiving or blessing sections, which flow into expositions of the meaning of salvation through Christ (Col 1:3–2:23; Eph 1:3–3:21). Particularly in the dense statements about salvation through Christ's death and resurrection (Col 1:12–23; 2:9–15; Eph 1:3–23;

2:4–22) references to God seem about as numerous as ones to Christ, and God seems emphatically represented as the ultimate author of redemption. The human need for salvation can be portrayed as a condition of alienation from God, while salvation is often represented as reconciliation, peace, or access in relation to God (Col 1:20–22; Eph 2:12, 14–18; 3:12). Colossians sometimes explains the redemptive power of Christ by declaring that God's fullness (*plērōma*) resided or resides in him (1:19; 2:9) and that believers have come to "fullness in him" (2:10). Ephesians describes the church as filled with the fullness (*plērōma*) of God (3:19) or as Christ's fullness (1:23) and as called to "grow up" into the fullness or maturity of Christ (4:13). In a striking way, Colossians speaks of grace (*charis*) as coming to believers from God only (1:2, 6; cf. 4:18), while Ephesians usually connects "grace" with both God and Jesus (e.g., 1:2, 6–7; 2:5–8; 3:7–8; 6:24). Ephesians speaks of God's love (*agapē*) for believers (1:4, 15; 2:4; 6:23) as well as Christ's love for them (3:19; 5:2, 25). Colossians speaks of believers once as "God's chosen ones, holy and beloved" (3:12).

Very often the writers use "in" (*en*) constructions to affirm that God acted in Christ to bring salvation (e.g., Eph 1:3, 4, 7, 9, 10, 11, 12, 17, 19, 20; 2:6–7, 10, 13, 15–16, 21, 22; 3:6, 11, 12, 21; 4:2, 32; Col 1:2, 4, 16–17, 19, 28; 2:6, 7, 10, 12, 13, 15; 3:3–4). In one passage, Ephesians speaks of Christ's death as a "sacrifice to God" (Eph 5:2). Both letters speak of faith (*pistis*) that has Christ as object (Eph 1:15; Col 1:4; 2:5). However, Eph 6:23 speaks of peace, love, and faith coming from both "God the Father and the Lord Jesus Christ," and Col 2:12 speaks of "faith in the power of God, who raised him [Christ] from the dead."

The language concerning God in these letters is closely related to worship and probably partly derives from actual early Christian liturgical traditions. Prayer, thanksgiving, and praise seem regularly directed not to Christ but to God (Col 1:3, 12; 3:16–17; Eph 1:3, 16–17; 3:14, 20–21; 5:20). A characteristic formulation appears in Col 3:16–17 (closely paralleled in Eph. 5:19–20):

> Let the word of Christ dwell in you richly; teach and admonish one another in all wisdom; and with gratitude in your hearts sing psalms, hymns, and spiritual songs to God. And whatever you do, in word or deed, do everything in the name of the Lord Jesus, giving thanks to God the Father through him.

Colossians gives special attention to the idea of thanksgiving, and three out of the letter's four references to God as Father appear in injunctions to the addressees to "give thanks" (1:3, 12; 3:17). Thankful worship of God also seems fundamental in Ephesians (1:16; 5:4, 20).

Paul as apostle is authorized and empowered by God (Col 1:1, 24–29; Eph 1:1; 3:2–3, 7–8), and missionary success hinges on God empowering both speakers and hearers (Col 4:3–4; Eph 6:19). Both letters stress the notion of the Christian gospel as a "mystery" that enables the salvation of Gentiles, a mystery concealed in all previous generations and now revealed to and through the church. Passive verbs referring to concealment imply that God was the one who concealed it in the past and now makes it known (Col 1:26–27; 2:2; Eph 3:3–12).

In the hortatory sections of the two letters, after transitional introductions (Col 3:1–4; Eph 4:1–6), Christ—often referred to as "the Lord"—is mentioned more often than God. God's wrath as eschatological punishment surely coming on "the sons of disobedience" is cited to warrant Christian avoidance of various vices (Col 3:6; Eph 5:6). As already noted, readers are told to offer thanks to God the Father in the name of the Lord Jesus Christ (Col 3:17: "the Lord"; Eph 5:20: "our Lord"). Ephesians calls readers to forgive one another "as God in Christ forgave you" and to become "imitators of God as beloved children" (4:32–5:1). The parenetic section in Ephesians concludes with exhortations to put on "the armor of God" (6:11, 13). Christian conduct can be defined as life in harmony with the will of Christ (Col 1:10; Eph 5:17) or the will of God (Col 1:9; 4:12; Eph 6:6).

God is quite often represented as the source of saving energy, power to raise and exalt Christ and believers with him (Col 1:11, 29; Eph 1:19–23; 3:7) and power to enable the body of Christ to grow (Col 2:19; cf. Eph 3:20). God is also portrayed as the one who chooses those who will be saved (Col 3:12) and designs their destiny (Eph 1:4–5). Moreover, it is God who has revealed salvation after ages of concealment and now enables believers to grasp that "mystery" (Col 1:25–27; Eph 1:8–10).

While Christ's death remains centrally important (Eph 1:7; 2:13–16; 5:2, 25–27; Col 1:20, 22; 2:11–15, 20), both letters seem to give greater prominence to affirmations about his glory or God's exaltation of him after his death, with related assertions about the empowerment of the church (e.g., Eph 1:3–4, 20–23; 2:5–7, 17–21; 3:11, 17–21; 4:7–16; 5:21–24, 29–32; 6:23–24; Col 1:13–19; 1:27–2:3, 2:6–10, 17, 19; 3:1–4, 9–11, 15–17).

A certain emphasis on God-guided violence appears in both letters, though the violence is centrally the event of Christ's death. Both speak directly of Jesus' blood (Col 1:20; Eph 1:7; 2:13) and cross (Col 1:20; Eph 2:16). More remarkable, however, are the interpretations of Christ's death as a military-like victory achieved by God: the erasing of a record against us and the stripping and overcoming of apparently hostile supernatural powers (Col 2:14–15) or the breaking down of a dividing wall and the abolition of the Jewish law (Eph 2:14–15). Of course, from the viewpoints of the authors, the final result is salvation for believers, to whom both letters are addressed. But non-Christian Gentiles, if they ever came across Colossians, might have been surprised by a claim that God won a quasi-imperial triumph over demonic powers (perhaps ones connected with pagan deities!). Likewise, some Jewish readers (whether Christian or non-Christian), with fresh memories of the Roman destruction of the walls and temple of Jerusalem, might have been troubled to find in Ephesians the claim that Jesus' death demolished their law for the sake of a very different sanctuary. Again, Eph 6:11–18, despite its orientation to a "gospel of peace," implies that believers fight an ongoing war with "the spiritual forces of evil in the heavenly places," alluding to ancient images of God as Divine Warrior (Yoder Neufeld 1997, 131–53). Thus, these letters delineate God with some distinctly bellicose features (cf. Lincoln and Wedderburn 1993, 47–48, 125–26).

At the same time, both letters speak of the results of God's saving work in terms of peace, forgiveness, reconciliation, reunification, and restored creation. The language of justification, so prominent in Galatians and Romans, has been set aside.

An absence of sustained argumentation or discussion of alternative viewpoints, among other things, marks the style of both letters. The writers seem entirely certain in all their statements, and no doubts are explicitly entertained. The author of Colossians implies that unnamed false teachers have raised questions about the adequacy of Christ in his readers' minds, but the solution to the problem is to hold fast to Christ and disregard such teachers as partisans of the flesh and human regulations. The rhetorical tone throughout is one of absolute assurance, as though the writers speak directly for God (cf. Hay 2000, 34). Their assertions are supported by frequent references to the authority of Paul (and other leaders associated with him), the gospel message and related traditions (including liturgical materials) already known in the churches, and to some extent (particularly in the case of Ephesians) the Jewish Scriptures.

The atmosphere of both letters is one of meditative confidence. Their often lengthy sentences flow like the waters of a great river, whose quiet waves suggest God's settled and reliable purpose. Or, to vary the analogy, if Galatians and 2 Corinthians call to mind the tension and struggle of Beethoven's Fifth Symphony, Colossians and more especially Ephesians evoke the serenity of that composer's Violin Concerto.

GOD AND CHRISTOLOGY

The Christology in the undisputed Pauline letters might be described, using language from a later Christian period, as "subordinationist." The Pauline gospel centers in Christ's death and resurrection; yet God is in charge from beginning to end (cf. Rom 1:16–3:20; 11:22–36; 1 Cor 8:6). Christ already reigns, yet at the end of time he will subject himself so that "God may be all in all" (1 Cor 15:20–28). Christ's saving work is ultimately the work of God (Rom 3:24–26; 2 Cor 5:19–21).

In Colossians and Ephesians, Christ is portrayed as approximately equal to, though not identical with, God the Father. No mention is made of Christ ever yielding up his kingdom to the Father. Indeed, the kingdom of Christ seems equivalent to that of God (cf. Col 1:13; 4:11; Eph 5:5).

The term "fullness" (*plērōma*) is familiar in the undisputed Pauline letters, but only in Colossians and Ephesians is it used to define Christ's status and relation to the Father. In him resides the whole fullness of God (Col 1:19; 2:9; cf. Eph 1:23). Just as God can be described as over and in "all things" (Eph 4:6), so also the risen Christ is "all and in all" (Col 3:11) and the one who "fills all things" (Eph 4:10). The closest New Testament parallel seems to be John 1:16: "From his [Christ's] fullness [*plērōma*] have we all received, grace upon grace."

On the other hand, Colossians stresses that the saving events were ones in which God was the ultimate actor and Christ the one through whom God has acted (1:12–23; 2:11–15). Salvation is a process of God reconciling the world to himself, forgiving sins. This has been fully accomplished through the death and resurrection of Christ; what remains is for people to appropriate the benefits of those events through steadfast faith and good works (e.g., 1:23; 2:6–7, 19; 3:1–2).

In Ephesians, the long opening blessing is a blessing of God the Father, who has acted for salvation through Christ. He destined "us" to be sons and daughters to him through Jesus Christ (1:5) and has revealed "his" purpose to unite all things in him. Prayer is offered that the God of Jesus Christ may fill the readers with knowledge and power. God made us alive through Christ "even when we were dead through our trespasses" and exalted "us" to a heavenly enthronement (2:4–6). In 2:13–16, somewhat greater emphasis is put on Christ as the one who initiated salvation by breaking down the wall of separation (the law) that divided Jews and Gentiles, but the object of salvation is to bring both human groups to God so that "both of us have access in one Spirit to the Father" (2:18). God has revealed and realized his eternal purpose of salvation in Christ (3:8–12), and the apostle bows his knees before the Father that his readers may be strengthened through the Spirit and that Christ may dwell in their hearts (3:14–19). Glory is to be given to God and to Christ forever (3:20–21).

Thus, in their "doctrinal" sections, both Colossians and Ephesians represent God as the ultimate author of salvation (cf. Hoppe 1992, 185). Christology does not displace theology, but interprets it. Christ is explicitly called "the image of God" only in Colossians (1:15), but both letters indicate that the message of divine salvation was concealed till the coming of Christ. Hence, in fundamental ways Christ can be understood only when his relationship to God is grasped; on the other hand, God is known through Christ and, evidently, adequately known only through Christ. The distinction between Christ and God is developed in functional rather than ontological terms (cf. Barclay 1997, 77–82).

The picture changes somewhat in the parenetic sections of the letters. Most of the ethical instruction in Colossians is explicitly linked with Christ as Lord (cf. de Oliveira 2000, 94–100). Here Christ is placed on something like an equal level with God the Father, indeed to such an extent that it becomes hard to distinguish one from the other. This is especially the case in the tables of household duties (Col 3:18–4:1; Eph 5:21–6:9). In ethical exhortations, Ephesians and Colossians seem to reflect church customs that made Christ or God the Father indifferently the authority to which believers must subject themselves.

In Ephesians, in contrast to Colossians, there are crucial expansions of the household tables involving the Jewish Scriptures and Christian redemption as warrants. The instruction to children about obeying parents is declared to be "right," and the author proceeds to quote "Honor your father and mother that it may be well with you and that you may live long on the earth" (Exod 20:12; Deut 5:16; the author adds a parenthetical comment that "this is the first commandment with a promise"). Readers are expected to know and respect Old Testament texts and to appreciate a divine declaration of purpose and assurance regarding long life on earth. Despite the apocalyptic images in 6:11–20, the writer of Ephesians assumes that his readers will be interested in a protracted existence in this world.

Most important, however, is the kerygmatic expansion of the commandments regarding husbands and wives: The love of husbands is to be modeled on Christ's cherishing love for the church, which involved his death to cleanse her perfectly (5:25–32). No reference is made in this paragraph to God the Father. Here Christ, not the Father, is the model of divine love that should guide the marriages and general conduct of believers.

Overall, both letters are both christocentric and theocentric.

GOD AND THE COMMUNITY OF SAINTS

Both letters underscore the saving work of God accomplished in Christ's death and resurrection in the past and also stress the present-time presence of God in the corporate and individual lives of believers. Just as the divine fullness (*plērōma*) "dwells bodily" in Christ, so believers "have come to fullness in him, who is the head of every rule and authority" (Col 2:9–10). Ephesians 1:22–23 declares that the church is "his [Christ's] body, the fullness of him who fills all in all." This already suggests that the church shares in the divine plenitude, a thought that becomes more explicit in the prayer of 3:19 that the letter's recipients come to know the love of Christ "so that you may be filled with all the fullness of God." Ephesians 4:13 speaks of Christians needing to grow up "to maturity, to the measure of the full stature [*plērōma*] of Christ."

One index of divine-human fellowship is the ease and frequency with which prayer is mentioned. Prayer is regularly directed to God in Colossians (1:3; 4:3), and readers are told in general to give thanks to God the Father through the Lord Jesus (Col 3:17). "Paul" and Timothy begin their letter by expressing their gratitude to God (1:3). They pray that the Colossians may be filled with divine wisdom and understanding and "all power, according to his glorious might" (1:11—the "his" may refer to God the Father, but might just as easily refer to Christ). Epaphras also prays for the spiritual maturation of the Colossians (4:12; cf. 1:28: "so that we may present everyone mature in Christ").

The writer of Colossians sums up the meaning of the gospel mystery as "Christ in you, the hope of glory" (1:27)—a confession of a kind of divine-human companionship in both present and future. The readers are to live in Christ (2:6) and they have "come to fullness in him" (2:10), just as Christ is the one in whom God's fullness resides (1:19; 2:9). Believers have been buried and raised with Christ (2:11–12) so that they currently share his heavenly enthronement at God's right hand (3:1–2). Yet their life with Christ in God is at present "hidden" (3:3); only in the eschatological future will they appear in glory with Christ (3:4). Through baptism they have already put on the new nature and bear the image of their creator (surely God, though the image seems also that of Christ, who is "all and in all!"—3:10–11). At the same time, they are exhorted to clothe themselves with Christian virtues (3:12–14).

Thus, Colossians affirms that in worship and daily living believers enjoy direct communion with Christ and God, although this is qualified by a sense of concealment (3:4) and a concept of their sharing divine glory in the future rather than the present. Perhaps this is related to the almost total silence about the Holy Spirit in Colossians. The term for "spirit" (*pneuma*) occurs only twice, in 1:8 and 2:5, and neither passage clearly refers to the Spirit of God. Moreover, Colossians says nothing about special gifts of God to individuals linked with responsibilities or offices in the congregation (in contrast to 1 Cor 12 and Eph 4:7–11, which, however, connects gifts with Christ rather than the Spirit). The adjective "spiritual" is also used twice in Colossians—in 1:9 and 3:16—but without clear reference to God's Spirit. Perhaps the author of Colossians maintains a quite un-Pauline virtual silence about the Spirit because the teachers he opposes (2:16–23) found it easier to defend their views by referring to the Spirit rather than to Christ (Schweizer 1982, 38–39).

By contrast, Ephesians uses the word "spirit" (*pneuma*) at least twelve times to refer to God's Spirit (1:17 is debatable). Two passages speak of "the Holy Spirit" (Eph 1:13; 4:30). Most of these passages speak of the Spirit's residing in or with believers, imparting knowledge of God (1:17), access to the Father (2:18), existence in the temple, which is "a dwelling place of God in the Spirit" (2:22), empowerment "in the inner person" (3:16), church unity (4:3), enthusiasm (5:18), divine protection (6:17), and power to pray (6:18). The Ephesians were sealed with the promised Holy Spirit, which ensures their eschatological inheritance (1:13–14; 4:30). Any wrongdoing on their part would "grieve" God's Spirit (4:30).

Further, quite apart from the use of Spirit language, the writer of Ephesians emphasizes that Christians are now living in the immediate presence of God. God has blessed them with every spiritual blessing (1:3), exalting them to sit with Christ in the heavenly places (2:5–6). Believers have learned from God the mystery of his will "with all wisdom and insight" (1:8). In their preconversion days, they were alienated from Christ and Israel and hence were "without God in the world" (2:12). Now, however, they enjoy evidently unlimited "access" to God, being members of God's household and spiritual sanctuary, the dwelling place of God. At one point God is praised as the one "who by the power at work within us is able to accomplish abundantly far more than all that we can ask or imagine" (3:20). God the Father "is above all and through all and in all" (4:6; cf. Col 3:11). Christians are able to clothe themselves with "the whole armor of God" and so face down all spiritual foes (6:11, 13).

In Ephesians, the concept of God's sovereign will to save is developed especially with ideas of time and predestination. God the Father chose believers "before the foundation of the world" (1:4) and prepared in advance the good works they perform (2:10). God's eternal purpose of uniting everything in Christ seems set from creation entirely apart from human sin (Perkins 1997, 46). Although, like Colossians, Ephesians speaks of a future eschatological fulfillment for believers, it does not speak of Christian existence as in any way "hidden" in the present age. The writer seems to think that God has blessed church members with virtually unlimited knowledge and power.

Yet the expressions of "realized eschatology" in these letters do not imply that believers are beyond suffering or sin. Paul's imprisonment is mentioned in both (Eph 3:1, 13; 6:20; Col 4:3, 18), and Col 1:24 even speaks of Paul "completing what is lacking in Christ's afflictions." While believers have undergone a spiritual transformation so that divine power works within them, the earnest and lengthy prayers and exhortations in both letters imply that church members remain subject to temptation and need to keep growing toward full maturity (Col 2:19; Eph 4:15–16). The concluding instructions in Eph 6:10–18 about ongoing warfare with "the spiritual forces of evil" provides a stern warning against pious complacency.

A GOD OF THE JEWISH SCRIPTURES
AND THE JEWISH PEOPLE?

It is generally recognized that New Testament writers took over the Jewish understanding of a monotheistic deity (Childs 1993, 365). Yet Colossians seems to go out of its way to conceal any sense of continuity with the Jewish Scriptures and religion. Ephesians, while it emphasizes links between Christianity and the Old Testament, does not dwell on the history of Israel. On their surfaces, both letters appear to ignore the religious situation and destiny of non-Christian Jews.

Colossians contains no quotations or unmistakable allusions to the Old Testament. A few of its phrases would probably recall the Jewish Bible to persons who knew it well: "Human commands and teachings" (2:22) recalls Isa 29:13, "at the right hand of God" (3:1) recalls Ps. 110:1, and "the image of its creator" (3:10) recalls Gen 1:26–27. The Christ hymn in the first chapter (1:15–20) seems clearly dependent on biblical and Hellenistic Jewish traditions about God's wisdom and word. Yet the writer makes no effort to identify the Jewish background of his thought.

On the other hand, in Col 4:10–11, "Paul" mentions a special trio of Jewish Christians first among those coworkers who send greetings to the Colossian church. He adds that they "are the only ones of the circumcision among my co-workers for the kingdom of God, and they have been a comfort to me." Mention of the kingdom may imply recognition of a continuity between pre-Christian Jewish hopes and Christian preaching. The passage also implies that the apostle feels emotionally close to these particular Jewish friends. Yet Col 3:11 seems to say that Christ has eliminated the Jewish-Gentile distinction, and 2:11 treats circumcision (or the Jewish law about it) as simply an anticipation of Christian baptism. The letter expresses no animosity against non-Christian Jews, but also no special concern for them. The God of Colossians, like the God of Genesis, is universal creator and redeemer, but he is not identified as the God of Israel past or present.

The God of Ephesians is linked much more straightforwardly with the Jewish Scriptures. There are explicit Old Testament quotations: in 4:8 (Ps 68:19), 5:31 (Gen 2:24), and 6:2–3 (Exod 20:12 and Deut 5:16). There are also a number of fairly obvious allusions: in 1:20 (Ps 110:1), 1:22 (Ps. 8:6), 2:12 (Isa 57:19), 4:25 (Zech 8:16), 5:2 (Exod 29:18; Ezek 20:41), 6:14 (Isa 11:5; 59:17), and 6:15 (Isa 52:7). The God of the church is plainly the God of the Old Testament, and the Old Testament has a positive relationship with God's work in Christ and the Christian community. On the other hand, the writer insists that the distinctive message of Paul, the mystery of the salvation of the Gentiles, was not made known to people in previous generations (3:4–6). References to "members of the same body" in 3:6 and "the commonwealth of Israel" and "covenants of promise" in 2:12 probably indicate that the writer thinks of the Jewish people as chosen by God, at least because they received promises pointing forward to Christ and the church. Yet Ephesians does not dwell on Christ's fulfillment of Old Testament promises, and the Jewish Scriptures are regarded as playing a supportive but hardly formative role in shaping church teaching (Lincoln 1982, 50). Further, there is no clear reference to the history of Israel or to any Old Testament individuals (the "apostles and prophets" in Eph 2:20 are probably all Christians). The author celebrates the uniting of Jews and Gentiles in the church and their access to the Father through Christ. There is no suggestion that non-Christian Jews enjoy saving access.

Of special importance is the attitude toward the law of Moses expressed explicitly in Ephesians and less directly in Colossians. Each letter offers only a single reference to the law, but the references come in pivotal soteriological contexts.

Ephesians 2:14–15 declares that Christ's death brought unity and peace between Gentiles and Jews by breaking down the wall of hostility that created enmity between them, and verse 16 proceeds to identify that wall with the law of Moses. More radical than the Paul of Galatians or Romans, the writer of Ephesians identifies the Mosaic legislation as not only impotent or temporary but as the essential obstacle to salvation (cf. Dahl 2000, 445; Gese 1997, 144–46). It is rather surprising that later on (Eph 5:31 and 6:2–3) the author cites with approval Pentateuchal laws about marriage and the honoring of parents; perhaps he considered such texts to be sources of insight but not binding as law on believers (cf. Moritz 1996, 219).

As for the law in Colossians, we find it alluded to in 2:11–15, which interprets Jesus' death with a series of extraordinary images. In the crucifixion, God is said to have erased or set aside "the record that stood against us, with its legal demands" (v. 14). The term for "record" (*cheirographon*) seems more general than Paul's regular term for the Mosaic law (*nomos*—a term never used in Colossians), but it seems likely that the writer has in mind every law or set of requirements that might lead people (Jews or Gentiles) to feel or actually be guilty. The author may have had pagan as well as Jewish religious laws in mind, but—given the stress on the Jewish law in the undisputed letters—it is hard to imagine that this passage does not also have in view the law of Moses (Schweizer 1982, 150–51). Colossians also asserts the idea, not paralleled in Ephesians, that the setting aside of the document that stood against us took place in the same moment that God decisively defeated the "rulers and authorities." Evidently the writer thinks of hostile supernatural beings (evil angels?) who made use of the "record" to oppress people and alienate them from God.

GOD AND THE WORLD BEYOND THE CHURCH

In both Colossians and Ephesians we find a striking and paradoxical combination of cosmic and ecclesiological foci. God is portrayed as creator, ruler, and reconciler of "all things." Yet for the most part each letter concentrates on teaching about the processes of redemption within the Christian community. Ephesians in particular has been characterized as displaying a decidedly "introversionist" tendency, encouraging a certain isolation of church members from nonbelievers (MacDonald 2000, 210–12).

Just as non-Christian Jews seem to be ignored in both letters, so too are non-Christian Gentiles—except as the pool of sinners from which church members have been drawn. Both letters employ harsh, stereotypical language to describe the pagan world out of which their readers have come: It is a world populated by "children of disobedience," persons enslaved to demonic powers or their own fleshly appetites (Col 3:5–6; Eph 2:2–3; 4:17–19). God's wrathful judgment hangs over them (Col 3:6; Eph 2:3). The language and imagery seem to a considerable degree drawn from Jewish apocalyptic traditions (many scholars have noted similarities between dualistic language in the Dead Sea Scrolls and Ephesians). Much of the point of such descriptions is to warn Christians that their pursuit of holiness demands a persisting rejection of the values and practices of pagan outsiders.

Still, both letters stress that their readers formerly belonged among those very outsiders (Col 1:21; Eph 2:3), and the readers are said to have been liberated and transferred to the community of the sanctified by grace (Eph 2:4–10). By implication, then, those presently on the outside may in the future join those on the inside. Ongoing missionary work among non-Christians is presupposed in both letters, especially in the symbolic person of Paul (see especially Col 4:3–4 and Eph 6:19–20). Colossians, more distinctly than Ephesians, also urges ordinary believers to interact with non-Christians in ways that may prompt conversion (Col 4:5–6; Macdonald 2000, 172–77, 317–24; Perkins 1997, 117–18). The Christian message is bearing fruit through the world (Col 1:6, 23), and Paul is known to have been commissioned to preach to all persons (Eph 3:8–9). Yet the references in both letters to church growth seem to give greater priority to internal spiritual development than to recruiting new members from the outside (cf. Meeks 1977).

At the theological level, both Colossians and Ephesians emphasize that God is the creator of everyone and everything, sometimes with language that seems drawn directly or indirectly from Hellenistic philosophy and religion (Pöhlmann 1973). The idea that God exercises sovereignty over all events, especially those related to salvation, is developed frequently in Colossians with the term "all" or "all things" (*ta panta*). God is both omnipotent and omniscient, and God has made subject to Christ *all* principalities and powers (Col 1:16; 2:10; Eph 1:20–23). Such statements establish that those inside the church have absolute security, but they also suggest that God's saving work has effects beyond the present Christian community.

In two remarkable passages, Ephesians seems to appropriate Hellenistic philosophical notions and formulae to describe God as father to the universe. Plato could speak of God as the world's father (Plato, *Timaeus* 28C, 37C, 41A). Philo of Alexandria often calls God father and maker (or ruler) of "the all" or the whole world (e.g., *Opif.* 72, 135; *Leg.* 1.18; 2.49; *Cher.* 44, 49; *Det.* 175; *Deus* 19; *Ebr.* 42, 131; *Conf.* 144; *Her.* 62; *Abr.* 21; cf. Josephus, *Ant.* 7.380). Sometimes Philo adds that as creator God necessarily also exercises providential care over everyone and everything, as parents care for their children (*Opif.* 10; 171–72).

In Eph 3:14–15, "Paul" bows in prayer before "the Father [*patēr*], from whom every family [*patria*] in heaven and on earth takes its name." Apparently this means that every human group on earth as well as every heavenly community (of angels?) has been given life by God (Lincoln 1990, 202–3).

In Eph 4:6, an elaborate confession of the oneness of God warrants a call to preserve unity within the church, but the idea of God as being "over, in, through, and in all" bears a likeness to cosmological ideas like those in a formula of Marcus Aurelius: "All things are from you, all things are in you, all things are to you" (*Meditations* 4:23). It is probably best to interpret the "all" in Eph 4:6 not restrictively (as though God's permeating presence is confined to the church) but to see the entire creed-like statement as declaring that God's kingdom is greater than the church. The church is commissioned to announce the mystery of God's love for all creation (Barth 1974, 2.471–72, 496–97; cf. Lincoln 1990, 240; Pokorný 1992, 166; and Best 1998, 371). One commentator on this passage infers that the church is "the eschatological outpost, the pilot project of God's purposes, and his people are the expression of this unity that displays to the universe his final goal" (O'Brien 1999, 286).

As God is creator and ruler of all (Eph 3:9; Col 1:15–17), so the salvation he accomplishes in Christ somehow embraces the entire universe. Colossians 1:19–20 says that in Christ the fullness of God "was pleased to dwell, and through him God was pleased to reconcile to himself all things, whether on earth or in heaven." Ephesians 1:10 speaks of the divine purpose set forth in Christ, a plan to sum up and unite in Christ everything in heaven and earth (Best 1998, 138–43). These statements resemble universalistic affirmations in the undisputed letters, notably 1 Cor 15:25–28 and Rom 11:32. The references to "all things" in Colossians and Ephesians being included in redemption also recall Paul's suggestive statements about the nonhuman creation in Rom 8:19–23 (cf. Dunn 1996, 102–4).

Where does all this leave Jews and Gentiles who are presently outside the church? Since both letters seem to leave no room for salvation outside the Christian community, the only hope for outsiders would seem to be that they will one day come into the church. If, however, God's work of salvation in Christ has already brought reconciliation to all things or aims at the "gathering up" of all things in Christ, it seems reasonable to infer that the writers of these letters thought that God would somehow in the future expand the church to encompass the universe.

Both letters contain both universalistic and particularistic statements about salvation through Christ, without clearly explaining how these are compatible. Perhaps the general viewpoint of these writers is something like this: Christ is the true head of both the universe and the church, but only Christians recognize this. The church is not a "third race" meant to exist indefinitely alongside communities of Jews and Gentiles, but is instead the "new humanity," a nonsectarian society composed of Jews and Gentiles that somehow represents all of humanity and God's purpose of finally leaving no one out. Nils Dahl in particular has written eloquently of Ephesians as offering a vision of the church as the kernel of a renewed universe, a vision that can inspire nontriumphalist criticism of exclusionary divisions within the church (Dahl 2000, 80–81).

It is often pointed out that both letters, while containing some remnants of futurist eschatology, give primacy to realized eschatology. Believers are already raised and exalted in heavenly regions through Christ (Col 3:1–4; Eph 1:20–23; 2:5–7). The future "glory" or "inheritance" of believers seems conceived largely as a revelation or amplification of benefits already essentially experienced. Yet if the writers of these letters did intend their readers to think in terms of a salvation reaching persons beyond the confines of the church of their own time, future eschatology would necessarily be of vital importance, not so much to reveal the full character of salvation as to expand the community of the saints.

Both letters dwell on the present revelation of the "mystery" of salvation through Christ in the church, but they do not claim that believers have answers to all possible questions. When and on what terms will non-Christians be reconciled? How did "the cosmic powers of this present darkness" (Eph 6:12) fall away from the truth and will they somehow share in the cosmic reconciliation? Are the structures of distinction and authority in the household tables permanently valid? How are they related to the ending of distinctions announced in Col 3:11? Why did God choose to conceal the saving revelation in Christ from previous generations, and what will be the fate of those generations? The writers of Colossians and Ephesians celebrate confidently the perfect revelation of God's salvation in Christ. They do not claim omniscience.

CONCLUSIONS

In these two letters, God the Father and Christ are regularly distinguished, yet so closely associated that God is adequately known only through the saving work of Christ and the ongoing life of the Christian community. God is represented as the ultimate and initiating actor in the drama of salvation, and monotheism is preserved. Yet Christ is indispensable mediator and Lord of the church, and he nowhere seems understood as inferior to the Father. The writers use dualistic language to describe conversion and the moral distance believers must preserve from mainly pagan neighbors. At the same time both letters stress linkages between creation and redemption and speak so expansively of the universal effects of God's work in Christ that a door of hope for the future salvation of everyone and everything is firmly held open.

SELECT BIBLIOGRAPHY

Barclay, John M. G. 1997. *Colossians and Philemon*. New Testament Guides. Sheffield: Sheffield Academic Press.

Barth, Markus. 1974. *Ephesians*. 2 vols. Anchor Bible 34 and 34A. Garden City, N.Y.: Doubleday.

Best, Ernest. 1998. *A Critical and Exegetical Commentary on Ephesians*. International Critical Commentary. Edinburgh: T. & T. Clark.

Childs, Brevard S. 1993. *Biblical Theology of the Old and New Testaments*. Minneapolis: Fortress.

Dahl, Nils A. 2000. *Studies in Ephesians*. Edited by Nils A. Dahl et al. Tübingen: Mohr (Siebeck).

de Oliveira, Anacleto. 2000. "Christozentrik im Kolosserbrief." Pages 72–103 in *Christologie in der Paulus-Schule: Zur Rezeptionsgeschichte des paulinischen Evangeliums*. Edited by Klaus Scholtissek. Stuttgarter Bibelstudien 181. Stuttgart: Katholisches Bibelwerk.

Dunn, James D. G. 1996. *The Epistles to the Colossians and to Philemon*. Grand Rapids: Eerdmans.

Gese, Michael. 1997. *Das Vermächtnis des Apostels: Die Rezeption der paulinischen Theologie im Epheserbrief*. Wissenschaftliche Untersuchungen zum Neuen Testament. Reihe 2, 99. Tübingen: Mohr (Siebeck).

Hay, David M. 2000. *Colossians*. Abingdon New Testament Commentaries. Nashville: Abingdon.

Hoppe, Rudolf. 1992. "Theologie in den Deuteropaulinen (Kolosser- und Epheserbrief)." Pages 163–85 in *Monotheismus und Christologie: Zur Gottesfrage im hellenistischen Judentum und im Urchristentum*. Edited by Hans-Josef Klauck. Quaestiones Disputatae 138. Freiburg: Herder.

Lincoln, Andrew T. 1982. "The Use of the OT in Ephesians." *Journal for the Study of the New Testament* 14:16–57.

———. 1990. *Ephesians*. Word Biblical Commentary 42. Dallas: Word.

Lincoln, Andrew T., and A. J. M. Wedderburn. 1993. *The Theology of the Later Pauline Letters.* New Testament Theology. Cambridge: Cambridge University Press.

MacDonald, Margaret Y. 2000. *Colossians and Ephesians.* Sacra Pagina 17. Collegeville, Minn.: Liturgical Press.

Meeks, Wayne A. 1977. "In One Body: The Unity of Humankind in Colossians and Ephesians." Pages 209–21 in *God's Christ and His People: Studies in Honour of Nils Alstrup Dahl.* Edited by Jacob Jervell and Wayne A. Meeks. Oslo: Universitetsforlaget.

Meyer, Paul W. 1996. "'The Father': The Presentation of God in the Fourth Gospel." Pages 255–73 in *Exploring the Gospel of John: In Honor of D. Moody Smith.* Edited by R. Alan Culpepper and C. Clifton Black. Louisville, Ky.: Westminster John Knox.

Moritz, Thorsten. 1996. *A Profound Mystery: The Use of the Old Testament in Ephesians.* Novum Testamentum Supplement 85. Leiden: E. J. Brill.

O'Brien, Peter T. 1999. *The Letter to the Ephesians.* Pillar New Testament Commentary. Grand Rapids: Eerdmans.

Perkins, Pheme. 1997. *Ephesians.* Abingdon New Testament Commentaries. Nashville: Abingdon.

Pöhlmann, Wolfgang. 1973. "Die hymnischen All-Prädikationen in Kol 1, 15–20." *Zeitschrift für die neutestamentliche Wissenschaft* 64:53–74.

Pokorný, Petr. 1992. *Der Brief des Paulus an die Epheser.* Theologischer Handkommentar zum Neuen Testament 10/II. Leipzig: Evangelische Verlagsanstalt.

Schweizer, Eduard. 1982. *The Letter to the Colossians: A Commentary.* Translated by Andrew Chester. Minneapolis: Augsburg.

Thompson, Marianne Meye. 2000. *The Promise of the Father: Jesus and God in the New Testament.* Louisville, Ky.: Westminster John Knox.

Yoder Neufeld, Thomas R. 1997. *'Put on the Armour of God': The Divine Warrior from Isaiah to Ephesians.* Journal for the Study of the New Testament: Supplement Series 140. Sheffield: Sheffield Academic Press.

11

The Savior God

The Pastoral Epistles

JOSEPH A. FITZMYER, S.J.

In the Pauline corpus, the epistle to Titus and the two epistles to Timothy stand apart from the rest. Although they bear the name of Paul, the apostle of Christ Jesus, their subject matter, language, and purpose differentiate them from the rest of the corpus in many ways. Since the time of P. Anton in the mid-eighteenth century they have been called "the Pastoral Epistles," not in the sense that they deal with bucolic topics, but because they are concerned with the growth and character of evangelized communities rather than the missionary expansion of the Christian church, which is the concern of the other letters of the Pauline corpus. They deal with the qualifications and ministries of "pastors" in the Christian church: the bishop, presbyters, and deacons. Yet their subject matter is not limited to such pastoral or ecclesiastical concerns, because other theological issues and matters of orthodoxy are addressed in them at times. The doctrinal teaching in these three epistles may be at a minimum in comparison with other Pauline writings; part of the reason for this minimal doctrinal content is the hortatory or parenetic concern of their author. Nevertheless, they also have a theology of their own, which is not inferior but concerned rather with the consolidation of a later stage of the growing church (Brox 1969, 52–54).

Although the three epistles have a certain homogeneity, they are not all of one piece. One detects a certain similarity in Titus and in 1 Timothy, but 2 Timothy stands out as somewhat different. It reads like a last will and testament along with a certain amount of instruction for pastors. Indeed, J. Murphy-O'Connor finds thirty items on which Titus and 1 Timothy agree against 2 Timothy, and even when they use the same terms, it is often with a different nuance (1991, 403–18).

Many New Testament interpreters consider the three Pastoral Epistles as pseudepigraphical, written by an unknown early Christian who was acquainted with and sympathetic to Paul's thinking. These epistles are thus understood as an expression of the way in which the apostle Paul was understood by a later generation of Christians toward the end of the first century A.D. Thus, an esteem for Paul led the author to grace with Paul's authority teachings important for the growing church, when Paul was no longer part of it. This is why both Titus and Timothy are treated as delegates of Paul in Crete and in Ephesus respectively, to neither of whom the title *episkopos* or *presbyteros* is ever given. They are, then, more than local bishops of these places. In the rest of this discussion, I too shall assume that the Pastoral Epistles are pseudepigraphical, and I shall refer to their author as "Paul."

Among topics other than ministerial or ecclesiastical that are dealt with in these epistles, there is an important teaching about God. Some of that doctrine finds parallels in other writings of the Pauline corpus, but a number of the affirmations are distinctive and merit due study.

All told, there are fifty-one instances in the Pastorals where *theos* is used in some form, either the noun itself or in compound adjectives such as *philotheos* and *theopneustos*. Moreover, there are several instances in 1 and 2 Timothy where *ho kyrios* appears (it is not used in Titus), where it may refer to God rather than the risen Christ; some occurrences are ambiguous, either God or Christ, and opinions about them differ among interpreters.

The rest of my remarks about God and his activity in the Pastoral Epistles will be made under four headings: (1) The Only God, (2) God as Father and Savior, (3) God and Christ Jesus, and (4) The Relationship of Human Beings to God.

THE ONLY GOD

Part of the reason why the Pastorals were composed was to offset the influence of contemporary folk religion in the Greco-Roman world of the eastern Mediterranean area. Polytheism or some form of henotheism prevailed there, and emperor worship was widespread. Consequently, the teaching in the Pastorals about the one God is a forthright rebuttal of such claims and a reaffirmation of the Christian monotheism based on its Jewish heritage.

This is evident from the way "Paul" emphasizes "the only God," the unique and universal God, who is sovereign and transcendent. In 1 Tim 1:17, he formulates a doxology thus: "To the King of the ages, immortal, invisible, the only God, be honor and glory forever. Amen." In so framing his praise, the Christian "Paul" reaffirms what the Shemaʿ of monotheistic Israel had proclaimed centuries before: "Hear, O Israel, Yahweh is our God, Yahweh alone" (Deut 6:4). He enhances his reaffirmation, however, with contemporary Hellenistic attributes of divinity so that it becomes a distinctively Christian expression of monotheism. God is "King of the ages," a title also used as a variant in Rev 15:4, and he is *aphthartos* (lit. "imperishable," a way of saying "immortal" [cf. 1 Tim 6:16]). This is a quality used of deities in Greek magical papyri. He is also *aoratos*, "unseen," another quality often used by Greek writers about gods.

An equally important passage is found at the end of the same epistle, when "Paul" charges Timothy to keep the commandment, "until the manifestation [*epiphaneia*] of our Lord Jesus Christ, which he [God] will bring about at the right time—he who is the blessed and only Sovereign, the King of kings and Lord of lords. It is he alone who has immortality and dwells in unapproachable light, whom no one has ever seen or can see; to him be honor and eternal dominion. Amen" (1 Tim 6:14–16). In this doxological affirmation, which spells out in more detail what the preceding passage already said, "Paul" lists seven attributes that express the uniqueness of God. Although R. E. Brown understands these titles as predicated of Christ (1997, 662), interpreters more commonly understand them as attributes of God, who will bring about the manifestation of Christ.

These verses have been interpreted often as a formulation borrowed from a Christian liturgy heavily indebted to a Hellenistic Jewish hymn or synagogue service. They have a hymnic rhythm, and many of the attributes are paralleled in Jewish writings and used of Yahweh; they could thus be reactions against the divinization of Roman emperors and their pretensions to universal rule. Spicq (1969, 572), however, argues rather in favor of a Pauline composition that utilizes Old Testament notions translated into Hellenistic Greek, but F. Young (1994, 49) rightly notes that, while it may be important to recognize the language of the Hellenistic synagogue, that may distract actually from the perspective this doxology is meant to introduce, namely, the offering of honor and glory to the unique God.

In either case, the title *dynastēs*, "sovereign," is parallel to Sir 46:5, 16; 2 Macc 1:24; 12:15, 28; 15:4, 23. Although the title "King of kings" has a long history, being used by rulers in the Assyrian, Egyptian, Parthian, and Persian worlds of antiquity (see Griffiths 1953), it is found also in Ezra 7:12 (for Artaxerxes), Ezek 26:7, and Dan 2:36 (for Nebuchadnezzar); it is predicated of Yahweh in 2 Macc 13:4; 3 Macc 5:35. Moreover, Deut 10:17 speaks of "the Lord your God" as "God of gods and Lord of lords, the great God, mighty and awesome"; see also Ps 136:3, which is echoed in Rev 17:14. In Rev 19:16, "King of kings and Lord of lords" is used of the rider on the white horse, "the word of God." Spicq lists the many Hellenistic parallels that can be found to these titles (1969, 573–74).

Another important passage in the Pastorals where the uniqueness of God is asserted unmistakably is 1 Tim 2:1–5. There "Paul" is urging Christians to pray, intercede, and give thanks for all human beings, but especially for kings and others in high positions: "This is right and is acceptable in the sight of God our Savior, who desires everyone to be saved and to come to the knowledge of the truth. For there is one God . . ." (1 Tim 2:3–5). Here the uniqueness of God is the basis for the divine universal salvific concern for all human beings.

Elsewhere in isolated statements, "Paul" attributes to "the only God" a number of other qualities. Chief among them is "the living God" (1 Tim 3:15; 4:10), which echoes a genuine Pauline phrase (Rom 9:26 [quoting Hos 1:10]); 2 Cor 3:3; 6:16; 1 Thess 1:9; cf. Acts 14:15). This epithet means that God is not a mere idol made by human hands, or an abstraction. It takes on a specific pregnant nuance in the Pastorals, when "the divine predicate 'the Living One' (*zōn*) is understood in a causative way; 'it is the living God who makes the promise of life (*epangelia zōēs* [4:8]) come true'" (Dibelius and Conzelmann 1972, 69). This quality, then, is "an integral element in Paul's monotheistic kerygma" (Goodwin 1996, 75).

Other attributes are "the blessed God" (*makarios*, 1 Tim 1:11; 6:15) and "our great God" (Titus 2:13)—not, to be sure, that that greatness implied other deities in a henotheistic sense, but rather that God is highly esteemed. God is also *apseudēs*, "one who does not deceive" (Titus 1:2).

"Paul" regards this unique God as one "who gives life to all things" (*tou theou tou zōogonountos ta panta*, 1 Tim 6:13), and so he speaks of God as creator of everything and source of all that is good. Consequently, he criticizes wayward Christians who advocate "abstinence from foods, which God created to be received with thanksgiving by those who believe" (1 Tim 4:3); for "everything created by God is good" (1 Tim 4:4). Indeed, it is "God who richly provides us with everything for our enjoyment" (1 Tim 6:17). So "Paul" acknowledges the providence of the Creator God.

He is also a powerful God (having *kratos aiōnion*, 1 Tim 6:16); consequently, "Paul" exhorts Timothy to "join with me in suffering for the gospel, relying on the power of God, who saved us" (2 Tim 1:8–9). Similarly, "Paul" reminds Timothy to "rekindle the gift of God that is within you through the laying on of my hands" (2 Tim 1:6). Thus, God is the source of the status that Timothy enjoys and of much good that Christian believers have.

To this unique God belongs the gospel with which "Paul" has been entrusted: "the glorious gospel of the blessed God" (1 Tim 1:11), which he calls "my gospel, for which I suffer hardship. . . . But the word of God is not chained" (2 Tim 2:9). He tends, then, to see the "gospel" as the "word of God," and it is not to be discredited (Titus 2:5). In these instances, neither "gospel" nor "word of God" is used in the sense of a written text, but they denote rather a divine message or instruction coming from its heavenly source. So "Paul" reiterates his view that everything created by God is good, "for it is sanctified by God's word and by prayer" (1 Tim 4:5), no doubt alluding to the Creator's view of what he had made as "good" in Gen 1:4, 10, 12, 18, 21. For these and other such reasons, "Paul" is concerned that "the name of God . . . may not be blasphemed" (1 Tim 6:1).

GOD AS FATHER AND SAVIOR

It may be surprising that "Paul" hails God as "Father" only in the opening greeting of these epistles: "Grace, mercy, and peace from God the Father and Christ Jesus our Lord" (1 Tim 1:2; 2 Tim 1:1; cf. Titus 1:4). This stands in contrast to the frequent appellation of God as "Father of our Lord Jesus Christ" in other letters of Paul (e.g., Rom 15:6; 2 Cor 1:3; 11:31; Col 1:3). It is not even "our Father," as in Rom 1:7; 1 Cor 1:3; 2 Cor 1:2; Phil 1:2; Phlm 3. The formulaic title of God as Father has been derived from the Old Testament, where Yahweh is portrayed as the father of corporate Israel (Exod 4:22–23; Deut 14:1; 32:6; Isa 30:9; Jer 3:4, 19; 31:9; Hos 11:1–3; Mal 2:10; Sir 51:10) and even as "our Father" (Isa 63:16; 64:8).

Yet if the name "Father" is rare in the Pastorals, there are other ways in which "Paul" makes up for that and stresses God's care for human beings, and chief among them is the distinctive use of "Savior." The epithet *theos sōtēr* occurs eight times in the entire New Testament, but six of them are in the Pastorals. (The other two are Luke 1:47 [echoing Hab 3:18] and Jude 25.) Significantly, there are no instances of its use in the rest of the Pauline corpus, which enhances the distinctiveness of this title in these epistles. This epithet stresses the essence of God's activity in salvation, showing how God's sovereignty is expressed in his will that all human beings be saved. Thus, Timothy and Titus are challenged to acknowledge this unique deity as "God our Savior."

The main occurrence of this epithet has already been cited above in the passage mentioning God's universal salvific will: "This is right and acceptable in the sight of God our Savior, who desires everyone to be saved and to come to the knowledge of the truth" (1 Tim 2:3–4). The phrase "God our Savior" appears again in uncomplicated passages such as 1 Tim 1:1; Titus 1:3; 2:10; 3:4.

In 1 Tim 4:10, however, "Paul" maintains that he has his "hope set on the living God, who is the Savior of all people, especially of those who believe." This passage is significant because it joins the concept of "Savior" with the notion of "the living God," but it also points up a problem in the use of *sōtēr*. The final words are not easy to interpret. If one says that "Paul" envisions God as "Savior of all people," how is one to understand "especially those who believe"? Does not the former assertion already include the latter? Are not believers already part of "all people"?

Part of this problem comes from the meaning of *sōtēr* in the Hellenistic world in which "Paul" lived; part of it comes also from the meaning of "salvation" that is involved. Each of these points needs further discussion, but before I begin that discussion, it is wise to introduce some further related passages.

In addition to 1 Tim 2:4, "Paul" also uses the verb *sōzō* of God's activity elsewhere: "the power of God, who saved us" (2 Tim 1:8–9); "he saved us" (Titus 3:5); and possibly in 2 Tim 4:18, where the subject of the verb *ho kyrios* is ambiguous but may refer to God. Finally, in Titus 2:11, "Paul" states that "the grace of God has appeared, bringing salvation to all" (*hē charis tou theou sōtērios*, lit. "the saving grace of God has appeared to all human beings"). These passages raise the question about what is meant by salvation in the Pastorals, where the abstract noun *sōtēria*, *sōtērion* does not appear, and in what way it is to be understood as universal.

In the contemporary Hellenistic world *sōtēr* meant "savior, deliverer, preserver." It was an epithet for gods such as Zeus, Apollo, Hermes, Asclepios, Isis, Sarapis, Artemis, and the Dioscuri; sometimes it was a title for humans, such as the Ptolemies and Roman emperors or governors. As a cultic epithet, Greeks and Romans used it to invoke such deliverers in time of need (illness, travail, sea storms, famine, and economic distress; see Spicq 1969, 315–16; Dibelius and Conzelmann 1972, 100–103). Josephus even tells us that he himself was hailed by Jews in Judea at the time of the revolt against Rome as *euergetēn kai sōtēra tēs chōras autōn*, "benefactor and savior of their land" (*Life* 47.244; cf. 50.259).

In the Old Testament, however, Yahweh too is recognized as Savior (*môšiaʿ*) of Israel in Isa 45:15; Zech 8:7 (cf. Ps 25:5; Mic 7:7; Hos 13:4); and at times Yahweh raises up human saviors for his people (Judg 3:9, 15; 6:36; 2 Kgs 13:5).

In the LXX of Isa 45:15, this epithet for God is rendered precisely as *sōtēr*, as it also is in Ps 25:5 and Mic 7:7; sometimes it uses instead the participle *sōzōn* (Hos 13:4; see also *Psalms of Solomon* 3:6; 8:33; 16:4; 17:3). Philo also speaks of God as *sōtēr te kai euergetēs*, "Savior and Benefactor" (*Spec.* 1.38.209; *Sobr.* 11.55). Moreover, in 1QM 14:5, the God of Israel is praised for "preserving mercy for his covenant and pledges salvation for the people he has redeemed." So the use of "Savior" for God in the pre-Christian Jewish world is well attested, and it acquires a specific Jewish nuance of the creator God as giver of life and providing for his people.

The upshot is that it is not easy to say whence "Paul" derives this distinctive epithet he uses for the one God, whether from his Old Testament or Jewish background or from the contemporary Hellenistic usage. Kelly thinks that there is "no need to regard it as a Christian correction of the growing custom of saluting the emperor as saviour" (1963, 40), but then how does one account for the frequent insistence on this notion in the Pastorals?

In what sense, however, does "Paul" say that God "saves"? S. M. Baugh answers that "Paul" uses the title in the Hellenistic sense of "a generous benefactor":

> The phrase "Savior of all people, especially believers" should not be interpreted as teaching a universal atonement. It is an assertion of the deity of the true and living God in the face of pagan notions of deity; and it asserts that the saviors looked to by the people with whom Paul and Timothy associated daily could not be compared with the true Benefactor of all people, the Living God, whose common grace embraces the whole world. (1992, 338)

He states further that although "eternal salvation" is the intended meaning of "to be saved" in 1 Tim 2:4, that meaning is different from "the earthly benefactions referred to in 1 Tim 4:10" (1992, 339). He translates *pantas anthrōpous* in 4:10 as "all sorts of peoples" (ibid.). Thus, the universality of eternal salvation is eliminated from 1 Tim 4:10, and all this is argued by Baugh in an article dominated by Arminian versus Calvinist concerns about "the Savior of all people." The upshot is that for Baugh, "Paul" is describing God as Savior in the sense that he bestows benefactions ("common grace") on "all sorts of peoples" during their time on earth, and that has nothing to do with "eternal salvation."

"Paul" does speak at times of God's benefactions to him in this life, which might fit the category of "common grace." A specific kind of salvation is found in 2 Tim 3:11, when "Paul" speaks of "the Lord" who rescued him from all the persecutions and sufferings that happened to him in Antioch, Iconium, and Lystra (recall the story of Paul in Acts 13:14, 50; 14:1, 5–8, 19). More than likely *ho kyrios* is to be understood as God (so Spicq 1969, 782; Kelly 1963, 199–200; Dornier 1969, 229; Bassler 1996, 165; but Marshall [1999, 785] understands it of Christ). One reason for interpreting the phrase for God is the allusion in the verse to Ps 34:20. This is, however, an isolated instance of such an earthly rescue or salvation ascribed to God in the Pastorals.

Such an interpretation of 1 Tim 4:10, though, is hardly correct. First, because *pantas anthrōpous* does not mean "all sorts of peoples"; it means "all human beings" and echoes the identical phrase in 1 Tim 2:4.

Second, even though the abstract noun "salvation" nowhere appears in the Pastorals, there is indication enough to show that "to be saved" has to do with "eternal life" or "the life to come," which differs from "the present life" (1 Tim 4:8) and "the present age" (Titus 2:12; 1 Tim 6:17; cf. 2 Tim 4:10). The closest one comes to a definition of what "salvation" would be is found in Titus 1:2, where "Paul" speaks of "the hope of eternal life that God, who never lies, promised before the ages began." Again, in Titus 3:7 he says, "having been justified by his grace, we might become heirs according to the hope of eternal life." Or again, "those who would come to believe in him [Jesus Christ] for eternal life" (1 Tim 1:16; cf. 1 Tim 6:12, 19). Possibly one should add 2 Tim 4:18, where "Paul" speaks apocalyptically: "The Lord will rescue me from every evil attack and save me for his heavenly kingdom." Here *ho kyrios* is ambiguous, possibly meaning God, and kingdom could refer to "the kingdom of God" (cf. Dan 4:3; Wis 6:4; 10:10; Matt 6:10). Or it could mean the risen Christ and his "kingdom" (Luke 23:42; 1 Cor 15:24; 2 Pet 1:11). In either case, it too would be a synonym for "eternal life." Moreover, F. Young has proposed plausibly that the oft-occurring phrase, *pistos ho logos*, "the saying is sure," is "invariably attached to a statement about salvation" (1994, 56), and her analysis of that salvation agrees with what is proposed here.

A fuller description of "salvation" must involve Christ's role in it; that raises yet another problem in the meaning of *sōtēr* in the Pastorals, where it is predicated also of the risen Christ (see the next section).

Third, a comment has to be made on *malista pistōn* (4:10), which the NRSV renders as "especially of those who believe." T. C. Skeat (1979, 174–75) has shown that *malista* can at times mean "in other words" or "that is to say" (see Titus 1:10; 2 Tim 4:13; Oxyrhynchus papyri 1411, 3253, 3302). He would translate the phrase in 1 Tim 4:10: "that is to say, all who believe in Him." With such a meaning, one sees that the final phrase of the verse is merely a precision, because the sense is hardly that God is the Savior of nonbelievers. So understood, 1 Tim 4:10 becomes a striking confirmation of 1 Tim 2:4. This passage, then, encapsulates well the teaching of "Paul" about the activity of the living God, who not only raised Christ from the dead (2 Tim 2:8) but through him promised life (2 Tim 1:1) to all believers. It also shows why "Paul" thinks of God as acting with power (2 Tim 1:8). The "main object in this passage, however, is not to discuss the deep issues of predestination and grace, but merely to make it clear beyond all doubting that those who make a genuine effort to practice *eusebeia* and lead a fully Christian life, placing their hope in the living God, will not be disappointed" (Kelly 1962, 102–3; cf. F. Young, 1994, 57–58).

GOD AND CHRIST JESUS

Although God is the Savior of all human beings in the primary sense in the Pastorals, Jesus Christ is also "Savior" by being the means through which God's salvific plan is implemented and revealed. In greeting Titus, "Paul" says, "Grace and peace from God the Father and Christ Jesus our Savior" (Titus 1:4). This appellation for Christ occurs again in a more pronounced way, as "Paul" records that God's purpose and grace have been "revealed through the appearing of our Savior Christ Jesus, who abolished death and brought life and immortality to light through the gospel" (2 Tim 1:10). Here salvation is spelled out as the abolition of death and introduction to life and immortality wrought by Christ Jesus and his gospel, another way of speaking about eternal salvation. Similarly, when "Paul" mentions God's merciful salvation wrought through the water of rebirth and renewal by the Holy Spirit, he adds, "This Spirit he poured out on us richly through Jesus Christ our Savior" (Titus 3:6). Hence, salvation is effected not just through the preached gospel but also through Christ and the Spirit poured out on humanity. In this instance, the salvific activity is seen coming from God through Christ and the Spirit. Again, in 1 Tim 1:15, "Paul" says, "The saying is sure and worthy of full acceptance, that Christ Jesus came into the world to save sinners."

In Titus 2:13, however, one meets one of the most problematic passages in the Pastorals: "We wait for the blessed hope and the manifestation of the glory of our great God and Savior, Jesus Christ" (*doxa tou megalou theou kai sōtēros hēmōn Iēsou Christou*). That Jesus Christ should be spoken of here as "our Savior" is not the problem, because it merely echoes the three foregoing passages where he bears this title, but that he seems to be called "our great God."

The meaning of the verse is, consequently, quite controverted. Three modes of interpretation have been suggested: (1) "The glory of our great God and of our Savior Jesus Christ." This translation distinguishes "our great God" from "our Savior Jesus Christ," and it would mean that Christians await the future glorious appearance of two figures. It is problematic because one definite article (*tou*) governs both *theou* and *sōtēros hēmōn* as a unit, with which the name *Iēsou Christou* stands in apposition. (2) "The glory of our great God and Savior, which [i.e., glory] is Jesus Christ." This translation respects the Greek syntactical unit and refers it to the Father, but it makes "Jesus Christ" stand in apposition to "glory"; he would be a personification of that glory. (3) "The glory of our great God and Savior Jesus Christ." This translation makes Jesus Christ the "great God and Savior," and it most accurately renders the Greek text, even if there is no other place in the Pastorals where the distinction between God and Christ is obscured, as it seems to be here. R. E. Brown (1994, 181–82) notes that Conzelmann, Jeremias, and Kelly have rejected the third interpretation, but "the majority (including Cullmann, Quinn, and Spicq) argue for it, accepting the fact that Jesus is here called "God." The NRSV, RSV, NJB, and REB follow the third interpretation, but they add as an alternative rendering in a footnote, "Or *of the great God and our Savior*," which is the first interpretation given above.

In addition to the four instances where the title "Savior" is extended to the risen Christ, God and Christ are often coupled as a pair, for example when

"Paul" sends his greetings of grace and peace (Titus 1:4; 1 Tim 1:2; 2 Tim 1:1) and when he identifies himself as an apostle of Christ Jesus "by the will of God" (2 Tim 1:1) or "by the command of God our Savior and of Christ Jesus our hope" (1 Tim 1:1). Moreover, "Paul" charges Timothy "in the presence of God and of Christ Jesus" to keep rules or commandments (1 Tim 5:21; 6:13; 2 Tim 4:1).

More significantly, however, "Paul" portrays Christ as the one through whom God's salvation, grace, or mercy comes to human beings, especially those who believe. The passage already quoted above about the "one God" continues immediately to explain Christ's role as part of the truth to which everyone is desired to come: "For there is one God; there is also one mediator between God and humankind, Christ Jesus, himself human, who gave himself a ransom for all" (1 Tim 2:5–6). Again, as in a passage already cited above: "This Spirit he poured out on us richly through Jesus Christ our Savior, so that, having been justified by his grace, we might become heirs according to the hope of eternal life" (Titus 3:6). Although this passage echoes the genuine Pauline teaching of justification by grace (Rom 3:24), only the Pastorals explicitly formulate Christ's role in it as *mesitēs*, "mediator," a teaching that Paul himself was striving to express in Gal 3:19–20.

The relationship of Christ to God in salvation is complicated by another notoriously difficult passage, where the Greek text is not uniformly transmitted in all manuscripts. In 1 Tim 3:16, "Paul" incorporates into the text what is widely regarded as a primitive Christian hymn or an early liturgical profession of faith, set forth in six rhythmic lines with antithetic parallelism (involving *sarx-pneuma*, *angeloi-ethnē*, *kosmos-doxa*) and assonance (*-thē* in the aorist passive verbs):

> Without any doubt, the mystery of our religion is great:
>   He was revealed in flesh,
>   vindicated in spirit,
>   seen by angels,
>   proclaimed among Gentiles,
>   believed in throughout the world,
>   taken up in glory.

Manuscripts S*, A*, C*, F, G, 33, 365 read the first word as the masculine relative pronoun *hos*, "who"; manuscript D*, followed by the Vetus Latina, reads the neuter relative (*ho*, *quod*); but manuscripts S^c, A^c, C², D², Psi, 1739, 1881, and the Koine text tradition read *theos*.

The six lines are an attempt to explain *mystērion*, "mystery," which is the essential content of Christian faith (see 1 Tim. 3:9), what has been hidden but what God has now revealed. The neuter relative would agree with this noun as its antecedent, but it is not possible that "mystery" is the subject of the following aorist passive verbs.

What would be the antecedent of the masculine relative pronoun? The last occurring masculine (toward the end of the preceding verse) is *stylos*, "pillar," which is hardly the subject, and before that *theou zōntos*, "the living God." The latter may seem to account for the variant reading *theos*, but that is an unlikely antecedent. For if "God" were the subject of the six-liner, a problem would be immediately apparent: How then would one square "revealed in flesh" with the assertion in 1 Tim 6:16 that God "dwells in unapproachable light, whom no one has ever seen or can see"? Or 1 Tim 1:17, "invisible"? For this reason, the RSV, NRSV, and many commentators have chosen to follow the first reading *hos*, understanding it as "He." The NAB literally renders it "Who" and interprets it in a footnote as Christ. The meaning, then, would be that Christ is the content of "the mystery of our religion." (The KJV and Luther's translation use "God" [see Zoba 1995].)

The mystery concerns Jesus Christ, who "was revealed in flesh," that is, "Christ Jesus, himself human" (*anthrōpos Christos Iēsous*, 1 Tim 2:5), whose manifestation *en sarki* comprehends the incarnation and the totality of his historic, earthly career as God's salvific envoy. Compare 1 Pet 3:18: "He was put to death in the flesh, but made alive in the spirit." He was "vindicated in spirit," that is, the human Jesus who ended his life by being crucified was actually declared in God's sight the righteous one (cf. Isa 45:25 LXX). The contrast of flesh and spirit "identifies the two spheres of existence, the one characterized by humanity (with all its limitations), the other characterized by its operative agent, the Holy Spirit" (Towner 1989, 91). He was "seen by angels," that is, the vindication of the risen Christ was witnessed by heavenly beings in his new abode (cf. Phil 2:10a; 1 Pet 3:22). He was "proclaimed among Gentiles," that is, preached as the risen Savior, Lord, and Messiah in the apostolic proclamation to the nations beyond Israel. He was "believed in throughout the world," that is, acknowledged in faith by human beings wherever news of him was preached as the Savior of all. He was "taken up in glory," that is, after his death he was victoriously and triumphantly assumed to the glorious presence of God the Father, where he reigns as the risen Lord.

THE RELATIONSHIP OF HUMAN BEINGS TO GOD

In this section, I shall try to bring together a number of not too closely related texts of the Pastorals that touch on the relationship of humanity to God. My comments are subdivided into three parts: (1) believers and nonbelievers, (2) "Paul," and (3) church officials.

Believers and Nonbelievers

A major concern, especially in Titus and 1 Timothy, is the preservation of the faith of Christians in face of false teaching. This is called "the faith of God's elect" (Titus 1:1). When "Paul" speaks of God's universal salvific will, he says that God desires everyone "to be saved and to come to the knowledge of the truth" (1 Tim 2:4). The "truth" is expressed then in the following verse about the "one God" and the "one mediator" (2:5). Those who acknowledge this truth are considered "God's elect" precisely because of their belief, and they are called *pistoi*, "those who believe" (1 Tim 4:3, 10, 12; 2 Tim 2:2).

"Paul" further demands that "those who have come to believe in God may be careful to devote themselves to good works" (Titus 3:8). Furthermore, he is aware that believers can become corrupted: "They profess to know God, but they deny him by their actions" (Titus 1:16); he castigates such people as "lovers of themselves, lovers of money, . . . rather than lovers of God" (*philotheoi*, 2 Tim 3:2, 4). "Paul" knows, however, that "God may perhaps grant that they [i.e., opponents of his delegate Timothy] will repent and come to know the truth" (2 Tim 2:25). He maintains too that "God did not give us a spirit of cowardice, but rather a spirit of power and love and of self-discipline" (2 Tim 1:7). "Paul" prays, "May the Lord grant mercy to the household of Onesiphorus, because he has often refreshed me" (2 Tim 1:16), where *ho kyrios* undoubtedly refers to God, as again in 1:18; 2:7, 22, 24.

In his concluding remarks in 2 Timothy, when "Paul" recalls the great harm done to him by Alexander the coppersmith, he adds, "The Lord will pay him back for his deeds" (4:14), where *ho kyrios* undoubtedly means God; the remark characterizes God's normal dealings with human beings. Similarly, a motive for Christian conduct is what "is pleasing in God's sight" (1 Tim 5:4). He gives an instance in the case of children or grandchildren making some payment to their parents. Similarly, "Paul" realizes that the real widow is one who "has set her hope on God [variant: the Lord]" (1 Tim 5:5). He recommends that Timothy urge the rich "not to be haughty, or to set their hopes on the uncertainty of riches, but rather on God who richly provides us with everything for our enjoyment" (1 Tim 6:17).

"Paul"

A special relationship to God is enjoyed by "Paul," who calls himself "a servant/slave of God" (Titus 1:1), using an epithet never found in the genuine Pauline letters or the Deutero-Paulines, where *doulos Christou* is used (e.g., Rom 1:1; Gal 1:10; Col 4:12). He is also "an apostle of Christ Jesus by the will of God" (2 Tim 1:1) and "by the command of God our Savior and Christ Jesus our hope" (1 Tim 1:1). Thus, he roots his apostolic activity in both God and Christ. For "in due time he [God] revealed his word through the proclamation with which I have been entrusted by the command of God our Savior" (Titus 1:3).

In encouraging Timothy, "Paul" writes, "I am grateful to God—whom I worship with a clear conscience, as my ancestors did—when I remember you constantly in my prayers night and day" (2 Tim 1:3). As he reflects on his approaching death, "Paul" admits, "From now on there is reserved for me the crown of righteousness, which the Lord, the righteous judge, will give me on that day, and not only to me but also to all who have longed for his appearing" (2 Tim 4:8). Here *ho kyrios* is at first sight ambiguous, possibly referring to either God or Christ, but in light of 4:1, where "Paul" speaks "in the presence of God and Christ Jesus, who is to judge the living and the dead" and where the singular participle *tou mellontos krinein* modifies *Christou Iēsou*, it probably should be taken as Christ the Lord.

Church Officials

"Paul" treats both Titus and Timothy as his delegates, who represent him in the churches of Crete and Ephesus and are charged "to put things in order" (Titus 1:5; 1 Tim 1:3). "I am writing these instructions to you so that, if I am delayed, you may know how one ought to behave in the household of God, which is the church of the living God, the pillar and bulwark of the truth" (1 Tim 3:14–15).

Timothy, accordingly, is addressed as "a man of God," an Old Testament epithet (Deut 33:1 [Moses]; 1 Sam 2:27; 9:6 [Samuel]; 1 Kgs 13:1; 2 Chr 8:14 [David]), but now it refers to a man of the unique God that the Christian "Paul" worships. He also tells Timothy that "all scripture is inspired by God and is useful for teaching, for reproof, for correction, and for training in righteousness so that everyone who belongs to God may be proficient, equipped for every good work" (2 Tim 3:16–17). The NRSV has garbled the text and missed the allusion to Timothy in *ho tou theou anthrōpos*, "man of God," the term "Paul" used of him explicitly above.

Moreover, "Paul" advises his delegate Timothy to remind Christians and "warn them before God [variant: the Lord] that they are to avoid wrangling over words, which does no good" (2 Tim 2:14). Timothy is likewise told to present himself "to God as one approved by him, a worker who has no need to be ashamed, rightly explaining the word of truth" (2:15).

In that community, "Paul" insists that the bishop must be "God's steward" (*theou oikonomon*, Titus 1:7), one called to "take care of God's church" (1 Tim 3:5), which is "the household of God' (1 Tim 3:15).

Moreover, "God's firm foundation stands, bearing this inscription: 'The Lord knows those who are his,' and 'Let everyone who calls on the name of the Lord turn away from wickedness'" (2 Tim 2:19, quoting Num 16:5 and a combined form of Greek Isa 26:13 and 52:11).

"Paul" ends 2 Timothy with his farewell: "The Lord be with your spirit" (4:22), where *ho kyrios* may refer to God, but a few manuscripts add after Lord "Jesus" or "Jesus Christ."

CONCLUSION

From the foregoing survey of statements made by "Paul" about God, one can see how rich and variegated the theocentric teaching of the Pastoral Epistles is. Great emphasis is put above all on the one God, whose uniqueness is expressed not only in imitation of the monotheism of Israel of old but also with Hellenistic divine attributes or titles: *aoratos* (unseen), *aphthartos* (imperishable), *apseudēs* (one who does not deceive), *makarios* (blessed), *dynastēs* (sovereign), and having *kratos aiōnion* (everlasting power).

Even though God is hailed as "Father" only in the opening greetings of the Pastoral Epistles, his distinctive title in these writings is *sōtēr*. The notion of "God our Savior" stresses divine activity in the salvation offered to all human beings, especially to those who believe, in terms particularly of eternal life. This activity of God is asserted in these writings over against a plethora of gods and human individuals often regarded as "saviors" or benefactors in the contemporary Greco-Roman world. That is why "Paul" insists that to "the only God" be honor and glory forever.

The title *sōtēr*, however, is extended also to the risen Christ in the Pastoral Epistles, because he is depicted as "the one mediator between God and humankind." In providing salvation for human beings, God has brought about "the manifestation of our Lord Jesus Christ at the right time." The extension of the title to Christ thus designates him as the agent of God's salvific activity.

"Paul" regards himself not only as the "servant/slave of God," but also as an apostle of Christ Jesus by "the will of God" or "the command of God." On behalf of "the gospel of the blessed God" he is called to suffer hardship, for this gospel is "the word of God," uttered for the instruction of humanity and to bring it to its salvific destiny.

As a result, human beings are themselves seen as related to God in many specific ways, but especially through "the faith of God's elect" they come "to be saved." Christians are thus called to manifest their "belief in God" and through good works to live so as to "be pleasing in God's sight" and share in their destiny of "eternal life."

Finally, as Spicq concludes, "These few references show to what extent the theology of the Pastorals is 'theocentric,' emphasizes the sovereignty of God, and stresses his initiative and constant role in governing humanity and the church. To him they ascribe the conception of a salvific plan, its historical implementation, and its realization by Christ and the Apostles, who transmit the knowledge of truth and justice in baptism. It is in the long run to God himself that this whole design of salvation is ordained" (1969, 245).

SELECT BIBLIOGRAPHY

Bassler, Jouette M. 1996. *1 Timothy, 2 Timothy, Titus.* Nashville: Abingdon.

Baugh, Steven M. 1992. "'Savior of All People': 1 Tim 4:10 in Context." *Westminster Theological Journal* 54:331–40.

Brown, Raymond E. 1994. *An Introduction to New Testament Christology.* New York: Paulist Press.

———. 1997. *An Introduction to the New Testament.* Anchor Bible Reference Library. New York: Doubleday.

Brox, Norbert. 1969. *Die Pastoralbriefe.* 4th ed. Regensburger Neues Testament 7/2. Regensburg: Pustet.

Dibelius, Martin, and Hans Conzelmann. 1972. *The Pastoral Epistles.* Hermeneia. Philadelphia: Fortress.

Donelson, Lewis R. 1986. *Pseudepigraphy and Ethical Argument in the Pastoral Epistles.* Hermeneutische Untersuchungen zur Theologie 22. Tübingen: Mohr (Siebeck).

Dornier, Pierre. 1969. *Les épîtres pastorales.* Sources bibliques. Paris: Gabalda.

Fee, Gordon D. 1988. *1 and 2 Timothy, Titus.* Peabody, Mass.: Hendrickson.

Goodwin, Mark J. 1996. "The Pauline Background of the Living God as Interpretive Context for 1 Timothy 4.10." *Journal for the Study of the New Testament* 61:65–85.

Griffiths, J. Gwyn. 1953. "*Basileus basileōn:* Remarks on the History of a Title." *Classical Philology* 48:145–54.

Kelly, J. N. D. 1963. *A Commentary on the Pastoral Epistles: I Timothy, II Timothy, Titus.* Harper's New Testament Commentaries. New York: Harper & Row.

Knight, George W. 1992. *The Pastoral Epistles: A Commentary on the Greek Text.* New International Greek Testament Commentary. Grand Rapids: Eerdmans.

Marshall, I. Howard, and Philip H. Towner. 1999. *The Pastoral Epistles.* International Critical Commentary. Edinburgh: T. &T. Clark.

Merkel, Helmut. 1991. *Die Pastoralbriefe.* 13th ed. Das Neue Testament Deutsch 9/1. Göttingen: Vandenhoeck & Ruprecht.

Murphy-O'Connor, Jerome. 1991. "2 Timothy Contrasted with 1 Timothy and Titus." *Revue biblique* 98:403–18.

Quinn, Jerome D. 1981. "Jesus as Savior and Only Mediator (1 Tim 2:3–6): Linguistic Paradigms of Acculturation." Pages 249–60 in *Fede e cultura alla luce della Bibbia.* Edited by J. D. Barthélemy. Turin: Elle di Ci.

———. 1990. *The Letter to Titus.* Anchor Bible 35. New York: Doubleday.

Roloff, Jürgen. 1988. *Der erste Brief an Timotheus.* Evangelisch-katholischer Kommentar zum Neuen Testament 15. Zürich: Benziger; Neukirchen-Vluyn: Neukirchener.

Skeat, T. C. 1979. "'Especially the Parchments': A Note on 2 Timothy 4:13." *Journal of Theological Studies* 30:173–77.

Spicq, Ceslas. 1969. *Saint Paul: Les épîtres pastorales.* 2 vols. 4th ed. Paris: Gabalda.

Towner, Philip H. 1989. *The Goal of Our Instruction: The Structure of Theology and Ethics in the Pastoral Epistles.* Journal for the Study of the New Testament: Supplement Series 34. Sheffield: Sheffield Academic Press.

Young, Frances M. 1994. *The Theology of the Pastoral Letters.* New Testament Theology. Cambridge: Cambridge University Press.

Zoba, Wendy Murray. 1995. "When Manuscripts Collide." *Christianity Today* 39 (October 23): 30–31.

12

God in Hebrews

Urging Children to Heavenly Glory

HAROLD W. ATTRIDGE

Although the "epistle" to the Hebrews focuses on the person and work of the heavenly high priest and his significance for a community of faith, God is the indispensable horizon within which discussion of such a priest makes sense and the ultimate focal point of such a priest's action. Hebrews, an anonymous homily from the third generation of the Christian movement (2:2), strives to reinvigorate addressees whose faith is apparently lagging in the face of external threats and obloquy (10:32–34; 13:13) and perhaps internal doubts about the reliability of eschatological promises (10:25). It ultimately affirms that all that is derives from God and to God all must be directed. Jesus is significant for members of his covenant community precisely because he enables others to be so directed, by the example that he sets and through the relationship with God that his faithful death enabled.

BASIC DOGMATIC CLAIMS

Although extracting systematic propositions from a text of the New Testament is a rather old-fashioned approach to theological analysis, Hebrews invites such an approach with its very plain propositional claims about God, which it apparently invites to be taken seriously.

Before launching into what it styles "much to say that is hard to explain" (5:11), which begins with the consideration of Melchizedek in chapter 7, Hebrews offers an ironic *captatio benevolentiae*, indicating that certain basic subjects need not be treated, including "faith toward God" (6:1). Yet the dismissal is ironic, because renewing faith in God is the ultimate goal of this "word of exhortation" (13:22). Not surprisingly, then, a definition of precisely that faith appears prominently in the midst of the catalogue of examples of fidelity in chapter 11. The fact that Enoch pleased God, earning him translation to heaven, elicits an explanation redolent of catechetical formulas. Enoch's faith, and the faith of anyone who would "approach" (*proserchomenon*, 11:6) God, consists in two articles of belief: that God is and that he rewards those who seek him. This is only one element of the complex portrait of faith that emerges in the chapter, but it is clearly fundamental.

Closely linked with the affirmation of the existence and providential character of God is the claim that God created all that is. The proem alludes to a doctrine of creation, but with a focus on the agent, the Son, through whom God acted in creation (1:2). The catalogue of heroes of faith begins on a similar note that intimates more details of the author's doctrine of creation: "By faith we understand that the worlds were prepared by the word of God, so that what is seen was made from things that are not visible" (11:3).

The precise details of the presupposed doctrine of creation remain elusive. *Creatio ex nihilo*, although possibly attested in Hellenistic Jewish sources (cf. 2 Macc 7:28), is probably not in view. Instead, the verse probably alludes to debates in contemporary Platonist circles about the interpretation of the *Timaeus*. Hebrews, like the Jewish philosopher and exegete Philo (*De opificio mundi*), affirms that the biblical doctrine of creation, whatever its temporal implications, above all asserts the dependence of the visible world on something outside of itself. Also like Philo, Hebrews probably equates the word (here *rhema*) of God with the realm of ideas, which gave and gives coherence to the phenomenal world.

Hebrews 11:2 uses a quasi-philosophical mode to affirm the dependence of all that is on a transcendent source. A more common device for conveying the same conviction is to use the ancient mythical portrait of God enthroned on high. Although much of Hebrews is concerned to expound what it means to affirm that the Son has, in the words of Ps 110:1, taken his seat at the "right hand" (1:3; 8:1; 10:12; 12:2), what is at the Son's left is the focal point of the heavenly court. There God sits on "the throne of the Majesty" (8:1), which is also a "throne of grace" (4:16).

The image of the heavenly throne is associated with the second article of faith mentioned in connection with Enoch's translation. The sovereign God rewards those who seek him. God is thus a God of mercy and grace, but the obverse of the coin is equally prominent. From that divine throne God also judges. God is explicitly labeled "judge of all" (12:23), to fall into whose hands is a fearsome thing (10:31).

The lapidary affirmation of a God of judgment in 10:31 uses one of Hebrews' favorite terms for God, namely, "living." Each of the four occurrences of the word as an epithet for God (3:12; 9:14; 10:31; 12:22) is associated with judgmental imagery or warnings to the addressees of the seriousness of their situation. Judgment is also the ultimate point of the portrait of the word of God as "living and active" (4:12). That word, issuing perhaps from the throne, penetrates even to the depths of the human mind and heart, indeed to the inmost depths of all creation, which it lays bare and which it is "able to judge" (*kritikos*, 4:12).

The portrait of God as ultimate judge concludes with another of the sermon's lapidary affirmations, that God is a "consuming fire" (12:29, alluding to Deut 4:24). That affirmation, whatever its biblical roots, summarizes the eschatological warning of Heb 12:25–29 and supports the admonition to worship God with reverence and fear (12:28; *eulabeias kai deous*).

As the sovereign judge, God is the object of propitiatory action (2:17). To effect such propitiation was the object of the ministry of any high priest (5:1). But ordinary priestly ministry could not do the trick. It took the personal sacrifice of the high-priestly Son to effect propitiation (9:23–28), precisely by establishing a new relationship between God and humankind (8:8–12; 10:1–10).

Thus, in the dogmatic framework that undergirds Hebrews, God exists as creator and sovereign Lord of the natural world and guarantor of the moral order, who stands in a special relationship to a covenant community.

A SHORT STORY OF GOD

The delineation of certain fundamental convictions that Hebrews conveys about God indicates something of the theistic horizon presupposed by the text, none of which is at all surprising. Hebrews' theology was widely shared by first-century Jews and Christians alike, and bears none of the revolutionary theological moves associated with Gnosticism or, as one recent student of the phenomenon, Michael Williams, styles it, "Demiurgic creationism."

The roots of Hebrews in the biblical tradition become even more apparent if we move from a consideration of the contours of basic dogmatic affirmations about God to the implicit narrative that Hebrews relates about the actions of God in history. The God to whom the Son leads and directs the members of his covenant community is not an abstract or remote entity, but a person related to and intimately involved with humankind.

The story of God that Hebrews evokes is as familiar as the text's basic dogmatic framework, but what Hebrews chooses to emphasize in that story has significance for the text's parenetic program. The creator's story begins, naturally enough, in the act of creation itself, or to be more precise, in the aftermath of creation. The one detail of the creation story that surfaces explicitly in Hebrews is the finale, when, as Gen 2:2 stipulates, "God rested on the seventh day" (Heb 4:4). While the fact of God's creative action is correlated with his sovereign sway over the created order, the divine sabbatical repose is paradigmatic for the faithful. The consummation of God's work in a Sabbath rest models what they may expect and identifies the goal toward which the homily urges them to strive (4:11). The reluctance of Hebrews to define more precisely "Sabbath rest," except in terms of other evocative imagery such as that of the festival in the heavenly Jerusalem (12:22-24), has elicited considerable modern commentary. Hebrews' reticence invites hearers with varied eschatological views to share the same formal hope, the hope of ultimately participating in God's own blessed state.

The story continues and follows a linear temporal sequence in the catalogue of the heroes of faith in chapter 11. The details of the scriptural narratives need not detain us. The ways in which God's action is described are of some potential significance. God "witnessed" or "testified" over the gifts of Abel that he was righteous (11:4). God's testimony is a constant in history, certifying the faith of those of old (11:2, 5, 39), sounding most emphatically as the miraculous confirmation of the proclamation of salvation (2:4).

God "called" Abraham and summoned him to go out to claim his inheritance (11:8). God's relationship with this patriarch and his family is one of the focal points of Hebrews' review of salvation history. Almost a third of the account (twelve verses of forty) treats Abraham, his wife, and their son. A faithful response to the divine call to go out and seek a new and heavenly homeland offers another paradigm for the faithful addressees, a model made explicit in 13:13–14. The stamp of divine approval that seals their belief and faithful action consists in the fact that God was "not ashamed to be called their God" (Heb 11:16, alluding to passages such as Exod 3:6).

The paradigmatic quality of God's relationship with Abraham also appears in the earlier references to the patriarch in Hebrews. The focus of those references is to the "promise" that God made to Abraham, initially defined as the promise of a numerous progeny (6:13–14). Hebrews toys with the notion of the divine promise, parsing it in such a way as to see it partially fulfilled in history (6:15) and partially fulfilled only in the eschatological consummation (11:13, 39). Hebrews will insist that a faithful God does fulfill promises.

The second major focus of the review of salvation history in chapter 11 is of course Moses. Hebrews' retelling of the exodus story focuses more on Moses and his virtue than on God, although God's involvement in the story of liberation does receive a passing mention in the brief reference to the visionary experience of Moses (11:27).

God's involvement with Moses is more apparent in an earlier passage in the text. Hebrews 3:1–6, already noted as a locus for the theme of God as creator, highlights God's special relationship with Moses. It does so, as part of the text's strategy of comparison or *synkrisis*, to underscore the "greater" fidelity of Jesus. Nonetheless, the framing of the relationship is important for our theme. Hebrews uses the son/slave trope, familiar from passages such as Gal 4:7 and John 8:34-36, to develop its contrast between Moses and Christ, but the framework for that relationship is the "household" over which God presides and which God calls into being. That image connotes a familial intimacy between God and the members of the household.

The image of the household provides an answer to a question that Hebrews does not directly address but that might be posed to a theology that consists only of the dogmatic framework and its focus on creation. Why is it that a majestic creator should be so interested in humankind as to initiate the soteriological process with which Hebrews is concerned? The simple answer is that God, the "one Father" from whom all come (2:11), is concerned with God's children. The NRSV's translation of that verse resolves a difficult exegetical problem, since the text specifies only that the sanctifier, presumably Jesus, and sanctified, the sons and daughters, come from "one" (*henos*). Nonetheless, that resolution is reasonable and foreshadows the familial language of chapter 3.

The "household" image bears fruit later in the text. Once the exposition of the nature and work of the heavenly high priest concludes, the author celebrates the fact that "we have a great priest over the house of God" (10:21). That in turn prepares the way for the final application of familial imagery in the exhortation of chapter 12. In that pericope, the homilist, citing Prov 3:11–12, deploys the proverbial topos of educative suffering as a consolation for the afflictions that the addressees may have to endure. The central point of that image, that such sufferings are simply the treatment that the "Father of spirits" (12:9) applies to his children, serves as encouragement to potentially beleaguered addressees.

God, then, is not simply a distant and aloof creator and judge, whose wrath awaits appeasement, but a Father intimately involved the history of a family on earth, whose aim is to share with that family a festive heavenly homeland.

A crucial stage in the relationship of God with God's people occurred at the establishment of the covenant at Sinai. Hebrews relates only three events from the larger story. The text notes (a) that God revealed to Moses a model or type of the earthly sanctuary (Heb 8:5, citing Exod 25:40), (b) that Moses inaugurated the covenant with the sprinkling of blood (Heb 9:18–22, citing Exod 24:8), and (c) that at Sinai a fearsome theophany accompanied the delivery of the law (Heb 12:18–21).

While these snippets from Exodus illustrate the involvement with God in history, they also serve the comparative program of Hebrews. The cult based on the revelation to Moses functioned as a "symbol" (*parabolē*) of the time of the true high priest's sacrifice (Heb 9:9). Moses' blood sacrifice established a principle that a covenant needs such an inaugural event, but the blood of "goats and calves" (Heb 9:12) was inferior to the blood of the Son, which inaugurated the new covenant. Similarly the dreadful theophany at Sinai is simply the foil for the bliss of the heavenly Jerusalem (Heb 12:22–24).

Sinai and the law associated with it, high points in the history of God's dealings with Israel, have their primary value for Hebrews as pointers to the "good things to come" (Heb 10:1). It is therefore significant that the most explicit description of the covenant is on the lips of God, as reported by Jeremiah, where the divine speaker contrasts what was done of old with what was to be (Heb 8:8–12, citing Jer 31:31–34), a new covenant written on the heart (Heb 8:10; 10:16).

The focal point for Hebrews' account of God's relationship with humankind is the death of Christ. Hebrews dwells on the action of Christ in offering himself to God as a sacrifice effective for cleansing conscience and inaugurating a covenant (Heb 9:14), but it is clear that this event was an act of divine initiative. The first dramatic affirmation of the incarnation, through the exegesis of Psalm 8 in Heb 2:8–9, holds that Christ was made lower than the angels, so that "by the grace of God" (*chariti theou*) he might taste death for all. The following verse continues and dramatically reaffirms the divine initiative in the event, with its claim that God fittingly "perfected" through suffering the author (*archēgos*) of salvation who would lead many children to glory.

It is hardly accidental that familial imagery emerges here for the first time. The whole short story of God in Hebrews revolves around that relationship between God and God's children. Through the windows on that story opened by Hebrews there emerges a picture of a God passionately involved not only with a single Son but with many children destined ultimately to share God's sabbatical rest.

IMAGING GOD

In drawing its verbal picture of God, Hebrews calls on a wide array of imagistic resources. One recent commentator, David A. deSilva, has drawn particular attention to one set of metaphors that run through the text, which tend to depict God as a typical Greco-Roman patron or benefactor, approached through the intermediation of a "broker" particularly intimate with the patron—in this case, the Son (3:6). Acting on behalf of the gracious patron, Jesus, the mediator (*mesitēs*, 8:6; 9:15; 12:24) provides help (2:18). By following in his footsteps and relying on his intercession (7:25), the clients of the heavenly patron "receive mercy and find grace to help in time of need" (4:16).

The virtues of loyalty and fidelity that they are encouraged to pursue are precisely those expected of dutiful clients.

The suggestion that such social imagery is part of our homilist's repertoire is helpful, yet it fails to capture the full complexity of Hebrews' portrait of God. Hebrews does indeed deploy this and other social images, some of which stand in playful tension with one another. The divine patron, for example, provides his benefactions as a legacy, or promised inheritance (9:15; cf. 1:14; 6:17). Yet it is the broker-Son whose death makes the testament valid (9:16–17), and through that death he himself becomes an heir (1:2–4)! Hence, the image of the Son qua broker is not developed without an ironic twist. Imagery derived from the social and legal realms indeed operates in Hebrews, but with some of the same innovative boldness that characterizes the image of the "anchor" that rests in no ordinary harbor but "enters the inner shrine behind the curtain" (6:19).

The review of the narrative of God's involvement with human history with which Hebrews works already suggests that the imagery of patronage, which Hebrews does indeed deploy, does not bear the whole weight of its reflections on God. Further examination indicates that the divine patron works in surprising ways. Most striking perhaps is the fashion in which the Lord of creation and Sovereign over human history enters into the world of his covenantal "clients" as one who speaks directly to them and, through the example of his Son, elicits from them a response.

GOD'S DIALOGUE WITH THE SON
AND HIS SIBLINGS

To portray God is often, as Xenophanes famously opined, to portray oneself, and so it is with the author of Hebrews. As a practitioner of sophisticated homiletic rhetoric, it is no surprise that Hebrews uses the word of God as a means to theological insight. It does so not simply through the scriptural texts on which its doctrinal and narrative depiction of God rests. No, this orator's focus on the word of God attends to the precise words and the qualities of God's voice, attending to what contemporary philosophers would call the divine "illocution." The preceding sketch of the narrative of salvation history assumed by Hebrews already calls attention to the characterization of God's speech acts in the text. The homilist's handling of God's spoken words will make this concern even more apparent.

Hebrews, that is, operates with the conceit that readers and hearers of Scripture can listen to God speaking, first to the Son and ultimately to all God's children. In this conceit, the character of God and of his scriptural speech provides the raw material for both reflection and parenesis. The technique thus models a response to the divine address and invites its hearers to share that response. In the development of this conceit resides the most creative theological work of this complex text.

The dialogue, which intersects but does not strictly follow the text's systematic and narrative axes, begins in the catena of scriptural citations in 1:5. There God addresses the Son in the words of Ps 2:7 and 2 Sam 7:14. These texts announce the Son's divine "begetting," whether that is simply equivalent to his eschatological enthronement at the right hand or an allusion to a pretemporal event in which God issues his word. God addresses the Son again in 1:13, in the words of Ps 110:1 that proclaim the Son's enthronement. In this dramatic fashion, the text begins its reflection on the central event of salvation history. The dialogue established in the scriptural catena (1:5–13) serves the needs of the program of *synkrisis* by indicating the Son's exalted position— above that of any angel. Of equal significance, these verses portray his relationship with God, a relationship begun with God's initiative, highlighted by God's role in "anointing" the Son (in the words of Ps 45:6–7 [LXX 44:7–8], cited in Heb 1:8–9).

The dialogue begun by God finds a response in the next chapter, which cites the words of the Son. The source of these words is not the sayings of the double or triple tradition of the Synoptic Gospels, nor the revealer discourses of John, but Scripture. The response consists of three brief statements. The first, in Heb 2:12, derives from Ps 22:22 [LXX 21:23], well-known from accounts of Christ's passion (cf. Mark 15:24, 34, and par.). The second and third citations both come from Isa 8:17–18, but the formula introducing the third indicates that the two verses are to be construed as independent utterances.

The resulting chiastic pattern frames a simple statement, "I will put my trust in him" (2:13), with two characterizations of the "many children" for whom the Son serves as "pioneer" (*archēgos*, 2:10). The first utterance, "I will proclaim your name to my brothers and sisters; in the midst of the congregation I will praise you" (2:12), establishes the solidarity between the Son and other children, which is the surface argument of the text at this point. It also efficiently scores three points significant for the text's theology. It first defines an important element of the Son's work, to proclaim the name of God, emphasizing the text's ultimate focus on God. It also defines the sphere where the response to the proclamation of God's name takes place, the congregation or *ekklēsia*, which certainly has a pregnant sense in Hebrews. The term will appear again at 12:23, referring to the community of "firstborn ones" enrolled in heaven. Hebrews 2:12 finally indicates what the Son's response to God's call is to be: singing God's praise. The final verse in this little triptych (2:13b, from

Isa 8:18), "Here I am and the children whom God has given me," also scores two points. The actions that Jesus claims for himself in the previous verses are not to be his alone, but shared with his "brothers and sisters," who also must trust in God and sing God's praise. Furthermore, those siblings are, like all else in the salvific process, also a gift of God.

The dialogue and response established in the first two chapters form a pattern at work throughout the text. The next instance of such dialogue reveals a passionate God who appeals to all who hear the call of Scripture "today" not to harden their hearts (Heb 3:8). God, speaking in the psalm, reports his own reaction to the rebellious members of the exodus generation: "As in my anger I swore, 'They will not enter my rest'" (Heb 3:11, citing Ps 95:11). There follows considerable exegetical play with the text of the psalm (Heb. 3:12–4:10), all of which emphasizes the immediacy of God's call to the addressees. Finally, the homilist himself articulates the desired response to that call to hear the divine voice in his exhortation to his addressees to hold fast, stay the course and enter God's "rest" (4:11).

A particularly striking feature of Psalm 95, quoted in Heb 3:7–11, is the characterization of God's speech as swearing an oath. The author of Hebrews, sensitive to the modes of God's speech, was particularly interested in cases of divine oaths. Two further examples caught his attention. The first comes at the end of the lengthy warning that precedes the exposition of the Melchizedek typology. Hebrews 6:13–14 appeals to Gen 22:16 to illustrate how God made his promise to Abraham. The overarching argument is that God's promises are to be trusted. What made the promise to Abraham particularly trustworthy was the oath, sworn on God's very self, that accompanied the promise. Hebrews here relies on the kind of reflection on divine swearing attested in Philo (*De sacrificiis* 91–94).

Discussion of the oath to Abraham anticipates the treatment of another even more significant oath—important because it is part of the dialogue at the heart of the inauguration of the new covenant—the address of God to the Son as priest forever according to the order of Melchizedek. Hebrews 5:6 first introduces that crucial verse from Ps 110:4, but exposition of its significance awaits the completion of the warning of chapter 6. The exposition, occupying chapter 7, culminates in a more extended citation of the psalm, which describes the divine speech act: "The Lord has sworn and will not change his mind, 'You are a priest forever.'" At that point, Heb 7:20–22, there is no need for further reflection on the importance of this divine line, nor on its character as an oath. What we anticipate is the dialogic response, but Hebrews once again creates suspense.

The next instance of God's speech is the prophecy from Jeremiah 31 in Heb 8:8–12. The introduction offers a typical analytical comment, reflecting again on the character of God's speech. The homilist indicates that the divine speaker "finds fault [*memphomenos*] with them" (i.e., members of the first covenant). The lengthy quote, however, does more than assign blame. The major linguistic act that God performs in this passage is to make a promise, referring, in language evocative of Hebrews' complex theme of "perfection" (*teleiosis*; cf., e.g., 5:9; 10:14), to yet another act that he would complete (*synteleso*), namely, a new covenant with the "house of Israel" and "house of Judah" (Heb 8:8, citing Jer 31[LXX 38]:31). The two major elements of this act of covenant creation, repeated in the concluding remarks on Christ's sacrificial death at 10:16–17, are that God will write his laws on the hearts and minds of the covenant people (Heb 8:10, citing Jer 31[LXX 38]:33) and that sins are remembered no more (Heb 8:12, citing Jer 31[38]:34).

Chapters 8 and 9 develop the image of the heavenly high priest, effecting final and permanent atonement for sins by his unique sacrifice, consummated by his entry to heaven, the "true tent" (8:2). This exposition culminates in a quotation of the Son's words, which ultimately constitute the response to his appointment by God as high priest. These words also show how God fulfills the promise recorded in the citation of Jeremiah, how, that is, God inscribes laws onto human hearts. God does so through dialogue with his Son, thereby providing a potent example for human beings to follow. The Son's words in Heb 10:5–6, like his earlier comments in chapter 2, come from Scripture—Ps 40:6–8 in its Greek form. They contrast the "burnt offerings and sin offerings" in which God does not take delight, with the Son's willing obedience, as he says, "See, God, I have come to do your will, O God."

The homilist's exegetical comment (10:8–10) underlines the importance of this bit of dialogue. As in earlier dialogues, Hebrews operates at several levels. The traditional contrast between external sacrifices and a faithful, obedient heart distinguishes the new and the old covenants, to the detriment of the latter. Thus, the comparative argument that serves as the framework for much of Hebrews continues. Of equal importance is the exemplary function of the Son's response to the divine initiative. Just as the Son's earlier words in chapter 2 modeled the kind of behavior expected of all God's sons and daughters, this final comment of the dutiful priestly Son models the fidelity that his siblings should exhibit. The example of virtue establishes the new covenant community.

A particularly telling indication of that exemplary function is the emphasis on the incarnate character of the Son's response to God. The second clause in the citation from the psalm, peculiar to the Greek version, reads, "but a body you have prepared for me" (Heb 10:5b, citing Ps 40:6). The final exegetical comment (10:10), that the conformity to the will (*thelema*) of God takes place in Christ's bodily (*soma*) sacrifice, picks up the verse from the psalm and hints at its parenetic application. It is this embodiment of God's will that constitutes the reality that casts its shadow back onto the old cult (10:1).

Christ's bodily sacrifice constitutes a fleshly way into the pure spiritual realm where God resides (10:19–20). The rest of Hebrews will spell out in more detail what that way of fidelity (10:19) entails for the heirs of the covenant/testament (9:15–17) established by his death.

The exposition of the way of fidelity continues to record God's voice. God's dialogue partner is now no longer the Son, who after chapter 10 remains silent, letting only his "blood" speak, more forcefully than that of Abel (12:24). God's words seem now to be addressed directly to the other children who follow the Son's way. Ominous words portend judgment: "Vengeance is mine, I will repay" (10:30, citing Deut 32:35). As at 2:13, Heb 10:30 cites a single verse as two, dividing Deut 32:35 from its sequel, "The Lord will judge his people." The separation takes note of the change in speaker, thus highlighting the divine voice in the first clause. Like all acts of divine discourse, the promise of 10:30 requires a response. The author, in effect, provides one on behalf of his community with the epigrammatic "It is a fearful thing to fall into the hands of the living God" (10:31).

The imminence of judgment reappears in the next composite citation in Heb 10:37–38, which combines Isa 26:20 and Hab 2:3–4, all in their LXX form. The reference to "my righteous one" (*ho dikaios mou*) and "my soul" (*hē psychē mou*) establish the speaker as God, who once again warns against falling back. The homilist again responds for the covenant community: "But we are not among those who shrink back and so are lost, but among those who have faith and so are saved" (10:39).

God speaks again in a final warning of eschatological catastrophe at 12:26, citing Hag 2:6 and 21: "Yet once more I will shake not only the earth but also the heaven." The homilist comments on the finality of the promised (*epēngeltai*) threat and then issues his last awestruck response, referring to "our" God as a consuming fire (Heb 12:29, citing Deut 4:24). The first-person pronoun is an addition to the quotation, rendering it the community's response to the promise of a final quake.

A warning tone and anxious response pervade the dialogical elements in the hortatory chapters at the end of Hebrews, but the homily does not conclude on such a somber note. In the midst of the warning, the homilist contrasts the situation of the members of the new covenant with those present at Sinai (12:18–24). The image of God as a moving and shaking judge is far too redolent of the theophany that led to Moses' confession "I tremble with fear" (Heb 12:21, citing Deut 9:19). The final exchange between God and the children in covenant relationship with him strikes a more encouraging note. Although specifically grounding an admonition not to be greedy (13:5), God's final word summarizes Hebrews' message of hope: "I will never leave you or forsake you" (Heb 13:5, citing Deut 31:6). The response on the part of the covenanters is clearly marked as such (Heb 13:6). Echoing the words of the *archēgos* of the covenant, who expressed himself in Hebrews through the words of the Psalms, "we" make bold to say the words of Ps 118:6 [LXX 117:6] in its Greek form: "The Lord is my helper; I will not be afraid. What can anyone do to me?"

The final exchange exemplifies what the addressees of Hebrews are invited to do as members of the new covenant: to act boldly, in the presence of God and humankind, offering "a sacrifice of praise to God, that is, the fruit of lips that confess his name" (Heb 13:15).

CONCLUSION

Hebrews, like the God whose word it celebrates, speaks in many and diverse ways about its subject, the relationship of God and God's covenant people. In addition to a basic dogmatic framework and a narrative account of God's dealings with his people, the homily uses a variety of metaphors and models for treating the reality of God. Elements of contemporary social relations offer glimpses into that reality, but do not convey the full sense of intimacy and immediacy that Hebrews associates with God. Hebrews understands God to have taken the initiative at every step in establishing and reestablishing a relationship with the covenant people.

As its opening line suggests, Hebrews finds particularly fruitful the notion that God has spoken and continues to speak in a vivid and compelling way. Unperturbed by the metaphysical problems of such claims, this homilist understands God to be doing what he himself aims to do: uttering a word that penetrates human hearts and minds.

The God who speaks through the dialogic oratory of the Psalms defines for a covenant people the goal toward which they strive and motivates through words of encouragement and warning their fidelity to that covenant. They can walk with assurance in the way of the covenant because in the words of Scripture they have overheard God talking to his Son and to them. They have heard him promise, as well as threaten. They have heard words of encouragement and consolation as well as words of warning. They have heard in the person of God's Son a model for their own dialogue with God, a paradigm for words of faith lived out in action. Through their listening to God's dialogue exalting his Son, they anchor their hope that the outcome of his life foreshadows their own, because, as Sarah recognized, the God who promises is "faithful" (Heb 11:11).

SELECT BIBLIOGRAPHY

Attridge, Harold W. 1989. *Hebrews.* Hermeneia. Philadelphia: Fortress.

deSilva, David A. 2000. *Perseverance in Gratitude: A Socio-Rhetorical Commentary.* Grand Rapids: Eerdmans.

Eisenbaum, Pamela M. 1997. *The Jewish Heroes of Christian History: Hebrews 11 in Literary Context.* Society of Biblical Literature Dissertation Series 156. Atlanta: Scholars Press.

Lane, William. 1991. *Hebrews.* 2 vols. Word Biblical Commentary 47A, B. Waco: Word.

Wider, David. 1997. *Theozentrik und Bekenntnis: Untersuchungen zur Theologie des Redens Gottes im Hebräerbrief.* Beihefte zur Zeitschrift für die neutestamentliche Wissenschaft 87. Berlin and New York: de Gruyter.

Williams, Michael. *1996. Rethinking "Gnosticism": An Argument for Dismantling a Dubious Category.* Princeton, N.J.: Princeton University Press.

Wolterstorff, Nicholas. 1995. *Divine Discourse: Philosophical Reflections on the Claim That God Speaks.* Cambridge: Cambridge University Press.

Wray, Judith Hoch. 1998. *Rest as a Theological Metaphor in the Epistle to the Hebrews and the Gospel of Truth: Early Christian Homiletics of Rest.* Society of Biblical Literature Dissertation Series 166. Atlanta: Scholars Press.

13

God Ever New, Ever the Same

The Witness of James and Peter

LUKE TIMOTHY JOHNSON

A consideration of *ho theos* (God) in the letters of James and 1 Peter, two of the so-called catholic or general epistles within the New Testament canon, must start from a candid recognition of how the indirect and partial character of the evidence frustrates any attempt at an adequate account. In light of the difficulties they present, it is the more pleasing that the witness of these compositions nevertheless turns out to be so complex and fascinating. This essay begins with a discussion of the critical questions presented by the letters, then seeks in turn to hear the distinctive voice of James and Peter, and concludes with a brief reflection on the implications of their witness.

PRELIMINARY QUESTIONS

How is the evidence indirect? We remember first the fact that both compositions are letters. They are general letters, to be sure, written not to single communities but to readers across a geographical area. Letters of any sort, however, represent part of a conversation between the implied sender and the implied readers. We are the indirect overhearers of this conversation. As has been stated often, present-day readers are in the position of those reading other people's mail. Even if the ancient composition is a letter in form only (as some moral essays were), use of this genre also implies that a subject is being treated in part, as fits the occasion for writing, rather than as a whole and in systematic fashion. Language about God is indirect in another way: The rhetoric of these letters is protreptic rather than didactic; rather than seeking to present an ordered teaching about God, it seeks to move readers to a renewed commitment to their profession of faith in God. Discourse about

God serves to shape the attitudes and actions of the first readers. When these letters speak of God, furthermore, they do so in the diction of prayer and exhortation, rather than in that of philosophy; we find in these letters first-order religious language, rather than the second-order reflection on such language that characterizes theology. The language of these letters gives rise to theology but does not derive from theology. When James and Peter speak of God, they speak out of the religious experiences and convictions that join them to their readers and form the shared context of their conversation. Access to that conversation is therefore also limited to the degree that the contemporary reader does or does not share those same experiences and convictions.

If the rhetorical character of the compositions sets limits to our expectations, so does their lack of context. Unlike some of Paul's letters, this correspondence does not yield specific information concerning the readers that might assist us in assessing the language used. Both letters are written to a readership larger than a single community and tell us next to nothing about the actual situation of the readers. We are able to conclude with a fair amount of certainty that 1 Peter was written to Gentile converts who were experiencing some degree of social ostracism, and that James was (in all likelihood) written to Jewish believers who likewise were facing various trials and testings. Beyond that, we are not able to go with any degree of confidence. Nor do we have other writings from these ascribed authors to fill out the evidence in these two letters. No other letter is attributed to James in the New Testament. If the author of 1 Peter is different from the author of 2 Peter, and if the words attributed to Peter by the Acts of the Apostles come from Luke rather than Peter—and I take both these protases to be correct—then 1 Peter also must be taken on its own.

But what of the obvious literary resemblances between the two writings? They are, after all, both general epistles. First Peter is sent to the "exiles of the Dispersion" (1 Pet 1:1) just as James addresses "the twelve tribes in the Dispersion" (Jas 1:1). Such designations evoke the symbolic world of Torah, and each composition makes heavy use of scriptural diction, citation, and allusion. First Peter 1:24 has a verbatim citation from Isa 40:6–8 in the LXX translation ("All flesh is like grass"), and the same passage is paraphrased by Jas 1:10–11 with reference to the passing away of the rich. Both Jas 5:20 and 1 Pet 4:8 cite Prov 10:12 ("love covers a multitude of sins"). Both letters quote Prov 3:34 ("God opposes the proud but gives grace to the humble") in strikingly similar fashion (see Jas 4:6; 1 Pet 5:5). The letters share other points of theme and diction. First Peter 1:6–7 instructs readers to rejoice if they should experience "various trials" (*poikilois peirasmois*) so that the "genuineness of your faith" (*to dokimion hymōn tēs pisteōs*) might be found "more precious than gold that, though perishable, is tested by fire," a sequence that is remarkably similar to

Jas 1:2–3. Likewise the language of Jas 1:18 concerning the word of truth that gives birth resembles 1 Pet 1:23, which says that the readers have been "born anew . . . through the living and enduring word of God." Similarly, 1 Pet 2:1–2 has the same transition, from putting off (*apothemenoi*) negative qualities to receiving a saving word, as does Jas 1:21.

Such similarities, if taken in isolation, might seem to support theories of literary dependence. Closer analysis, however, reveals that each of these writings has as many points of resemblance to the letters of Paul as they do to each other. The rhetorical climax in Jas 1:2–4 resembles that in Rom 5:3–4 more than it does 1 Pet 1:6–7, and James's use of the example of Abraham (Jas 2:21–24) is much closer to Paul (Rom 4; Gal 3) than it is to 1 Peter's reference to Sarah and Abraham (1 Pet 3:6). Similarly, 1 Peter's catena of Scripture passages in 2:4–10 is very close to Paul in Rom 9:25–33, with no parallel to James, and its language about the death, resurrection, and exaltation of Christ (2:24; 3:18–22) has multiple parallels in Paul (Rom 6:2; Phil 2:10–11; Col 2:15) and none in James. The elements that 1 Peter and James do share, furthermore, are turned to distinctive use in the respective compositions. First Peter has domestic, ecclesial, and, above all, christological interests that are not shared by James. Note that the passage concerning the testing of faith is given by Peter a specifically christological turn lacking in James: "to result in praise and glory and honor when Jesus Christ is revealed" (1 Pet 1:7). The living and enduring word of God is identified as "the good news that was announced to you" (1 Pet 1:25), and the admonition "Humble yourselves therefore under the mighty hand of God, so that he may exalt you in due time" (5:6), which so palpably resonates Jas 4:10, is used by 1 Peter to exhort younger people to submit to the older within the community (1 Pet 5:5).

No evidence compels the conclusion that James and 1 Peter were pseudonymous in composition and (as a result) composed significantly later than the extant letters of Paul. The same scarcity of data that limits our ability to place these compositions in the circumstances of first-generation Christianity also resists their inclusion within some developmental scheme that demands their being read as second-century productions. Nothing is lost and much is gained if we imagine them as voices contemporary to Paul, parts of the rich and complex conversation that the experience of Jesus as risen Lord generated among his followers as they sought to grasp not only what had happened to them but also the nature of the one at work in their transforming experience. Perhaps reading them this way can help us grasp how that *koinōnia* of faith and mission to which Paul attests was expressed by the "right hand of fellowship" among himself, Peter, and James, a fellowship that at once recognized the diversity of ministries among them as well as the one God enabling those ministries (Gal 2:9–10), and was also expressed in a similar way by of diverse literary expressions pointing to the experience of a single God who was at once always new and always the same.

THE WITNESS OF THE LETTER OF JAMES

It might be argued that James is the most thoroughly *theological*—as opposed to *christological*—writing in the New Testament. Apart from the greeting (1:1), the name of Jesus appears only once (2:1). James tells no stories about Jesus and bears no trace of those elements of the *kerygma* (the death and resurrection of Jesus, the sending of the Holy Spirit) that are so well attested elsewhere in the canon. The *pneuma* that God makes dwell in humans (Jas 4:5) is probably not the Holy Spirit, though it might be stretched to mean that. The opinion that James is only a lightly baptized Jewish composition, however, is shown to be wrong when one looks more closely. Not only does James have many points of resemblance to other Christian literature, its diction makes sense only within the messianic movement associated with Jesus. His epithets make clear that for James, Jesus is Messiah (*Christos*, 1:1; 2:1) and the *kyrios* (1:1; 2:1) to whom he owes particular allegiance as slave (*doulos*, 1:1). Calling Jesus *kyrios* and associating his "name" (2:7) with "glory" (*doxa*) suggests also that James acknowledges Jesus as the powerful risen one. Indeed, James's use of the title *kyrios* is richly ambiguous. It probably refers to God as the Yahweh (=LXX *kyrios*) of Scripture (see Isa 40:3; Ps 117:1) in passages such as 1:7; 3:9; 4:10, 15; 5:4, 11; and possibly 5:10. But it may also apply to Jesus as the risen one in 5:7, 8, 14, 15. Particularly impressive is James's use of the expression *parousia tou kyriou* in 5:8; in the New Testament, it is virtually a technical term for the return of Jesus (see 1 Thess 2:19; 3:13), whereas it is never used of Yahweh in the Old Testament.

James makes especially strong use of Jesus' teaching. He speaks of "the faith of Jesus Christ" (2:1) as the measure for the faith of the readers, and the most striking parallels are those between statements in James and sayings of Jesus found in the Synoptic tradition (see Jas 2:5 and Luke 6:20; Jas 2:13 and Matt 5:7; Jas 4:8 and Matt 5:8; Jas 3:18 and Matt 5:9; Jas 1:5 and Matt 7:7; Jas 4:11–12/5:9 and Matt 7:1; Jas 5:12 and Matt 5:34). Such statements from Jesus occur in close conjunction with James's thematic use of Leviticus 19 throughout the letter (Lev 19:12 = Jas 5:12; Lev 19:13 = Jas 5:4; Lev 19:15 = Jas 2:1; Lev 19:16 = Jas 4:11; Lev 19:17b = Jas 5:20). The two sets of teaching come together in 2:8, when James cites as the "royal law" the commandment of love of neighbor, which derives from Lev 19:18 and is confirmed by Jesus in Mark 12:31; Matt 22:39; Luke 10:27. The faith expressed through the sayings of the Messiah Jesus is in deep continuity with the revelation of God in Torah.

In contrast to the relatively little explicit attention paid to Jesus, James has a rich set of statements concerning God. The term *theos* occurs fifteen times (1:1, 5, 13, 20, 27; 2:5, 19, 23 (2); 3:9; 4:4 (2), 6, 7, 8). James places the term "Father" (*patēr*) in apposition to *theos* in 1:17, 27, and 3:9. Notably, he never calls God "Father of Jesus Christ." In addition to *theos*, at least some of James's references to "Lord" (*kyrios*) refer to God rather than to Jesus (see 1:7; 3:9; 4:10, 15; 5:4, 11). In 108 verses, then, James mentions God some twenty-four times. This is properly designated a theocentric composition.

James's language about God appears largely in the form of warrants and premises for his moral exhortation. The thoroughly hortatory character of this writing can be discerned directly from its grammar. In 108 verses, there are some fifty-nine imperatives (forty-six in the second person, thirteen in the third person)! But by no means are these random or disconnected. James attaches to his imperatives a variety of explanatory clauses, either by way of participles (1:3, 14, 22; 2:9, 25; 3:1), or *gar* ("for") clauses (1:6, 7, 11, 13, 20, 24; 2:11, 13, 26; 3:2, 16; 4:14) or *hoti* ("because") clauses (see 1:12, 23; 2:10; 3:1; 4:3; 5:8, 11). Statements about God occur in these clauses as support and motivation for James's moral instruction. To grasp the significance of James's language about God, therefore, the very grammar of the composition demands that we place it in the context of his moral exhortation.

When James is compared to other ancient wisdom literature, its distinctiveness quickly becomes apparent. First, James deals exclusively with morals rather than with manners; second, he addresses an intentional community rather than a household; third, he is egalitarian rather than hierarchical; fourth, James is communitarian rather than individualistic. This is not a writing that represents a ruling elite or a scribal tradition within a stable, traditional culture. Instead, James stands over against the dominant culture with an emphasis on group solidarity and moral rigor as opposed to conformity to societal norms. James has a sectarian ethic that is defined as much by what it opposes as by what it affirms, and is marked by considerable eschatological urgency: Judgment is coming soon (5:9), when the wicked will be punished (5:1–6) and the righteous rewarded (1:12).

The social location suggested by James is that of a sectarian movement that identifies itself with the poor and opposes the wealthy. This opposition is expressed and supported by the dualistic character of James's moral exhortation and theological perspective. The contrast between the rich and the poor (1:9–11; 2:1–6) is articulated in moral terms as a contrast between the "innocent/righteous" (*dikaios*, 5:6) and the oppressor (2:6), between the arrogant and the lowly (4:6). Other moral contrasts are between truth (1:18) and error (1:16), war (4:1–2) and peace (3:17–18), meekness (1:21) and anger (1:20), justice (1:20; 3:18) and anger (1:20), envious craving (3:16; 4:1–3) and generous self-giving (1:17; 4:6). Likewise, James places in opposition the hearer of the word and the doer of the word (1:22, 25), the one who forgets and the one who remembers (1:25), the perfect (or mature) and the lacking (or unstable, 1:4, 6–11). So also he distinguishes between wisdom (1:5; 3:13) and foolishness (1:26), filthiness (1:21, 27) and purity (1:27; 4:8), blessing and curse (3:9), saving and destroying (4:12), death and life (1:16), the indwelling spirit (4:5) and that which is earthbound and unspiritual (3:15).

These moral contrasts are placed by James within a religious framework that is equally dualistic and expressed by spatial imagery of "above and below" and of "raising and lowering." He speaks of a wisdom from above (1:5, 17). This wisdom demands of humans a submission or lowering/humbling, to which God responds with a lifting up/exalting of the meek person (4:7–10). To this James opposes a wisdom from below, which he calls "earthly, unspiritual, devilish" (3:15), and which is sponsored by the devil (4:7). This wisdom from below causes people to elevate themselves through boasting and arrogance (3:14; 4:6). And just as God raises the lowly (4:10), so God resists the arrogant (4:6). James's religious dualism is most explicitly expressed in the verse that can be taken as the thematic heart of the letter: "Adulterers! Do you not know that friendship with the world is enmity with God? Therefore whoever wishes to be a friend of the world becomes an enemy of God" (4:4). This short—and in many respects shocking—syllogism points to the organizing logic of James's symbolism. We see that the terms for God (*theos*) and world (*kosmos*) are opposed as the objects of human allegiance and commitment (friendship). James's readers are assumed to know of the irreconcilable character of this opposition, and that allegiance to one or the other is a matter of free choice rather than destiny ("whoever wishes to be a friend of the world . . .").

We gain further insight into the contrast when we see that in each of the three other times James uses the term *kosmos*, he consistently opposes it to *theos*. In 3:6, the tongue is described as a "world of iniquity" among the body's members that leads one to bless God and curse one created in God's image (3:9). In 2:5, the "poor in the world" are said to be "rich in faith." These passages show us that "the world" for James is a system of meaning or measurement: Those who in the value system of the world are poor are also, in the value system of faith, rich. Finally, in 1:27, James defines a religion that is "pure and undefiled before God, the Father" as one that remains "unstained by the world." These are the measures between which humans can choose to live (which is what ancients meant by "being friends with"). The world's measure is clearly delineated by James as one that sees life as a closed system in which humans are in competition for being and worth. Its logic is that of envy, which seeks to win by eliminating the competition (4:1–3), whether through the banal assumption that gaining a profit can also secure a tomorrow (4:13–16) or through the arrogant assertion of raw power over the helpless, leading to their death (5:1–6). James presents Abraham as the example of the one who lives as the "friend of God," because his faith enabled him to perceive reality as God did and act accordingly. By the measure of the world, Abraham should have regarded Isaac as his possession, his guarantee of securing the blessing promised by God. But Abraham saw reality as one shaped by the giver of every good and perfect gift (1:17) and was willing to give back Isaac as gift to the one who lifts up the lowly and to the humble "gives a greater gift" (or "grace" in the NRSV, 4:6).

What makes James truly distinctive among sectarian writings is that he turns his moral critique inward. He does not condemn the world so much as hold in contempt those in the assembly who want both to profess faith in God and to live by the measure of the world. These he calls "double-minded" (1:8; 4:8), and the goal of his exhortation is to make them single-minded once more, to realize that it is impossible to be friends with everyone. The incompatibility of friendship with God and the world is suggested also by James's use of the prophetic image of the adulteress (in the Greek) in 4:4. The prophets so called Israel when it abandoned its covenant with the Lord (see Hos 3:1; Ezek 16:38; Isa 57:3; Jer 3:9). James therefore challenges his readers to that simplicity which consists in genuine faith in God expressed by wholehearted love toward the neighbor.

Who then is this God toward whom the human heart should be turned? James contains an unusually rich set of statements. Like all Jews—and like his colleague Paul (see Rom 3:30)—James takes it as axiomatic that God is one (2:19). But he mocks the so-called faith that consists in such a bare assertion of monotheism. This one God makes the demons shudder (2:19). God, in other words, is the powerful Lord of Israel. James reaches deeply into the symbolic world of Torah when he names God "Lord of hosts" (5:4). Some of James's statements move in the direction of a negative theology, asserting what God is not: With God there is no change or shadow of alteration (1:17), God neither tempts anyone nor is tempted by evil (1:13), God's righteousness is not worked through human anger (1:20). These negative ascriptions do not result from a philosophical position but from the religious conviction concerning the infinite moral distance between humans and God. God's changelessness in 1:17 does not describe a state of being but rather a moral consistency which is the opposite of that of fickle, two-minded humans. God "works" justice, but not through human anger (1:20). And God's goodness cannot be mixed with moral ambiguity or mischief (1:13). James does not deny the role of superhuman forces in influencing freedom: The wisdom from below is "devilish" (3:15), and the devil is to be resisted (4:7), but humans remain responsible for their evil desires and deeds. They cannot claim, "I am being tempted by God" (1:13) as a way of evading that responsibility.

James's positive statements assert God's powerful presence to creation and, above all, to humanity. Thus, God is not only "light" but is the "Father of lights" (1:17), an expression that points to God as the source of all being. James 3:7 alludes to Gen 1:26–28 and God's creation of all things. James 3:9 is the New Testament's only explicit assertion—outside of christological statements—that humans are created in the image of God. Perhaps James's most powerful and paradoxical statement of God's creative power is 1:18: "The Father of lights" here gives birth to humans as "a kind of first fruits of his creatures," and does so by his "own purpose" and "the word of truth." The statement is capable of almost endless meaning. We note first the striking image of a father "birthing": The verb *apokuein* can be rendered no other way, especially since it deliberately opposes the "giving birth to death" by human desire in 1:15. Second, we see that humans are to function within God's creation as representatives, the "firstfruits" who stand for the entire harvest. Third, we observe how God's deliberate purpose in creating humans stands opposed to the "desire" by which humans run amok (1:14–16). Fourth, we can ponder the ambiguity of "the word of truth." To what does James refer? As commentators have seen from the start, the word of truth might mean the word by which God creates the world anew at every moment (Gen 1:26–30); or, it might mean the word of Torah by which God revealed the divine will to humans (LXX Ps 118:43); or, it could refer to the word of the gospel (2 Cor 6:7; Col 1:5). The impossibility of deciding exclusively for one or the other of these options is precisely the most important point about James's theological perspective: The God who is now at work among them is the same as has always been at work, the one God revealed through creation, through covenant, through gospel.

The same rich ambiguity attends James's statements concerning the perfect law of liberty (2:8–11) through which God has revealed God's will for humans and on the basis of which humans will be judged (2:12–4:12). James states powerfully, "There is one lawgiver [*nomothetēs*] and judge [*kritēs*] who is able to save [*sōsai*] and destroy [*apolesai*]" (4:12). The divine origin and authority of the law could scarcely be stated more clearly. But what does James mean by this *nomos?* The term certainly encompasses Torah as narrative, wisdom, and prophecy, as shown by James's citations from each of those sections of the Old Testament, and by his invitation to gaze into the perfect law (1:22–25) in order to see the exemplars for authentic human response to God in the figures of Abraham and Rahab, who display the works of faith (2:21–26), Job, who displays the endurance of faith (5:11), and Elijah, who shows the prayer of faith (5:17). And it includes the moral commandments of the Decalogue and Leviticus 19 (see above and Jas 2:11). The "royal law," however, is that of love for neighbor (2:8), and as we have seen, that law is stated both in Torah (Lev 19:18) and by the Lord Jesus.

God does not leave humans with only a verbal norm. The word of truth is also an "implanted word" able to save souls (1:21), and God has made a "spirit" (*pneuma*) contrary to the envious one of the devil to dwell in humans (4:5). God remains always in control of human affairs (4:15) and declares as righteous and as friends those whose faith in him is expressed in action (2:23). In all this activity among humans, God reveals a nature that is merciful and compassionate; indeed, these terms define God (5:11). Thus, God promises the crown of life to those who love him (1:12; 2:5); has chosen the poor of the world to be rich in faith and heirs of the kingdom (2:5); regards true religion as including the visitation of orphans and widows in their distress (1:27), even as God also hears the cries of the oppressed (5:4), raises up the sick (5:15), answers the prayers of those who ask in faith (1:5–6; 5:16) rather than wickedly (4:3), and forgives the sins of those who confess them (5:15). This is a God who approaches those who approach him (4:8), who lifts up the lowly (4:10), and enters into friendship with humans (2:23; 4:4). But this is also a God who opposes the proud and arrogant who exalt themselves by their oppression of others (4:6; 5:6).

Most distinctive is James's understanding of God as gift giver. The letter makes the point explicitly three times. In 4:6, James derives from the text of Prov 3:34: "God opposes the proud but gives grace [*charis* = favor/gift] to the humble." In contrast to those who seek to gain by taking away, God gains by gifting: "But he gives all the more grace." That this is not an accidental conclusion is shown by James's very first characterization of God in 1:5, where he affirms that God "gives to all generously [*haplōs*] and ungrudgingly [*mē oneidizontos*]." Finally, there is the programmatic statement in 1:17, "Every generous act of giving, with every perfect gift, is from above, coming down from the Father of lights, with whom there is no variation or shadow due to change." Taken together, the propositions assert that God's giving is universal, abundant, without envy, and constant. To have faith in this God, therefore, is to see the world as an open system, in contrast to the zero-sum game imagined by envy: The creating and revealing and saving God drenches the world constantly with gifts.

Because God is in active relationship with creation rather than isolated from it, human existence can be described in terms of a story with both God and humans as characters. The story has a past, defined in terms of the gifts God has already given: creating humans in God's image, revealing God's will in the law and the prophets and in the "faith of Jesus Christ," implanting in humans the "word of truth," the "wisdom from above," and "the spirit." The story also has a future, which consists of God's response to human behavior in the world in the *parousia* of the Lord: God will reward the innocent and merciful and persevering, who have spoken and acted according to the "royal law of liberty." In contrast, God will punish the wicked oppressors who blaspheme the noble name associated with God's people. James's world, in other words, is not only open spatially, but also temporally.

Critical to an appreciation of James's theological language is seeing how his theological propositions stand as warrants and premises for his moral exhortation. James does not contain a series of statements about God that simply stand juxtaposed to moral commands. The two kinds of statements are intricately related. Moral exhortation is always grounded in James's understanding of the human relationship to God. Precisely this makes his affirmation of the constant, universal, ungrudging, and abundant gift-giving by God so central, for it is this understanding of reality that enables James to advocate a life of intracommunitarian concern and solidarity rather than one of competitive envy.

THE WITNESS OF 1 PETER

If analysis of James's language about God demands its being placed in relation to that letter's moral instruction, such instruction in 1 Peter must likewise be seen in relation to this letter's statements about Jesus Christ. In this composition, Christology is central. Reading James, we are struck by the continuity and consistency in what God does and who God is. In 1 Peter, the note of newness is everywhere sounded, and that newness is directly connected to the pivotal role of Jesus. Several examples can illustrate the point.

We have seen that Jas 1:18 speaks of God "giving birth" to humans through a word of truth. But in 1 Pet 1:3 we read that by his great mercy God has "given us a new birth [*anagennēsas*] into a living hope through the resurrection of Jesus Christ from the dead." It is not a birth but a rebirth, and it is accomplished through the resurrection of Jesus. This rebirth extends also to the reshaping of the symbols of Torah. Peter takes over the notion of "inheritance" (*klēronomia*) as the reality hoped for, and redefines it in light of the resurrection as something "imperishable, undefiled, and unfading, kept in heaven for you" (1 Pet 1:4).

A second example: In Jas 5:10, the prophets are mentioned as examples of suffering and patience, but in 1 Pet 1:10–11 the prophets appear as those who "prophesied of the grace that was to be yours [making] careful search and inquiry, inquiring about the person or time that the Spirit of Christ within them indicated when it testified in advance to the sufferings destined for Christ and the subsequent glory." The significance of prophecy is predictive, and the spirit at work in the prophets of old is, we note, the *pneuma christou* ("the Spirit of Christ"). In 1 Peter, moreover, it is not the suffering of the prophets that serves as an example to the readers, but the suffering of Christ (2:21).

A third example: James 1:10–11 echoes Isa 40:6–7 to make a point about the transitory character of wealth. Just as the flower fades, "It is the same way with the rich; in the midst of a busy life, they will wither away." In 1 Pet 1:23–25, the use of Isa 40:6–9 is quite different. Peter extends the citation to include the words, "but the word of the Lord endures forever" (Isa 40:9), and identifies it with the gospel: "That word is the good news that was announced to you" (1 Pet 1:25). The point of the citation and identification, furthermore, is once more the newness of their experience of God: "You have been born anew [anagennēmenoi], not of perishable but of imperishable seed, through the living and enduring word of God" (1 Pet 1:23).

The complexity of 1 Peter's language about God is signaled from the start by the letter's greeting. Peter identifies himself as "an apostle of Jesus Christ" (1:1), that is, as one commissioned by the Messiah Jesus. By itself, this could refer to Peter's designation as an apostle during Jesus' ministry. But in the identification of the readers, Peter continues, "who have been chosen and destined by God the Father and sanctified by the Spirit to be obedient to Jesus Christ and to be sprinkled with his blood" (1 Pet 1:2). Here, God the Father, Spirit, and Jesus Christ are both linked and distinguished. Jesus' blood can be sprinkled on the readers—clearly not literally but symbolically, as a sign of the effect of his death. They are sanctified by the Spirit (whose?). These relations are made more complex by 1:3, where Peter blesses "the God and Father of our Lord Jesus Christ." God is not only "Father" in the senses derived from Torah, that is, as creator or as the begetter of the people Israel. In a very specific sense this God is "Father" of Jesus the Messiah. Taking this designation seriously means at the very least to see everything attributed to Jesus as derived ultimately from "God" as well, since the Son is minimally the agent of the Father and maximally a different sort of presence of the Father. To speak about "God" in 1 Peter therefore demands speaking as well about Jesus Christ and about the Spirit. Although the language needed to clarify these relations is still three centuries away, it is obvious how 1 Peter both enables and demands that sort of ontological analysis. Precisely because the relations between Father, Son, and Spirit remain here implicit and unexamined, statements about all three are pertinent to our perception of God. For the purposes of this essay, then, a brief consideration of 1 Peter's pneumatology and Christology is not a distraction but rather a recognition of this composition's distinctive way of speaking about *ho theos*.

What Peter says about spirit has its own ambiguities. Note, for example, the way the letter speaks about the death and resurrection of Jesus: He was "put to death in the flesh [sarki], but made alive in the spirit [pneumati]" (3:18). The NRSV catches some of the ambiguity by placing a definite article ("the spirit") where the Greek has none, but then also leaving "spirit" uncapitalized.

What does the text say? Is it that Christ was made alive with respect to his spirit? Or is it that he was made alive through the Spirit (of God)? The choice is not made easier by the following phrase: "in which also he went and made a proclamation to the spirits in prison" (3:19). The "in which" refers to the spirit, and the most obvious way to read this would be: "being brought back to life as Spirit, he went in that state to proclaim to the imprisoned spirits." This reading is supported by 4:6: "For this is the reason the gospel was proclaimed even to the dead, so that, though they had been judged in the flesh as everyone is judged, they might live in the spirit as God does." In these passages, language about *pneuma* denotes a mode of existence that is not exclusive to God. When, however, Peter speaks of the readers being "sanctified by [or 'in,' *en*] the Spirit" (1:2), the logic moves in the other direction. The phrase could as easily be translated "in a spirit of sanctification," without the capital letter and the definite article. In this case, however, the NRSV properly nudges us toward seeing this spirit as the "Holy Spirit," because sanctification is exclusively a prerogative of God.

Three final mentions of the spirit move us even closer to the activity of God and to the distinctive way in which Peter points to continuity within the new experience of God among his Gentile readers. Peter uses the explicit title "Holy Spirit" in 1:12 with reference to the gospel: "It was revealed to them [the prophets] that they were serving not themselves but you, in regard to the things that have now been announced to you through those who brought you good news by the Holy Spirit sent from heaven—things into which angels long to look!" The conviction that the preaching of the gospel was accompanied by the powerful working of the Holy Spirit is scarcely unique to Peter (see Acts 10:44; Rom 15:19; Gal 3:2; 1 Thess 1:5; Heb 2:4). But this statement is immediately preceded by another concerning the prophets, who "prophesied of the grace that was to be yours [making] careful search and inquiry, inquiring about the person or time that the Spirit of Christ within them indicated when it testified in advance to the sufferings destined for Christ and the subsequent glory" (1 Pet 1:10–11). Once more, the NRSV translation makes a choice where there are several options. The Greek could be rendered, "the messianic spirit." By capitalizing "spirit" and giving it a definite article, the NRSV provides a very strong reading—in my estimation, correctly. Peter intends his readers to understand that the same Holy Spirit that inspired the prophets of old is now at work in the gospel. But even more: That Holy Spirit was from the beginning connected to the Messiah, who is now understood to be Jesus. The distance between old and new is collapsed even as it is stated. Such foreshortening helps us understand the otherwise startling way in which Peter applies the epithets of the historical Israel directly and without more ado to his Gentile readers in 2:9–10. They are indeed the ones who had not been shown mercy but were now being shown mercy (by God). But if the "Spirit of Christ" had been at work in all prophecy, then in one sense these Gentile believers had been in view all along in the words of the prophets. Finally, Peter asserts that if his readers suffer "for the name of Christ," they will be blessed and the Spirit of God [*pneuma tou theou*] will rest upon them" (4:14).

The Christ has in fact, according to Peter, been "destined [or 'foreknown,' *proegnōsmenou*) before the foundation of the world, but was revealed [that is, 'made known,' *phanerōthentos*] at the end of the ages for your sake" (1:20). These passive voices indicate that the one knowing and the one revealing is God. And as God is the source of the Christ, so is God the goal of the Messiah's work. Peter continues, "Through him you have come to trust in God" (1:21). Like Paul, Peter focuses primarily on the basic elements of the kerygma: the suffering and death of Jesus Christ, his resurrection and exaltation, and his future appearance. Thus, Peter's readers have been purified by the blood of Jesus Christ (1:2) and have been purchased in ransom by his precious blood (1:19). Jesus suffered in the flesh (4:1), suffered once for sins, the righteous for the unrighteous, in order to bring them to God (3:18). Jesus not only suffered for them (2:21), but did so in a manner that left them an example of how they might suffer (2:21–23), not because of wrongdoing, but in the name of Christ (4:14). Jesus was also resurrected from the dead (1:3, 21), made alive in the Spirit (3:18, 21) and is exalted at the right hand of God with angels subject to him (3:22). He will appear again (1:7, 13).

Even in the present, however, Jesus is the object of love and faith: "Although you have not seen him, you love him; and even though you do not see him now, you believe in him and rejoice with an indescribable and glorious joy" (1:8). Jesus not only brings them to God (3:18), but it is through him also that spiritual sacrifices acceptable to God are offered in the assembly (2:4). Depending on how we understand "you have tasted that the Lord is good" (2:3)—does *kyrios* here refer to Christ or to *ho theos?*—Peter may also be suggesting that they can approach the risen Jesus: "Come to him, a living stone" (2:4).

The intensity of their personal relationship with the risen Jesus, not to mention Peter's sense of Jesus' present status, is revealed not only in expressions such as "love him" and "believe in him" but also in the imperative: "in your hearts sanctify Christ as Lord" (3:15 NRSV), or "sanctify the Lord Christ in your hearts." The fact that a textual variant has *theos* ("God") rather than *Christos* ("Christ") as the object of this sanctification only makes the point more emphatically: In 1 Peter, just such a close relation between the two is implied. Christ Jesus now shares the eternal glory of God (5:10). It does not surprise us, therefore, to hear Peter say in 4:11, after listing all the things that *God* is doing for them, "so that God may be glorified in all things through Jesus

Christ [*dia Iēsou Christou*]. To him [i.e., Jesus Christ] belong the glory and the power forever and ever. Amen."

The answer to the question of how 1 Peter speaks about God must include all of the above. But statements about Christ and the Spirit by no means exhaust the subject. Like James, Peter has a range of remarkable explicit statements about *ho theos*, so many, in fact, that more than a mere (and partial) catalogue of them is not possible in the present essay. We can organize these statements into titles or epithets, actions, ascribed qualities, and attitudes/ actions directed toward God. These are drawn both from Peter's direct statements and from the implications of the Scriptures he cites.

Peter calls God "Father" in the greeting (1:2), and we have seen how this title is given one specification in 1:3 when God is called "Father of our Lord Jesus Christ." But that title for God is available to others besides Jesus. First Peter 1:17 has, "if you invoke as Father . . . ," indicating that this was a way in which all Christians could designate God. Peter also uses the epithet "the God of all grace" in 5:10, "the shepherd and guardian of [their] souls" in 2:25, and "the chief shepherd" in 5:4. Each of these epithets, as we shall see, corresponds to God's actions.

Everything Peter says about *ho theos* points to a power that later language would identify as proper to a person (*prosōpon*). This composition has no negative theology, no criticism of its first-order language of ascription that would provide a cautionary hedge around anthropomorphism. But attention paid to the sort of personal qualities and actions attributed to *ho theos* makes it clear that this is a "person" far beyond any capacity known by humans. God is first the one who knows. Peter speaks of God's "foreknowledge" twice, with reference to the status of his readers as the elect sojourners of the Diaspora (1:1) and to the destiny of Christ (1:20). From his citation of Ps 34:13–17, we learn that God sees the righteous and hears their prayers (3:12). It is a function of God's knowledge that he can be designated as judge. In 1:17, Peter says that God judges people according to their deeds *aprosōpolēmptōs* ("impartially"). By attributing "no respect for persons" to God rather than to humans, Peter again resembles Paul (see Rom 2:11) more than James (see Jas 2:1, 9). In 2:23, Peter states that in his suffering Jesus made no threat in return, but "entrusted himself to the one who judges justly [*dikaiōs*]." And in 4:5, he asserts that those who continue to live riotously (that is, in the way his readers used to before their conversion) "will have to give an accounting to him who stands ready to judge the living and the dead." The claim that God knows from before the creation of the world (1:20), sees the works of humans without discrimination, and judges both dead and living, is to state that *ho theos* is transcendent, that is, so far beyond the created order as to be intimately present to all things. It is in this connection that Peter's language about *pneuma* is pertinent (see the discussion above).

God also wills. First Peter speaks of God's will in connection with the ordering of reality to which humans should conform in attitude and behavior. It is God's will that they live in accord with God's desires (4:2), that they silence their critics by doing good (2:15), that they suffer for doing good rather than doing evil (3:17; 4:19), that pastors shepherd their flock willingly (5:2). God's desires are expressed in action. God creates the world (1:20) and actively intervenes in creation through words (1:25; 4:11) that are alive and enduring (1:23). Scripture speaks some of these words and teaches how God acts to do his will, as in "laying in Zion a stone" (2:6; Isa 8:14), or turning his face against those who do evil (3:13; Ps 34:16), or waiting patiently during the days of Noah (3:20; Gen 6:11–22), or opposing the proud even as he gives grace to the lowly (5:5; Prov 3:34). Peter emphasizes the *call* of God, who has summoned (*kalein*) the Gentiles "out of darkness into his marvelous light" (2:9), who has called them for the very purpose of receiving a blessing (3:9) and to be holy as he is holy (1:15), who has, finally, called them to his eternal glory in Christ (5:10). Those whom God has so called are his elect or chosen ones (1:2; 2:4). It is to them above all that God announces the good news (1:25; 4:17).

God's actions for those whom he has chosen—his people (2:10), his flock (5:2), his servants (2:16), his house (4:17)—are not verbal only. In one of the composition's most striking statements, Peter says, "Cast all your anxiety on him, because he cares for you" (5:7). God's care for humans is expressed through a variety of gifts ("graces"). God gives them credit for suffering innocently (2:20), and God gives grace to the humble (5:5). Peter correctly summarizes by speaking of "the God of all grace" in 5:10 and testifying to "the true grace of God" (5:12). God's favor is shown in that mercy (2:10) by which they have been given a share in an inheritance and blessing (1:4; 3:9) that goes beyond that of the land, wealth, or posterity, a blessing that consists in life (4:6), expressed first through the resurrection of Jesus (1:3, 21) and then through the rebirth or regeneration of God's chosen ones (1:3, 23), now through the protection God shows them (1:5). All this is God's way of saving their lives (or souls, 1:9–10) and leading them to God's own glory that is shared by Christ (1:21; 4:11; 5:10). In the present, God "will himself restore, support, strengthen, and establish" them (5:10).

In all of these actions, the qualities of God are revealed: God's great mercy (1:3), power (1:5), holiness (1:16), life (1:23), sweetness (2:3), light (2:9), justice (2:23), patience (3:20), grace (4:10), and strength (4:11). Those who have been brought to God by Christ (3:18), therefore, respond by declaring God blessed (1:3), submitting to his mighty hand (5:6), fearing him (2:17), praying to him (3:21), directing their faith toward him (1:21) as well as their hope (3:5), and seeking in every way to glorify God (2:12; 4:11, 16).

CONCLUSION

In the middle of the second century, the question of God became critical for Christians. In the face of the challenge posed by various forms of Gnosticism, it was necessary to articulate more clearly the rich, evocative, but also deeply ambiguous language of the New Testament concerning *ho theos*. Above all, the church had to decide how radical the new experience of God through Jesus Christ really was. Was its experience so new that Jesus could only be truly perceived as the manifestation of a god totally other than the creator god? Such was the claim of Marcion. And if the claim was that the experience of Jesus was somehow continuous with the revelation of God in Torah, then how was it new? Was not the logical corollary of continuity a form of Christianity in which God's activity in Jesus was collapsed entirely to the precedents of Torah? Such seems to have been the position of the Ebionites. The challenge to orthodoxy was to recognize both continuity and discontinuity while avoiding these extreme expressions of each.

What do we learn through Jesus about the identity and nature of God? To answer this question, the Gnostics wanted to read only Paul—and only according to the key to Paul provided by their convictions. The Ebionites wanted to read anything but Paul. Neither James nor 1 Peter by themselves provide a direct or adequate answer to the question. But they suggest that Paul's statements should be read within the context of the entire canon, and when so read, do not appear idiosyncratic. Together with other canonical witnesses, they offer invaluable testimony to two central convictions out of which any true statement about *ho theos* must be based. God is ever new, says Peter, even while being the same. Yes, says James, and God is always the same even while ever new.

SELECT BIBLIOGRAPHY

First Peter

Achtemeier, Paul J. 1989. "Newborn Babes and Living Stones: Literal and Figurative in 1 Peter." Pages 207–36 in *To Touch the Text*. Edited by Maurya P. Horgan and Paul J. Kobelski. New York: Crossroad.
———. 1996. *1 Peter: A Commentary on First Peter*. Edited by Eldon Jay Epp. Hermeneia. Minneapolis: Fortress.
Dalton, William J. 1989. *Christ's Proclamation to the Spirits: A Study of 1 Peter 3:18–4:6.* 2d ed. Analecta Biblica 23. Rome: Biblical Institute Press.
Elliott, John H. 1966. *The Elect and the Holy*. Novum Testamentum Supplements 12. Leiden: E. J. Brill.
———. 1981. *A Home for the Homeless: A Sociological Exegesis of 1 Peter*. Philadelphia: Fortress.

Talbert, Charles. H., ed. 1986. *Perspectives on First Peter.* Macon, Ga.: Mercer University Press.

Thurén, Lauri. 1995. *Argument and Theology in 1 Peter: The Origins of Christian Paraenesis.* Journal for the Study of the New Testament: Supplement Series 114. Sheffield: Sheffield Academic Press.

James

Adamson, James B. 1989. *James: The Man and His Message.* Grand Rapids: Eerdmans,.

Cargal, Timothy B. 1993. *Restoring the Diaspora: Discursive Structure and Purpose in the Epistle of James.* Society of Biblical Literature Dissertation Series 144. Atlanta: Scholars Press.

Hartin, P. J. 1991. *James and the Q Sayings of Jesus.* Journal for the Study of the New Testament: Supplement Series 47. Sheffield: Sheffield Academic Press.

Johnson, Luke Timothy. 1985. "Friendship with the World and Friendship with God: A Study of Discipleship in James." Pages 166–83 in *Discipleship in the New Testament.* Edited by Fernando F. Segovia. Philadelphia: Fortress.

———. 1995. *The Letter of James.* Anchor Bible 37A. New York: Doubleday.

Penner, Todd C. 1996. *The Epistle of James and Eschatology: Re-Reading an Ancient Christian Letter.* Journal for the Study of the New Testament: Supplement Series 121. Sheffield: Sheffield Academic Press.

Ward, R. B. 1968. "The Works of Abraham: James 2:14–26." *Harvard Theological Review* 61:283–90.

———. 1969. "Partiality in the Assembly." *Harvard Theological Review* 62:87–97.

14

God and Time
in the Apocalypse of John

DAVID E. AUNE

While God is frequently referred to in the Apocalypse of John as the focal presence in numerous scenes set in the heavenly throne room and is the primary recipient of the worship and hymns of praise offered by members of the heavenly court, he is only given a speaking role twice in the entire book. The first instance is at the conclusion of the prologue (1:8): "'I am the Alpha and the Omega,' says the Lord God, 'who is and who was and who is to come, the Almighty'" (the NRSV, I think incorrectly, does not enclose the last phrase in quotation marks as I have done here). The second instance occurs in a climactic position in the eschatological drama that constitutes the focus of Rev 4:1–22:9. Following the destruction of the first heaven and the first earth and the appearance of the new heaven and the new earth, God is given a longer speech (21:5–8), near the middle of which we find two further titles uttered as self-predications: "I am the Alpha and the Omega, the Beginning and the End" (v. 6b; I have capitalized the last two nouns, though the NRSV does not).

The two passages just quoted have a striking similarity that I want to explore further in this essay, written in honor of my esteemed colleague and friend, Paul J. Achtemeier. Both passages contain self-predications introduced by "I am" (egō eimi). "'I am the Alpha and the Omega,' says the Lord God, 'who is and who was and who is to come'" (1:8), and "I am the Alpha and the Omega, the beginning and the end" (21:6). These two "I am" sayings contain three divine titles, all of which are found in other contexts in the Apocalypse of John, and all of which appear to have temporal as well as cosmological aspects. A closely related title that does not appear in these two "I am" sayings is "the First and the Last," which is associated with two titles we have already encountered: "the Alpha and the Omega" and "the Beginning and the End" (Rev 22:13), suggesting that it is part of a set. In this essay, I will argue that this series

of interrelated temporal metaphors which function as divine titles were specifically crafted by the author to encapsulate his apocalyptic vision of God as the
sovereign and almighty One who at the end restores both the cosmos and
humankind to the pristine perfection of the beginning.

There are, then, four divine titles in the Apocalypse of John that appear to
have an implicit relationship to the notion of time: (1) "[he] who is and who
was and who is to come," which occurs three times in a tripartite form—twice
in the form just quoted (1:4, 8) and once in a slightly modified form as "who
was and is and is to come" (4:8)—and twice in the related bipartite form "who
are and who were" (11:17; 16:5), (2) "the First and the Last" (1:17; 2:8; 22:13),
(3) "the Beginning and the End" (21:6; 22:13), and (4) "the Alpha and the
Omega" (1:8; 21:6; 22:13).

There are several arresting features about these titles that are of obvious
interest. First, with the exception of the first (which is a temporal continuum
in both its three-part and two-part forms), these titles are expressed in terms of
two extremes of a continuum embracing all that lies between. Second, while the
first title is applied exclusively to God in the Apocalypse and the second is
applied exclusively to Christ, the third and fourth are applied both to God (1:8)
and to Christ (21:6; 22:13). What may appear as a blurring of the distinction
between God and Christ is in fact an attempt to use conceptions of God to characterize Christ, a theological move that needs closer examination. Third, there
is a tendency for some of these titles to cluster, for two are found together in
1:8 and 21:6, while three are found side by side in 22:13. This suggests that, in
these three passages at least, these titles are in some sense synonymous as well
as mutually interpretive. Fourth, each of these titles is used as a self-predication
of God or Christ following "I am" (*egō* [*eimi*]; 1:8, 17; 21:6; 22:13, au. trans.):

1:8   "'I am [*egō eimi*] the Alpha and the Omega,' says the Lord God, 'who is and
        who was and who is to come, the Almighty.'"
1:17   "I am [*egō eimi*] the First and the Last and the Living One, and I was dead
        but behold I am living forever."
21:6   "And he said to me, 'It is finished. I am [*egō (eimi)*] the Alpha and the
        Omega, the Beginning and the End.'"
22:13   "I [*egō*] (am) the Alpha and the Omega, the First and the Last, the Begin-
        ning and the End."

The titles "the Alpha and the Omega" and "the Beginning and the End" are,
in fact, used *only* in "I am" self-predications. Fifth, it is striking that none of
these titles occur elsewhere in the New Testament or other early Christian literature prior to the third century C.E.

After exploring the significance of each of the four divine titles individually,
I will examine the possible relationships between these titles and the concep-

tions of time characteristic of Jewish apocalypses in general and the Apocalypse of John in particular.

FOUR DIVINE TITLES

The One Who Is and Who Was and Who Is to Come

This striking tripartite formula occurs twice in this form (1:4, 8) and once in a slightly revised form exhibiting a more chronological arrangement: "who was and is and is to come" (4:8). A variation also occurs in two occurrences of a bipartite form of the title using just the first two of the three predicates: "who are and were" (11:17; 16:5). In each context, the predicates are used of God alone, a fact which suggests that some God-language was thought appropriate only for God. Surprisingly, neither the tripartite nor bipartite versions of this formula occur elsewhere in early Jewish or early Christian texts before the third century. The predicate "the One who is" (*ho ōn*), however, occurs with some frequency in Greco-Jewish texts ultimately based on the LXX version of Exod 3:14 (Josephus, *Ant.* 8.350; LXX Jer 1:6; 4:10; 14:13; 39:17 [variae lectiones]; Philo, *Moses* 1.75; *Somn.* 1.231; *Deus* 110). In these Hellenistic Jewish contexts, the predicate is used in an ontological rather than a temporal sense, and can therefore be translated as "the Existent One."

The predicate "the One who is" also occurs in some comparatively late pagan philosophical and magical texts, though the latter may well have been the result of the pagan fascination with Jewish divine names. The possible temporal significance of the phrase only becomes evident when it is associated in the Apocalypse with the predicates "the One who was" (*ho ēn*) and "the One who was and who is coming" (*ho ōn kai erchomenos*). Further, the final predicate, "the One who is to come," gives the whole not only a temporal, but more specifically an eschatological significance.

Very similar to the tripartite title in the Apocalypse of John is Plato's discussion of the traditional Greek way of referring to God (the principle of unity in the cosmos, not identical with Zeus, the foremost Olympian deity) using past, present, and future forms of the verb "to be" found in *Timaeus* 37e: "We say that it [Eternal Being] was and is and will be [*legomen gar dē hōs ēn estin te kai estai*]." Plato, however, rejects this as a naive and inaccurate way of speaking of Eternal Being:

> All these [days, nights, months, years] are all divisions of time, just as "was" [*to ēn*] and "shall be" [*to estai*] are generated forms of time, though we apply these terms reflexively though improperly and incorrectly to the eternal being. For we say that "he is" or "he was" or "he will be," though actually only "he is" [*to esti*] is appropriate.

Of the many other texts which indicate that the verbal reference to past, present, and future was indeed a traditional way of using temporal categories to refer to the eternality of the divine being (e.g., Plato, *Laws* 4.715e; Plutarch, *De Iside et Osiride* 354c; *Asclepius* 134.25–26), I will cite just three of the relevant parallel texts. Pausanias 10.12.10 preserves a hexameter formula, which he attributes to the female priestesses of Zeus at the famous oracle at Dodona: "Zeus was, Zeus is, Zeus shall be." The Zeus who can be so described, however, is not the Zeus of Greek mythology (the normal Greek view is that the cosmos is eternal while the gods came into existence in time) but rather an attempt to transfer the name of the central Olympian deity of traditional Greek myth and cult to the god of the philosophers, who is identical with the basic principle of the universe (i.e., with the universe itself) and who was thought to provide it with a basic and inclusive unity. According to the *Asclepius* 14.17–18: *deus aeternus nec nasci potest nec potuit; hoc est, hoc fuit, hoc erit semper*, "the eternal God neither can nor could have come to be; that which is, which was, which always will be." Here the past, present, and future forms of *sum* are explicitly used to indicate the eternality of God. The third text is fragment 14(21) of Empedocles: "From them [fire, air, water] comes all that was and is and will be hereafter." In this instance, the tripartite formula is not used of God but of the basic principle underlying the cosmos, regarded as God in philosophical tradition. Here it is clear that the tripartite formula is understood in a temporal manner as a metaphor for the eternity of God. With regard to Revelation, it has been frequently noticed that the third predicate of the tripartite formula has been modified from a future form of the verb "to be" (*eimi*), either *estai* or *essetai*, to the present substantival participle *ho erchomenos*, "the One who comes."

Martin McNamara has argued that the Aramaic equivalent to the tripartite divine name found in Rev 1:4, 8; 4:8 is in some way dependent on similar formulations found in several Targumic texts. One example he cites is *Exod. Rab.* 3:14: "R. Isaac [ca. 300 C.E.] said: The Holy One Blessed be He said to Moses: Say to them: 'I am he who was and I am he (who is) now and I am he (who will be) forever.' Wherefore is it said thrice, 'I am.'" He suggests that an even closer parallel can be found in *Tg. Ps.-J.* Deut 32:39: "When the Memra of the Lord will be revealed to redeem his people he will say to all the nations: 'See now that I am He who is and who was and I am he who will be and there is no other God beside me.'" McNamara's view that the author of the Apocalypse was dependent on these Targumic traditions rather than on LXX Exod 3:14 or on the pagan Hellenistic tradition discussed above, however, is problematic because of the late date of the Targums. It is worth noting that the Targums agree with the Hellenistic parallels in using the future tense of the verb "to be" in the formula, suggesting dependence on the Hellenistic parallels discussed above, while the author of the Apocalypse has substituted a present participle with future significance: "the One who is coming." What really matters, of course, is not where the tripartite formula comes from, but how and why the author has modified it and what it means in the Apocalypse of John.

The tripartite and bipartite versions of the formula occur in a variety of contexts in the Apocalypse, each of which sheds some light on the meaning or function of the title. The first occurrence of the tripartite formula is in the epistolary salutation in Rev 1:4–5: "Grace to you and peace from him who is and who was and who is to come, and from the seven spirits who are before his throne, and from Jesus Christ, the faithful witness, the firstborn of the dead, and the ruler of the kings of the earth." While the form of this salutation is very similar to that of the salutations found in the superscriptions to the Pauline letters, the content is distinctive. A typical Pauline or Deutero-Pauline salutation (though some are expanded and varied), would be "grace and peace from God our Father and the Lord Jesus Christ" (e.g., 1 Cor 1:3; 2 Cor 1:2; Phil 1:2; 2 Thess 1:2; Eph 1:2). The inclusion of the tripartite divine title in the superscription of Rev 1:4, in the slot where Christians familiar with the Pauline letters would expect a more conventional salutation, suggests that the author is making a special point of emphasizing this particular divine title.

Similarly in Rev 1:8, where the tripartite title is repeated, this time in one of just two brief speeches attributed to God in the entire book, the reader or hearer cannot miss the importance and distinctiveness of the formula, for here it is framed by two other divine titles in the form of a complex "I am" saying: "'I am the Alpha and the Omega,' says the Lord God, 'who is and who was and who is to come, the Almighty.'" The author is fond of clusters of three elements and has used this group of three titles to mutually reinforce one another. "The Alpha and the Omega" (see below) is an abbreviated metaphor for the comprehensiveness expressed in a different way than the tripartite formula. The designation "Almighty" (*pantokratōr*), again juxtaposed with the tripartite formula in Rev 4:8, occurs some 170 times in the LXX as a translation for the Hebrew word *tsĕbā'ôt* (hosts), a traditional Israelite epithet of God linking him to warfare, found frequently in the Old Testament in the archaic phrase *yhwh tsĕbā'ôt*, "Lord of hosts." The Greek term *pantokratōr*, which means "all powerful" or "all mighty," was chosen by the LXX translators to convey the meaning they found in *tsĕbā'ôt* in the third century B.C.E.; it also represents the significance the author of the Apocalypse attributes to "the Alpha and the Omega" as well as the tripartite formula.

In a hymnic context in Rev 4:8, the tripartite formula appears in a slightly revised form in a more chronological order: "Holy, holy, holy, the Lord God the Almighty, who *was* and *is* and *is to come*." While the first part of this acclamation closely follows the Hebrew text of Isa 6:3 (where the LXX transliterates rather than translates *tsĕbā'ôt*), the tripartite formula represents an addition by the author of the Apocalypse, perhaps based on traditional Jewish exegesis of Exod 3:14 and Deut 32:39, though nowhere in Jewish literature does the *Qĕdussah*, or *sanctus*, occur with the tripartite formula.

The bipartite formula "who are and who were" occurs in two other hymnic contexts, in Rev 11:17 and 16:5. The omission of the epithet "who is to come" is probably due to the fact that from a dramatic perspective, God has *already* visited the earth in judgment earlier in the narrative of each passage (11:18a: "The nations raged, but your wrath *came*"; 16:5: "You are just in these your judgments"), as well as in salvation (11:18b: "[the time came] for rewarding your servants"). In 11:17, God is also addressed as the "Lord God Almighty," so that the title *pantokratōr* actually occurs in company with the tripartite formula in two of its three occurrences (1:8; 4:8) and with the bipartite version of the formula in this context (11:17). In Rev 16:5, the bipartite title "who are and who were" is followed by a relatively rare predicate: "Holy One" (*hosios*).

The results of this sequential discussion of the uses of the tripartite and bipartite formulas in their respective contexts are two: (1) The epithet "who is to come," present in three occurrences of the tripartite formula (1:4, 8; 4:8), is missing in the bipartite versions (11:17; 16:5), presumably because the judgment of God has already come in the narrative context. This suggests that "who is to come" is a divine epithet narrowly focused on a divine visitation in eschatological judgment and salvation. (2) The title most frequently associated with the tripartite and bipartite formula is "Almighty," a traditional title of God in early Judaism, which suggests the author's primary understanding of the significance of the tripartite and bipartite formulas.

The Alpha and the Omega

This divine title, which does not occur earlier than the Apocalypse of John, is used twice of God (1:8; 21:6) and once of Christ (22:13). In all three instances it is a predicate nominative in an "I am" statement. The author clearly intends the reader to associate this title with the other antithetical titles, for it is found with "the Beginning and the End" in 21:6 and with "the First and the Last" and "the Beginning and the End" in 22:13. The context of the divine self-predications "I am the Alpha and the Omega, the Beginning and the End" in Rev 21:6 is extremely significant, for it is part of 21:5–8, the second speech attributed to God in the Apocalypse (the first is in 1:8), a divine utterance that follows the destruction of the first heaven and the first earth.

Since alpha and omega are the first and last letters of the Greek alphabet, the author apparently intends an association with the speculation that surrounded the letters of the alphabet. In later Jewish alphabet symbolism, ʾemet, the Hebrew word for "truth," was interpreted as a designation of God as the beginning, middle, and end (*Tg. Yer. Sanh.* 18a). Yet the basic conception must surely have been Hellenistic in origin (see Plato, *Laws* 4.716A; Josephus, *Against Apion* 2.190), since mu is the twelfth letter of the twenty-four-letter Greek alphabet (as close to the middle as possible, given the even number of letters). While aleph and tau are the first and last letters of the Hebrew-Aramaic alphabet, mem is not the middle letter of these alphabets but the thirteenth of twenty-two letters.

Hellenistic alphabet speculation also involved the vowels. The Greek alphabet had seven vowels, *aeēiouō*, thought by some to constitute the true name of God. According to Eusebius (*Preparation for the Gospel* 519d): "[The Hebrews] say also that the combination of the seven vowels contains the enunciation of one forbidden name, which the Hebrews indicate by four letters and apply to the supreme power of God, having received the tradition from father to son that this is something unutterable and forbidden to the multitude." While the Tetragrammaton (lit. "four letters") refers to the four Hebrew consonants in *yhwh*, the unspoken name of God, reference to the seven Greek vowels similarly involves the belief that *aeēiouō* somehow contains the pronunciation of that unutterable divine name. This tradition is also preserved in *PGM* XIII.39: "Write the great name with the seven vowels," and again in *PGM* XXI.11–12: "Your name which is seven-lettered in harmony with the seven vowel sounds." The seven vowels can also be used in self-predications following "I am," as in *Papyri graecae magicae* III.661: "I am *aeēiouō aeēiouō*."

In *On Style* 2.71, a first-century C.E. essay mistakenly attributed to Demetrius of Phaleron (late fourth century B.C.E.), there is a reference to Egyptian priests who used the seven vowels in singing hymns in praise of the gods. Again (despite the supposed Egyptian provenance of the tradition) the mention of seven vowels indicates that *Greek* vowels are in view, and it is likely that this tradition preserves the notion that the seven vowels are construed as a divine name, as they frequently do in the magical papyri (nearly all of which originated in Egypt). Alpha and omega can be understood as an abbreviation of the seven vowels by contraction, one common ancient type of abbreviation in which the first and last letters of a word, or the first two and last two letters of a word, are used as an abbreviation of the entire word.

The temporal significance of "the Alpha and the Omega" seems to have been left in the dust. However, the phrase must have been polyvalent, since, when juxtaposed with "the Beginning and the End" (21:6) and "the First and the Last" and "the Beginning and the End" (22:13), it seems to take on the notions of preeminence and superiority. In *PGM* IV.487–88, the significance of the seven vowels is construed in terms of priority or preeminence: "First origin of my origin, *aeēiouō*, first beginning [*archē prōtē*] of my beginning."

The First and the Last

The divine title "the First and the Last" (*ho prōtos kai ho eschatos*) occurs three times in the Apocalypse, always as the predicate of an "I am" declaration, and always a self-predication of the exalted Christ (1:17; 2:8; 22:13). Since this title is associated with two others in 22:13, which are used elsewhere of God in the Apocalypse (the Alpha and the Omega and the Beginning and the End), it is appropriate to explore its significance in this essay. This title is almost certainly based on the Hebrew text of Isa 44:6b (cf. 48:12), which is an "I am" self-predication of "the Lord, the King and Redeemer of Israel, the Lord of Hosts," which can be literally translated "I am the first and the last" (for whatever reason, the LXX never uses the term *eschatos* to translate ʾachărôn). The context is a lengthy speech attributed to God (42:14–44:23), which contains a section toward the end (44:6–8) in which God emphasizes the fact that he is absolutely sovereign and that there are no other gods beside him. The fact that the author of the Apocalypse presents the exalted Jesus as claiming this predication of himself is significant christologically, for from the perspective of the Old Testament such a predication is appropriate only to the God of Israel.

Revelation 1:17–18, in the context of an appearance of the exalted Jesus, is in the familiar form of an oracle of assurance: "Stop being afraid. I am the First and [*kai*] the Last, even [*kai*] the Living One. I died and behold I am alive for evermore" (my translation). It is possible, with the NRSV, to translate the clause "I am the First and the Last and the Living One" (here I have capitalized the titles) under the assumption that the self-predication has a tripartite form. However, the fact that the bipartite title "the First and the Last" occurs without elaboration in 22:13 suggests that the *kai* following the bipartite form in 1:17 is epexegetical, implying that "the First and the Last" is also the Living One. The phrase "the Living One" appears to be a double entendre, for it is immediately interpreted by reference to the death and resurrection of Jesus, yet "the Living One" primarily calls to mind the numerous Old Testament references to God as "the living God" (Deut 5:26; 1 Sam 17:26, 36; Jer 10:10; 23:36; Dan 6:27). Further, the phrases "the One who lives forever" and "the God who lives forever" are used by the author to refer to God four times in the Apocalypse (4:9, 10; 10:6; 15:7), indicating its relative importance.

The second occurrence of the title in Rev 2:8, though expressed in the third person, clearly refers back to the previous use of the title in 1:17–18 in the inaugural christophany: "These are the words of the First and the Last, who was dead and came to life." Here it is clear that "who was dead and came to life" is not a title but rather a particular way of identifying Jesus as "the First and the Last." The third and final occurrence of the title is the "I am" predication of the exalted Jesus in 22:13: "I am the Alpha and the Omega, the First and the Last, the Beginning and the End." Here, finally, all three of these antithetical titles occur in the same context, mutually defining one another. Since the exalted Jesus has the last word here, the functional equivalency between himself and God is intentionally emphasized. Each of these antithetical titles attempts to capture a divine characteristic by implying that, since he is both extremes he encompasses the continuum defined by the antithesis. Since "the Alpha and the Omega" is twice attributed to God in "I am" sayings (1:8; 21:6) and "the Beginning and the End" is also a definite self-predication in part of a short speech attributed to God in 21:6, it is clearly the author's purpose to identify the exalted Jesus with God.

The Beginning and the End

As we have seen above, this epithet is a self-predication of God in the "I am" statement of Rev 21:6, and is similarly a self-predication of the exalted Jesus in the "I am" statement of Rev 22:13. From the standpoint of narrative strategy, it is not only clear that the author wants us to understand that God and the exalted Jesus are somehow functionally identical, but also that the categories for conceptualizing the cosmic significance of Jesus are based on language primarily associated with God. This title, which is sometimes found in extra-biblical sources with a reference to the middle—"the Beginning and the Middle and the End"—is drawn from Hellenistic philosophical and religious traditions and has cosmological as well as temporal signification. The Derveni papyrus, found preserved through carbonization in a Macedonian grave and dating to ca. 350 B.C.E., contains a fragment from an earlier Orphic poem: "Zeus is the beginning, Zeus is the middle, all things are fulfilled by Zeus." A similar Orphic fragment is preserved in Plato, *Laws* 4.715E: "God . . . holds the beginning and the middle and the end of all things which exist," a statement quoted by a number of early Christian authors (Ps.-Justin, *Cohort.* 25; Irenaeus, *Haer.* 3.25.5; Hippolytus, *Haer.* 19.6; Clement Alex., *Strom.* 2.22; Origen, *Contra Celsum* 6.15). God is referred to as "the beginning and end of all things" by both Philo (*Plant.* 93) and Josephus (*Ant.* 8.280), but this title is rarely found in early Christian writers. "Beginning and End" is also a divine epithet found in many magical texts, including the Greek magical papyri. In *PGM* IV.2836–37, part of a hexameter hymn to Hekate (a Greek goddess who acquired cosmic significance in some circles): "Beginning and end [*archē kai telos*] are you [Hekate], and you alone rule all. For all things are from you and you alone rule all." Here, remarkably, Hekate is assigned a cosmic significance that is expressed through a different metaphor in *Orphic Hymns* 1.7, where she is designated as "key-bearing mistress of the entire cosmos." The last line quoted above from *PGM* IV.2837 is significant as a gloss interpreting one way of construing the title "the Beginning and the End": "For all things are from you and you alone rule all."

Summary

To this point I have discussed four titles for God and/or Christ that I have argued are similar in both form and meaning. Three of the four titles use different metaphors to conceptualize a continuum bounded by extremes: the Alpha and the Omega, the First and the Last, the Beginning and the End. Only "the One who is and who was and who is to come" (and its variations) does not fit this pattern. This last title does not consist of elements that frame a continuum so much as points plotted along a temporal continuum based on the ancient perception of the three basic tenses of the Greek verb: past, present, and future. As observed above, this was a widespread metaphor for expressing the eternality of the cosmos or of the one God (capitalized in translations of Greek sources only when understood as equivalent to the cosmos). As we have noted, the author of the Apocalypse has modified the third term of this traditional formulation by substituting "the One who comes" for the more conventional Hellenistic phrase "the One who will be." This title in the Apocalypse is based on the three basic tenses of the Greek language—past, present, and (implied) future—or just on past and present.

BIBLICAL AND APOCALYPTIC
PERSPECTIVES ON TIME

In this section, I want to review some of the work on the biblical conceptions of time to determine their utility for our investigation of the four divine titles focused on in this essay.

Conceptions of Time in Biblical Theology

The theological significance of the biblical conception of time has been a topic of major interest explored by a number of Old Testament and New Testament scholars associated with the biblical theology movement during the middle third of the twentieth century. Many of these scholars, however, tended to underrate apocalypticism and hence ignored the temporal perspectives of biblical (and extrabiblical) apocalypses and apocalyptic passages. Reacting against the history-of-religions school's conception of the faith of Israel and early Christianity as syncretistic amalgams of the myths, ideas, and practices of pagan societies and cultures in their environment, these scholars identified theological features and presuppositions of the faith of Israel and the early church that they considered historically and culturally unique. In their view, uniqueness was itself a strong argument for truth. This perspective pervades the nine-volume *Theological Dictionary of the New Testament*, a major monument of the biblical theology movement (1933–1973; English translation, 1964–1974).

Not surprisingly, adherents of the biblical theology movement found the Hebrew conception of time, inherited by early Christianity, to be in sharp contrast to (as well as superior to) the Greek view. In Oscar Cullmann's classic book *Christ and Time: The Primitive Christian Conception of Time and History* (1945; English translation, 1950), he contrasted Hebrew and Greek conceptions of time, proposing that the former was linear, the latter cyclical. For primitive Christianity and biblical Judaism, he argued, the most appropriate metaphor for time was the "upward sloping line" moving irreversibly toward the goal of complete fulfillment. The midpoint of this upward sloping line is the Christ event, from which all preceding and subsequent events receive meaning (the division of Western time into "Before Christ" and "Anno Domini" is one expression of the historical centrality of the Christ event). The two ideas which most clearly express the New Testament concept of time, he argued, were expressed by two Greek words for time: *kairos*, referring to a point of time, that is, time defined by its content, and *aiōn*, designating a duration or extent of time that could be understood as limited or unlimited. According to Cullmann, time and eternity are not contrasted, as in Greek philosophy (e.g., Plato, *Timaeus* 37D), but time is contrasted with endless time.

In *The Fullness of Time* (1952), John Marsh argued that a cyclical, abstract conception of time was characteristic of Greek thought (represented by the Greek word *chronos*), a perspective which deprived history of any real significance. On the other hand, "realistic" time located an event by its content and was, he claimed, the hallmark of the Hebrew conception of time inherited by early Christianity (represented by the Greek term *kairos*). In a short appendix, Marsh criticized Cullmann's linear model since it implies a concept of "chronological time," which he thought was lacking in the Old Testament. He further found that the linear view is misleading, since the end of the linear process (the Christ event) has appeared in the middle of the line as the center of history rather than at the end of the line (a point of view that Cullmann had developed at great length). Both Marsh and Thorlief Boman (a Norwegian Old Testament scholar influenced by Johannes Pedersen) thought that neither the line nor the circle (nor any other spatially oriented metaphor) adequately conveys the Hebrew conception of time. Marsh was also critical of the cataclysmic view of history (by which he apparently means the apocalyptic view), since once the end occurs, the process leading up to it ceases to have significance.

In the early 1960s, James Barr published two monographs that severely critiqued the linguistic methodology characteristic of many articles in the *Theological Dictionary of the New Testament*, as well as several studies on the Greek and Hebrew conceptions of time written by several biblical scholars. Barr used three basic lines of argument. First, attempts to connect the Hebrew and Greek conceptions of time with the aspectual verbal system of Hebrew and the temporal verbal system of Indo-European (specifically Greek) were methodologically invalid. Second, Greek and Hebrew words have distinct semantic meanings that must not be blended by an "illegitimate totality transfer," that is, words are not "concepts" that contain all latent semantic meanings in all contexts. Third, not all Greek conceptions of time were cyclical, while cyclical conceptions of time are also found in the Hebrew Bible. Momigliano, in essential agreement with Barr, argued that a cyclical view of time is absent from the histories of Herodotus and Thucydides, while on the other hand, the Israelite festival of Passover is a prime example of cultic and cyclical time.

Malina's Model of Ancient and Modern Time

The problem of time in the Apocalypse of John has been raised more directly by Bruce Malina, who objects to labeling the book an "apocalypse" and has questioned the propriety of using the term "eschatology" to describe the temporal perspective of the work. Both terms, he argues, are modern theological concepts imposed anachronistically on the Apocalypse. What scholars label "eschatology" was not concerned with life after death or the future, he maintains, but with life in the present. Since John's prophecy has just two temporal dimensions, past and present, there is nothing particularly "eschatological" about it.

Malina's view of the conception of time in the Apocalypse is based in part on earlier research on social conceptions of time in the ancient and modern world published in a 1989 article entitled "Christ and Time: Swiss or Mediterranean?" Here he presents a model for understanding the conception of time held by an ancient Mediterranean person, using a variety of modern social scientific studies. He argues that, unlike modern Americans, who have a highly abstract notion of time and a predominantly *future* orientation, ancient Mediterranean peasants had a primarily *present* orientation, dividing time into *experienced* time and *imaginary* time. Experienced time is the perception of duration within the horizon of actual experience (i.e., a broad conception of "the present"), which focuses on processes that include the recent past, the present, and that which is forthcoming (i.e., the unfolding or developing horizon of the experienced present). Imaginary time, on the other hand, refers to everything that does not exist in the present, namely, the past and the future.

In a second set of antithetical conceptions, Malina argues that modern Americans have a "linear separable time" that is monochronic (they can do only one thing at a time), while traditional peoples have a social time conception that is polychronic (they can do several things at once). The ancient Mediterranean had no conception of "linear separable time" and could not experience urgency based on scheduled time. The social time of traditional peoples had both "cyclical" and "procedural" dimensions. Cyclical time is rooted in the regular motion of the sun, moon, and stars, and is pegged to recurrent human activity; procedural time perceives the experience of singular and infrequent occurrences such as biological processes that must be brought to completion (e.g., marriage, birth of a firstborn son, old age).

Malina then presents a third set of antitheses, consisting of modern "abstract historical and operational time" over against "traditional historical and operational time." The latter understands historical time primarily for its present significance (like "imaginary time"), while "modern historical time" (a post-Renaissance development in the West) is a sense of history that assumes people in the past were different from people in the present.

In the following chart, I have simplified Malina's relatively complex model of Mediterranean time to call attention to the basic three sets of antithetical features of the ancient or traditional and modern conceptions of time described above.

Malina's Antithetical Conceptions of Time

Modern Conceptions	Ancient Mediterranean Conceptions
Modern abstract time	Traditional experienced and imaginary time
Modern linear separable time	Traditional cyclical and procedural time
Abstract historical and operational time	Traditional historical and operational time

One of the strengths of Malina's approach is that he does not rely on simple graphic metaphors, such as the line, circle, or spiral, but rather provides a detailed verbal description of the ways in which he thinks time was conceptualized by both ancients and moderns. He observes that the distinction biblical theologians make between linear time and cyclical time is not very clear, for the so-called linear time of the Bible is actually cyclical, but in the sense that the cycle occurs only once, not indefinitely. Malina's antithetical constructions of time are remarkably similar to Marsh's "chronological" time versus "realistic" time dichotomy (the latter was designated "psychological" time by Boman).

While "chronological" time was characteristic of Greek thought and "realistic" time of Hebrew thought for Marsh, corresponding to Cullmann's characterization of the Greek conception of time as "cyclical" and the Jewish and early Christian conception of time as "linear," Malina lumps all ancients together (Greeks, Romans, Hebrews), arguing that they had a *present* orientation consisting of *experienced* and *imaginary* time, while modern Americans have an *abstract* notion of time with a *future* orientation. In the end, such simplistic antithetical conceptions are problematic, for most of the social constructions of time discussed by Malina (and many that are not) are found in both the modern and ancient worlds, though in widely varying proportions and differing from culture to culture. The antithetical conceptualization of temporal constructs is a rhetorical strategy to privilege one side of the antithesis over the other. The biblical theologians explicitly regarded the Hebrew conception of time as superior to the Greek conception, while Malina implicitly regards ancient experiential conceptions of time as superior to modern abstract conceptions.

Malina's rejection of the terms "apocalyptic" and "eschatology" as modern temporal conceptions imposed on ancient thought is based in part on a misrepresentation of their meaning in modern scholarship. Scholars generally use these terms to refer, not to the distant future, but rather to the imminent future transformation of the world, that is, the end of history. Further, Malina's insistence that ancients were *present* oriented (though he defines the "present" broadly to consist of "this generation," that is, forty years) is based on the reductionist view that language about the future really functions exclusively to control and direct present social behavior. Eschatological language certainly does function in this way, but it functions in other ways as well.

Reflections on Models for Time

While time and space provide the basic grid for the human perception of reality, both can be conceptualized in an astonishing variety of ways. Time, unlike space, involves change, and the experience of the movement of time is often conceptualized through the spatial metaphors of the line or the circle, often thought to be antithetical. As a counterpart to Cullmann's "upward sloping line," it is equally possible to conceive of time as a "downward sloping line," that is, as headed in a negative degenerative direction that includes cultural and moral decline. This is essentially the conception of time reflected in Jewish apocalyptic literature, but is also the view of the seventh-century B.C.E. Greek poet Hesiod. In *Works and Days* (109–201), he describes five successive races of humans, each representing a further decline in culture and morality. A similar decline is implicit in Daniel's vision of four sequential empires represented by four beasts, each worse than the last (Dan 7:1–8). There are two features implicit in the linear time model (whether straight, upward, or downward sloping): (1) Primacy is placed on the past or on what is perceived as the first in a series of events, that is, past events are implicitly understood as the causes of present and future events. (2) The linear sequence consisting of three isolable dimensions of time (past, present, future) implies that each temporal category is consistent with the other.

There are, of course, other possible metaphors. The spiral, for example, suggests that there are cyclical movements of events that are never identically repeated, combining the progressive character of the linear metaphor with the repetitive character of the cyclical metaphor, and of course the spiral can go up or down. The spiral is a metaphor appropriate for the repeated historical cycles of apostasy-punishment-repentance-deliverance narrated in the book of Judges (for no cycle is exactly repeated in the narrative), or the sin-exile-return cycle in prophetic passages in the *Testaments of the Twelve Patriarchs*, or the lengthy eschatological vision that understood human history as a series of six dark rain showers, or times of falsehood, and six bright rain showers, or times of truth (*2 Bar.* 53:1–74:4). The dark showers that follow the bright showers represent the future, consisting of a period of warfare and chaos culminating in the assembly of hostile nations that will be judged by the Messiah and punished or rewarded depending on how they have treated Israel (71:1–72:6). The final bright showers represent the period following the Messiah's complete victory over all opposition in the world, when he sits down in peace forever on the throne of his kingdom, introducing an apparently permanent idyllic period (73:1–74:4).

The "zigzag" (proposed by Steensgaard) can be used to convey the perception of sudden changes in history, reflecting (for example) the notion that while the God of Israel intervenes to judge and to save, people are free to obey or disobey (since history is not predetermined), thus changing the course of history continually, giving it a "zigzag" character, though this can also be conveyed through the spiral. One could perhaps even conceptualize time under the metaphor of a line of dashes, that is, by a series of events separated from each other by the fact that each is perceived as having a beginning and an end. However, these metaphors must be recognized for what they are: crude ways of understanding time, a dimension of reality that can be conceptualized in a great number of ways.

Summary

Each in their own way, the proposals of the biblical theologians and of Bruce Malina represent general conceptions imposed on, rather than elicited from, the biblical text, and to that extent they are unsatisfactory. Time is a phenomenon that can be conceptualized in a multiplicity of ways, and various social and psychological constructions of time can exist side-by-side without any perception of conflict or contradiction. When I make an appointment with my physician for 3:15 P.M., I understand that to mean strict clock time, and I will probably arrive at least ten minutes early. After sitting in the waiting room for thirty to sixty minutes, I will eventually be ushered into an inner cubicle to wait another eternity (perhaps fifteen to twenty minutes) for the appearance of the physician. This time lag, which makes everyone who experiences it unhappy, occurs for the simple reason that the physician is not operating according to time on his watch, but rather must complete a series of tasks defined by the specific complaints of a series of patients. Between this abstract time of my world and the experiential time of the physician's world, the nurse-receptionist, pretending that the arrival of the physician is imminent, is the one who mediates between two very different conceptions of time.

RESTORATION IN THE APOCALYPSE OF JOHN

The four divine titles reviewed above cohere particularly well with the notion of restoration that is characteristic of Jewish apocalyptic literature in general and the Apocalypse of John in particular. Restoration is a concept that has an essentially temporal character and that can be imagined as a cycle that occurs just once, returning to the place where it began.

Throughout the ancient world, both east and west, the imagined past was commonly considered the primary basis for assessing the legitimacy of the present and envisioning the shape of the future. There is a continuing debate about the legitimacy of the second of two rival concepts of history in the Greek world: While the notion of history as deterioration from an original Golden Age is widely accepted as representing the ancient Greek view, the notion of history as progress from primitive beginnings is often considered an anachronistic view attributed to the Greeks. Ancient thinkers such as Democritus, Aristotle, and Protagoras are sometimes thought to have conceived of history as holding out the possibility of the infinite progress of human culture (the second notion), but the problem with that assessment lies in the probability that they understood progress as the attainment of perfection within a closed or limited ideal. At any rate, viewing the ideal past as paradigmatic for the present as well as the future was particularly characteristic of apocalyptic eschatology, which was preoccupied with the problem of evil. Salvation, the ultimate solution to the negative impact of evil on individuals and society, was not thought to occur through divine intervention in history but rather through the elimination of history by the destruction of the old world order and its replacement by a new order. The ultimate solution of the human predicament was projected into the eschatological future, where both the punishment and salvation of responsible moral agents would be meted out by God. Salvation, the positive aspect of the solution, was the divinely arranged restoration of individuals within their social matrices to the ideal state they had enjoyed at the beginning. The conception that the End should recapitulate the perfect and paradigmatic Beginning forms the basic horizon of the apocalyptic view of history, for the imperfections of the present constitute a low point between the perfections of the distant past and the perfections of the imminent future.

Apocalyptic eschatology centers on the expectation of God's imminent intervention into human history to save his people and punish their enemies by destroying the existing cosmic order and by restoring or recreating the cosmos to its original pristine perfection. It is the world view characteristic of apocalypses, a literary form that flourished between 250 B.C.E. and 150 C.E., when Palestine was successively dominated by the Greeks (both the Ptolemies and the Seleucids) and then the Romans.

The restoration theme in apocalyptic literature has both nationalistic and universalistic aspects, both of which are represented in the Apocalypse of John. Nationalistic restoration includes such elements as the restoration of sovereignty over the land of Palestine, the restoration kingship (i.e., the reestablishment of theocratic monarchy in the ideal form of the Davidic messiahship), the regathering of the twelve tribes of Israel, and the final restoration of the city of Jerusalem and the temple. Universalistic restoration, on the other hand, lacks an ethnic focus, but rather envisions the restoration of creation, the restoration of Edenic conditions, and the restoration of human society generally.

While various constituent themes of national restoration are found in the Apocalypse of John, the constituent themes of universal or cosmic restoration are of direct and particular relevance for understanding the four titles of God or Christ. Particularly significant is the speech of God in the Apocalypse (Rev 21:5–8), at the center of which we find the self-predications "I am the Alpha and the Omega, the Beginning and the End" (v. 6). The immediate context indicates that these titles must be understood within the framework of cosmic restoration. Revelation 21:5–8 is arguably the most important single passage in the Apocalypse, for here the central message of the book is articulated by God himself, including emphases on his sovereignty and power, the trustworthiness of the revelation transmitted by John, and the salvation or judgment awaiting the conquerors and the enemies of God respectively. The summative character of the passage is indicated by the fact that it is a pastiche of words and phrases drawn from elsewhere in the book. It is carefully composed of seven sayings:

(1) Then the One sitting on the throne said, "Behold I am making everything new" (v. 5a).
(2) He also said, "Write, for this message is trustworthy and true" (v. 5b).
(3) He also said to me, "It is finished" (v. 6a).
(4) "I am the Alpha and the Omega, the Beginning and the End" (v. 6b).
(5) "I will freely give some water to the one who is thirsty from the well of living water" (v. 6c).
(6) "Those who conquer will inherit these things, for I will be their God and they will be my children" (v. 7).
(7) "But as for the cowards and the unbelievers and the abominable and murderers and the immoral and sorcerers and idolaters and all who lie, they will experience the lake that burns with fire and sulphur, which is the second death" (v. 8).

Here the phrase "I am making everything new" emphasizes God's role in the recreation or renewal of a fallen cosmos, while "It is finished" refers not to the end of the first heaven and the first earth but rather to the completion of God's planned restoration of the world to its original perfection. Despite the relative infrequency of references to God as creator in the Apocalypse (4:11; 10:6; 14:7), this passage alludes to Isa 43:19 ("Behold I am doing a new thing") but reinterprets it to emphasize God's role as renewer or recreator. Revelation 21:5–8 follows the brief narrative mention of the appearance of the new heaven and the new earth, following the apparent destruction of the first heaven and the first earth, and the descent of the holy city Jerusalem (21:1–3).

In the Apocalypse of John, the focus of the new or renewed creation is the New Jerusalem (21:1–22:9), which represents a combination of the eschatological themes of national restoration (the restoration of Jerusalem and of the twelve tribes) with the two focal themes of universal restoration (renewal of creation and the restoration of paradise). In Rev 21:12, the New Jerusalem is described as having a wall with twelve gates, each inscribed with the names of "the twelve tribes of the sons of Israel." This implies that the New Jerusalem is not simply a city but rather the center for a reinhabited land. The expectation of the eschatological restoration of Jerusalem has antecedents in the eschatological Jerusalem of Ezekiel, which has twelve gates, three on each side, named after the twelve tribes of Israel (Ezek 48:30–35), as well as in the reconstructed apocalypse found in many fragmentary copies at Qumran entitled "Description of the New Jerusalem" (inspired by Ezekiel), which also depicts the eschatological Jerusalem as having twelve gates named after the twelve tribes of Israel (4Q554 frag. 1, I.9–II.11). Similarly in the Temple Scroll, the twelve gates of the eschatological Jerusalem are named after the twelve tribes of Israel (11QTemple 39.12–13; 40.11–14), anticipating the final realization of one of the central concerns of Jewish eschatology, the restoration of all Israel, which is repeatedly mentioned in postexilic Old Testament texts and early Jewish literature. However, in none of these texts is the eschatological restoration of Jerusalem, carefully linked to the restoration of the people, made part of the cosmic restoration as it is in the Apocalypse of John.

In the Apocalypse of John, the restoration of Jerusalem is also linked to the restoration of paradise. In Rev 2:7 (cf. 22:14), this is suggested in the promise that the exalted Christ will grant the conqueror the privilege of eating of the tree of life in the paradise of God. Revelation 22:2 uses Edenic imagery (refracted through Ezek 31:8–9) to describe the New Jerusalem, for the Apocalyptist describes how, on either side of the river of living water flowing through the city, there are trees of life, each with twelve kinds of fruit, each producing fruit monthly.

CONCLUDING OBSERVATIONS

In the hermeneutically significant speech of God in Rev 21:5–8, placed in the narrative context of the restoration of creation through replacement and restoration of paradise through the renewed access to the tree of life in the New Jerusalem, the divine titles "the Alpha and the Omega" and "the Beginning and the End" (21:6) appear to be linear conceptions for understanding God's relationship to his creation. Yet since the line proceeds from the original creation to a new creation and from a paradise lost to a paradise regained, the "line" is essentially a "circle" which ends up where it began.

If we regard Rev 21:5–8 as a passage of central significance in the theology of the Apocalypse, the title "the Alpha and the Omega" there is paired elsewhere with "the One who is and who was and who is to come," used of God in 1:8, and later used as a self-predication of Christ in 22:13, where it occurs in conjunction with "the First and the Last" and "the Beginning and the End" (the latter also applied to God in 21:6).

The exclusive use of the title "the One who is and who was and who is to come" to God in the Apocalypse perhaps needs some qualification. In biblical tradition, Yahweh is "the coming One," a tradition based in part on the Sinai tradition. God "comes" to *judge* (Pss 95:13; 97:9; Isa 30:27; 66:15–16; Jer 21:13; Mic 1:3; Mal 3:1–2) as well as to *save* (Isa 35:4; 40:10–11; 59:20; Ezek 43:1-5; Ps 49:2; Zech 2:10; 14:5). This opens the possibility, then, that the tripartite name serves as a theological motto for the Apocalypse of John, signifying that the eternal God is about to visit the world to bring both judgment and salvation.

Yet in the Apocalypse of John, though God is identified as "the One who is coming," there is not a single explicit reference to God as "coming." It is rather his wrath that "comes" (11:18). But as we have seen, the omission of the third predicate, "the One who is to come," in Rev 11:17–18 and 16:5 from the normally tripartite formula suggests that, at least from a narrative perspective, God has in fact "come" in judgment in the plagues of the seven trumpets and in the plague unleashed by the third bowl angel. However, these "comings" cannot be identified with the final and climactic coming of God to judge the world. Two different verbs meaning "to come" (*erchomai* and *hēkō*) are used to refer to the impending coming of Christ (1:7; 2:5, 16, 25; 3:3 [twice], 11; 16:15; 22:7, 12, 20). However, four of these texts cannot refer to the Parousia but rather must refer to a "coming" in judgment, which must be understood as preliminary to the final and climactic Parousia of Christ (2:5, 16; 3:3 [twice]). The difference is that God "comes" to judge the wicked with preliminary plagues, while Christ "comes" to judge the Christian community. In these texts, the author of the Apocalypse uses language traditionally applied to God as a basis for exploring the function and significance of Christ.

SELECT BIBLIOGRAPHY

Aune, David E. 1987. "The Apocalypse of John and Graeco-Roman Revelatory Magic." *New Testament Studies* 33:481–501.

———. 1999. "Qumran and the Book of Revelation." Pages 622–48 in vol. 2 of *The Dead Sea Scrolls after Fifty Years: A Comprehensive Assessment*. Edited by P. W. Flint and J. C. VanderKam. 2 vols. Leiden: E. J. Brill.

Barr, James. 1961. *The Semantics of Biblical Language*. Oxford: Clarendon.

———. 1962. *Biblical Words for Time*. London: SCM.

Boman, Thorlief. 1960. *Hebrew Thought Compared with Greek*. Philadelphia: Westminster.

Cullmann, Oscar. 1964. *Christ and Time: The Primitive Christian Conception of Time and History*. Translated by Floyd Filson. Rev. ed. Philadelphia: Westminster.

Dodds, E. R. 1973. "The Ancient Conception of Progress." Pages 1–25 in *The Ancient Concept of Progress*. Oxford: Clarendon.

Gurvitch, Georges. 1964. *The Spectrum of Social Time*. Dordrecht: D. Reidel.

Lloyd, G. E. R. 1976. "Views on Time in Greek Thought." Pages 117–48 in *Cultures and Time*. Edited by Louis Gardet. Paris: Unesco.

Malina, Bruce J. 1989. "Christ and Time: Swiss or Mediterranean?" *Catholic Biblical Quarterly* 51:1–31.

———. 1995. *On the Genre and Message of Revelation: Star Visions and Sky Journeys*. Peabody, Mass.: Hendrickson.

Marsh, John. 1952. *The Fullness of Time*. New York: Harper & Brothers.

McNamara, Martin. 1966. *The New Testament and the Palestinian Targum to the Pentateuch*. Rome: Pontifical Biblical Institute.

Momigliano, Arnaldo. 1969. "Time in Ancient Historiography." Pages 13–41 in *Quarto Contributo alla storia degli studi classici e del monto antico*. Storia e Letteratura 115. Rome: Edizioni di storia e letteratura.

Stanford, W. B. 1964. "The Significance of the Alpha and Omega in Revelation 1.8." *Hermanthena* 98:43–44.

Steensgaard, Peter. 1993. "Time in Judaism." Pages 63–108 in *Religion and Time*. Edited by Anindita Niyogi Balsley and Jitendranath N. Mohanty. Leiden: E. J. Brill.

15

Preaching and Ministry
in the Service of the God of the Bible

Elizabeth Achtemeier

It is a signal pleasure to contribute to this volume honoring the scholarly work and service to the church of my beloved husband. For almost fifty years, he has preached, taught, and written out of the biblical, apostolic faith of the Christian church. This article is my attempt to stand also in that faith and to set forth what it implies for the preaching and ministry of the ordinary preacher in the twenty-first century.

THE ONE GOD OF THE BIBLE

The God of the New Testament—the God and Father of our Lord Jesus Christ—is the God of Abraham, Isaac, and Jacob, of prophets and psalmists, of wisdom writers and historians, in short, the God of the Old Testament. One deplores the fact that it is still necessary to make such a statement. Yet much of recent biblical scholarship and church practice ignores the commonality of the two testaments' witness to God. We hear frequently these days of B.C.E. and C.E. as if the church's witness does not encompass the testimony of the Old Testament in its understandings. Similarly, there seems to be great reluctance to speak of an Old Testament and a New, the thirty-nine books of the former being called instead just "the Hebrew Scriptures." To be sure, one wants to acknowledge that the Old Testament is Israel's book, but by the grace of God, the Old Testament—the book of the old covenant—is also the church's book through Jesus Christ, whose new covenant (or testament) was promised already by Jeremiah (see Jer 31:31–34). To ignore the integral relationship of the two testaments is a denial of the centuries-long fact that the church has a canon. Such ignorance cuts off the first two-thirds of the sacred history from the New Testament's final third, and above all, it denies to the church the complete witness to God's revelation of himself in the life of his people.

Throughout the New Testament, the integral relation of old and new covenants is manifested. Matthew repeatedly speaks of the fulfillment of Old Testament prophecy in the life of our Lord, and the first sentence of that gospel identifies Jesus as "the son of David, the son of Abraham." When Peter preaches, in the accounts in Acts, he has to quote the Psalms. The list of the heroes of faith in Hebrews begins with Abel and Enoch and Abraham. Paul cannot lay out the message of salvation in Christ apart from God's plan for the Jews. As for our Lord himself, his roles and titles all serve as fulfillments of the Old Testament: He is the Messiah, the Suffering Servant, the prophet like Moses, the royal Son of God, the priest after the order of Melchizedek, the Good Shepherd, the word of the Old Testament incarnated.

Repeatedly, theological motifs sounded first in the Old Testament echo and illumine the New. We cannot fully understand Jesus' stilling of the storm without its precedent in God's conquering of the chaotic *tehom* in Genesis 1, and in the prophetic writings and psalms. Equally the motifs of darkness and light, so prominent in the gospel and epistles of John, find their beginning in the first book of the Old Covenant. The identification of the church as the kingdom of priests and a holy nation rests on Exodus 19, without which Paul's term for the church as "the Israel of God" (Gal 6:16) makes no sense. Our adoption as children of God, our redemption, our justification, our worship as our "work" for God, our servanthood, and our pilgrimage toward a place of rest all find their explanation in Israel—as do covenant and kingdom of God, the Day of the Lord, and much of eschatology. The lists could be elaborated almost endlessly.

All of this is by way of saying that Old Testament and New belong together, as our one canon or "measure," and the modern attempts of both scholars and clergy to separate the two deprive the church of the fullness of God's revelation of himself. Jesus Christ is not some mysterious revelatory figure suddenly dropped from the blue. He is the fulfillment and reinterpreting revelation of the 1700 years of revelation given before through Israel's history with God, and the church cannot know who Christ is and therefore who God is, nor can it know who it is, unless it keeps the testaments inseparably joined. The Old Testament itself is an unfinished book unless it be continued in the New, and the New Testament is an opaque book unless it be seen to grow from the Old. The church is the wild branches grown from the root of Israel (Rom 11:13–24); the same is true of the church's scriptures in the New Testament.

Perhaps one of the reasons this volume of essays can be titled *The Forgotten God* is because of the widespread ignorance among both clergy and laity, not only of much of the New Testament but also principally of the Old. That ignorance is the rot that eats away at the foundations of the church in our day, and until the rot is excised and replaced with firmer biblical foundations, the institutional church will continue to totter and, perhaps in the future, even fall. What follows in this particular essay, therefore, is my attempt to reconstruct some of the foundation, in order that we may know the God of the Scriptures through his word, both preached and written.

GOD KNOWN THROUGH A NARRATIVE

Perhaps the most important fact about the Bible for preachers is that the living God makes himself known through a historical narrative. That is not to say that everything written in the Scriptures is "pure history," if one can even speak of such a thing. Every biblical narrative is interpreted narrative, given not as a coldly factual account but as a confession of faith. But all of the Bible's writings, including the psalms and prophets, the wisdom writings and epistles and apocalypses, have as their context an ongoing story that has a beginning in God and that moves toward God's completion of it.

The fact that God chooses to reveal himself through an ongoing narrative is the mirror of his nature. The Lord is an active God, working always toward his future kingdom, in what I would like to call a *Heilswirkung*, a working-out of salvation. Preachers and lay people these days have fallen into the habit of discussing God as if he were some sort of a passive object out there (cf. Eve's conversation with the serpent in Genesis 3). The Lord is talked about, evaluated, even judged, and urged upon us as an object of belief, to be found and trusted and accepted; thus, we are the subjects, discussing an object, God. But we have turned upside down the understanding of Scripture. God is the subject in the Scriptures' narrative, acting always toward and for us creatures, who are the objects of his concern, his judgment and love, his mercy and grace. And that action is all written out for us in the ongoing *Heilswirkung* that makes up the content of the Bible.

The narrative of God's actions has its clearly delineated focal points in the Old Testament. God creates a world that is very good, but when it is corrupted by human sin, he sets out through his people Israel to make it very good again. There follow Israel's slavery, the exodus, the wilderness wandering, the gift of the promised land, the Davidic kingship, the prophets, the exiles, and the promises of future salvation in a new age, with the psalmists, wisdom writers, and seers recording their responses to it all.

With the birth of Jesus at Bethlehem, the whole word of God to Israel is gathered up and incarnated, and the announcement is made that the new age of the kingdom of God, promised in the Old Testament, has broken into human history in the person of our Lord. In Jesus' ministry in Galilee and

Judea, the powers of God's new age work their teaching and healing and preaching. At his death, the sin and corruption of the old age struggle for supremacy and lose. And on Easter morn, death itself and the power of sin are broken and vanquished by God in Christ, the sole victor. With the gift of the Spirit of God in Christ to the disciples at Pentecost after the Lord's ascension, the good news of God's new age of victory is carried forth, to Judea and Samaria and the ends of the earth. A man named Saul is transformed by the risen Christ to be Paul the apostle and to establish or guide churches in Galatia and Asia Minor and Macedonia. Letters are sent by sea and on Roman roads. Oral traditions are gathered into gospels. And little churches, following the traditions of Paul or John, of Hebrews or James or Matthew, gather as points of light in the midst of the darkness of a pagan world. Persecution by the state and by the Jews does not silence their gospel. And John of Patmos looks forward to the full coming of the kingdom, when there is a new heaven and a new earth, and all the kingdoms of this world have become the kingdom of our Lord and of his Christ.

The Bible's narrative is a story—an ongoing history of God's working—coursing through two thousand years, and every text in the Scriptures has as its context that ongoing *Heilswirkung*. It seems perverse, therefore, for any preacher to turn the story into a set of propositions, to which assent is then sought if the listener wants to be called a Christian. Propositional preaching paralyzes an action or characteristic of God, transforms it into a dogma, and makes it then an object to be believed on the preacher's advice. Woe, then, to the poor parishioner who will not accept the advice! But what has really happened is that the preacher has usurped the action of God toward the congregation and has replaced it with a dead truth to be accepted. Or barring that, the preacher transforms the story into a psychological or sociological "truth" to be used in the analysis of society's ways.

The narrative that comes to us through the Scriptures is neither dead dogma nor psychological or sociological truth, however. It is action-bearing word of God. When God speaks his word and works his works through the Bible's witness, he does not just convey new information or tell of an interesting event. He continues to work in the life of the gathered congregation. The word of God in the Bible is an active, effective force, which brings about a new situation. For example, in Genesis 1, God says, "Let there be light," and light is created. Or in Isaiah 55, the word of God does not return to him void, but accomplishes that which God purposes. The word works, bringing about that of which it speaks. And the amazing thing about the Bible is that the action of God's Word is not limited to the biblical world. As the great Lutheran preacher Paul Scherer remarked one time, "God didn't stop acting when his book went to press." The word of God, spoken through the Scriptures, continues to act in the lives of all who will hear it, transforming them and bringing about in their persons and their society a new situation. The word of the past becomes contemporary in our present, continuing to work out God's purpose of salvation in our lives and world, until finally that kingdom of God will be realized fully in God's plan for history and nature.

Every congregation and every person is a little participant in that ongoing *Heilswirkung*. We all stand in God's stream of salvation history, which moves from its beginning in God's alpha toward his omega. We inherit in that stream all the traditions of faith that have gone before us, and we help shape all the way of the faithful who will come after. We can deny the stream. We can try to dam up its flow. We can fight its course and try to divert it into our own corrupted puddles. Or we can move with God's onflowing work until the earth is as full of the knowledge of him as the waters cover the sea.

Surely every preacher and pastor needs to convey to his or her people, through pulpit and ministry, their participation in the ongoing flow of God's work toward his kingdom's goal, their place in the communion of saints and their inheritance of all the traditions of that blest communion that has gone before them, their importance in the continuing cosmic work being done by the Lord, and their promised place in the kingdom that is surely coming. Then perhaps parishioners will find some meaning in their lives, which are so full of the aimlessness and turbulent trouble or quiet desperation of our society.

PREACHING AS SACRAMENTAL

Because the God and Father of our Lord Jesus Christ is the active God, working always toward his goal of the kingdom, preaching has as its purpose not only the instillment of a sense of God's ongoing history in his people's lives but primarily a transformation of their lives. Preaching is sacramental. That is, it is God's work toward us. In the usages of the church, sacrifices are the praise and offering, the thanksgiving and service that we render to God. But sacraments are the life-giving actions that God does toward us. And preaching has as its purpose the conveyance of that action by the Lord.

It has been noted far too often that most of the preaching that takes place in the United States leaves people pretty much as they are. In the worst cases, the pulpit simply entertains a congregation or gives them an emotional high. Unfortunately, many of the newly popular contemporary "praise" services serve that purpose: The popular music, the clapping, the sentimental prayers, the exuberant expressions of praise, draw the people into crowd excitement that raises spirits but changes personalities not at all. More prevalent still, therapeutic preaching serves to assure the congregation that they are loved and accepted as they are and are really fine people who perhaps need just a little psychological adjustment to be happy. Moralizing preaching, so widespread in the land, simply conveys little stories with moral points about how to get along in life, much like a *Reader's Digest* article or an Aesop fable. In all such pulpi-teering, a congregation remains unchanged, and the active word of God is unheard from the biblical text.

If the word of God is active, effective force, however, bringing about a new situation—if it is truly, as Jeremiah says (23:29), like a hammer that breaks rocks in pieces or like a fire burning in one's bones—then the purpose of a ser-mon is so to convey that work that it is given freedom to act and to change its hearers. The sermon becomes the medium of God's action on his people, and they are left, not as they wish, but as God purposes.

That implies of course that the concentration of the sermon is on what God is doing in and through any selected biblical text. The old saying, "Preach about twenty minutes and preach about God" is not outdated. If we want to see lives changed, we have to preach about God, for the Lord alone is able to make us new creatures in Jesus Christ. It is very easy to tell what is wrong about our lives and in our world. A twelve-year-old can do that, and any one of us can read the morning headlines. But it takes a preacher to tell what God is doing about it—a genuine preacher, an evangelist of the good news of Jesus Christ.

God's action through the biblical word preached in the sermon may be quite varied on any Sunday morning. The Lord may simply deepen the faith of some saint in the congregation—and every congregation has such a person or per-sons. He may increase our love for one another so that we are bound more truly into a community, or send us forth into greater service to our society. The Lord may call our lifestyle into serious question and bring the terrifying weight of his judgment upon us. He may comfort us in some distress. He may erase some guilt or forgive some sin, or flood our hearts with his Spirit. The Lord may even overwhelm a parishioner with an awesome sense of his glory and majesty so that there is the momentary feeling of standing with one foot in heaven. Or God may tenderly assure us that underneath always are his ever-lasting arms. And that work of God through his word calls forth all our responses in his worship—our repentance, our confession of faith, our praise and petitions and thanksgivings, and above all our surrender and our commit-ment of our lives to him alone. Whatever God chooses to do with his people through the words of his preacher, those people do not remain the same per-sons they were when they entered the church. God's word, faithfully preached, transforms human lives and congregations when God so wills by his Spirit. And God uses that transformation in his ongoing plan of salvation.

A NEW WORLDVIEW

Perhaps the most sweeping transformation that is wrought by God's Spirit in a congregation through the preaching of the active, biblical word, however, is the change in the congregation's total worldview, and until that change takes place, genuine Christian discipleship is almost impossible.

We live in an almost totally secular society—that is, we live in a society in which the God to which the Bible witnesses is no longer considered necessary or seen to have a hand, and there is no way in which the modern United States can be considered to be a Christian nation or, in Abraham Lincoln's words, "an almost chosen nation." The anchor ropes that formerly held us to the biblical worldview have been severed, and our society is adrift on a sea of multiple deities, multiple opinions, multiple worldviews.

It was not always thus, of course. Society used to furnish the context for learning Christian faith. Every schoolchild read in McGuffy's readers that he or she was created by God. Biblical parlance was common in daily converse. Lawyers who could quote the Bible in court were viewed with favor. School programs regularly celebrated Christmas. Most public gatherings opened with prayer. Churches were looked to for ethical guidance. An agreed-upon set of values informed home and marriage and social relations. And underneath it all lay a common story, not only of nationhood but also of faith, which bound much of the populace together as a community.

None of that is now the case. As theologian Douglas John Hall has written, "Automatic Christianity is finished," and Christian faith is no longer heard and learned, either from society or, very often, family. Indeed, the ignorance of the Scriptures and of basic Christian doctrine in most families is appalling: Add to that the breakdown of all authority and ethics in the 1960s, the systematic elimination from the public square and schools of all mention of Christianity, the concerted attacks on Christian influence by many organizations, including sometimes the government, and the increasing incursion of other faiths into our society, and the church remains alone as a small, noninfluential, divided, and sometimes warring entity that more or less preserves the biblical narrative. Yet the Bible's narrative and the worldview that arises out of it are indispensable for Christian living, and it is those that every preacher is called to proclaim.

Who is the God who confronts us through the biblical word? He is, in the confession of both Israel and our Lord, "one" (Deut 6:4; Mark 12:29). So he cannot be identified with the multiple *numina* that inhabit nature or with the deities of other religions. He cannot be found in any place at any time or in any object. Indeed, he insists that he be worshiped only where he has put his name—in the temple in Jerusalem in the Old Testament, in his only begotten Son, who replaces the temple (John 2:19–21), in the New. Because his name is "the Holy One," he is other than anything or anyone in creation, and it is forbidden to worship him in "anything that is in heaven above, or that is in the earth beneath, or that is in the water under the earth."

To a society that will worship almost anything these days or that will dabble in almost any form of "spirituality," such exclusive holiness and oneness comes across as limiting and offensive. Many modern Americans seek a god that they define, a deity accessible to their needs and experience, when they want to be "religious." It is unsettling to modern autonomous views that God is the one who decides who he is and when and where he will reveal himself, because that takes control out of human hands and reserves it for the lordship of God.

That the triune God of the Bible is Lord, however—King, majestic Sovereign—is a basic statement of the Bible's witness. "Jesus is Lord" is the earliest confession of the church in the letters of Paul (Rom 10:9; 1 Cor 12:3; Phil 2:11). God created all that is through his incarnate Word, Jesus Christ. He owns the totality of existence as its Maker. And he rules over it all, as the Lord of all history and nature, asking from his total creation conformity to his will and intention for it.

That is a direct assault on our society's views of persons, however. The common view of most is that we are autonomous selves, beholden to no one other than our own persons, self-motivated, self-directed, self-fulfilling, free to assert our own will and to satisfy our own desires as we see fit. That we owe our very breath of life to the faithful sustenance of God is ignored. That we are made in his image and therefore never free of that relationship is doubted. And that we are responsible to the Lord for living our lives as he intends is shoved aside for the belief that we can define our own right and wrong.

In fact, in present "postmodern" viewpoints, there is no absolute standard of right and wrong, or, for that matter, of truth and falsehood. Everything is culturally conditioned or relative to the individual. One person's "truth" or "right" is just as good as another's. No absolute standards exist and all persons decree their own. So there is agreement on conduct or fact only if it is enforced by the most powerful. No common founding story or set of values holds communities of family and society together.

As for world society, in the views of many, its course is largely determined by the power plays of government and politicians, by military might or by the economic pressures of multinational corporations. Police coercion enforces peace in a world where there is no agreed-upon good. And humanity becomes the terrified observer of who has won the struggle for power. To hear that God rules over all of that turmoil is therefore incredible to many, just as is the proclamation that he is directing it all toward his kingdom goal.

Similar secular views mark the common understandings of nature. While our scientists have not yet quite figured out what happened at the "big bang," many persons are quite certain that the natural world runs automatically. Natural laws direct the course of nature's evolution and yearly cycle, and the only ones who can solve all nature's mysteries are our experts, although our hopes in their salvation of us have faded a little lately. But God does not interfere in nature's laws—miracles and resurrection are fables. To hear from the Scriptures that God not only created the world but also sustains all its processes, using them in his purpose, is therefore quite absurd to the thinking of many twenty-first century souls, just as is the biblical view that nature too is in need of redemption.

The God of the Bible is nevertheless Redeemer, because nature is fallen, as well as we, and we all need to be rescued (Rom 8:19–23). The term "redeemer" has always to do with a buying back from slavery. So the natural world, writes Paul, is in bondage to decay and corruption and "waits with eager longing" (Rom 8:19) for God's final salvation—his restoration of its goodness that he created in the beginning. In the same manner, we human beings are enslaved to sin and death, turned in upon ourselves, dying subversives of God's kingly rule in every area of human life, and except we be delivered into the "glorious liberty of the children of God" (Rom 8:21) by the cross and resurrection, our end is finally anarchy and the extinction of death.

In a society and among individuals, however, who feel no responsibility toward God and very little toward neighbor, and who therefore have no thought of the reality of sin, the message that we are enslaved and in need of deliverance comes across as nonsense. As has become faddish among some radical feminists, the cross is deemed as nothing more than brutish child abuse by a patriarchal tyrant-God, and the belief in the resurrection is dismissed as mythical speculation, with the thought that the final end of human beings is to be absorbed back into some great soul of nature.

The God of the Bible is a triune God, encompassing relationships within himself among the three Persons of the Father, Son, and Holy Spirit. And all through the biblical story, his will is to make a community that embodies in itself his love and justice, his peace and righteousness. With Abraham, he sets out to make that new people, into whose community he hopes to draw all the nations of the earth. Despite Israel's failure ever to be a holy people, the Lord nevertheless finds in their descendant, Jesus Christ, the cornerstone of that universal people, bound together by a common redemption and given his Spirit, by whose power every member of that new covenant community may live in faithfulness, and certain hope of eternal life, and love for God and neighbor. The Lord dwells in the midst of that community, sometimes judging it and bringing upon it distress, but always enclosing it in a merciful grace beyond all failure. The Lord's relation with that community called the church is so personal, so intimate, so forgiving, so ever-wakeful and guiding, that he is called its Father, Husband, Comforter, and Protector. And God's will is that the community reach out until it draws all peoples into its fellowship.

To hear that God's purpose, according to the Scriptures, is to make a new faithful and righteous community, however, goes against the rampant individualism of our time. Persons who believe that they are rulers unto themselves, with responsibility only for their own welfare, status, and material success, have neither time nor patience for the life and growth of a community of God. And when they hear that community transcends all boundaries of nationality, race, gender, situation, and even death, and that we are all bound together in "one great fellowship of love throughout the whole wide earth" and even heaven, they dismiss the idea as an impossible dream and return to their busy rounds.

In other words, a Christian preacher who is proclaiming the word of God from the Bible is uttering a message that carries a worldview very different from that held by most in our society. The message comes across as intrusive of the worldview of this age—as intrusive as was God's call to Abraham or Amos's message at the king's sanctuary in Bethel or Jesus' entrance into Jerusalem. The message contradicts all of the presuppositions of a postmodern society and introduces it to a God-haunted and God-ruled world unknown to most modern folk, and it reveals the preacher to be maintaining thoughts that many people find ridiculous.

Moreover, the Christian preacher is addressing such views to an audience that finds in itself very little reason to change. On the whole, most congregations are comfortable as they are, and they lack any motivation whatsoever to alter their way of living. Life is reasonably satisfactory, and despite occasional upheavals and sufferings, the god of the public imagination can always be called upon to bail them out of difficulty or to sustain them through some trial. What many want from the pulpit, therefore, is the assurance that they are okay, that God is on their side, and that finally, everything will turn out all right.

This is not to say that there is not a great deal of pain out there in any congregation. Just underneath the surface of the modern person's autonomous will to self-control and self-fulfillment there are an aimlessness and lack of any lasting purpose, and the biblical proclamation of an everlasting divine plan that includes every human life and that moves on toward a universal goal can instill meaning in lives found otherwise meaningless. Haunting every soul who believes that he or she is responsible to self alone and who has experienced the corruption of every form of community in marriage and family and among friends and social groupings, there are to be found a deep sense of loneliness and a longing to belong to something or someone. And the Christian necessity of a community called the church for the expression and maintenance of faith can enclose the lonely in a welcoming fellowship which at the same time proclaims that every individual belongs to a God of loving and personal relationship. Common to every comfortable and self-supporting individual in our prosperous society is nevertheless the experience of suffering—mental or physical or spiritual—and finally every person faces the blank, dark extinction of death. The biblical message of a God of undergirding, everlasting arms can therefore give comfort where none else is possible, and the proclamation of the victory of the resurrection can ease tears beside a grave and give an inextinguishable hope of life. Thus, the Christian preacher has some fertile ground in which to plant the seed of the gospel, even in our secular society. Unfortunately, however, many pulpits these days are sites of quick fixes, of momentary assurances, of therapeutic sentiments, of surface treatments of the biblical message, designed to alleviate suffering during at least the hour of worship so that the preacher is greeted warmly at the church door after the service. What is needed instead is that deep exploration into the biblical word that can change whole worldviews and that can be the medium of God's work of transformation in the lives of a congregation.

ENGAGING THE BIBLICAL TEXT

How can a preacher so enter into a biblical text that it shapes the entire sermon into a vehicle God may use in his saving work? As everyone knows, there are multiple exegetical and homiletical helps on the market these days to aid the faithful preacher. Some of them are good, some are very bad—canned sermons and sermon outlines and illustrations numbering among the worst, because they replace the preacher's own wrestling with the text. But from the many good periodicals and books and commentaries available, a preacher may learn a lot. He or she may be aided in setting a text in its historical, literary, sociological, and geographical context. The preacher may learn of the biblical customs and laws mentioned in the text or become familiar with its characters. She or he may be shown the meaning of unfamiliar terms or even the wider theological tendencies of the biblical author. Perhaps two of the most helpful reference books on the market are HarperCollins' *Bible Dictionary* and one-volume *Bible Commentary*. Both furnish quick references to a lot of background material. Unfortunately, there are preachers who ignore even that, seizing a text in order to spin off on their own spiritual, allegorical, or moralizing three points that then bear little relation to the message of the text at hand. Such preachers could at least preach the words of a good commentary, the *Interpretation* series being among the best. But, of course, that too is not the word of

God and is no substitute for the Scriptures themselves. So how does a preacher engage the biblical text?

The truth is that the text of the Bible speaks its own message, by the work of the Holy Spirit, if it is allowed to do so, and the first step in hearing that message is the abandonment of one's own thoughts and presuppositions about the text. I suppose every faithful biblical preacher has had the experience of beginning to formulate an exposition of some biblical passage and then finding that the text itself is leading the thought of a sermon in an entirely different direction than that initially intended. The message of the text pushes itself to the fore and literally runs away with the course of thought. And the expositor finds that it is not he or she who is speaking and writing, but the Word of God himself. So the beginning step in biblical preaching is the abandonment of one's own views. As Karl Barth has written in a passage I have often quoted:

> The gospel is not in our thoughts or hearts; it is in Scripture. The dearest habits and best insights that I have—I must give them all up before listening. I must not use them to protect myself against the breakthrough of a knowledge that derives from Scripture. Again and again I must let myself be contradicted. I must let myself be loosened up. I must be able to surrender everything. (1991, 78)

Some Japanese homileticians have termed such an exercise "meditation," in which one simply abandons oneself in favor of reading and meditating on the words of the text itself, over and over again, at length. I have often found myself, when beginning to prepare a sermon, doing nothing but sitting for an hour and meditating, and often that exercise is accompanied by prayer for the enlightenment of the Holy Spirit. But there are further steps that may be taken in order to get into the text.

One of the most helpful, in my opinion, is the exercise of rhetorical criticism, which is the examination of the structures of the language in the text. Rhetorical examination takes note of parallels, of questions, of exclamations, of key words, of beginnings and endings and inclusios, and especially of repetitions in a text.

For example, suppose we are dealing with Deut 8:7–18, which is the stated text in the three-year lectionary for Thanksgiving Day in Year A. Two sets of repetitions in that text sound its principal concern: "the LORD your God" vv. 7, 10, 11, 14, 18, 19, 20) and "[lest you] forget" (vv. 11, 12, 14, 19), with the corollary "remember" (v. 18). The main concern of the text, judging from its repetitions, is that Israel not "forget" the Lord her God and all that he has done for her when she enjoys the plenty of the promised land, but that Israel "remember." And surely that is the concern of our Thanksgiving too—our remembrance of the deeds of the Lord on our behalf and therefore our thankfulness for them. Often this text is used by preachers to lay a great guilt trip on a congregation and to point out that they are enjoying a prosperity not known to the rest of the world's population. But the thrust of the text is remembering and so thanksgiving.

Consider another text in which repetition of key words plays such a large part: Isa 42:1–9, which includes the first Servant Song in Second Isaiah (vv. 1–4) joined to the beginning verses of the next long announcement by the prophet (vv. 5–8). It is specified as the Old Testament reading for the first Sunday after Epiphany in Year A of the three-year lectionary. What is the repeated key word in 42:1–4? "Justice" (*mishpat*), meaning God's just order in the world, in verses 1, 3, and 4. "Justice" is what the Servant will establish and is that for which the "coastlands" wait (v. 4). Thus, in verses 6 and 7, the actions that Israel the Servant will perform as a "covenant" to the people and light to the nations are the actions of justice, the establishment of the one Lord's righteous order. And the nature of some of those actions is spelled out in verse 7. "Justice" therefore forms the principal subject of the sermon, and linked with the New Testament and our life, becomes that which Jesus Christ brings.

In analyzing structures of texts, the help for every preacher is the little word "for"—*ki* in the Hebrew, *hoti* in the Greek, having the meaning of "because" or sometimes "that." It crops up in the hymnic structures of the Bible, and its function is to give the reason for the statement that precedes it. Thus, we read in Psalm 98: "O sing to the LORD a new song, / *for* he has done marvelous things. / His right hand and his holy arm have gotten him the victory [v. 1]. . . . Let the floods clap their hands; / let the hills sing together for joy / at the presence of the LORD, *for* he is coming to judge the earth" (vv. 8–9). The reasons for the praise from all creation are clearly delineated by the phases beginning with "for," and those must be the reasons for any praise called for in the sermon.

The hymns found in the New Testament share the same structure: "Lord, now lettest thou thy servant depart in peace, / according to thy word; / *for* mine eyes have seen thy salvation (Luke 2:29–30 KJV); "Blessed be the Lord God of Israel; / *for* he hath visited and redeemed his people (Luke 1:68 KJV). The reasons for Simeon's peace in the face of death and Zechariah's blessing of the Lord both are highlighted by the beginning word "for." And the same helpful "for" is found in the triumphant hymns of Rev 19:1–3 and 19:6–8. Those *ki* and *hoti* phrases aid the preacher enormously in ferreting out the Scriptures' reasons for praise of the Lord, and those become the biblical basis for the congregation's praise also.

In the structure of any passage, the word "for" should not be separated from the words that precede it. For example, "for" at the beginning of Matt 20:1 shows that it must not be separated from 19:30, and the repetition of 19:30 in 20:16 confirms that judgment. Similarly, "for" does not mark the beginning of a strophe or stanza in the Bible's poetry, despite the stanza divisions in English translations, and those divisions can be all important in grasping the meaning of a text. These are but a few examples of the usefulness of rhetorical analysis in the attempt to get inside a biblical text.

In analyzing a text, its immediate context too can be all important. To cite just one example, the well-known lines in Mic 6:8 belong with what goes before in 6:1–7, which has the form of a court case. God presents his case in verses 1–5, and his charge is that his people say he has "wearied" them (v. 3). Israel replies in verses 6–7, and the question is, How are Israel's words to be interpreted? Is Israel "wearied" with the Lord? And so are the questions in verses 6–7 spoken in weariness or in the sarcasm that believes that nothing will satisfy the Lord? I believe they are. But to that weary sarcasm the Lord replies in verse 8, in the great patience of his mercy.

Not only are the contexts of a biblical text important but also its cross references, listed in a center column or in footnotes in many Bibles. If the preacher will take the time and trouble to hunt those down, or refer to a concordance, that exercise can be an enormous help in understanding both how the Scriptures themselves have interpreted a passage ("the Scriptures interpret the Scriptures"), and how the passage forms a trajectory on through the sacred history. For example, in the court case of Jer 2:4–13, which is the stated Old Testament text for Proper 17 in Year C of the Revised Common Lectionary, the Lord describes himself as "the fountain of living waters," accusing Israel of rejecting his everlasting waters of life in order to dig for itself worthless cisterns in the desert that can hold no water. If we turn to a concordance and look up "living," we are directed to John 4:10–14, where Jesus tells the Samaritan woman that he can provide "living water"—"a spring of water welling up to eternal life." Similarly, in John 8:38, the Lord speaks of "living water" flowing out of the heart of anyone who comes to him. The pairing of the Old and New Testament texts thus gives the immediate indication of where, like Israel, a congregation may find the waters of eternal life. The preacher can therefore illumine Israel's situation in the time of Jeremiah in the late seventh century B.C. and show how it is also the story of our modern lives in Jesus Christ.

All of this digging into a biblical passage—analyzing its structure and examining its context and tracing its trajectory—insures almost inevitably, if the work is carefully and faithfully done, that the preacher will preach from the biblical text and not from his or her own opinion or view. What happens in the process is that, God willing by his Spirit, the text speaks with its own voice and conveys its own word of God.

The amazing thing, however, is that the deeper one works into a biblical text, the more contemporary it becomes, and the word speaks not just of the past but of our present, working its influence in the here and now. Indeed, we find our lives writ large on the pages of the Bible, and it becomes not only Israel's story and the early church's story, but also ours. I think that is the secret of biblical preaching—that it need not be the illumination of a text and then of an application to our lives, but that it is immediately the portrayal of us in relation to our God, with the text speaking immediately to us from a story that is the real story of our lives. Certainly we are Israel, redeemed from slavery to sin and death by the cross and resurrection, adopted as God's sons and daughters as was Israel, set free into the foretaste of the glorious liberty of the children of God, brought to the table of the covenant, as was Israel, given the commandments of our Lord, and set on our journey toward God's promised place of rest, as was Israel. And certainly we are those at the table of the covenant, as were the first disciples, hearing that one of us will betray our Lord, sleeping and uncaring as he goes to his execution, forgiven after his resurrection when he breathes his Spirit upon us, and sent forth to baptize all nations in his triune name. One of the geniuses of African-American piety has always been that it has found its story mirrored in the Bible's story and so lived in the strength and hope of that amazing grace. And we, like them, should know that we too can sing, "Were you there when they crucified my Lord?" For we were there in fact, and it causes us too "to tremble." But we also can sing, "My Lord, what a morning!" because we are there too at the first rays of dawn on resurrection morning.

To preach biblically involves an unstinting trust in the power and effectiveness of the biblical word. When we take our place in the pulpit and preach that amazing biblical word of God, we have to trust that God's word is indeed powerful and that it will not return to him void, but that it will, by God's Spirit, work his will in the gathered congregation. If that trust is present, and the biblical text has been engaged and become the real story of human life, then every self-serving reason for preaching drops out of consideration and we—even we unworthy servants—may in fact become the heralds of the good news of the gospel.

THE WORK OF THE WORD IN MINISTRY

In order to be the channel of God's work by which a congregation is given a totally new, biblical worldview, certainly a preaching ministry must also be a teaching ministry. Every sermon, with its text, is but a moment in the ongoing *Heilswirkung* of God, and a congregation must be introduced to and educated in the whole sweep of that biblical history. Otherwise they cannot grasp either the setting of any particular biblical passage or the total story of God's deeds and words. Implied, therefore, is systematic and continuous Bible study, both corporate and private, led by the pastor or a well-trained associate. Clergy sometimes complain that it is very difficult to get their people to attend Bible study groups, and often the reason is that the examination of the Bible is so dull or superficial. The leader of the group therefore needs to look to his or her own understanding of the Scriptures and ask if there is being communicated the excitement of finding the story of our lives in relation to God's working in the Scriptures' pages. A minister who is not excited about the Bible will engender no excitement about it among her or his people. But it is also true that sometimes Bible study should start on the simplest level, with illustrations of time lines and historical settings and memorization of the order of the books of the Bible.

Certainly part of the function of the pulpit can also be that of instruction. Every biblical passage needs its context explained before it is read from the lectern. Occasionally, the preacher may want to preach a sermon that covers the whole span of God's work in the Bible's story. I have sometimes asked preachers if they could tell the whole story of the Bible in a twenty-minute sermon, which is not a bad exercise to attempt every two or three years. It also can be helpful to preach through one biblical book; for example, preaching through the continuous story of Genesis or Exodus gives a sense of the flow of the Bible's history, just as preaching through Ephesians can give an understanding of the whole of its thought.

Biblical instruction in the church school should not be simply turned over to a religious educator with a curriculum or to untrained teachers. And serious teacher-training over a length of time should be a sine qua non. Only if teachers themselves are properly educated can they educate, and perhaps they can be motivated to learn if they realize that they are dealing with the words of God that are a matter of eternal life or death. Biblical drama can teach, if it is anchored in the Scriptures, and confirmation classes can lay foundations. As a resource, every church should have a good library stocked not only with entertaining and inspirational books, but also with books that teach.

Few things can anchor a congregation more firmly in biblical understandings than its worship. It is crucial that the Psalms and prophetic writings and New Testament quotations are used in calls to worship and prayers and doxologies, over and over again, for repetition in worship instills the word of God deeply in hungering souls. There is something perverse when the language of liturgy abandons well-known words for the "new," or when the congregation is suddenly introduced to a new version of the Scriptures that drastically alters the past words they have come to know so well. Faithful church members have whole lifetimes of memories and emotions and beliefs attached to the Christmas story or the Lord's Prayer or some psalms, and to alter drastically the language of those is to cut the people off from the foundations of their faith. This is not to say that there can never be anything new introduced into the worship of a congregation. Sometimes the old has been misguided or erroneous. But liturgies undergird lives, and foundations must not be ignored or too quickly replaced.

Equally important are the hymns that the congregation is asked to sing. In the first place, they are instructional, as Charles Wesley emphasized. As a congregation learns to sing, so too it often learns to believe, and the great hymns of the church that encapsulate the thought and language of the Bible serve to instill those in a congregation's minds and hearts, instructing the children and adults alike. For example, "The Church's One Foundation" is full of biblical allusions. Not only are good hymns instructional, however, but they are expressions of faith and allow the gathered people to offer to God in praise and dedication, prayer and thanksgiving, petition and repentance, love in return for his love. The words of the great hymns center on God, in contrast to many of the new hymns, which are concerned mostly with human beings, and indeed, which sometimes substitute praise of our ways for the praise of the Lord's. In all of worship, as in all of life, the triune God should be the subject, for worship is the "reasonable service" (Rom 12:1) of the people who belong to him.

If a congregation is to find its life and worldview transformed by the gospel of Jesus Christ, then the pastoral ministry, the shepherding of a congregation, must also find its foundation and growth in the Scriptures. I think so often of George Buttrick, former pastor of Madison Avenue Presbyterian Church in New York City, in which I served as a youth leader for two years. Buttrick's whole thought in relation to his people was saturated with the Scriptures' words. Every incident, every question that arose was seen by him in the Bible's light, because that light flooded his heart and thought and determined his pastoral actions. His was a model, I think, of a pastor guided by a lifelong study of the Scriptures that had transformed him into a true servant of his Lord. The faithful pastor who immerses himself or herself in the word of God will, when God so wills, undergo the same transformation.

We pastors and preachers are called, writes Paul, as "servants of Christ and stewards of the mysteries of God" (1 Cor 4:1)—servants and stewards of those mysterious words and that largely forgotten worldview of the Scriptures. They reveal to us an amazing history of grace in which the Lord God is always at work, guiding our sin-pocked world toward the full completion of his good kingdom on earth, even as it is in heaven. And we, even we, can be instruments in that work if we trust him. "For it is required of stewards that they be trustworthy" (1 Cor 4:2).

SELECT BIBLIOGRAPHY

Achtemeier, Paul J. 1999. *Inspiration and Authority*. Grand Rapids: Eerdmans.

Anderson, Ray S. 1997. *The Soul of Ministry*. Louisville, Ky.: Westminster John Knox.

Barth, Karl. 1991. *Homiletics*. Translated by G. W. Bromiley and D. E. Daniels. Louisville, Ky.: Westminster/John Knox.

Baxter, Richard. 1956. *The Reformed Pastor*. London: SCM.

Doberstein, John W. 1986. *Minister's Prayer Book*. Philadelphia: Fortress.

HarperCollins Bible Dictionary. 1996. Edited by Paul J. Achtemeier. San Francisco: HarperSanFrancisco.

Interpretation: A Bible Commentary for Teaching and Preaching (series). Paul J. Achtemeier, New Testament editor. Louisville, Ky.: John Knox (1979–present).

Long, Thomas. 1989. *The Witness of Preaching*. Louisville, Ky.: Westminster John Knox.

Neuhaus, Richard John. 1992. *Freedom for Ministry*. Grand Rapids: Eerdmans.

Peterson, Eugene. 1987. *Working the Angles: The Shape of Pastoral Integrity*. Grand Rapids: Eerdmans.

Plantinga, Cornelius, Jr. 1995. *Not the Way It's Supposed to Be: A Breviary of Sin*. Grand Rapids: Eerdmans.

Stewart, James S. 1974. *A Faith to Proclaim*. Grand Rapids: Baker.

Thielicke, Helmut. 1975. *Encounter with Spurgeon*. Grand Rapids: Baker.

Torrance, Thomas F., et al. 1999. *A Passion for Christ: The Vision That Ignites Ministry*. Edinburgh: Handsel.

Willimon, William. 1992. *Peculiar Speech: Preaching to the Baptized*. Grand Rapids: Eerdmans.

Paul J. Achtemeier: Career

BORN

- September 3, 1927, Lincoln, Nebraska, the son of the Reverend Arthur R. and Clara B. Achtemeier

EDUCATION

- A.B. (summa cum laude) Elmhurst College, Elmhurst, Illinois, 1949
- B.D. (magna cum laude) Union Theological Seminary, New York, 1952. Named Traveling Fellow, 1952
- Th.D. Union Theological Seminary, New York, 1958 (awarded the fellowship granted to the graduating student who showed the most promise for "contributions to theological culture")

ADDITIONAL STUDY

- Princeton Theological Seminary, 1950
- University of Heidelberg, Germany, 1952–1953
- University of Basel, Switzerland, 1953–1954

PROFESSIONAL CAREER

- Instructor in biblical literature and Greek, Elmhurst College, 1956–1957
- Assistant Professor of New Testament, Lancaster Theological Seminary, 1957–1959; Associate Professor, 1959–1961; Kunz Professor of New Testament, 1961–1973

- Professor of New Testament, Union Theological Seminary in Virginia, 1973; Herbert Worth and Annie H. Jackson Professor of Biblical Interpretation, 1979–1997; granted emeritus status by the board of the seminary on July 1, 1997
- Tutor, Graduate School of Ecumenical Studies of the World Council of Churches, Chateau de Bossey, Switzerland, 1963–1964
- Visiting Professor of New Testament at Pittsburgh Theological Seminary, 1968, and at Lutheran Theological Seminary, Gettysburg, Pa., 1971–1972
- University Seminary Associate, Columbia University (N.Y.), 1972–1980
- First Annual Staley Distinguished Christian Scholar, Rollins College, Winter Park, Fla., January 1972
- Staley Foundation Distinguished Christian Scholar, Northwest Christian College, Eugene, Oreg., February 1973
- Rosenstiel Fellow, Notre Dame University, Notre Dame, Ind., Spring 1974
- Staley Foundation Distinguished Christian Scholar, Rollins College, Winter Park, Fla., April 1982
- Staley Foundation Distinguished Christian Scholar, Elmhurst College, Elmhurst, Ill., March, 1984
- Staley Foundation Distinguished Christian Scholar, Newberry College, Newberry, S.C., March 1985
- Staley Foundation Distinguished Christian Scholar, Ferrum College, Ferrum, Va., March 1986
- Lecturer, Evangelical Round Table, Eastern College, St. Davids, Pa., June 4–6, 1986
- Professor Achtemeier has lectured and preached in a number of colleges and seminaries, Protestant and Catholic, in the United States and abroad, and has spoken to many groups of pastors and laypeople, Protestant, Catholic, and Orthodox

MEMBERSHIPS

- American Council of Learned Societies, Conference of Executive Secretaries (1977–1980)
- American Theological Society (elected 1975)
- Chicago Bible Translation Project, advisory board (1995–present)
- Columbia University Seminar on New Testament Studies (1972 to its disbanding)
- Committee on Faith and Order, Pennsylvania State Council of Churches (1961–1973)
- Council on the Study of Religion (1977–1980)
    Nominating Committee (1978–1980)
- Catholic Biblical Association
    Executive Committee (1975–1977; 1984–1985)
    Special Projects Committee (1976–1979)
    Vice President (1984)
    President (1985)
    Computer Committee (1993–1994)

- Philadelphia Seminar on Christian Origins
- Scholars Press
  Board of Directors (1977–1980)
  Executive Committee (1977–1980)
  Financial Advisory Board (1984–1986)
  Advisory Board for Scholars Press Preservation Project (1984–present)
- Society of Biblical Literature
  Chairman, Synoptics Section (1971–1976)
  Associate in Council (1972–1974)
  Nominations Committee (1976–1977)
  Executive Secretary (Chief Executive Officer) (1977–1980)
  Investment Committee (1985–1995)
  Chairman (1992–1995)
  Pauline Theology Group (Steering Committee 1985–1995)
  President-elect (1988)
  President (1989)
  Member, Search Committee for Assistant Director (1989–1990)
  Member, Search Committee for Executive Director (1995–1997)
  Member of Council (1996–present)
  Chairman, Finance Committee (1995–present)
  Member, Constitution Revision Committee (1999–present)
- Studiorum Novi Testamenti Societas (elected 1972)
- World Alliance of Reformed and Presbyterian Churches, North American Area (1961–1972)
  Recording Clerk, Administrative Committee (1963–1970)

ECUMENICAL ACTIVITIES

- Member of the Roman Catholic/Reformed-Presbyterian Bilateral Consultation, National Level, which was involved in discussions on "The Shape of the Unity We Seek."
- Member of the Reformed/Roman Catholic Dialogue, World Level, which was involved in discussions on "The Presence of Christ in Church and World."
- Member of the panel of New Testament scholars, sponsored by the United States Lutheran-Roman Catholic Dialogue, investigating the topic, "Peter in the New Testament." The results were published in book form in 1973 by Paulist Press/Augsburg Press under same title (edited by R. E. Brown, et al.).
- Member of the panel of New Testament scholars, sponsored by the United States Lutheran-Roman Catholic Dialogue, investigating the topic, "Mary in the New Testament." The results were published in book form in 1973 under the same title by Paulist Press/Fortress Press (edited by R. E. Brown, et al.).
- One of twenty-three international experts in the field of the inspiration of the Bible invited by the Pontifical Athenaeum Regina Apostolorum of Rome to participate in an International Encounter on the Inspiration of Scripture, September 18–20, 2001, in Rome.

Paul J. Achtemeier: Publications

BOOKS

The Old Testament Roots of Our Faith. With Elizabeth Achtemeier. Nashville: Abingdon, 1962. Reprint, Philadelphia: Fortress, 1979. Rev. ed., Peabody, Mass.: Hendrickson, 1995.

To Save All People. With Elizabeth Achtemeier. Philadelphia: United Church Press, 1967.

An Introduction to the New Hermeneutic. Philadelphia: Westminster, 1969.

Epiphany. Proclamation: Aids for Interpreting the Lessons of the Church Year. With Elizabeth Achtemeier. Philadelphia: Fortress, 1973.

Mark. Proclamation Commentaries. Philadelphia: Fortress, 1975. Rev. and enlarged ed., Philadelphia: Fortress, 1986.

Invitation to Mark. Garden City, N.Y.: Doubleday, 1978.

The Inspiration of Scripture: Problems and Proposals. Philadelphia: Westminster, 1980. *L'Inspiration de l'Ecriture; Problemes et Propositions*. Collection Loi et Evangile. Translated by Michel Desjardins. Montreal: Editions Fides, 1985. Enlarged ed.: *The Inspiration and Authority of Scripture*. Peabody, Mass.: Hendrickson, 1999.

Advent, Christmas. Proclamation 2: Aids for Interpreting the Church Year. With J. Leland Mebust. Philadelphia: Fortress, 1981.

Romans. Interpretation: A Bible Commentary for Teaching and Preaching. Atlanta: John Knox, 1985.

Pentecost. Proclamation 3: Aids for Interpreting the Church Year. Philadelphia: Fortress, 1986.

The Quest for Unity in the New Testament Church: A Study in Paul and Acts. Philadelphia: Fortress, 1987.

Easter. Proclamation 4: Aids for Interpreting the Lessons of the Church Year. With Elizabeth Achtemeier. Minneapolis: Fortress, 1991.

Commentary on 1 Peter. Hermeneia. Minneapolis: Fortress, 1996.

Introduction to the New Testament, Its Literature and Theology. With Marianne Meye Thompson and Joel B. Green. Grand Rapids: Eerdmans, 2001.

A Commentary on the Four Gospels (co-authored). Mahwah, N.J.: Paulist Press, 2001.

Paul's Gospel: The Resurrection as the Center of the Apostle's Theology. Nashville: Abingdon (forthcoming)

ARTICLES

"St. Paul and the Necessity of the Cross." *Theology and Life* 1 (1958): 181–88.
"The Servant Motif in the New Testament." *Theology and Life* 2 (1959): 74–77.
"The Son of Man Must Suffer." *Theology and Life* 2 (1959): 198–205.
"The Significance of Christian Suffering." *Theology and Life* 2 (1959): 279–87.
"Some Theological Books for the Laity." *Theology and Life* 3 (1960): 66–69.
"The Historical Jesus: A Dilemma." *Theology and Life* 4 (1961): 107–19.
"The Church and the Kingdom of God." *Theology and Life* 5 (1962): 187–98.
"Person and Deed: Jesus and the Storm-Tossed Sea." *Interpretation* 16 (1962): 169–76.
"Is the New Quest Docetic?" *Theology Today* 19 (1962): 355–68.
"Righteousness in the New Testament." Pages 91–99 of vol. 4 of *The Interpreter's Dictionary of the Bible*. Edited by George Arthur Buttrick. 4 vols. Nashville: Abingdon, 1962.
"Historical Perspectives in the New Testament." *Lancaster Seminary Occasional Papers* 3 (1964): 39–75.
"Reflections on an Ecumenical Year." *Theology and Life* 8 (1965): 62–73.
"How Adequate Is the New Hermeneutic?" *Theology Today* 23 (1966): 101–19.
"The New Hermeneutic." *Lancaster Seminary Bulletin* 2 (1967): 21–31.
"Hermeneutics and Historical Reality." *The Voice of St. Mary's Seminary* 45 (1967): 19–24.
"Toward the Isolation of Pre-Markan Miracle Catenae." *Journal of Biblical Literature* 89 (1970): 265–91.
"On the Historical-Critical Method in New Testament Studies: Apologia Pro Vita Sua." *Perspective* 11 (1970): 289–304.
"Gospel Miracle Tradition and the Divine Man." *Interpretation* 28 (1972): 174–97.
"The Origin and Function of the Pre-Markan Miracle Catenae." *Journal of Biblical Literature* 91 (1972): 198–221.
"Carlston's *Parables*: A Review Article." *Andover Newton Quarterly* 16 (new series) (1975–1976): 227–31.
"Miracles and the Historical Jesus: Mark 9:14–29." *Catholic Biblical Quarterly* 37 (1975): 471–91.
"Jesus and the Disciples as Miracle Workers in the Apocryphal New Testament." Pages 149–86 in *Aspects of Religious Propaganda in Judaism and Early Christianity*. Edited by Elisabeth Schüssler Fiorenza. Notre Dame, Ind.: University of Notre Dame Press, 1976.
"The Lukan Perspective on the Miracles of Jesus: A Preliminary Sketch." *Journal of Biblical Literature* 94 (1975): 547–62. Reprinted, pages 153–67 in *Perspectives on Luke-Acts:* Danville, Va : Association of Baptist Professors of Religion, 1978. Perspectives in Religious Studies: Special Series 5. Edited by Charles H. Talbert. Macon, Ga.: Mercer University Press, 1981.
"An Exposition of Mark 9:30–37." *Interpretation* 30 (1976): 178–83.
"Introduction and Annotations to Acts, I, II Timothy, Titus." *The New English Bible: Oxford Study Edition*. New York: Oxford University Press, 1976. Rev. ed., 1991.
"Mark as Interpreter of the Jesus Traditions." *Interpretation* 32 (1978): 339–52. Reprinted, pages 115–29 in *Interpreting the Gospels*. Edited by James Luther Mays. Philadelphia: Fortress, 1981.
"'And He Followed Him': Miracles and Discipleship in Mark 10:46–52." *Semeia* 11 (1978): 115–45.
"An Imperfect Union: Reflections on Gerd Theissen, *Urchristliche Wundergeschichten*." *Semeia* 11 (1978): 49–68.

"'He Taught Them Many Things': Reflections on Marcan Christology." *Catholic Biblical Quarterly* 42 (1980): 465–81. Reprinted, *Affirmation* 1, no. 6 (1980): 5–20.

"The Ministry of Jesus in the Synoptic Gospels." *Interpretation* 25 (1981): 157–69.

"Resources for Pastoral Ministry in the Synoptic Gospels." Pages 145–85 in *A Biblical Basis for Ministry*. Edited by Earl E. Shelp and Ronald Sunderland. Philadelphia: Westminster, 1981.

"Roman Catholic-Reformed Dialogue: Evaluation." *Reformed World* 36 (1981): 212–20.

"Paul and the Apostolic Office." *Reformed World* 36 (1981): 299–305.

"Epilogue: The New Testament Becomes Normative." Pages 367–86 in *Understanding the New Testament*. Written by Howard Clark Kee. 4th ed. Englewood Cliffs, N.J.: Prentice-Hall, 1983.

"It's the Little Things That Count: Enigmatic Biblical Passages (Mark 14:17–21; Luke 4:1–13; Matthew 18:10–14)." *Biblical Archaeologist*, Winter 1983, 30–32.

"An Apocalyptic Shift in Early Christian Tradition: Reflections on Some Canonical Evidence." *Catholic Biblical Quarterly* 45 (1983): 231–48. Reprinted pages 293–318 in *A Companion to the Bible*. Edited by Miriam Ward, RSM. New York: Alba House, 1985.

"How the Scriptures Were Formed." Pages 3–17 in *The Authoritative Word*. Edited by Donald K. McKim. Grand Rapids: Eerdmans, 1983 (reprint of chap. 3, *The Inspiration of Scripture*).

"'Some Things in Them Hard to Understand': Reflections on an Approach to Paul." *Interpretation* 38 (July 1984): 254–67.

"The Bible and the Word of God." Pages 2–5 in *Bible Studies: Cooperative Uniform Series*. December 1984–February 1985. Crawfordsville, Ind.: Geneva Press, 1984 (reprint of pages 162–65 in *The Inspiration of Scripture*).

"An Elusive Unity: Paul, Acts, and the Early Church." 1985 Presidential Address at the Catholic Biblical Association. *Catholic Biblical Quarterly* 48 (1986): 1–26.

"An Exposition of Revelation 5." *Interpretation* 40 (1986): 283–88.

"The Authority of the Bible: What Then Shall We Preach?" *TSF Bulletin* 10 (1986): 19–22. Reprinted, pages 105–12 in *Evangelicalism: Surviving Its Success*. Vol. 2 of *The Evangelical Round Table*. Edited by David Allen Fraser. St. Davids, Pa.: Eastern Baptist College and Eastern Baptist Theological Seminary, 1987.

"New Testament Canon." Pages 1–13 in *Adult Biblical Interdependent Learning*. East Troy, Wis.: ABIL Foundation, 1986.

"I Peter." Pages 1279–85 in *Harper's Bible Commentary*. Edited by James L. Mays. New York: Harper & Row, 1988. Reprinted, pages 1168–74 in *HarperCollins Bible Commentary*. Rev. ed. New York: HarperCollins and the Society of Biblical Literature, 2000.

"Newborn Babes and Living Stones: Literal and Figurative in 1 Peter." Pages 207–36 in *To Touch the Text: Biblical and Related Studies in Honor of Joseph A. Fitzmyer*. Edited by Maurya P. Horgan and Paul J. Kobelski. New York: Crossroad/Continuum, 1989.

"I Peter." Pages 345–51 in *The Apocrypha and the New Testament*. Vol. 2 of *The Books of the Bible*. Edited by Bernhard W. Anderson. New York: Charles Scribner's Sons, 1989.

"Omne verbum sonat: The New Testament and the Oral Environment of Late Western Antiquity." 1989 Presidential Address, Society of Biblical Literature. *Journal of Biblical Literature* 109 (1990): 3–27.

"Romans 3:1–8: Structure and Argument." Pages 77–87 in *Christ and His Communities: Essays in Honor of Reginald H. Fuller*. Edited by Arland J. Hultgren and Barbara

Hall. Cincinnati: Forward Movement Publications, 1990. Reprinted, *Anglican Theological Review*. Supplementary Series 11 (1990): 77–87.

"Grace and the Shattering of Illusions: Jesus and Mark's Gospel." Pages 47–57 in *Evangelism in the Reformed Tradition*. Edited by Arnold B. Lovell. Decatur, Ga.: CTS Press, 1990.

"Finding the Way to Paul's Theology." Pages 25–36 in *Thessalonians, Philippians, Galatians, Philemon*. Vol. 1 of *Pauline Theology*. Edited by Jouette M. Bassler. Minneapolis: Augsburg Fortress, 1991.

"Mark." Pages 541–57 in vol. 4 of *The Anchor Bible Dictionary*. Edited by D. N. Friedman. New York: Doubleday, 1992.

"Suffering Servant and Suffering Christ in I Peter: A Proposal." Pages 176–88 in *The Future of Christology: Essays in Honor of Leander E. Keck*. Edited by Abraham J. Malherbe and Wayne A. Meeks. Minneapolis: Fortress, 1993.

"Romans, the Letter of Paul to the." Pages in 659–62 in *The Oxford Companion to the Bible*. Edited by Bruce M. Metzger and Michael D. Coogan. New York: Oxford University Press, 1993.

"Unsearchable Judgements and Inscrutable Ways: Reflections on the Discussion of Romans." Pages 521–34 in *Society of Biblical Literature 1995 Seminar Papers*. Edited by Eugene H. Lovering. Atlanta: Scholars Press, 1995. Reprinted pages (Reprinted and revised) 3–21 in *Looking Back, Pressing On*. Vol. 4 of *Pauline Theology*. Edited by E. Elizabeth Johnson and David M. Hay. Symposium Series, Society of Biblical Literature. Atlanta: Scholars Press, 1997.

"Perspectives on Homoerotic Practice." *Presbyterian Outlook* 178, no. 2 (1996): 10–11.

"The Continuing Quest for Coherence in the Theology of St. Paul: An Experiment in Thought." Pages 132–45 in *Theology and Ethics in Paul and His Interpreters: Essays in Honor of Victor L. Furnish*. Edited by Eugene H. Lovering and Jerry L. Sumney. Nashville: Abingdon, 1996.

"Gods Made with Hands: Idolatry and the New Testament." *Ex Auditu* 15 (1999): 43–61.

"Miracles in the New Testament and in the Greco-Roman World." *Aufstieg und Niedergang der römischen Welt* Part II, vol. 26/2 (forthcoming).

SERMONS

"Christian Security." *Pulpit* 33 (1962): 17–19.

"The Uncomfortable Incarnation." *Pulpit* 37 (1966): 20–22.

"On Telling a Story." *Pulpit* 40 (1969): 20–22.

"The Hidden God." Pages 12–19 in *Preaching in the Witnessing Community*. Edited by H. G. Stuempfle Jr. Philadelphia: Fortress, 1973.

TRANSLATIONS

Bauer, Walter. "The Old Testament, the Lord, and the Apostles." Chap. 9 of *Orthodoxy and Heresy in Earliest Christianity*. Edited by Robert A. Kraft and Gerhard Krodel. Philadelphia: Fortress, 1969.

Marxsen, Willi. *The Beginnings of Christology: A Study in Its Problems*. Philadelphia: Fortress, 1969.

Pannenberg, W. "Universal History and Hermeneutics." Pages 89–127 in vol. 5 of *God and Christ: Existence and Providence*.

Rendtorff, R. "Reflections on the Early History of Prophecy in Israel." Pages 14–34 in *History and Hermeneutics*. Vol. 4 of *Journal for Theology and the Church*. Edited by Robert W. Funk, et al. New York: Harper & Row, 1967.

BOOK REVIEWS
Over 75 reviews in a wide range of scholarly publications.

EDITORIAL ACTIVITY
Books
General editor, *Harper's Bible Dictionary* (new edition 1985).
General editor, *HarperCollins Bible Dictionary* (rev. and enlarged ed. of *Harper's Bible Dictionary*), 1996.
New Testament editor, Interpretation: A Bible Commentary for Teaching and Preaching, John Knox Press, 1979–present.
Coeditor, Biblical Scholarship in North America, Scholars Press
Coeditor, Interpreting the Prophets, Fortress, 1987.
Coeditor, Interpreting the Gospels, Fortress, 1981.
Editorial committee, Centennial Publication Series of the Society of Biblical Literature, Scholars Press.
Editorial board, Scholars Press Reprints and Translations
Editorial consultant, *Harper's Bible Commentary*, 1988.

Periodicals
Editorial board, *Interpretation* (1973–1992).
Associate editor, *Interpretation* (1980–1983).
Editor, *Interpretation* (1984–1990).
Associate editor, *Catholic Biblical Quarterly* (1981–1989, 1996–present).
Editorial board, *Journal of Biblical Literature* (1975–1977, 1980–1984).

Records
A symposium on the theme "The Bible Today: An Open-Ended Discussion by Biblical Scholars, Ministers and Laymen," (four LP records) released by United Church Press, 1967. Discussion by a panel of five persons.

Cassette
"A New Perspective on Reality (2 Cor. 5:14–20)." *Thesis Theological Cassettes.* Vol. 3 no. 11, 1972.

Index of Personal Names

Index of Scripture and Ancient Sources

Old Testament

Apocrypha

New Testament

Old Testament Pseudepigrapha

Dead Sea Scrolls and Related Texts